Social Science

Based on Latest NCERT

Authors

Kriti Arora

Susmita Dhar

ARIHANT PRAKASHAN

(School Division Series)

卐 ADMINISTRATIVE & PRODUCTION OFFICES

Regd. Office

'Ramchhaya' 4577/15, Agarwal Road, Darya Ganj, New Delhi -110002
Tele: 011- 47630600, 43518550; Fax: 011- 23280316

卐 **Head Office**

Kalindi, TP Nagar, Meerut (UP) - 250002, Tel: 0121-7156203, 7156204

卐 SALES & SUPPORT OFFICES

Agra, Ahmedabad, Bengaluru, Bareilly, Chennai, Delhi, Guwahati, Hyderabad, Jaipur, Jhansi, Kolkata, Lucknow, Nagpur & Pune.

PO No. : TXT-59-T066307-08-25

Published By Arihant Publications (India) Ltd.

For further information about the books published by Arihant, log on to www.arihantbooks.com or e-mail at info@arihantbooks.com

Follow us on    

卐 PRICE ₹ 305.00

PRODUCTION TEAM

Publishing Managers
Mahendra Singh Rawat & Keshav Mohan

Project Head
Ashwani

Cover Designer
Bilal Hashmi

Inner Designer
Ankit Tyagi

Page Layouting
Mayank Saini

Proof Readers
Mukul Kaushik
Manish Kumar

Inside the Book

Our Pasts-II (History)

Our Environment (Geography)

Social and Political Life-II (Civics)

Key Features

Social Science Class 7

Chapter Intro

A quick information about the coverage of the chapter to explain students about what they are going to study.

CHAPTER 1

Introduction : Tracing Changes Through a Thousand Years

The world map has undergone significant changes due to changes in political, geographical and cultural situations in different periods. Apart from this, the names of different place have also changed over different time periods. There are many sources used by historians for getting information about these changes. These changes also included the emergence of new political and social groups, empires and religions.

Knowledge Plus

Additional but informational matter related to given concept. It helps & motivate students to explore more beyond their books.

KNOWLEDGE PLUS Dance forms, other than Kathak, which are recognised as classical at present are **Bharatanatyam** (Tamil Nadu), **Kathakali** (Kerala), **Odissi** (Odisha), **Kuchipudi** (Andhra Pradesh) and **Manipuri** (Manipur).

Boxed Matter

Information given in the boxes cover some important facts related to the concept given.

Types of Land

According to Chola inscription, there were several types of land as follows

- ***Vellanvagai*** This type of land belong to non-Brahmana peasant proprietors.
- ***Shalabhoga*** This type of land was meant for the maintenance of school.
- ***Devadana, Tirunamattukkani*** This type of land was gifted to temples.

Try These

A set of 3-5 Questions given in between the text, helps students to remain connected with the text while studying. They can instantly assess themselves for their understanding.

Try These

1. **What does the term 'foreigner' mean in the past?**
2. **Name two sects of Islam.**
3. **What are some sources that give information about our past?**
4. **They are the place where all old and new documents and manuscripts are kept. What are being referred to here?**

NCERT Folder

To make students completely understand NCERT books, answers of all the NCERT Exercises have been given in each chapter in NCERT Folder. Accuracy, Detailing and Simplicity of Answers are the major features of this section.

NCERT FOLDER

Covering Intext Questions and Exercises of NCERT

NCERT ON PAGE 3

Q.1 Can you think of any other words whose meanings change in different context?

Ans. The word whose meanings change in different context is 'Dharma'.

In ancient times, it meant 'righteousness' or 'duty' but today it has changed and means 'religion'.

Likewise, caste was earlier based on occupation but over the centuries it has become based on birth.

NCERT ON PAGE 4

Q.2 Compare the following

1. In the middle of the 13th century, a scholar wanted to copy a book. But he did not have enough paper. So, he washed the writing off a manuscript he did not want, dried the paper and used it.

NCERT ON PAGE 10

Q.4 Why do you think rulers made such claims?

Ans. Rulers made the exaggerated claims of conquests to show themselves as powerful warriors.

Q.5 Did you notice that the names by which languages are known have changed over time ?

Ans. Names of following languages have changed over time

Lahori - Punjabi
Telangani - Telugu
Gujari - Gujarati
Mabari - Tamil
Gauri - Bengali
Hindawi - Hindi

NCERT ON PAGE 11

Q.6 Find out whether and for how long your state was part of these pan-regional empires.

1 **Cartographer** It refers to a skilled person who makes maps.
2 **Chronicle** It refers to a written record of historical events describing them in order in which they happened.
3 **Manuscripts** These are handwritten records of the past and are in the form of books.
4 **Archive** It refers to a place where documents and manuscripts are stored.
5 **Patron** It refers to an influential wealthy individual who supports another person, an artist, a poet or a noble.
6 **Ulama** It refers to learned theologians and jurist of Islam.
7 **Periodisation** It is the process of dividing history into various periods with similar characteristics.

Terms in Footnote

Meaning or definition of important words/terms given on the pages.

Mind Map

A quick revision visual tool for the complete chapter.

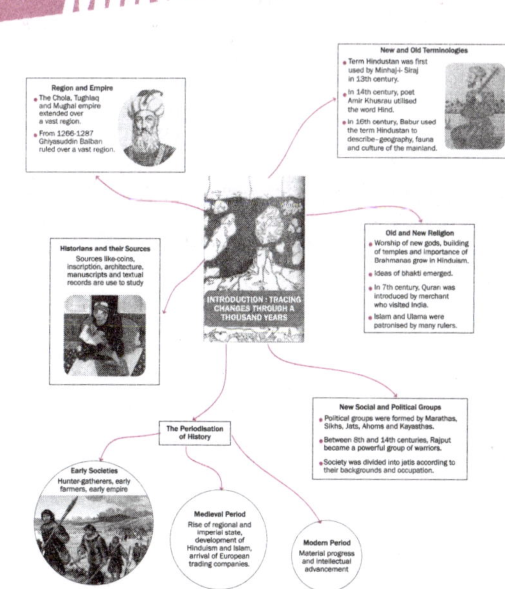

CHAPTER 1

Introduction : Tracing Changes Through a Thousand Years

The world map has undergone significant changes due to changes in political, geographical and cultural situations in different periods. Apart from this, the names of different place have also changed over different time periods. There are many sources used by historians for getting information about these changes. These changes also included the emergence of new political and social groups, empires and religions.

Maps play an important role in studying history. For example, maps provide detailed information about the Indian sub-continent and the changes that occurred over time.

With changing times, maps have also evolved. The map of the Indian sub-continent made in the 1720s by a French **cartographer**[1] was very different from the map made in 1154 CE by **Al-Idrisi**. The map made by French cartographer was used by European sailors and merchants on their voyages.

The science of cartography has also evolved over time. When historians read documents, maps and texts from the past, they have to keep in mind the context of different historical backgrounds in which information about the past was produced.

1.1 New and Old Terminologies

As the context in which the information is produced changes over time, the language and meaning of the words have also changed. For example,

- The term 'Hindustan' today is understood as 'India'i.e. the modern nation-state. However in 13th century, it was used by **Minhaj-i-Siraj** to refer the areas of Punjab, Haryana and lands between the Ganga and Yamuna under the Delhi Sultanate.
- In the early 16th century, Babur used the term 'Hindustan' to describe the geography, the fauna and the culture of the inhabitants of the sub-continent. This description is similar to the one given by 14th century poet **Amir Khusrau** who used the term 'Hind'.
- The term 'foreigner' was used in the Medieval period for any unknown person coming to a village, who was not a part of that society or culture. However, today the term 'foreigner' refers to someone who is not an Indian. The term *'pardesi'* in Hindi and *'ajnabi'* in Persian are used for the term *'foreigner'*.

1.2 Historians and their Sources

Historians use different types of sources like coins, inscriptions, architecture and textual records for studying history.

The number of textual records increased during the period between 700 to 1750 and the paper gradually became cheaper and widely available.

Paper was widely used to write Holy texts, **chronicles**[2] of rulers, letters and teachings of saints, petitions and judicial records, and for registers of accounts and taxes.

Manuscripts

Manuscripts[3] were another source of information collected by wealthy people, rulers, monasteries and temples, and placed in libraries and **archives**[4]. They provide a lot of detailed information to historians but they are difficult to use.

As **scribes** used to copy manuscripts by hand, it often led to small changes in the text of the manuscripts.

These small changes grew over time until the manuscripts of the same text became different from each other. Sometimes, authors also revise their work. For example, **Ziauddin Barani** wrote his chronicle first in 1356 and revised it two years later. Both versions were different from each other.

1 **Cartographer** It refers to a skilled person who makes maps.
2 **Chronicle** It refers to a written record of historical events describing them in order in which they happened.
3 **Manuscripts** These are handwritten records of the past and are in the form of books.
4 **Archive** It refers to a place where documents and manuscripts are stored.

1.2 New Social and Political Groups

A number of developments took place during the period between 700 and 1750. These included the following

- New technologies like the **Persian wheel** in irrigation, the **spinning wheel** in weaving and **firearms** in combat emerged during this period.
- New food and beverages were introduced in the subcontinent like potatoes, corn, chillies, tea and coffee.
- During this period the Rajput group became important. The name 'Rajput' is derived from 'Rajaputra, meaning the son of a ruler.
- Between 8th and 14th centuries, the term 'Rajput' was commonly used for a group of warriors who belonged to **Kshatriya** caste. Rajputs were known for their loyalty and bravery.
- Other groups such as the Marathas, Sikhs, Jats, Ahoms and Kayasthas also became politically important during this period.
- Forests were cleared during this period to expand agriculture in the country. As a result, many forest-dwellers were forced to migrate, while some became peasants. These peasants were required to pay taxes and offer goods and services to local lords.
- Society was divided into **jatis** or **sub castes** during this period and they were ranked according to their backgrounds and occupations.

  Ranks were varied according to the power, influence and resources controlled by members of the jati. The status of the same jati could be different from area to area.

  Jatis framed their own rules to manage their members. An assembly of elders called **Jati Panchayat** was responsible for enforcing these rules.

1.3 Region and Empire

The Chola, Tughlaq, and Mughal empires extended their influence over vast and diverse regions. For example, according to a Sanskrit Prashasti, **Ghiyasuddin Balban** (1266-1287) ruled over a vast empire that extended from Bengal (Gauda) in the East to Ghazni (Gajjana) in Afghanistan in the West, and all of South India.

These dynasties were able to build pan-regional empires however not all these empires were equally stable.

After the decline of Mughal empire in the 18th century, several regional states re-emerged. However, extended pan-regional (across regions) rule changed the overall nature of these regions in terms of governance, language, culture and economic management.

Over the thousand years from 700-1750, various regions experienced the influence of larger pan-regional forces that integrated them, while maintaining their distinct characteristics.

Try These

1. **What does the term 'foreigner' mean in the past?**
2. **Name two sects of Islam.**
3. **What are some sources that give information about our past?**
4. **They are the place where all old and new documents and manuscripts are kept. What are being referred to here?**

1.4 Old and New Religions

Many changes occurred in religious traditions during the period between 700 to 1750. In Hinduism, these included worship of new deities, construction of temples by royalty and growing importance of Brahmanas.

Brahmanas earned great respect in society for their knowledge of Sanskrit texts. They were supported by new rulers.

Idea of Bhakti and new religions also emerged during this period. Teachings of Quran were introduced by merchants who came to India in the 7th century. Quran is the Holy book of Muslims. Many rulers were **patrons**[5] of Islam and **Ulama**[6].

Muslims are divided into two sects. These are **Shia Muslims** who consider Ali as their leader and **Sunni Muslims** who accept authority of Khalifas (early leaders).

1.5 Periodisation of History

Historians divide history into different periods to make study of history easier. British historians divided history into **Hindu**, **Muslim** and **British** period. It was done on the basis of religion of the rulers.

Only few historians follow this **periodisation**[7]. Most of the historians divide history on the basis of economic and social factors.

---

5 **Patron** It refers to an influential wealthy individual who supports another person, an artist, a poet or a noble.
6 **Ulama** It refers to learned theologians and jurist of Islam.
7 **Periodisation** It is the process of dividing history into various periods with similar characteristics.

Mind Map

Region and Empire

- The Chola, Tughlaq and Mughal empire extended over a vast region.
- From 1266-1287 Ghiyasuddin Balban ruled over a vast region.

New and Old Terminologies

- Term Hindustan was first used by Minhaj-i- Siraj in 13th century.
- In 14th century, poet Amir Khusrau utilised the word Hind.
- In 16th century, Babur used the term Hindustan to describe–geography, fauna and culture of the mainland.

Historians and their Sources

Sources like-coins, inscription, architecture, manuscripts and textual records are use to study

Old and New Religion

- Worship of new gods, building of temples and importance of Brahmanas grow in Hinduism.
- Ideas of bhakti emerged.
- In 7th century, Quran was introduced by merchant who visited India.
- Islam and Ulama were patronised by many rulers.

New Social and Political Groups

- Political groups were formed by Marathas, Sikhs, Jats, Ahoms and Kayasthas.
- Between 8th and 14th centuries, Rajput became a powerful group of warriors.
- Society was divided into jatis according to their backgrounds and occupation.

The Periodisation of History

Early Societies

Hunter-gatherers, early farmers, early empire

Medieval Period

Rise of regional and imperial state, development of Hinduism and Islam, arrival of European trading companies.

Modern Period

Material progress and intellectual advancement

NCERT FOLDER

Covering Intext Questions and Exercises of NCERT

NCERT ON PAGE 3

Q.1 Can you think of any other words whose meanings change in different context?

Ans. The word whose meanings change in different context is 'Dharma'.

In ancient times, it meant 'righteousness' or 'duty' but today it has changed and means 'religion'.

Likewise, caste was earlier based on occupation but over the centuries it has become based on birth.

NCERT ON PAGE 4

Q.2 Compare the following

1. In the middle of the 13th century, a scholar wanted to copy a book. But he did not have enough paper. So, he washed the writing off a manuscript he did not want, dried the paper and used it.
2. A century later, if you bought some food in the market, you could be lucky and have the shopkeeper wrap it for you in some paper.

   When was paper more expensive and easily available in the 13th or 14th century?

Ans. The paper was more expensive and easily available in the 14th or 13th century because

- In the 13th century, a scholar had to wash a manuscript to rewrite on the same manuscript. This shows that paper was expensive in the 13th century.
- In the 14th century, any one could get food wrapped in paper in the market. This suggests that paper was easily available and not expensive in 14th century.

NCERT ON PAGE 8

Q.3 Of the technological, economic, social and cultural changes described in this section, which do you think were most significant in the town or village in which you live?

Ans. Among the technological, economic, social and cultural changes, introduction of Persian wheel in irrigation was the most significant development. It was used for lifting water from wells. It helped in efficient use of water.

NCERT ON PAGE 10

Q.4 Why do you think rulers made such claims?

Ans. Rulers made the exaggerated claims of conquests to show themselves as powerful warriors.

Q.5 Did you notice that the names by which languages are known have changed over time ?

Ans. Names of following languages have changed over time

Lahori - Punjabi
Telangani - Telugu
Gujari - Gujarati
Mabari - Tamil
Gauri - Bengali
Hindawi - Hindi

NCERT ON PAGE 11

Q.6 Find out whether and for how long your state was part of these pan-regional empires.

Ans. Yes, my state Delhi has been a part of the Mughal empire for about 235 years. Mughal rule was established by Babur in 1526 by defeating Ibrahim Lodi.

From 1707,the empire began to decline as later mughals were not very powerful. By this time, Delhi had come under British Colonial Rule.

Q.7 Do you remember what Amir Khusrau had to say regarding Sanskrit, knowledge and Brahmanas?

Ans. Yes, I remember. According to Amir Khusrau, Sanskrit did not belong to any single region.

Common people did not know Sanskrit, only Brahmanas could read and write Sanskrit.

NCERT ON PAGE 14 (IMAGINE)

Q.8 You are a historian. Choose one of the themes mentioned in this chapter,such as economic, social or political history, and discuss why you think it would be interesting to find out the history of that theme.

Ans. As a historian, I would choose economic history because it would be interesting to know how society functioned without money.

Also, I am curious to know how money was introduced and how it changed society.

EXERCISES

Q.1 Who was considered a 'Foreigner' in the past?

Ans. Foreigner was any stranger in a village who was not a part of that society or culture.

Q.2 State whether true or false.

(a) We do not find inscriptions for the period after 700.

(b) The Marathas asserted their political importance during this period.

(c) Forest-dwellers were sometimes pushed out of their lands with the spread of agricultural settlements.

(d) Sultan Ghiyasuddin Balban controlled Assam, Manipur and Kashmir.

Ans. (a) False (b) True (c) True (d) False

Q.3 Fill in the blanks.

(a) Archives are places where .... are kept.

(b) .... was a 14th century chronicler.

(c) ...., ..., ..., ... and ...... were some of the crops introduced into the sub-continent during this period.

Ans. (a) manuscripts

(b) Ziauddin Barani

(c) Potatoes, corn, chillies, tea, coffee

Q.4 List some of the technological changes associated with this period.

Ans. The technological changes associated with this period were as follows

- Use of Persian wheel in irrigation.
- Use of spinning wheel in weaving.
- Use of firearms in battlefield.

Q.5 What were some of the major religious developments during this period?

Ans. Some of the major religious developments during this period were as follows

- People started worshiping new deities.
- Rulers helped in the construction of temples.
- Importance of Brahmanas, the priest class, grew.
- Sanskrit became the language of learned Brahmanas and were patronised by emperors.
- Merchants and migrants brought Holy Quran with them.
- Idea of bhakti emerged.

Q. 6 In what ways has the meaning of the term 'Hindustan' changed over the centuries?

Ans. The term 'Hindustan' has changed over the centuries in the following ways

- In the 13th century, Minhaj-i-Siraj used the term 'Hindustan', to refer to the areas of Punjab, Haryana and the land between Ganga and Yamuna rivers. This region was under Delhi Sultanate.
- The poet Amir Khusrau used this term in his poems in 14th century.
- In the 16th century, Babur used the term 'Hindustan' to describe the geography, the fauna and the culture of the inhabitants of the sub-continent.
- Today, Hindustan is understood as "India" the modern nation-state.

Q.7 How were the affairs of Jati regulated?

Ans. The affairs of Jati were regulated in the following ways

- Society was divided into jatis on the basis of their background and occupation.
- Jatis framed their own rules and regulations to manage the conduct of their members.
- The regulations of Jatis were enforced by an assembly of elders called Jati Panchayat. But Jatis had to follow their village rules also.

Q.8 What does the term 'Pan-regional empire' mean?

Ans. Pan-regional empire refers to a significant empire that has control over multiple regions and small kingdom of the sub-continent.

The Cholas, Khaljis, Tughlaqs and Mughals are prominent examples of pan-regional empire in the medieval period.

Q.9 What are the difficulties historians face in using manuscripts?

Ans. There are several difficulties historian face in using manuscripts such as

- Manuscripts were handwritten and palm leaves were used in early days. It was difficult to maintain them.
- There was no printing press in those days. So people copied manuscripts by hand. They were known as scribes. Different handwriting made the reading of manuscripts hard.
- Sometimes scribes introduced small changes in the original manuscript by mistake. This made the copied manuscripts very different from the original ones.

Q.10 How do the historians divide the past into periods? Do they face any problems in doing so?

Ans. The historians divide the past into periods based on the economic and social factors which characterise them.

But they faced problem in doing so because economic and social changes keep taking place, so definite boundaries can't be drawn.

Q.11 Find out where records are kept in your village or city. Who writes these records? Is there an archive? Who manages it? What kinds of documents are stored there? Who are the people who use it?

Ans. In our city, the records are kept in Tehsil. These records are written by government officials.

The archive manager maintains them. Documents related to past are stored there. The people who use it are research scholars and the historians.

REVIEW EXERCISE

Including Competency Based Questions

Part I

Multiple Choice Questions (MCQs)

1. What is meant by archaeology?
(a) The study of paintings
(b) The study of buildings
(c) The study of politics
(d) The study of remains of our past

2. From which region did Al-Idrisi belong?
(a) Arab (b) France
(c) Germany (d) Sri Lanka

3. Maps are drawn by which of the following?
(a) Painter (b) Sailors
(c) Cartographer (d) Historians

4. The word foreigner today means someone not an Indian. In the medieval period, it means .... Diksha
(a) peasants (b) city-dweller
(c) forest dweller (d) stranger

5. Which of the following is/are source(s) of History?
(a) Monuments
(b) Coins
(c) Artefacts and paintings
(d) All of the above

6. When paper became cheap it was used to write .... . Diksha
(a) Holy texts
(b) Chronicles of rulers
(c) Letters and teachings of saints
(d) All of the above

7. Archive was a place where .... were kept for future references.
(a) coins (b) grains
(c) manuscripts (d) books

8. Ziauddin Barani was a chronicler of which century?
(a) 15th (b) 14th
(c) 18th (d) 17th

9. In which period the number and variety of textual records increased dramatically?
(a) 600 to 700 (b) 700 to 800
(c) 800 to 1200 (d) 700 to 1750

10. Through the period of 700 to 1750 AD, which of the following became cheaper?
(a) Paper (b) Grains
(c) Potatoes (d) Clothes

11. Two qualities attributed to Rajput were .... . Diksha
(a) valour and sense of justice
(b) extreme valour and sense of loyalty
(c) justice and extreme valour
(d) truth and justice

12. Name the dynasties which was/were able to build a pan-regional empire.
(a) Cholas and Khaljis (b) Mughals
(c) Tughlaqs and Mughals (d) Both (a) and (c)

13. Pan-regional means ....
(a) one regional unit
(b) spanning single region
(c) not belonging to lands but seas
(d) spanning diverse regions

14. When did the Mughal empire decline?
(a) 18th century (b) 19th century
(c) 20th century (d) 17th century

15. In which century British historians divided the history of India into three periods i.e. Hindu, Muslim and British?
(a) 18th century (b) 17th century
(c) 16th century (d) 19th century

16. In which century did the Ghiyasuddin Balban rule?
(a) 14th century (b) 13th century
(c) 12th century (d) 16th century

17. **Identify the following with the help of information given below.** **Competency Based**

I. Collective belief in a supernatural agency.

II. Many changes occurred in it during medieval period.

III. Personal and collective belief.

Codes

(a) Jatis (b) Religion
(c) language (d) Empire

18. **Identify the following with the help of information given below.** **Competency Based**

I. This group became important between 700 and 1750.

II. Their name means 'son of a ruler'.

III. It is known for extreme valour and loyalty.

Codes

(a) Marathas (b) Sikhs (c) Kayasthas (d) Rajputs

19. **Choose the correct statement(s) among the following.**

I. Manuscripts were placed in archives.

II. Akbar used the term 'Hind' in 14th century.

III. Ziauddin Barani wrote his first Chronicles in 1356.

Codes

(a) Only I (b) I and II
(c) Only III (d) I and III

20. **Choose the incorrect statement(s) among the following**

I. Scribes used to copy manuscripts by hand.

II. Foreigner is antonym of Pardesi and Ajnabi.

III. Jat was the caste of scribes and secretaries.

Codes

(a) I and III (b) I and II
(c) II and III (d) Only III

21. **Arrange the following events in chronological order.** **Competency Based**

I. Decline of Mughal empire.

II. Ghiyasuddin Tuqhlaq Sultan of Delhi.

III. British historians divided History into three periods.

IV. Ideas of Quran introduced in India by merchants.

Codes

(a) II, IV, III, I (b) IV, III, II, I
(c) IV, II, I, III (d) I, II, IIII, IV

Answers

1. (d)	**2.** (a)	**3.** (c)	**4.** (d)	**5.** (d)
6. (d)	**7.** (c)	**8.** (b)	**9.** (d)	**10.** (a)
11. (b)	**12.** (d)	**13.** (d)	**14.** (a)	**15.** (a)
16. (b)	**17.** (b)	**18.** (d)	**19.** (d)	**20.** (c)
21. (c)				

Match the Following

1.

	List I		List II
A.	Amir Khusrau	1.	Chronicler
B.	Ziauddin Barani	2.	Khalifas
C.	Shia	3.	Ali
D.	Sunni	4.	Termi Hind

Codes

	A	B	C	D		A	B	C	D
(a)	4	1	3	2	(b)	3	4	1	2
(c)	4	1	2	3	(d)	3	1	2	4

2.

	List I		List II
A.	Minhaj-i-Siraj	1.	Court poet
B.	Amir Khusrau	2.	Delhi Sultan
C.	Manuscripts	3.	Prophet Mohammad's son-in-law
D.	Ghiyasuddin Balban	4.	A chronicler
E.	Kayasthas	5.	Archives
F.	Ali	6.	Sub-castes

Codes

	A	B	C	D	E	F		A	B	C	D	E	F
(a)	4	1	5	2	6	3	(b)	3	4	1	2	6	5
(c)	4	1	6	2	3	5	(d)	3	1	2	6	4	5

Ans. 1. (a) 2. (a)

Assertion-Reason

1. **Assertion** (A) Historians read different manuscript versions of same text.

Reason (R) Scribes copied manuscripts and also introduced small changes in it.

Codes

(a) Both A and R are true and R is the correct explanation of A
(b) Both A and R are true, but R is not the correct explanation of A
(c) A is true, but R is false
(d) A is false, but R is true

2. **Assertion** (A) British historians divided the history of India into three periods.

Reason (R) Historians accepted the rich diversity of Indian sub-continent.

Codes

(a) Both A and R are true and R is the correct explanation of A

(b) Both A and R are true, but R is not the correct explanation of A

(c) A is true, but R is false

(d) A is false, but R is true

Ans. 1. (a) Both A and R are true, and R is the correct explanation of A.

2. (c) A is true, but R is false

Fill in the Blanks

1. Historical .... exist in a variety of languages and forms.

2. 'Hindustan' was used in the .... by Minhaj-i-Siraj, a chronicler who wrote in Persian.

3. Term 'Hind' was coined by Amir Khusrau in the ....

4. .... were collected by wealthy people.

5. Persian wheel was used in ....

Ans. 1. records 2. 13th century 3. 14th century 4. Manuscripts 5. irrigation

True/False

1. Jatis framed their own rules and regulations to manage the conduct of their members.

2. Persian wheel was used in transportation.

3. Rajput was the caste whose people were spinning wheel in weaving clothes.

4. In the middle of 19th century, history of India was divided into three period.

Ans. 1. True 2. False 3. False 4. True

Picture Based Question

1. There is a image of wheel shown in figure given below. Who introduced wheel in irrigation ?

(a) Arabs (b) Turks

(c) French (d) Persian

Ans. 1. (d) Persian

Case Based Question

1. Read the passage given below and answer the questions that follow.

There was no printing press in those days so scribes copied manuscripts by hand. If you have ever copied a friend's homework you would know that this is not a simple exercise. Sometimes, you cannot read your friend's handwriting and are forced to guess what is written. As a result, there are small but significant differences in your copy of your friend's work. Manuscript copying is somewhat similar. As scribes copied manuscripts, they also introduced small changes - a word here, a sentence there. These small differences grew over centuries copying until manuscripts of the same text became substantially different from one another.

(i) Who collected manuscripts for the record ?

(a) Wealthy people

(b) Rulers

(c) Temples

(d) All of the above

(ii) Where were manuscripts and documents stored ?

(a) Hall (b) Archive

(c) Treasury (d) Granary

(iii) What is the reason for substanial differences in manuscripts of the same text?

(a) Better handwriting

(b) Introduction of small changes by scribes over centuries

(c) Existence of multiple original manuscripts

(d) None of the above

(iv) Why was copying a friend's homework compared to the process of manuscript copying?

(a) To highlight importance of handwriting skills

(b) To emphasise the simplicity of manuscript copying.

(c) To illustrate the challenge of deciphering handwriting.

(d) To promote use of printing

Ans (i) (d) All of the above

(ii) (b) Archive

(iii) (b) Introduction of small changes by scribes over centuries

(iv) (c) To illustrate the challenge of deciphering handwriting.

Part II

Very Short Answer Type Questions

1. What was Al-Idrisi known for?

Ans. Al-Idrisi was known for historical cartography.

2. Name the poet who used the term 'Hind' for the first time.

Ans. Amir Khusrau used the term 'Hind' in his poems.

3. Who ruled Delhi in 13th century?

Ans. Ghiyasuddin Balban ruled Delhi in 13th century according to a Sanskrit text/Prashasti.

4. Which areas were included in Hindustan by Minhaj-i-Siraj in his writings?

Ans. Minhaj-i-Siraj used 'Hindustan' to refer the areas of Punjab, Haryana and the lands between the Ganga and Yamuna.

5. Name the Mughal Emperor who used Hindustan to describe the geography, the fauna and the culture of the inhabitants of the sub-continent.

Ans. Mughal Emperor Babur used the term Hindustan to describe the geography, the fauna and the culture of the inhabitants of the sub-continent.

6. What sources do the historians use for the study of a particular period of history ? Diksha

Ans. Coins, inscriptions, architectures and textual records are some sources used by historians for the study of a particular period of history.

7. Who used to copy the manuscripts in the early Medieval period ? Diksha

Ans. The scribes used to copy the manuscripts in the early Medieval period.

8. Who were known as scribes?

Ans. Scribes were those professionals who used to copy manuscripts by hand .

9. Which is the Holy book of Islam?

Ans. Quran is the Holy book of Islam.

10. Name the countries that comprises the Indian sub-continent.

Ans. The Indian sub-continent comprises of India, Afghanistan, Pakistan, Nepal, Sri Lanka, Maldives, Bhutan and Bangladesh.

11. Name the warrior clan that became popular between 8th and 14th centuries. Diksha

Ans. Rajputs were the warrior clan that became popular between 8th and 14th centuries.

12. Why forest dwellers had to migrate? Competency Based

Ans. Forest dwellers had to migrate because of change in their habitat. As forests were cleared to extend agriculture.

13. Which varna or sub-castes were able to learn the Sanskrit language?

Ans. The Brahmanas were known for their ability to learn Sanskrit.

14. What do you mean by Jati Panchayat?

Ans. Jati Panchayat is an assembly of elders who enforces rules of jatis. Jatis frame their own rules and regulations.

15. What was the stretch of Delhi Sultan Ghiyasuddin Tughlaq empire?

Ans. Delhi Sultan Ghiyasuddin Tughlaq empire stretched from Bengal (Gauda) in the East to Afghanistan (Gajjana) in the West and included all South India.

16. When did the merchants and the migrants brought the teachings of Quran in India?

Ans. In the 7th century, the merchants and migrants brought the teachings of Quran in India.

17. How many sects are there in Islam?

Ans. There are two sects in Islam – Shia and Sunni.

18. Who was the legitimate leader of the Muslim community according to Shia Muslims?

Ans. Prophet Muhammad's son-in law Ali was the legitimate leader of the Muslim community according to Shia Muslims.

19. What is meant by Caliph or Khalifas?

Ans. Caliph is the title given to the head of the Muslim community. Sunni Muslims accepted the authority of the Khalifas.

20. What is the meaning of Ulama?

Ans. Ulama means learned theologians and jurists of Islam.

21. British historians divided History into how many periods?

Ans. British historians divided Indian History into three periods which are Hindu, Muslim and British.

Short Answer Type Questions

1. What are the differences between the region of Hindustan of 13th century and the modern India?

Ans. In 13th century, Minhaj-i-Siraj used the term 'Hindustan' to refer to areas of Punjab, Haryana and land between Ganga and Yamuna. It only included Northern plains of modern day India.

Today, modern India along with Punjab and Haryana includes Jammu and Kashmir in North, deserts of Rajasthan, states of North East and South and Islands of Andaman and Lakshadweep.

2. How historians work in interpreting and analysing historical events?

Ans. Historians rely on different types of available sources of history to interprete and analyse historical events.

These are maps, inscriptions, coins, poetry, ornaments, paintings, chronicles, architecture and textual records.

Many historians analyse the changes in the social, political and economic aspects of the society to analyse events. Manuscripts in archives are also of great help for historians in throwing light upon the events and happenings of history.

3. Paper became cheaper in the later years of medieval period. How it affected people? **Competency Based**

Ans. Paper became cheaper in the later years of medieval period. It affected people as they started using it to write holy texts, chronicles of rulers, letters and teachings of saints, petitions and judicial records, and for registers of accounts and taxes.

This led to many written records being found from this period.

4. Explain about division of groups into Jatis during the medieval period. How did Jatis manage the conduct of their member?

Ans. In the medieval period as society became divided, people were grouped into Jatis or sub-castes. They were ranked on the basis of their backgrounds and their occupations.

Jatis framed their own rules and regulations to manage the conduct of their members. These regulations were enforced by an assembly of elders. Jatis were also required to follow the rules of their villages which were governed by a chieftain.

5. How the views of Shias are different from that of Sunnis?

Or **State the difference between Shia Muslims and Sunni Muslims.** **Diksha**

Ans. The views of Shias are different from that of Sunnis as Shia Muslims followed the teachings of Prophet Mohammad's son-in law, Ali and regarded him as the legitimate leader of the Muslim community. On the other hand, Sunni Muslims accepted the authority of the early leaders (Khalifas) of the community and the succeeding Khalifas.

6. "As a result historians have to read different manuscript versions of the same text to guess what the author had originally written." What were the reasons for this?

Ans. Manuscripts provide a lot of detailed information to historians but they are difficult to use. As scribes used to copy manuscripts by hand, it often led to small changes in the text of the manuscripts. These small changes grew over time until the manuscripts of the same text became different from each other.

Thus, historians had to guess sometimes what the author had originally written.

Long Answer Type Questions

1. "Historians today have to be careful about the terms they use because these towns means different things in the past." Support the statement using examples. **Competency Based**

Ans. Historians have to be careful about the terms they use because these terms means different things in the past. For example,

- The term 'Hindustan' today is understood as 'India' i.e. the modern nation-state. However in 13th century, it was used by Minhaj-i-Siraj to refer the areas of Punjab, Haryana and lands between the Ganga and Yamuna under the Delhi Sultanate. In the early 16th century, Babur used the term 'Hindustan' to describe the geography, the fauna and the culture of the inhabitants of the sub-continent. This description is similar to the one given by 14th century poet Amir Khusrau who used the term 'Hind'.
- The term 'foreigner' was used in the medieval period for any unknown person coming to a village, who was not a part of that society or culture. However, today the term 'foreigner' refers to someone who is not an Indian. The term *'pardesi'* in Hindi and *'ajnabi'* in Persian are used for the term *'foreigner'*.

2. What major changes were noticed between 700 AD and 1750 AD?

Or **Why was the period of thousand years between 700 AD and 1750 AD termed as a period of economic, political, social and cultural changes ?** **Diksha**

Ans. The period of thousand years between 700 AD and 1750 AD termed as a period of economic, political, social and cultural changes due to the following changes

- New technologies like the Persian wheel in irrigation, the spinning wheel in weaving and firearms in combat emerged during this period.
- New food and beverages were introduced in the subcontinent like potatoes, corn, chillies, tea and coffee.
- During this period the Rajput group became important. The name 'Rajput' is derived from 'Rajaputra, meaning the son of a ruler. Other groups such as the Marathas, Sikhs, Jats, Ahoms and Kshatriyas also became politically important during this period.
- Society was divided into jatis or sub castes during this period and they were ranked according to their backgrounds and occupations.

3. Describe the major developments in the religious traditions during 700 AD to 1750 AD.

Ans. Many major developments occurred in religious traditions during the period between 700 to 1750 AD.

These were as follows

- In Hinduism, these developments included worship of new deities, construction of temples by royalty and growing importance of Brahmanas.
- Brahmanas earned great respect in society for their knowledge of Sanskrit texts. They were supported by new rulers.
- Idea of Bhakti and new religions also emerged during this period. Teachings of Quran were introduced by merchants who came to India in the 7th century. Quran is the Holy book of Muslims. Many rulers became patrons of Islam and Ulama.

Picture Based Questions

1. Answer the question based on following picture.

(i) What is the picture all about?

Ans. The picture shows a scribe.

(ii) What is he doing?

Ans. He is making a copy of a manuscript.

(iii) Why is it called miniature?

Ans. This is called miniature because of its smaller size (10.5 cm by 7.1 cm).

(iv) What were the two features of miniatures?

Ans. The two features of miniatures were

(i) Miniature is used to illustrate the text of manuscripts.

(ii) Miniatures are so beautiful that collectors often took the manuscripts apart and sold just the miniatures.

2. On the basis of the given picture, answer the following questions.

Figure I

Figure II

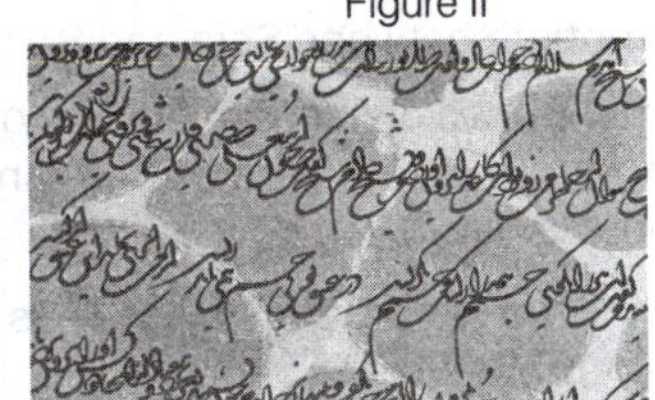

(a) What do the above figures shows?

Ans. Both the figures show the handwriting of Persian and Arabic languages.

(b) What are the differences that one can make out from the two given figures?

Ans. First figure is cursive and easy to read, it is called the nastaliq style.

Second figure is denser and more difficult to understand, it is called as shikaste style.

Case Based Questions

1. Read the passage given below and answer the following questions.

Language and Region

In 1318, the poet Amir Khusrau noted that there was a different language in every region of this land: Sindhi, Lahori, Kashmiri, Dvarsamudri (in Southern Karnataka), Telangani (in Andhra Pradesh), Gujari (in Gujarat), Ma'bari (in Tamil Nadu), Gauri, (in Bengal). Awadhi (in Eastern Uttar Pradesh) and Hindawi (in the area around Delhi). Amir Khusrau went on to explain that in contrast to these languages there was Sanskrit which did not belong to any region. It was an old language and *"common people do not know it, only the Brahmanas do"*.

Make a list of the languages mentioned by Amir Khusrau. Prepare another list of the names of languages spoken today in the regions he mentioned. Underline names that are similar and circle those that are different. Did you notice that the names by which languages are known have changed over time?

Ans.

Region	Language spoken today	Is it similar or different
Kashmir	Kashmiri	Same
Lahore/West Punjab	Punjabi	Different (Lahori)
Sindh	Sindhi	Same
Andhra Pradesh	Telugu	Different (Telangani)
Karnataka	Kannad	Different (Dvarsamudri)
Gujarat	Gujarati	Different (Gujari)
Bengal	Gauri	Different (Bengali)
Eastern Uttar Pradesh	Awadhi	Same
Delhi	Hindi	Different (Hindawi)

Yes, the languages have changed over time. For example, today Punjabi is spoken in Lahore whereas Lahori was spoken in the past.

2. Read the passage given below and answer the following questions.

One group of people who became important in this period were the Rajputs, a name derived from "Rajaputra", the son of a ruler. Between the eighth and fourteenth centuries, the term was applied more generally to a group of warriors who claimed Kshatriya caste status. A chivalric code of conduct – extreme valour and a great sense of loyalty – were the qualities attributed to Rajputs by their poets and bards. Other groups of people such as the Marathas, Sikhs, Jats,

Ahoms and Kayasthas (a caste of scribes and secretaries) also used the opportunities of the age to become politically important.

(i) **What were the qualities attributed to the Rajputs by their poets and bards, and why were these qualities significant?**

Ans. The qualities attributed to the Rajputs by their poets and bards were extreme valour and a great sense of loyalty.

These qualities were significant as they formed a great code of conduct, contributing to the political importance of the Rajputs between the eighth and fourteenth centuries.

(ii) **How did other groups like the Marathas, Sikhs, Jats, Ahoms and Kayasthas take advantage of the opportunities of the age to become politically important?**

Ans. Other groups, like the Marathas, Sikhs, Jats, Ahoms, and Kayasthas, took advantage of the opportunities of the age to become politically important by utilising their resources and positions to gain significance in the political landscape.

(iii) **How did the term "Rajaputra" evolve to represent a broader group of warriors?**

Ans. Over time, between the eighth and fourteenth centuries, the term "Rajaputra" evolved to denote a broader group of warriors. Initially referring to the son of a ruler, it began to be applied more generally to a group of warriors who claimed Kshatriya caste status, contributing to the importance of the Rajputs in that historical period.

Map Based Question

1. **Compare either Map 1 or Map 2 with the present day map of the sub-continent listing as many similarities and differences as you can find.**

Map 1

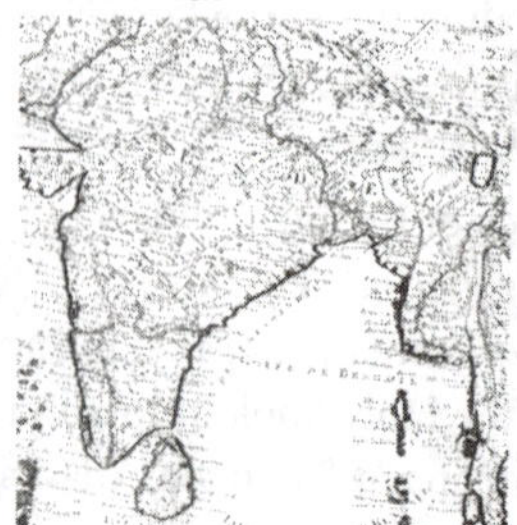
Map 2

Ans. Map 1 and 2 represent two different times. Map 1 was made in 1154 CE by Al-Idrisi, an Arab geographer. This section is a detail of the Indian sub-continent from his larger map of the world.

Map 2 was made by a French cartographer in the year 1720. Both maps are quite different from each other, even though, they represent the same area.

In Map 1, we find South India at the place where we would expect to find North India and Sri Lanka is the island at the top. The place names are in Arabic. Some familiar places like Kannauj in Uttar Pradesh have been spelt as Qannauj.

In comparison to this, Map 2 was made nearly 600 years after Map 1. By that time information about the sub-continent had changed a lot. This map appears to be more familiar to us. The coastal areas, particularly are more detailed.

ASSESSMENT EXERCISE

Multiple Choice Questions (MCQs)

1. Which of the following is the meaning of foreigner during medieval period?
(a) Someone who is not an Indian
(b) Someone who is not a part of society
(c) People of Africa
(d) None of the above

2. How the historians decipher the original work of manuscripts?
(a) Read different versions of the same text
(b) Read only original manuscripts.
(c) Do not read one versions
(d) Both (a) and (b)

3. Which of the following period is recognised as period of great mobility?
(a) 700 to 1750
(b) 1000 to 2000
(c) 600 to 1600
(d) 500 to 1500

Subjective Questions (VSA, SA & LA)

1. How jatis were ranked during medieval period?
2. Which script praise the Delhi Sultan Ghiyasuddin Balban?
3. What was term Hindustan meant to Babur?
4. What were the regions of span of Chola and Khalji dynasty?
5. How can you say that Pan regional rule had altered the character of the regions?
6. Differentiate between Shia and Sunni Muslims.
7. How did British divided the history of India on the idea that the religion of rulers was the only important historical change?
8. How can we say that languages has changed considerably over the years?
9. How do the beliefs change with the alteration of society?
10. Write about the use of new technologies made their appearance during 700 and 1750.

Kings and Kingdoms

CHAPTER 2

Between the 7th and 12th centuries, many new dynasties emerged in different parts of the sub-continent. In this chapter, we will learn about the political development and military conquest of various dynasties, and a detailed study of the Cholas.

2.1 Emergence of New Dynasties

During the period between 7th and 12th centuries, many new dynasties emerged in India like the Rashtrakutas, Cholas, Cheras, Pandyas, Chandelas, Palas, etc. Kings of these dynasties acknowledged big landlords and warrior chiefs as their subordinates or ***samantas***.

Samantas were expected to do the following

- to bring gifts for their kings.
- to be present at king's court.
- to provide the king with military support.

As *samantas* gained power and wealth, they declared themselves to be ***maha-samanta*** or ***maha-mandaleshvara*** Sometimes, they also declared themselves as independent from their kings.

For example, Rashtrakutas in the Deccan were the subordinates of Chalukyas of Karnataka. In the mid-eighth century, **Dantidurga**, Rashtrakuta chief overthrew his Chalukya king and performed a ritual called ***hiranya-garbha*** (the golden womb). It was done to demonstrate his rebirth as a Kshatriya.

Sometimes men from trading families used their military skills to develop kingdoms. For example, **Kadamba Mayurasharman** and the **Gurjara-Pratihara Harichandra** were Brahmanas. They gave up their traditional occupations and established kingdoms in Karnataka and Rajasthan, respectively.

2.2 Administration in the Kingdoms

Many of the new kings adopted titles like ***maharaja-adhiraja*** (great king, overlord of kings) and ***tribhuvana-chakravartin*** (lord of the three worlds). However, they shared power with Samantas, association of peasants, traders and Brahmanas.

Revenue was collected in these kingdoms from producers like peasants, cattle-keepers, artisans and traders as 'rent' which was a part of what they produced.

These resources were used to finance king's establishment, construction of temples and forts, and fight wars.

Revenue was collected by people from influential families and these positions were hereditary.

2.3 Prashastis and Land Grants

Prashastis[1] contain details about the ruler but this information may not always be true. Rulers often depict themselves as warriors.

Prashastis were composed by Brahamanas in exchange of grants of land as reward from the rulers. Land grants given to them were recorded on copper plates.

Unlike the writers of *Prashastis*, an author named Kalhana criticised the rulers and their policies in his account. He used a variety of sources, including inscriptions, documents, eyewitness accounts and earlier histories to write his account.

---

1 Prashasti It is a kind of inscription which means 'in praise of'.

2.4 Wars for Acquiring Wealth

The rulers of new dynasties that emerged between 7th and 12th centuries were involved in **warfare**[2] to take control of other areas. The rulers of Gurjara- Pratihara, Rashtrakuta and Pala dynasties were involved in a long struggle for control over Kannauj which was known as **Tripartite struggle**.

Rulers tried to demonstrate their power by building large temples. Extremely rich temples were targeted in any attack.

For example, **Mahmud of Ghazni** (Afghanistan) attacked India 17 times and targeted wealthy temples like Somanth of Gujarat. He created a grand city at Ghazni with the wealth he looted from India.

Other rulers involved in warfare included the Chahamanas (later called Chauhans) who ruled over Delhi and Ajmer. They tried to expand their control in the West against Chalukyas of Gujarat and in the East against Gahadavalas of Uttar Pradesh.

Prithviraja III was the most famous Chauhan ruler who defeated an Afghan ruler named Sultan Muhammad Ghori in 1191.

2.5 The Cholas

From Uraiyur to Thanjavur

Muttaraiyar was a small family that had power in Kaveri delta. They were subordinates of Pallava kings of Kanchipuram.

Vijayalaya who belonged to the Chola family of Uraiyur, captured the delta from the Muttaraiyar in the middle of 19th century. He built the town of Thanjavur and temple of Nishumbhasudini goddess at this place.

The successors of Vijayalaya conquered neighbouring regions and the Chola kingdom grew in size and power. The territories of Pandyas to the South and Pallavas to the North were also made part of Chola kingdom.

Rajaraja I became king in **985**. He was the most powerful king of Chola dynasty. He reorganised the administration of the empire. His son **Rajendra I** also continued his policies. He even invaded Sri Lanka and countries of South-East Asia by developing navy.

Grand Temples and Bronze Sculptures

The temples of Thanjavur and Gangaikonda-cholapuram that were built by Rajaraja and Rajendra are prominent examples of great architecture of Cholas. **Settlement**[3] grew around these temples.

Chola temples were centres of craft production. The **bronze images** of Chola are considered amongst the finest in the world. These include both images of deities and devotees.

Rulers provided lands to the temples. The produce of this land was used to maintain lives of people who worked at the temple. In this way, temple were the centres of economic, social and cultural life.

Agriculture and Irrigation

New developments in agriculture were responsible for many achievements of the Cholas. They used water of the **Kaveri river** for irrigation purposes. For large-scale cultivations, the Cholas had to clear the forests and level the land.

They had to built **embankments**[4] in the delta region to prevent flooding and canals had to be constructed for carrying water to the fields. In many areas, two crops were grown in a year.

In some cases, they used artificial irrigation methods like construction of wells and tanks for collecting rainwater.

Try These

1. **What was called 'Brahmadeya'?**
2. **Name the Chola ruler who developed navy.**
3. **At the time of Cholas, this tax was levied in the form of forced labour. Identify the tax.**
4. **Who is the king related to Gwalior Prashasti?**

2 **Warfare** It refers to the process of military struggle between two nations or groups of nations.
3 **Settlement** It refers to a place that a group of people have built to live.
4 **Embankments** It refers to a wall of stone that is built to stop a river from flooding.

2.6 The Administration of Chola Kingdom

In the kingdom of Cholas, settlements of peasants that were known as *'ur'* became prosperous with the spread of irrigation agriculture. Groups of these villages formed larger units called ***nadu***.

The village council and the *nadu* performed several administrative functions like collecting taxes and delivering justice.

Rich peasants exercised control over the affairs of the *nadu* under the supervision of the Central Chola government. Titles like ***muvendavelan*** (a velan of peasant serving three kings) and ***araiyar*** (chief) were given to rich landowners by the Chola kings.

Land grants were given to Brahmanas that were known as **Brahmadeya**. Thus, a large number of Brahmana settlements emerged in the Kaveri valley as in other parts of South India.

Each *Brahmadeya* was looked after by an assembly or sabha of prominent Brahmana landholders. Their decisions were recorded in inscription, mostly on the stone walls of temples. The sabha had separate committees with different responsibilities like irrigation works, gardens, temples, etc.

The inscriptions from **Uttaramerur** in Chingleput district, Tamil Nadu, give information about the way in which Sabha was organised. The sabha had separate committees to look after irrigation work, gardens, temples, etc.

There were associations of traders that were known as **Nagarams**. They occasionally performed administrative functions of the state.

Types of Land

According to Chola inscription, there were several types of land as follows

- ***Vellanvagai*** This type of land belong to non-Brahmana peasant proprietors.
- ***Shalabhoga*** This type of land was meant for the maintenance of school.
- ***Devadana***, ***Tirunamattukkani*** This type of land was gifted to temples.
- ***Pallichchhandam*** This type of land was donated to Jaina institutions.
- ***Brahmadeya*** This type of land is gifted to Brahmanas.

Mind Map

Administration in the Kingdoms

- The new kings adopted titles like Maharaja-adhiraja and Tribhuvana-Chakravartin.
- Rulers shared power with Samantas peasants, Traders and Brahmans.
- Resources used to finance king's establishment, construction of temples, forts and fight wars.

Emergence of New Dynasties

- Between 7th and 12th centuries, following dynasties emerged
  - Rashtrakutas
  - Palas
  - Chalukyas.
  - Cheras
  - Chandelas
- Rashtrakuta chief Dantidurga performed a ritual called hiranyagarbha and became king.
- Samantas declared themselves as Maha-samanta or Maha-mandaleshvara.

KINGS AND KINGDOMS

The Cholas

- Rajaraja I was the most powerful king of Chola dynasty.
- Chola temples were centres of craft production.
- Rulers provided land to the temples.

Wars for Acquiring Wealth

- Tripartite struggle – Rulers of Gurjara-Pratihara, Rashtrakuta and Pala dynasties involved in a war to acquire Kannauj.
- Mahmud of Ghazni attacked India 17 times and targeted wealthy temples.
- The Chauhan ruler Prithviraj III defeated Sultan Muhammad Ghori in 1191.

Prashastis and Land Grants

- Contain details about the rulers.
- Composed by Brahmanasin exchange of grants of land as rewards from the rulers.
- Kalhana did not praised rulers in his account like in prashastis. He used sources like inscriptions, documents, eyewitness accounts and earlier histories.

The Administration of Chola Kingdom

- Kings adopted titles like *maharaja -adhiraja* and *tribhuvana-chakravartin.*
- Revenue was collected from producers like peasants, cattle-keepers, artisans and traders.
- Nadu is large unit of settlements are formed by peasants.
- Titles like, Muvendavelan and Araiyar given to rich landowners by the Chola Kings.

NCERT FOLDER

Covering Intext Questions and Exercises of NCERT

NCERT ON PAGE 17

Q.1 Do you think being born as a Kshatriya was important in order to become a ruler during this period ?

Ans. No, being born as a Kshatriya was not important in order to become a ruler during this period. For instance, Rashtrakutas were not Kshatriyas but they could become rulers after performing a ritual. Gurjara-Pratihara Harichandra was a Brahman but could establish his own kingdom in Rajasthan.

NCERT ON PAGE 18

Q.2 In what ways was this form of administration different from the present day system ?

Ans. This form of administration is different from the present day system as the King, was the head of the state and he was regarded as the Lord of the three worlds. He was assisted by Samantas. These positions were hereditary. Whereas, today heads of the states are elected by the people. People take part in administration and exercise their choice through vote.

Q.3 Are any such taxes collected today?

Ans. No, any such taxes are not collected today. Taxes collected are very reasonable today and used for the development of the country and welfare of the citizens. Earlier rulers used to collect unreasonable taxes for maintaining their luxurious life and common people had to pay such taxes.

NCERT ON PAGE 19

Q.4 Also, see if you can find some of the areas mentioned in the inscription on Map 1. Other rulers made similar claims as well. Why do you think they made these claims ?

Ans. Rulers made these exaggerated claims to depict themselves as brave and victorious warriors. They used to spread messages of their superiority and military capabilities through these inscriptions. It was done to make their enemies fearful.

NCERT ON PAGE 27

Q.5 Do you think women participated in these assemblies? In your view are lotteries useful in choosing members of committees?

Ans. No, women could not participate in these assemblies because only owners of land could participate and women were never given ownership of land.

No, I don't think lotteries are useful in choosing members of the committees because then it would be based on chance. People with knowledge and experience may get missed out and people with no experience may hold power.

Q.6 Were there any Brahmanas in this hamlet? Describe all the activities that were taking place in the village. Why do you think temple inscriptions ignore these activities?

Ans. No, there were no Brahmanas in this hamlet. Such hamlets were only for people engaged in menial occupations.

The activities that were taking place in the village were

- Labourers were engaged in menial (unskilled/low) occupations.
- Little chickens moved about in groups.
- Children were carrying little puppies.
- A female labourer put her baby to sleep on a sheet of leather.
- Pulaiya women were singing as they were husking the paddy.

The temple inscriptions recorded only the praise of the king and kingdom, and therefore the inscriptions ignored other such activities of hamlet.

Q.7 You are present in an election for a sabha. Describe what you see and hear ?

Ans. Here's a description of what I might see and hear during an election for a sabha.

All male adults of the society are present in a temple hall. The eldest males are deciding who is eligible to become a member of the sabha. A group of young boys is assisting these elders in providing a list of people interested in becoming members. The group of eldest people is now deciding the final members for election.

A member is disqualified to become a member because he did not have knowledge of Vedas. The names of those who are eligible, are written on small tickets of palm leaf. These tickets are put into an earthenware pot, from which a young boy was asked to take out the tickets.

EXERCISES

Q.1 Match the following.

	Column A	Column B
A.	Gurjara-Pratiharas	1. Western Deccan
B.	Rashtrakutas	2. Bengal
C.	Palas	3. Gujarat and Rajasthan
D.	Cholas	4. Tamil Nadu

Codes

	A	B	C	D		A	B	C	D
(a)	1	2	3	4	(b)	2	1	3	4
(c)	3	1	2	4	(d)	3	2	4	1

Ans. (c)

Q.2 Who were the parties involved in the "Tripartite struggle"?

Ans. Gurjara-Pratiharas, Rashtrakutas and Pala Dynasties were involved in Tripartite struggle to gain control over Kannauj.

Q.3 What were the qualifications necessary to become a member of a committee of the sabha in the Chola empire?

Ans. The qualifications necessary to become a member of a committee of the sabha in the Chola empire were

- They should own land from which land revenue is collected.
- They should be between 35 and 70 years of age.
- They should have knowledge of the Vedas.
- They should be well or well aware in administrative matters and honest. Anyone who has been a member in last three years cannot become a member.
- They should submit accounts of their family and the relatives.

Q.4 What were the two major cities under the control of the Chahamanas?

Ans. The two major cities under the control of the Chahamanas were Delhi and Ajmer.

Q.5 How did the Rashtrakutas become powerful?

Ans. Initially, Rashtrakutas were subordinates to the Chalukyas of Karnataka. Gradually, they gained power and wealth. In the mid-8th century Dantidurga, a Rashtrakuta chief, overthrew his Chalukya overlord. He performed a ritual called *hiranya-garbha* with the help of Brahmanas. This ritual was then, considered to lead the rebirth of the sacrificer as Kshatriya, even if he was not a Kshatriya born.

Q.6 What did the new dynasties do to gain acceptance ?

Ans. New dynasties did the following things to gain acceptance

- The rulers recorded their activities in inscriptions. Brahmanas were given land in exchange of inscriptions they wrote. To impress the king they often praised the kings and exaggerated the reality. These inscriptions created a positive image among the common people.
- Rulers built grand temples to demonstrate their power and wealth. These temples attracted people from other kingdoms as well.

Q.7 What kind of irrigation works were developed in the Tamil region?

Ans. Following irrigation works were developed in Tamil region to control the overflow of several channels of Kaveri river

- Embankment were build to prevent flooding.
- Canals were constructed to carry water to the fields.
- Huge tanks to collect rainwater were built.
- Wells were dug for irrigation purpose.

Q.8 What were the activities associated with Chola temples?

Ans. The activities associated with Chola temples were

- Settlements emerged around the temples.
- Land grants were given to temple by kings and others. The produce of such land went for the livelihood of priests, garland makers, cooks, sweepers, musicians, dancers, etc.
- Temples were not only places of worship but also the hub of economic, social and cultural life as well.
- Temples were centres of craft production. Craftsmen used to make bronze image of deities and devotees.

Q.9 Contrast the elections in Uttaramerur with present-day Panchayat elections.

Ans. The difference between the election in Uttaramerur and present-day Panchayat elections are

In Uttaramerur	Panchayat election of present-day
The names of the persons eligible were written on small tickets of palm leaves.	The names of the members are printed with a symbol allotted to them on a paper called ballot paper.
The tickets were put into an earthenware pot.	The voter is verified from the voter list, then he is given the ballot paper.
One young boy was asked to take out the tickets, one by one for each committee.	The voter puts a stamp on the allotted sign of any chosen candidate. Candidate with maximum stamps in front of his name used to win.
It was an informal process. Women did not take parts in elections.	It is a formal process. All the protocols are strictly followed. Men and women both take part in elections.

Q.10 **Look at map below and find out whether there were any kingdoms in the state in which you live.**

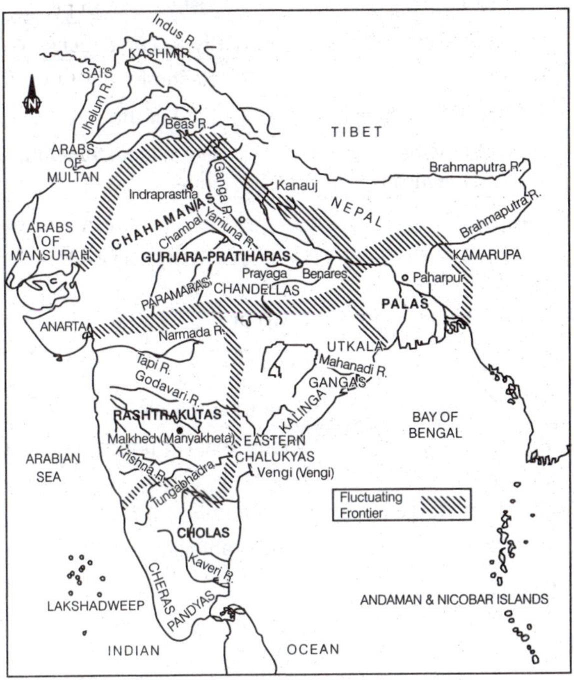

Ans. According to the map, there was a kingdom in my state named Indraprastha. I live in Delhi.

Q.11 **Compare the temple shown in this chapter with any present day temple in your neighbourhood highlighting any similarities and differences that you notice?**

Ans. After comparing the temple shown in this chapter with a temple in my neighbourhood, I noticed the following similarities and differences

Temples stated in chapter	Present day temples
Pyramidal in shape	Like the shape of a cone with narrow at the top.
Images on the walls	No images on the walls.
Settlements and land nearby	Settlements nearby
Several persons were employed	Only the priests and a helpers.
Worship of gods and goddesses	Worship of gods and goddesses
Domination of Brahmanas	Domination of Brahmanas
Crafts were associated	No crafts work seen

Q.12 **Find out more about taxes that are collected at present. Are these in cash, kind, or labour services.**

Ans. Taxes that are collected today are Goods & Services tax, Water tax, Income tax, Wealth tax, Sales tax, Property tax, Excise tax, VAT (Value Added Tax), Service tax, Education tax. These taxes are collected in cash and not in kind or labour services.

REVIEW EXERCISE

Including Competency Based Questions

Part I

Multiple Choice Questions (MCQs)

1. Who were Maha-Samantas?
(a) Samantas who gained wealth
(b) Samantas who wrote good text
(c) Samantas who became more powerful
(d) Both (a) and (c)

2. In the mid-8th, Dantidurga overthrew his Chalukya overlord and became the chief of
(a) Rashtrakuta (b) Chola
(c) Brahmana (d) Samanta

3. Prashastis were composed by Diksha
(a) kings only (b) learned Samantas
(c) brahmanas (d) army men

4. Kings rewarded Brahmanas grants of
(a) money (b) land (c) gold (d) big palace

5. Where did Sultan Mahmud of Ghazni came from ?
(a) Afghanistan (b) Arab (c) Persia (d) China

6. Who built the temple of Goddess Nishumbhasudini at Thanjavur ?
(a) Vijayalaya (b) Palas of Eastern India
(c) Dantidurga (d) Rajaraja and Rajendra

7. Who was the most powerful Chola ruler? Diksha
(a) Vijayalaya (b) Rajaraja I
(c) Rajendra I (d) Virarajendra

8. Settlements of peasants were known as Diksha
(a) Panchayat (b) Nadu
(c) Mandal (d) Ur

9. Brahmanas received land grants called as
(a) Jagir (b) Devadana
(c) Brahmadeya (d) Mandala

10. What is Vetti?

(a) Revenue (b) Rent (c) Tax (d) Gold

11. Who was Nagabhatta?

(a) Chola ruler (b) Pratihara king
(c) Malava king (d) Rashtrakuta ruler

12. The prashasti found in Gwalior about Pratihara king Nagabhatta was written in which language?

(a) Sanskrit (b) Urdu
(c) Hindi (d) Persian

13. Kailash temple of Ellora was built during the period of

(a) Rashtrakutas (b) Cholas
(c) Palas (d) Pratiharas

14. He was a Brahmana who gave up his traditional occupation and established his own kingdom in Karnataka. **Competency Based**

Identify the ruler from the following options.

(a) Gurjara-Pratihara Harichandra
(b) Kadamba Mayurasharman
(c) Nagabhatta
(d) None of the above

15. Which of the following statements is/are correct ? **Competency Based**

I. Vijayalaya built the town Thanjavur.
II. Rajaraja I was the son of Rajendra I.
III. Group of villages formed the larger unit called Ur.

Codes

(a) I and II (b) I, II and III
(c) Only I (d) II and III

16. Which of the following statements is/are incorrect? **Competency Based**

I. Prithviraja III defeated Muhammad Ghori in 1191.
II. History of Kings of Kashmir was written by Kalhan in Sanskrit.
III. Tripartite struggle for Kannauj was held for supermacy in South India.

Codes

(a) Only I (b) I and II
(c) Only III (d) All of these

17. What is the correct sequence of Chola rulers?

I. Rajaraja I II. Rajendra I
III. Rajendra II IV. Vijayalaya

Codes

(a) I, II, III, IV (b) IV, II, III, I
(c) I, IV, III, II (d) IV, I, II, III

Answers

1. (d)	**2.** (a)	**3.** (c)	**4.** (b)	**5.** (a)
6. (a)	**7.** (b)	**8.** (d)	**9.** (c)	**10.** (c)
11. (b)	**12.** (a)	**13.** (a)	**14.** (b)	**15.** (c)
16. (a)	**17.** (a)			

Match the Following

1.

	List I		List II
A.	Maharaja-Adhiraja	1.	Rajaraja
B.	Kalhana	2.	Kashmir
C.	Temple of Thanjavur	3.	Lord of the three kings
D.	Tribhuvana Chakravartin	4.	Great king, over lord of kings

Codes

	A	B	C	D		A	B	C	D
(a)	4	2	1	3	(b)	3	4	1	2
(c)	4	1	2	3	(d)	3	1	2	4

2.

	List I		List II
A.	Prashastis	1.	Rashtrakuta Chief
B.	Ur	2.	A long sanskrit poem depicting kings rule
C.	Dantidurga	3.	Settlements of peasants
D.	Brahmadeya	4.	Land grants given to Brahmanas

Codes

	A	B	C	D		A	B	C	D
(a)	2	3	1	4	(b)	3	4	1	2
(c)	4	1	2	3	(d)	3	1	2	4

Ans. 1. (a) 2. (a)

Assertion-Reason

1. **Assertion** (A) Gurjara-Pratihara, Rashtrakuta and Pala dynasties fought for control over Kannauj.

Reason (R) Tripartite struggle was the conflict to show domain over the whole Ganga Valley.

Codes

(a) Both A and R are true and R is the correct explanation of A
(b) Both A and R are true, but R is not the correct explanation of A
(c) A is true, but R is false
(d) A is false, but R is true

2. **Assertion** (A) Prashastis were written to describe achievements of kings.

Reason (R) Nagabhatta's Prashasti was found in Thanjavur, Tamil Nadu.

Codes

(a) Both A and R are true and R is the correct explanation of A
(b) Both A and R are true, but R is not the correct explanation of A
(c) A is true, but R is false
(d) A is false, but R is true

Ans. 1. (a) Both A and R are true and R is the correct explanation of A

2. (c) A is true, but R is false

Fill in the Blanks

1. Kadamba Mayurasharman and the Gurjara-Pratihara Harichandra were .... who gave up their traditional professions.
2. Prashastis were written by learned ...... in ...... language.
3. Kalhana wrote a long poem in Sanskrit containing the history of kings who ruled over ....
4. Some rich landowners of Chola rule were honoured with the titles like .... and ....

Ans. 1. Brahamanas 2. Brahmanas, Sanskrit
3. Kashmir 4. Muvendavelan, Araiyar

True/False

1. Kadamba Mayurasharman and the Gurjara-Pratihara Harichandra were Brahmanas who gave up their traditional professions and took to arms.
2. The produce of the temple land went into maintaining all the specialists employed in the temple.
3. Only after 4th century, area of Tamil Nadu was opened up for large scale cultivation.
4. Brahmanas often received land grants called as Jagir.

Ans. 1. True 2. True 3. True 4. False

Picture Based Questions

1. **The artwork depicted in the image at Ellora was attributed to which dynasty?**

(a) Pala (b) Rashtrakuta (c) Chola (d) Chahamanas

2. **What material was used to create the sculpture of a girl from Chola period as, depicted in the picture below.**

(a) Bronze (b) Copper (c) Gold (d) Silver

Ans. 1. (b) Rashtrakuta 2. (a) Bronze

Case Based Question

1. **Read the passage given below and answer the questions that follow.**

For centuries, rulers belonging to the Gurjara-Pratihara, Rashtrakuta and Pala dynasties fought for control over Kannauj. Because there were three "Parties" in this long-drawn conflict, historians often describe it as the "Tripartite Struggle". Rulers also tried to demonstrate their power and resources by building large temples. So, when they attacked one another's kingdom, they often chose to target temples, which were sometimes extremely rich. One such ruler is Mahmud of Ghazni, Afghanistan.

He raided the sub-continent 17 times (1000–1025) with a religious motive. His targets were wealthy temples, including that of Somnath, Gujarat. Much of the wealth Mahmud carried away was used to create a splendid capital city at Ghazni.

(i) What did Mahmud of Ghazni do with the wealth he carried away from the sub-continent?
(a) Built a navy
(b) Created a splendid capital city
(c) Invested in education
(d) Distributed among the poor

(ii) What term is commonly used to describe the conflict over Kanauj in the passage?
(a) The Hundred-Year War
(b) The Pala Strife
(c) The Tripartite Struggle
(d) The Long-drawn Clash

(iii) What was the primary motive for Mahmud of Ghazni's seventeen raids in the sub-continent?
(a) To seek knowledge.
(b) To conquer and unite India under one rule.
(c) To plunder India's wealth
(d) To establish peaceful relations with neighbouring states.

(iv) Mahmud of Ghazni raided the sub-continent 17 times with a religious motive. What was his primary target during these raids?
(a) Royal palaces
(b) Educational institutions
(c) Wealthy temples
(d) Military fortifications

Ans (i) (b) Created a Splendid Capital City
(ii) (c) The Tripartite Struggle
(iii) (c) To Plunder India's wealth
(iv) (c) Wealthy temples

Part II

Very Short Answer Type Questions

1. What did the *samantas* declare themselves later?

Ans. As *samantas* gained power and wealth, they declared themselves to be *Maha-Samanta* or *Maha-Mandaleshvara*.

2. Who was Dantidurga?

Ans. Dantidurga was a Rashtrakuta chief who overthrew his Chalukya king. He performed a ritual called *hiranya-garbha*.

3. Who was given the task of collecting revenue in newly emerged dynasties?

Ans. People from influential families were given the task of collecting revenue. This position was often hereditary.

4. Name the 12th century Sanskrit poet from Kashmir.

Ans. Kalhana was the 12th century Sanskrit poet from Kashmir.

5. Why did the rulers choose temples as their targets when they attacked upon one another's kingdom during medieval era ? **Competency Based**

Ans. The rulers choose temples as their targets when they attacked upon one another's kingdom during medieval era because attack on temples was considered as attack on king who had built it and it was seen as a challenge to king's authority.

6. What really made Mahmud of Ghazni to attack India?

Ans. Religious motives made Mahmud of Ghazni to attack India 17 times.

7. Who opposed the expansion of Chahamanas towards West and East?

Ans. The Chalukyas of Gujarat and Gahadavalas of Western Uttar Pradesh opposed the Chahamanas.

8. Who defeated Prithviraja III in 1192?

Ans. Sultan Muhammad Ghori defeated Prithviraja III in 1192.

9. Name the most distinctive craft associated with Chola temples. **Diksha**

Ans. Making bronze sculptures is the most distinctive craft associated with Chola temples.

10. Which images were created in Chola bronze art?

Ans. Images of deities and devotees were created in Chola bronze art.

11. What was the use of embankments in the delta region?

Ans. Embankments were built in the delta region to prevent flooding.

12. What is the meaning of *nadu*?

Ans. Groups of villages that formed larger units were called as *nadu*.

13. What type of taxes were collected by Cholas according to the inscriptions?

Ans. According to the inscription, Cholas used to collect *Vetti* (tax in the form of forced labour) and Kadamai (tax as a land revenue) and many other taxes.

14. What is the meaning of Sabha?

Ans. An assembly of prominent Brahmanas, landholders looking after the Brahmadeya land grants was called Sabha.

15. What is the meaning of *Nagarams*?

Ans. Associations of traders which occasionally performed administrative function in towns were known as *nagarams*.

16. Name the famous caves having a wall carving of Vishnu as Narsimha, the man-lion, done during the Rashtrakuta period. **Diksha**

Ans. Ellora Caves have a wall carving of Vishnu as Narsimha, the man-lion, done during the Rashtrakuta period.

Short Answer Type Questions

1. Explain about the new class of rulers that emerged in the period of 7th century.

Ans. During the 7th century, a new class of rulers emerged. They were the subordinates or *samantas* under the influence of big landlords or warrior chiefs. Gradually, they themselves gained power and wealth and declared themselves to be *maha-samantas* or *maha-mandaleshvara* (the great lord of a circle or region). Sometimes, they asserted their independence from their overlords.

2. Who was Dantidurga? How he became a Kshatriya?

Ans. Dantidurga was a Rashtrakuta chief in Deccan. Initially, Rashtrakutas were the subordinates of Chalukyas of Karnataka.

Dantidurga became a Kshatriya after performing a ritual called *hiranya-garbha*. It literally means the 'golden womb'. This ritual was performed with the help of Brahmanas. It was thought to lead to the rebirth of the sacrificer as a Kshatriya, even if he was not by birth.

3. What titles were adopted by the kings?

Ans. Many of the new kings adopted high-sounding titles. These titles were Maharaja-Adhiraja meaning great king, overlord of kings or Tribhuvana Chakravartin meaning the lord of the three worlds and so on.

However, they often shared power with their Samantas as well as with association of peasants, traders and Brahmanas.

4. From whom the resources were obtained during 7th to 12th centuries and how they were used?

Ans. The resources were obtained during 7th to 12th centuries from producers like peasants, cattle-keepers, artisans and traders as 'rent' which was a part of what they produced.

These resources were used to finance king's establishment, construction of temples and forts, and fight wars. Revenue was collected by people from influential families and these positions were hereditary.

5. How was Kalhan's writing different and ahead of times?

Ans. Kalhan's writing was different and ahead of his times as he followed a critical approach. He was a sanskrit poet from Kashmir. He has written about history of kings of Kashmir. He did not write just to praise the kings. He wrote in a balanced way, highlighting both benefits and drawbacks of rulers' policies.

He used different sources like inscriptions, documents, eye witness accounts and earlier histories in his account.

6. What is a Prashasti? What was the use of it?

Ans. A Prashasti is an inscription from medieval India. It was used to praise and commemorate rulers, their achievements and virtues.

Prashastis served as a means to glorify and record the achievements of kings and dynasties, often in a religious or political context. Brahmanas were given land grants for writing prashastis. Hence, they used to impress kings with their work.

7. Who were the best remembered Chola Kings? Which regions or areas were attacked by Rajendra I?

Ans. Rajaraja I and Rajendra I are the best remembered Chola rulers. Rajaraja I became king in 985 and expanded control over most of the Pandyas and the Pallava territories. He reorganised the administration of the empire.

Rajaraja's son Rajendra I continued his father's policies. He even invaded the Ganga valley, Sri Lanka and countries of South-East Asia, by developing a navy for these expeditions.

8. Who built the two famous temples of Thanjavur and Gangaikondacholapuram? How was these maintained?

Ans. Rajaraja I and his son Rajendra I built the big and grand temples of Thanjavur and Gangaikondacholapuram.

Both these temples were considered the best examples of architectural and sculptural works. Land given to these temples were cultivated and the produce were used to maintain and look after the specialists working there. They were priests, musicians, dancers, cooks, helpers, garland makers, sweepers, etc.

9. What do inscriptions of the Cholas refer to as four hundred taxes? **Competency Based**

Ans. The inscriptions of the Cholas refer to more than 400 terms for different kinds of taxes. The most common among them is Vetti, taken not in cash but in the form of forced labour and Kadami or land revenue. Other taxes were on covering the roof of the houses, the use of a ladder to climb palm trees, a cess on succession to family property, etc.

10. What were the achievements of Nagabhata?

Ans. Nagabhata was a Pratihara king. His achievements were written on a prashasti found in Gwalior.

These were

- He had conquered regions of Andhra, Saindhava (Sind), Vidarbha (part of Maharashtra) and Kalinga (part of Orissa).
- He won a battle against Chakrayudha (the ruler of Kannauj).
- He defeated the king of Vanga (part of Bengal), Anarta (part of Gujarat), Malava (part of Madhya Pradesh), Kirata (forest peoples), Turushka (Turks), Vatsa and Matsya.

Long Answer Type Questions

1. How did the Cholas rise to power ? **Diksha**

Ans. Cholas rose to power after defeating Muttaraiyar in Kaveri delta.

Muttaraiyar was a family of minor chief who held power in the Kaveri delta. The family was subordinate to the Pallava kings of Kanchipuram.

Vijayalaya belonged to the ancient chiefly family of the Cholas from Uraiyur. He captured the Kaveri delta from the Muttaraiyar in the middle of the 9th century. He also built the town of Thanjavur and a temple for goddess Nishumbhasudini there. The successors of Vijayalaya conquered neighbouring areas.

Thus, the empire grew in size and power. The territories of the Pandyan and the Pallava kings were included in this kingdom. Rajaraja I, considered the most powerful Chola ruler expanded the Chola empire. He constructed big temples to show the prosperity and wealth of the kingdom.

2. Give an account of the splendid temples and the sculptures of the Cholas.

Ans. Cholas ruled South India and parts of South-East Asia. They built many splendid temples and sculptures in their kingdom.

The temples of Thanjavur and Gangaikondacholapuram that were built by Rajaraja and Rajendra are prominent examples of great architecture of Cholas. Settlement grew around these temples.

Chola temples were centres of craft production. The bronze images of Chola are considered amongst the finest in the world. These include both images of deities and devotees.

Rulers provided lands to the temples. The produce of this land was used to maintain lives of people who worked at the temple. In this way, temple were the centres of economic, social and cultural life.

3. Describe the agriculture and irrigation works of the Cholas.

Ans. New developments in agriculture were responsible for many achievements of the Cholas. They used water of the Kaveri river for irrigation purposes. For large-scale cultivations, the Cholas had to clear the forests and level the land.

They had to built embankments in the delta region to prevent flooding and canals had to be constructed for carrying water to the fields. In many areas, two crops were grown in a year. In some cases, they used artificial irrigation methods like construction of wells and tanks for collecting rainwater.

4. Give an account of the administration of the Chola Empire.

Ans. In the kingdom of Cholas, settlements of peasants that were known as *'ur'* became prosperous with the spread of irrigation agriculture. Groups of these villages formed larger units called *nadu*.

Rich peasants exercised control over the affairs of the *nadu* under the supervision of the Central Chola government. Titles like *muvendavelan* and *araiyar* were given to rich landowners by the Chola kings.

Land grants were given to Brahmanas that were known as *Brahmadeya*. Each Brahmadeya was looked after by an assembly or sabha of prominent Brahmanas. The sabha had separate committees with different responsibilities. Their decisions were recorded in inscription, mostly on the stone walls of temples. The sabha had separate committees to look after irrigation work, gardens, temples, etc.

There were associations of traders that were known as *nagarams*. They occasionally performed administrative functions of the state.

5. "Irrigation works require planning – organising labour and resources, maintaining these works". Explain the statement in the light of the Chola period. **Competency Based**

Ans. During the Chola period, irrigation works were a critical component of the region's agricultural and economic development. For expanding agriculture, Chola rulers developed many irrigation facilities. Embankments were built to prevent flooding and canals were constructed to carry water to the fields.

Careful planning was done to ensure proper irrigation to all regions. People who were given land grants could collect taxes. These taxes were used to maintain and construct irrigation facilities. Thus, we can conclude that irrigation works required planning in organising labour and maintenance which the Chola dynasty successfully did. Irrigation techniques used by them are still used today.

Picture Based Question

1. Look at the picture given below and answer the following questions.

(i) What is depicted in the image?

Ans. The image depicts a set of copper plates recording a grant of land made by a ruler in the ninth century.

(ii) In what languages is the inscription on the copper plates written?

Ans. The inscription on the copper plates is written partly in Sanskrit and partly in Tamil.

(iii) What is the purpose of the copper plates in the historical context?

Ans. The copper plates serve as a record of a grant of land made by a ruler in the ninth century. They function as an official document authenticating the transfer of land ownership.

(iv) How is the authenticity of the document ensured?

Ans. The authenticity of the document is ensured by the royal seal that secures the ring holding the copper plates together.

Case Based Questions

1. Read the following passage given below and answer the question that follows.

This is a part of the Tamil section of a land grant given by the Cholas

We have demarcated the boundaries of the land by making earthen embankments, as well as by planting thorny bushes. This is what the land contains: fruit-bearing trees, water, land, gardens and orchards, trees, wells, open spaces, pastureland, a village, anthills, platforms, canals, ditches, rivers silt-laden land, tanks, granaries, fish ponds, beehives and deep lakes.

He who receives the land can collect taxes from it. He can collect the taxes imposed by judicial officers as fines, the tax on betel-leaves, that on woven cloth, as well as on vehicles. He can build large rooms with upper stories made of baked bricks, he can get large and small wells dug, he can plant trees and thorny bushes, if necessary, he can get canals constructed for irrigation. He should ensure that water is not wasted and that embankments are built.

(i) **List all the possible sources of irrigation mentioned in the inscription and discuss how these might have been used.**

Ans. The possible sources of irrigation mentioned in this inscription are wells, canals, ditches, tanks, rivers and deep lakes. Embankments were built, so that extra water of the river does not flood nearby area. Seasonal water could be stored in tanks, etc. Later this, water could be used for irrigation.

(ii) **How were the records of land grants kept in the 9th century ?**

Ans. Land grants were recorded on copper plates in 9th century. These were partly written in Sanskrit and partly in Tamil.

(iii) **What type of taxes can the recipient of the land collect?**

Ans. Recipient of land can collect taxes imposed by judicial officers such as fines, tax on betel-leaves, on woven cloth and on vehicles.

2. Read the extract below and answer the question that follows.

While inscriptions tell us about kings and powerful men, here is an excerpt from the Periyapuranam, a 12th century Tamil work, which informs us about the lives of ordinary men and women.

"On the outskirts of Adanur was a small hamlet of Pulaiyas (a name used for a social group considered 'outcastes' by Brahmanas and Vellalas), studded with small huts under old thatches and inhabited by agrarian labourers engaged in menial occupations.

In the thresholds of the huts covered with strips of leather, little chickens moved about in groups, dark children who wore bracelets of black iron were prancing about, carrying little puppies .... In the shade of the marudu (arjuna) trees a female labourer put her baby to sleep on a sheet of leather, there were mango trees from whose branches drums were hanging and under the coconut palms, in little hollows on the ground, tiny-headed bitches lay after whelping. The red-crested cocks crowed before down calling the brawny Pulaiyar (plural) to their day's work and by day, under the shade of the kanji tree spread the voice of the wavy-haired Pulaiya women singing as they were husking paddy ...

(i) **Why do we have limited information about lives of ordinary people?**

Ans. We have limited information about the lives of the ordinary people because the inscriptions were written by Brahmanas and they used to consider several groups as outcastes. Lives and hardships faced by these people were ignored. Brahmanas only wrote about good things of the kingdom to impress the kings and get huge grants of land.

(ii) **Who considered Pulaiyas 'outcastes' ?**

Ans. Pulaiyas were considered as 'outcastes' by Brahmanas and Vellalas. They used to live in the outskirts of the villages. They were agrarian labourers engaged in menial occupations.

Map Based Questions

1. Look at the map given below and answer the following questions.

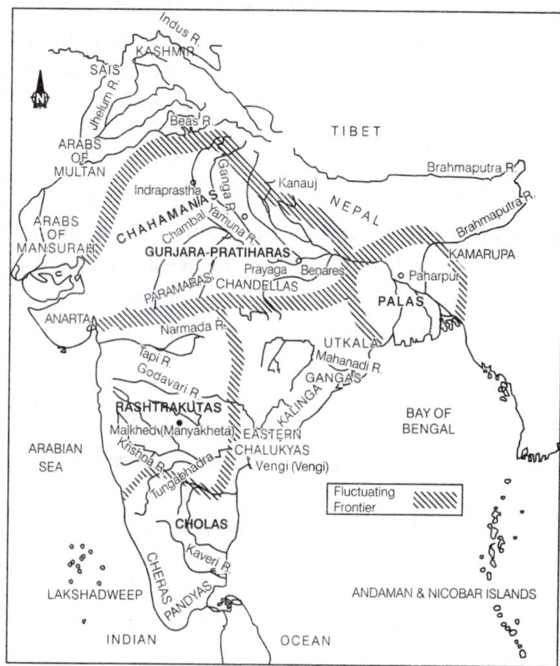

(i) **Can you identify the present day states over which they exercised control.**

Ans. (i) Gurjara-Pratiharas - Madhya Pradesh and Uttar Pradesh
(ii) Rashtrakutas - Maharashtra
(iii) Palas - Bengal
(iv) Cholas - Andhra Pradesh
(v) Chahamanas - Delhi, Rajasthan

(ii) **Look at map and find out whether there were any kingdoms in the state in which you live.**

Ans. Yes, there were kingdoms in the following states

States	Kingdoms
West Bengal	Palas
Orissa	Utkalas, Gangas, Kalinga
Tamil Nadu	Cholas and Pandyas
Madhya Pradesh	Gurjara-Pratiharas, Chandellas, Paramaras
Kerala	Cheras
Maharashtra	Rashtrakutas
Karnataka	Rashtrakutas
Gujarat	Anarta
Rajasthan	Chahamanas

(iii) Look at the map and suggest reasons why these rulers wanted to control Kannauj and the Ganga valley.

Ans. Rulers wanted to control Kannauj and the Ganga valley because of their strategic location and fertile land. These places were well connected by rivers making transportation easier. They lie in Doab region making them an ideal location for agriculture.

(iv) Look at the map and discuss why the Chahamanas may have wanted to expand their territories.

Ans. Chahamanas may have wanted to expand their territories because expansion brings with it the opportunity to control and tax new lands and resources. This includes taxing agricultural production, trade and other economic activities in the conquered regions, which contributes to the dynasty's wealth.

2. Locate the following on an outline map of India.

(i) Gurjara-Pratiharas (ii) Rashtrakutas
(iii) Palas (iv) Cholas
(v) Chahamanas

Ans.

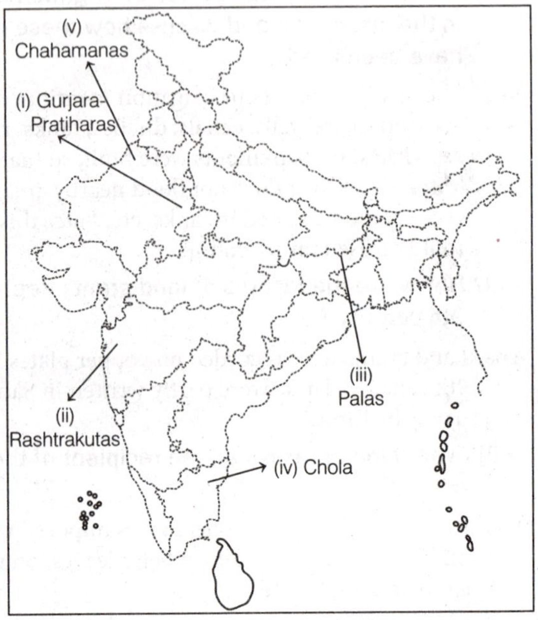

(v) Chahamanas
(i) Gurjara-Pratiharas
(iii) Palas
(ii) Rashtrakutas
(iv) Chola

ASSESSMENT EXERCISE

Multiple Choice Questions (MCQs)

1. As Samantas gained power and wealth they declared themselves to be

(a) Super-Samanta (b) Khap-Samanta
(c) Maha-Samanta (d) None of these

2. Which of the following performed a ritual called *hiranya-garbha*?

(a) Harichandra (b) Dantidurga
(c) Brahmanas (d) Mahmud Ghazni

3. During which of the following ruler, most frequently mentioned tax was vetti?

(a) Rashtrakuta (b) Gurjara-Pratihara
(c) Chola (d) Pala dynasties

4. Chauhans ruled over the region around Delhi and Ajmer. Which of the following dynasty opposed them to expand?

(a) Pratihara (b) Chalukyas
(c) Gahadavalas (d) Both (a) and (b)

Subjective Questions (VSA, SA & LA)

1. What were the extension of ruled areas by Mahmud of Ghazni?

2. Write the name of ruler who defeated Afghan ruler Muhammad Ghori in 1191.

3. Pandyan and the Pallava territories were part of which kingdom?

4. What were the functions performed by the village council and the Nadu?

5. In the emergence of new dynasties, what were the functions of Samantas or subordinates?

6. Why several rulers tried to control Kanauj in the Ganga valley? Write about Kitab-al-Hind.

7. Write a short note on Temples and Bronze sculpture.

8. Write about the benifits of Kaveri branches. How did it help Chola dynasty?

Delhi : 12th to 15th Century

CHAPTER 3

In 12th century, Delhi became the capital of **Tomara Rajputs**. They were defeated by the Chauhans (Chahamanas) of Ajmer in the middle of 12th century.

Under Tomaras and Chauhans, Delhi became an important commercial centre. Many rich Jaina merchants lived in Delhi and constructed a number of temples. Coins known as **Dehliwal**, were minted here and had wide circulation.

3.1 Delhi under Sultans

The information about Delhi Sultans can be obtained from histories known as ***tarikh*** (singular)/***tawarikh*** (plural) which were written in Persian, the language of administration under the Delhi Sultans.

The authors of tawarikh were learned men including secretaries, administrators, poets and courtiers. They advised rulers on governance and emphasised just rule.

They used to live in cities and wrote for Sultans in the hope of rewards. They advised rulers to maintain an 'ideal' social order based on **birthright** and **gender distinctions**.

In the beginning of 13th century, Delhi was transformed into a capital under Delhi Sultanate that controlled vast areas of the sub-continent.

In 1236, Sultan Iltutmish's daughter Raziyya became Sultan of Delhi. According to **Minhaj-i Siraj**, a **chronicler**[1] she was more able and qualified than all her brothers but they were not comfortable at having a queen as ruler. They thought that the queen's rule went against the ideal social order created by God, in which women were supposed to be sub-ordinate to men.

The nobles were also dissatisfied with her attempts to rule independently. Thus, she was removed from the throne in 1240.

The Rulers of Delhi

1. Rajput Dynasties	
Tomaras	**Early 12th century-1165**
• Ananga Pala	1130-1145
Chauhans	**1165-1192**
• Prithviraj Chauhan	1175-1192
2. Early Turkish Rulers	**1206-1290**
• Qutubuddin Aybak	1206-1210
• Shamsuddin Iltutmish	1210-1236
• Raziyya	1236-1240
• Ghiyasuddin Balban	1266-1287
3. Khalji Dynasty	**1290-1320**
• Jalaluddin Khalji	1290-1296
• Alauddin Khalji	1296-1316
4. Tughluq Dynasty	**1320-1414**
• Ghiyasuddin Tughluq	1320-1324
• Muhammad Tughluq	1324-1351
• Firuz Shah Tughluq	1351-1388
5. Sayyid Dynasty	**1414-1451**
• Khizr Khan	1414-1421
6. Lodi Dynasty	**1451-1526**
• Bahlul Lodi	1451-1489

3.2 Administration under Khaljis and Tughluqs

The early Delhi Sultans, especially Iltutmish, appointed their special slaves as governors to consolidate their kingdom. These slaves were called ***bandagan*** in Persian language and they were purchased for military service.

They were carefully trained to work in most important political offices in the kingdom. The Sultans trusted them as they were totally dependent upon their masters.

1 **Chronicler** It refers to a person who writes accounts of important or historical events.

The **Khaljis** and **Tughluq** continued to use *bandagan* and raised ordinary people who were their **clients**[2], to high political positions. They were appointed as generals and governors.

However, this created political instability because slaves and clients were loyal to their masters and patrons but not to their **heirs**. New Sultans had their own servants. Thus, there were conflicts at the time of succession of new kings between the old and new nobles.

The authors of Persian *tawarikh* criticised the Delhi Sultans for appointing low caste people to high offices.

Law and Order

The Khaljis and Tughluqs appointed military commanders as governors of territories. These territories were called **iqta**[3] and their holder was called ***iqtadar*** or ***muqti***.

The duty of the *muqtis* was to lead military campaigns and maintain law and order in their iqtas. In return for their military services, the *muqtis* collected the revenues from the territories assigned to them, as salary. They also paid their soldiers from these collected revenues.

For maintaining effective control over muqtis, their office was not inheritable and they were shifted to another *iqta* regularly after a short period of time. These conditions were imposed during the rule of Alauddin Khalji and Muhammad Tughluq.

Accountants were appointed by the state to check the revenue collected by *muqtis*. They ensured that only the taxes allowed by the state were collected and only the required number of soldiers were maintained.

Taxes and Land Revenues

Under Alauddin Khalji, assessment and collection of land revenue was done by the state instead of the local chief, and they were also forced to pay taxes. There were three types of taxes

(i) On cultivation called ***Kharaj*** (50% of the produce)

(ii) On cattle

(iii) On houses

Control over Distant Areas

Large parts of the sub-continent remained outside the control of Delhi Sultans. The Sultanate could not extend control over distant provinces like Bengal and forested areas of Gangetic plain. These areas were under the local chieftains.

Attacks by Mongols

In 1219, the **Mongols** under Genghis Khan invaded Transoxiana in North-East Iran and after that attacked the Delhi Sultanate.

Mongol attacks on the Delhi Sultanate increased during the reign of Alauddin Khalji and in the early years of Muhammad Tughluq's rule. Thus, the two rulers had to maintain a large standing army in Delhi which was a big administrative challenge.

Try These

1. **What are the sources of information on Delhi Sultans?**
2. **During whose reign, the system of Bandagan came into existence?**
3. **How many taxes were levied by the Delhi Sultans?**
4. **It is a type of coin which was minted at Delhi. Identify the coin.**

3.3 Sultanate in the 15th and 16th Centuries

After the **Tughluqs**, the Sayyid and Lodi dynasties ruled Delhi and Agra until **1526**. By this period, independent rulers had control over Jaunpur, Bengal, Malwa, Gujarat, Rajasthan and entire South India.

New ruling groups like **Afghans** and the **Rajputs** also emerged during this period. Some of the states established in this period were small but they were powerful and well administered.

Administration under Sher Shah Sur

Initially, **Sher Shah Suri** (1540-45) managed a small territory for his uncle in Bihar. Eventually, he defeated the Mughal emperor Humayun (1530-40, 1555-56), captured Delhi and established his own dynasty.

He introduced an administration that include many administering methods of Alauddin Khalji and made them more efficient. Sher Shah's model of administration was followed by the great emperor Akbar (1556-1605) when he consolidated the Mughal Empire.

2 **Client** It refers to a person who is under the protection of some other person.

3 **Iqta** It refers to land territory of different sizes.

Delhi under Sultans

- Information can be obtained from histories known as Tarikh/Tawarikh.
- The administrative language was Persian.
- In 13th century, Delhi was transformed into capital.
- In 1236, Raziyya Sultan became the ruler, she was removed from throne in 1240.

Rulers of Delhi

- Tomaras – Early 12th century to 1165
- Chauhans – 1165-1192
- Eary Turkish Rulers – 1206-1290
- Khalji Dynasty – 1290-1320
- Tughlaq Dynasty –1320-1414
- Sayyid Dynasty – 1414-1451
- Lodi Dynasty – 1451-1526

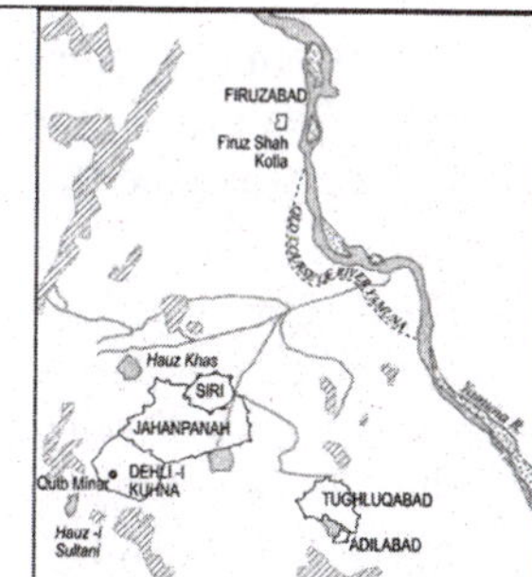

Administration under Khaljis and Tughlaqs

- Slave practice prevailed, which was started by Iltutmish.
- The salves were called Bandagan.
- Under Khaljis and Tughlaqs territories were called Iqta and their holder called Iqtadar or Muqti.
- Accountant were appointed to check the amount collected by Muqti.
- Khaljis and Tughlaqs maintained a large army as Mongols under Genghis Khan invaded frequently.

Sultanate in the 15th and 16th Centuries

- The Tughlaqs, Sayyid and Lodi dynasties ruled Delhi and Agra until 1526.
- Afghans and Rajputs emerged in this period.
- Suri dynasty established by Sher Shah Suri ruled Delhi for a short period of time.

Attacks by Mongols

- Genghis Khan invaded Tansoxiana in North-East Iran in 1219 and later attaked Delhi Sultanate.
- His model of administration was followed by Akbar to consolidate Mughal Empire.

Administration under Sher Shah Sur

- He include the methods of Alauddin Khalji in his administration.
- His model of administration was followed by Akbar to consolidate Mughal Empire.

Taxes and Land Revenues

- Kharaj (On Cultivation)
- On Cattle
- On houses

NCERT FOLDER

Covering Intext Questions and Exercises of NCERT

NCERT ON PAGE 33

Q.1 Express Minhaj's ideas in your own words. Do you think Raziyya shared these ideas? Why do you think it was so difficult for a woman to be a ruler ?

Ans. Minhaj-i Siraj believed that rule by women is against the natural order created by God, where women are subordinate to men. He questioned how a woman could possess excellent qualities when she is not in the category of men.

Raziyya, on the other hand, did not share these ideas as she proudly mentioned her as a woman on inscription and coins. While other female rulers changed their names and pretended to be a male.

I think it was difficult for a woman to be a ruler because society considered women as inferior and incapable of leadership.

NCERT ON PAGE 37

Q.2 You are a peasant in Alauddin Khalji's or Muhammad Tughluq's reign and you cannot pay the taxes demanded by the Sultan. What will you do?

Ans. If I am not able to pay the taxes imposed by the Sultan, I would first talk to other villagers facing the same problem. Together, we will request the local leaders to reduce our taxes or give us more time to pay. If that doesn't work, I would borrow money from moneylender and then pay the taxes.

EXERCISES

Q.1 Which ruler first established his or her capital at Delhi?

Ans. Tomara Rajputs were the first rulers who established their capital at Delhi.

Q.2 What was the language of administration under the Delhi Sultans?

Ans. Persian was the language of administration under the Delhi Sultans.

Q.3 In whose reign did the Sultanate reach its farthest extent?

Ans. The Delhi Sultanate reached its farthest extent during the reign of Muhammad Tughluq.

Q.4 From which country did Ibn Battuta travel to India?

Ans. Ibn Battuta travelled from Morocco, Africa to India.

Q.5 According to the "Circle of Justice", why was it important for military commanders to keep the interests of the peasantry in mind?

Ans. According to the "Circle of Justice" it was important for military commanders to keep the interests of the peasantry in mind because peasants are the source of revenue in the state. If they are prosperous and happy, only then revenue can be generated which is used to give salaries of the soldiers. Thus, prosperity and happiness of the peasants was directly linked to the well-being of the state.

Q.6 What is meant by the "internal" and "external" frontiers of the Sultanate?

Ans. Internal frontiers of the state refers to the hinterland of the Garrison towns in Bengal and Sindhs. During internal campaigns, forests were cleared in the Ganga-Yamuna doab and hunter gatherers were expelled from their habitat.

External frontiers refer to Southern India. Military expeditions to external frontiers were started during the reign of Alauddin Khalji and reached its peak under Muhammad Tughluq.

Q.7 What were the steps taken to ensure that *muqtis* performed their duties? Why do you think they may have wanted to defy the orders of the Sultans?

Ans. The following steps were taken to ensure that *muqtis* performed their duties

- Accountants were appointed by the state to check the amount of revenue collected by the muqtis.
- It was ensured that the *muqti* collected only the taxes prescribed by the state and that he kept the required number of soldiers.
- Their office was not inheritable and sometimes they were assigned *iqtas* for a short time span and transferred regularly. The state maintained tight control over *muqtis*.
- *Muqtis* might have wanted to defy the orders of the Sultans because harsh conditions of service were imposed on them.

Q.8 Do you think the authors of Tawarikh would provide information about the lives of ordinary men and women?

Ans. No, I think authors of tawarikh would not provide information about the lives of ordinary men and women because of the following reasons

(i) Authors of Tawarikh lived in cities (mainly Delhi) and hardly ever in villages. So, they had no idea about ordinary people residing in villages.

(ii) They often wrote for Sultans in the hope of rich rewards. So, they wrote only good things to impress the Sultan.

(iii) Authors favoured 'high born' people and ignored ordinary men and women.They advised rulers to preserve an 'ideal' social order based on birthright and gender distinctions.

Q.9 Raziyya Sultan was unique in the history of the Delhi Sultanate. Do you think women leaders are accepted more readily today?

Ans. Raziyya Sultan was unique in the history of the Delhi Sultanate because she was the first woman to became the ruler of the Sultanate. She was more able and qualified than all her brothers.

Yes, I think women leaders are accepted more readily today because of democracy. Now, the world has become open minded in terms of gender equality and don't mind having a woman as their leader. Many women have proved that they can be at the top as leaders.

Q.10 Why were the Delhi Sultans interested in cutting down forests? Does deforestation occur for the same reasons today?

Ans. The Delhi Sultans were interested in cutting down forests to give land to the peasants and extend agriculture. Also, new fortresses and towns were established to protect trade routes and to promote regional trade. They also cleared forests in order to safeguard their borders and for quick movement of the army.

In today's world, deforestation occurs due to development goals like construction of roads, railways, houses and industries. So, we can say that deforestation occur for the same reasons today only the perspective has been changed.

Q.11 Find out whether there are any buildings built by the Delhi Sultans in your area. Are there any other buildings in your area that were built between the 12th and 15th centuries? Describe some of these buildings, and draw sketches of them.

Ans. Yes, there are buildings built by the Delhi Sultans in my area. These are as follows

- **Quwwat-ul-Islam Mosque** It was built by Qutubuddin Aybak.It is situated in Qutub Complex.
- **Qutub Minar** It was built by Qutubuddin Aybak. It is the highest tower in India, with five storeys and projecting balconies. The first three storeys of the Qutub Minar are made of red sandstone and the last two are made of marble and sandstone.
- **Tomb of Hazarat Nizamuddin Auliya** It was built by Muhammad bin Tughluq. The tomb is a square-shaped chamber covered with dome shaped roof and crowned with an ornamental lotus cap.

REVIEW EXERCISE

Including Competency Based Questions

Part I

Multiple Choice Questions (MCQs)

1. What were the coins minted during 12th century under Tomaras called?

(a) Tawarikh (b) Muqtis
(c) Rupiya (d) Dehliwal

2. Which ruler first established his capital at Delhi?

(a) Tomara Rajputs (b) Chauhans
(c) Lodi (d) Sayyid

3. When did Raziyya Sultan sat on the throne?

(a) 1235 (b) 1236
(c) 1237 (d) 1238

4. Raziyya Sultan ruled during the period of

(a) 1206-1201 AD (b) 1236-1240 AD
(c) 1210-1236 AD (d) 1266-1287 AD

5. Who was the first slave king of Delhi Sultanate?

(a) Qutubuddin Aybak (b) Iltutmish
(c) Raziyya Sultan (d) Alauddin Khalji

6. Territories under the Khalji and Tughluq's were known as

(a) *Jagir* (b) Kingdom
(c) *Iqta* (d) Mandala

7. Which of the following was not the kind of taxes levied during the Delhi Sultanate?

(a) Kharaj (b) Taxes on cattles
(c) Taxes on houses (d) Taxes on sales of grains

8. After Tughluqs, the Sayyid and Lodi dynasties ruled from

(a) Bengal and Jaunpur (b) Gujarat and Rajasthan
(c) Entire South (d) Delhi and Agra

9. **Sher Shah fought and defeated which of the following Mughal rulers?**

(a) Babur (b) Jahangir
(c) Humayun (d) Aurangzeb

10. **Inscriptions, coins and architecture provide a lot of**

(a) money (b) costly metals
(c) information (d) rewards

11. **Who was Minhaj-i-Siraj?**

(a) Chronicler (b) Historian
(c) Samanta (d) Sultan

12. **A fortified town is called as**

(a) Hinterland (b) Jagir
(c) Garrison town (d) Court room

13. **Who was Ibn Battuta?**

(a) Irani traveller
(b) African traveller
(c) Afghani traveller
(d) Chinese traveller

14. **Queen Rudramadevi (1262-1289) belonged to which dynasty?**

(a) Lodi dynasty (b) Slave dynasty
(c) Kakatiya dynasty (d) Khalji dynasty

15. **Read the following statements and identify the position from the given functions.**

I. They were the military commanders who were also appointed as the Governor of territories.
II. Their duties included the maintenance of law and order. **Competency Based**

Codes

(a) Samanta (b) Chieftain
(c) Muqtis (d) Clients

16. **Choose the correct statement(s) given below.** **Competency Based**

I. Tughluq dynasty was succeded by Lodi dynasty.
II. Muhammad Tughluq issued token currency.
III. Raziyya succeeded Iltumish in 1240.

Codes

(a) I and II (b) Only II
(c) I, II and III (d) Only III

17. **Choose the correct statement(s) given below.** **Competency Based**

I. Alauddin Khalji became king in 1296.
II. Officers who collected revenue and maintain law during Khalji were called muqtis.
III. Kharaj was tax on cattles.

Codes

(a) Only I (b) I, II and III
(c) I and II (d) I and III

18. **Arrange the following in correct sequence of accession in Delhi.**

(i) Prithviraj Chauhan (ii) Alauddin Khalji
(iii) Ananga Pala (iv) Muhammad Tughluq

Codes

(a) (i), (ii), (iii), (iv) (b) (iii), (i), (ii), (iv)
(c) (i), (iii), (iv), (ii) (d) (iii), (i), (iv), (ii)

19. **Arrange the dynasties of Sultanate period in chronological order.**

(i) Slave dynasty (ii) Tughluq dynasty
(iii) Lodi dynasty (iv) Sayyid dynasty
(v) Khalji dynasty

Codes

(a) (i), (ii), (v), (iv), (iii) (b) (v), (i), (ii), (iii), (iv)
(c) (i), (v), (ii), (iv), (iii) (d) (i), (ii), (v), (iii), (iv)

Answers

1. (d)	**2.** (a)	**3.** (b)	**4.** (b)	**5.** (a)
6. (c)	**7.** (d)	**8.** (d)	**9.** (c)	**10.** (c)
11. (a)	**12.** (c)	**13.** (b)	**14.** (c)	**15.** (c)
16. (b)	**17.** (c)	**18.** (b)	**19.** (c)	

Match the Following

1.

	List I		List II
A.	Tawarikh	1.	Territories of different size
B.	Inscriptions, coins	2.	Persian language
C.	Minhaj-i-Siraj	3.	Chronicler
D.	Iqta	4.	Historical information

Codes

	A	B	C	D		A	B	C	D
(a)	2	4	3	1	(b)	2	3	1	4
(c)	1	2	3	4	(d)	3	4	2	1

2.

	List I (Kings)		List II (Dynasties)
A.	Raziyya	1.	Sur dynasty
B.	Sher Shah	2.	Chauhans
C.	Khizr Khan	3.	Tomars
D.	Ananga Pala	4.	Sayyid dynasty
E.	Prithviraj	5.	Slave dynasty

Codes

	A	B	C	D	E		A	B	C	D	E
(a)	5	1	4	3	2	(b)	2	3	1	5	4
(c)	1	2	3	4	5	(d)	3	4	5	1	2

Ans. 1. (a) 2. (a)

Assertion-Reason

1. **Assertion** (A) The Khaljis and Tughlugs raised the people of humble birth to high political positions.

   Reason (R) Bandagan were loyal to their heirs.

   Codes

   (a) Both A and R are true and R is the correct explanation of A
   (b) Both A and R are true, but R is not the correct explanation of A
   (c) A is true, but R is false
   (d) A is false, but R is true

2. **Assertion** (A) Alauddin Khalji raised a large standing army and imposed tax on cultivation.

   Reason (R) Mongols attacked Delhi Sultanate after 1219.

   Codes

   (a) Both A and R are true and R is the correct explanation of A
   (b) Both A and R are true, but R is not the correct explanation of A
   (c) A is true, but R is false
   (d) A is false, but R is true

Ans. 1. (c) A is true, but R is false
2. (a) Both A and R are true and R is the correct explanation of A

Fill in the Blanks

1. Muhammad Tughluq shifted his capital to ....
2. The ruler of Delhi between 1414-1421, Khizr Khan was of .... dynasty.
3. Tawarikh were written in .... language.
4. Iqtadar was also known as ....
5. Emperor .... followed the administration model of Sher Shah Suri, when he consolidated the Mughal Empire.

Ans. 1. Daulatabad 2. Sayyid
3. Persian 4. muqti
5. Akbar

True/False

1. Ideal social order was based on birthright and gender distinctions.
2. Delhi first became the capital of a kingdom under the Tomara Rajputs.
3. Internal frontier was aimed at military expeditions into Southern India.
4. Citizens were known as *bandagan*.
5. Soldiers were paid salaries in cash in the reign of Alauddin Khalji.

Ans. 1. True 2. True 3. False
4. False 5. True

Case Based Question

1. **Read the passage given below and answer the following questions.**

   "Care was taken that the muqti collected only the taxes prescribed by the state and that he kept the required number of soldiers.Under Alauddin Khalji the state brought the assessment and collection of land revenue under its own control. The rights of the local chieftains to levy taxes were cancelled and they were also forced to pay taxes.

   The Sultan's administrators measured the land and kept careful accounts. Some of the old chieftains and landlords served the Sultanate as revenue collectors and assessors. There were three types of taxes (1) on cultivation called kharaj and amounting to about 50% of the peasant's produce, (2) on cattle and (3) on houses."

   (i) What were the land holders called during the period of Khalji and Tughluqs?

   (a) Muqti (b) Iqta
   (c) Bandagan (d) Zamindars

   (ii) Who brought collection of land revenue under the state's control?

   (a) Muhammad Tughluq
   (b) Alauddin Khalji
   (c) Iltutmish
   (d) Khizr Khan

   (iii) What was the other obligation of local chieftains, apart from paying taxes?

   (a) Religious rituals
   (b) Military service
   (c) Cultural events
   (d) Educational programmes

   (iv) Who decided the amount of tax imposed during Khalji and Tughluqs ?

   (a) Peasants (b) Landlords
   (c) Sultans (d) Iqtadars

Ans (i) (a) Muqti (ii) (b) Alauddin Khalji
(iii) (b) Military service (iv) (c) Sultans

Part II

Very Short Answer Type Questions

1. What was Dehliwal?

Ans. Dehliwal was a kind of coin minted in Delhi.

2. Who was the first woman ruler in Delhi Sultanate and when did she become Sultan?

Ans. Sultan Iltutmish's daughter Raziyya Sultan was the first woman ruler and in 1236 she became Sultan.

3. What was Iqta?

Ans. Iqta was territories of varying sizes under the control of *muqtis* or *iqtadars*.

4. Who were *muqtis*?

Ans. *Muqtis* were the Governors of the territories. They were also known by the name of *iqtadar*.

5. What is Kharaj?

Ans. Kharaj is the kind of tax on cultivation.

6. Under whose reign did the Mongols invaded the Delhi Sultanate?

Ans. Under the reign of Alauddin Khalji and Muhammad-bin-Tughluq, Mongols invaded the Delhi Sultanate.

7. Who was the leader of Mongols that invaded Transoxiana in Iran?

Ans. Genghis Khan was the leader of Mongols who invaded Transoxiana in Iran.

8. Who was the successor of Muhammad Tughluq?

Ans. Firuz Shah Tughluq was the successor of Muhammad Tughluq.

9. Which dynasty ruled for the shortest span of time in Delhi Sultanate ? Competency Based

Ans. Khalji dynasty ruled for the shortest span of time in Delhi Sultanate. It ruled for 30 years. Jalaluddin Khalji and Alauddin Khalji were the only two Khalji kings of Delhi.

Short Answer Type Questions

1. Who was Raziyya? Why was she not accepted as a Sultan despite being talented ?

Ans. Raziyya was the daughter of Sultan Iltutmish. She became Sultan of Delhi in 1236.

According to Minhaj-i-Siraj, she was more able and qualified than all her brothers. However, she was not accepted as Sultan because it was believed that women were subordinate to men. Many nobles and religious leaders resisted her rule because they believed that only men should be Sultans. They could not submit before a female Sultan.

2. What changes did Alauddin Khalji introduce in administration of the state?

Ans. Alauddin Khalji introduced the following changes in administration of the state.

- Alauddin Khalji brought the assessment and collection of land revenue under his control.
- He cancelled the rights of the local chieftains to levy taxes and they were rather asked to pay taxes. The Sultan's administrators measured the land and kept careful accounts.
- Some of the old chieftains and landlords were allowed to serve the Sultanate as revenue collectors and assessors.

3. How did the Khaljis and Tughluqs help the people of humble birth? How did it lead to instability in the Sultanate?

Ans. The Khaljis and the Tughluq's raised people of humble birth, who were often their clients, to high political positions. They were appointed as generals and governors.

However, the slaves and clients were loyal to their masters and patrons but not to their heirs. When heirs became the new rulers, they neglected such appointed men of high posts. This led to conflict between old and new mobility and rebellions, which led to instability in the Sultanate.

4. "Since they were totally dependent upon their master, the Sultan could trust and rely upon them". Who is being referred here as trustworthy? Explain. Competency Based

Ans. A slave is being referred here as trustworthy and reliable. A slave was considered better than a son as he was fully dependent on his master and was thus loyal to him.
A slave could never ask for authority or any hereditary claims like son. Son's claims to the throne, often leads to power struggles and instability. For example, Aurangzeb killed his brother Dara Shikoh and arrested his father Shah Jahan and declared himself as emperor.

5. Which types of taxes were there during Delhi Sultanate? Who was assigned the duty of collecting taxes?

Ans. There were three kinds of taxes during Delhi Sultanate. These were

- Tax on cultivation (known as kharaj) which was about 50% of the peasant's produce.
- Tax on cattle
- Tax on houses

At the time of Alauddin Khalji, the state brought the assessment and collection of land revenue under its own control. Thus, the rights of the local chieftains to levy taxes were cancelled and they were forced to pay taxes.

6. Who was Sher Shah Sur? What was remarkable about his administration?

Ans. Sher Shah Sur (1540-45) was a manager of a small territory for his uncle in Bihar. Eventually, he defeated the Mughal emperor Humayun (1530-40, 1555-56), captured Delhi and established his own dynasty.

The remarkable thing about his administration was that he introduced an administration that include many administering methods of Alauddin Khalji and made them more efficient. Sher Shah's model of administration was followed by the great emperor Akbar (1556-1605) when he consolidated the Mughal Empire.

Long Answer Type Questions

1. Describe the administration of Delhi under Alauddin Khalji .

Ans. The administration under Alauddin Khalji had the following characteristics

- *Muqtis* were under strict control of the state. They had to work under strict conditions of service as their position was transferable and not hereditary.
- Accountants were appointed by the state to check the amount of revenue collected by the *muqtis*. Care was taken that the *muqti* collected only the taxes prescribed by the state and that he kept the required number of soldiers.
- The state brought the assessment and collection of land revenue under its own control. The rights of the local chieftains to levy taxes were cancelled and they were also forced to pay taxes.
- The Sultans administrators measured the land and kept careful accounts.
- A large standing army in Delhi was placed because of constant threat of Mongol invasion on the Delhi Sultanate.

2. How the information about Delhi Sultans can be obtained? Also describe the rule of Delhi Sultanate in the 15th and 16th centuries.

Ans. The information about Delhi Sultans can be obtained from histories known as *tarikh* (singular)/*tawarikh* (plural) which were written in Persian, the language of administration under the Delhi Sultans.

During 15th and 16th centuries, the Sayyid and Lodi dynasties ruled Delhi and Agra until 1526. By this period, independent rulers had control over Jaunpur, Bengal, Malwa, Gujarat, Rajasthan and entire South India.

New ruling groups like Afghans and the Rajputs also emerged during this period. Some of the states established in this period were small but they were powerful and well administered.

Case Based Questions

1. Read the passage given below and answer the question that follows.

The Circle of Justice

Fakhr-i Mudabbir wrote in the 13th century,
A king cannot survive without soldiers and soldiers cannot live without salaries. Salaries come from the revenue collected from peasants. But peasants can pay revenue only when they are prosperous and happy. This happens when the king promotes justice and honest governance.

(i) Do you think the 'Circle of Justice' is an appropriate term to describe the relationship between the king and his subjects?

Ans. Yes, circle of justice is an appropriate term to describe the relationship between the king and his subjects.

It highlights the interdependence between the ruler and the subjects. A king's just and honest governance leads to the prosperity and happiness of the peasants, which, in turn, helps in collection of revenue to pay salaries to soldiers, ensuring the king's survival.

(ii) How did the king pay the salaries of the soldiers?

Ans. The king paid the salaries of the soldiers through the revenue collected from the peasants.

(iii) What were the expectations of the peasants from the king ?

Ans. Peasants expected a happy and prosperous life. They needed a honest government who promoted justice and main tained law and order. Taxes collected should be reasonable and just.

2. Read the passage given below and answer the question that follows.

Officials of Sultan Muhammad Tughluq

Sultan Muhammad Tughluq appointed Aziz Khummar, a wine distiller, Firuz Hajjam, a barber, Manka Tabbakh, a cook and two gardeners, Ladha and Pira, to high administrative posts. Ziyauddin Barani, a mid-14th century chronicler, reported their appointments as a sign of the Sultan's loss of political judgement and his incapacity to rule.

(i) Why do you think Barani criticised the Sultan?

Ans. Barani criticised the Sultan because he appointed common men with no experience to high administrative posts. He believed that individuals without the necessary qualifications or experience could lead to mismanagement, corruption and incompetence in the government. He questioned Sultan's political judgement.

(ii) What are the slaves purchased for military service called?

Ans. Slaves purchased for military service are called *bandagan* in Persian. They were carefully trained for handling important offices of the kingdom.

3. Read the passage given below and answer the question that follows.

Chieftains and their Fortifications

Ibn Battuta, a 14th-century traveller from Morocco, Africa, explained that chieftains sometimes fortified themselves in mountains, in rocky, uneven and rugged places as well as in bamboo groves. In India, the bamboo is not hollow, it is big. Its several parts are so intertwined that even fire cannot affect them and they are on the whole very strong. The chieftains live in these forests which serve them as ramparts, inside which are their cattle and their crops. There is also water for them within, that is, rain water which collects there. Hence, they cannot be subdued except by powerful armies, who entering these forests, cut down the bamboos with specially prepared instruments.

(i) Describe the ways in which the chieftains arranged for their defence.

Ans. Chieftains arranged for their defence by fortifying themselves in mountains, rocky, uneven terrain and dense bamboo groves. These locations were selected for their defensive advantages. The bamboos are thick and intertwined, providing strong protection. They collected rainwater for survival in such conditions. These defences allowed chieftains to resist attacks except from very powerful armies.

Map Based Question

1. In the given map, centres of Alauddin Khalji's campaign into South India are marked. Identify and write their names.

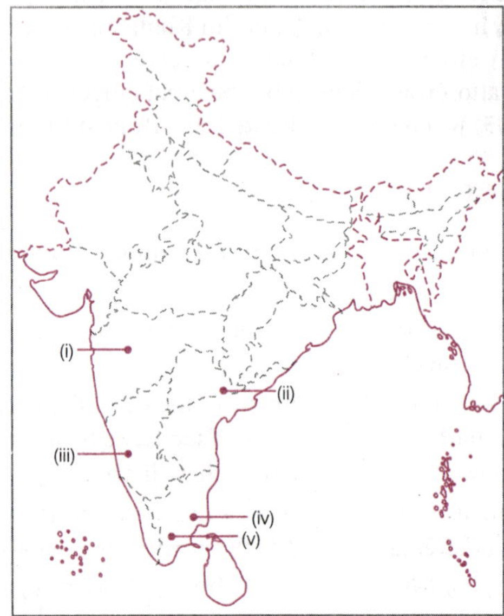

Ans. (i) Devagiri (ii) Warangal (iii) Dwarasamudra (iv) Thanjavur (v) Madurai

ASSESSMENT EXERCISE

Multiple Choice Questions (MCQs)

1. In which of the following centuries Delhi became an important city?
   (a) 10th century (b) 12th century
   (c) 5th century (d) None of these
2. On which of the following Raziyya mentioned that she was the daughter of Iltutmish?
   (a) Coins
   (b) Inscriptions
   (c) Both (a) and (b)
   (d) None of the above
3. What percentage of the peasant's produce was taxed under the category of cultivation known as kharaj?
   (a) 25% (b) 50%
   (c) 75% (d) 100%
4. Which ruler first established his capital at Delhi?
   (a) Chauhan rulers (b) Turkish ruler
   (c) Khalji dynasty (d) Tomara Rajput rulers

Subjective Questions (VSA, SA & LA)

1. What were the coins called that were minted in Delhi during the rule of Tomaras and Chauhans?
2. Who were not happy when Raziyya become Sultan?
3. Who were the authors of tawarikh?
4. Who constructed a new garrison town, Siri for his soldiers?
5. What happened after humble beginnings of Muhammad Tughluq's reign?
6. Who were the *iqtadar*? Write about their role in the military.
7. Write in detail about the need of reliable governors and administrators by Delhi Sultanate.
8. What were the steps taken by Alauddin Khalji to save their dynasty from the attack of Mongols?
9. Who was Raziyya Sultan and how did her rule go against the social order?

The Mughals
(16th to 17th Century)

By the middle of 16th century, the **Mughals** expanded their kingdom from Agra and Delhi. In the 17th century, they controlled nearly all of the sub-continent. Their administration and ideas of governance had a long-lasting impact on the succeeding rulers.

4.1 The Mughals

The Mughals were the descendants of Genghis Khan from their mother's side. Genghis Khan was the Mongol ruler who ruled over parts of China and Central Asia.

From their father's side, the Mughals were the successors of Timur who was the ruler of Iran, Iraq and modern-day Turkey.

However, they did not like to be called Mughal or Mongol because Mongol leader Genghis Khan's memory was associated with the massacre of many people.

On the other hand, Mughals were proud of their Timurid **ancestry**[1] as they had conquered Delhi in 1398. The Red Fort in Delhi was the residence of the Mughal emperors.

4.2 Mughal Military Campaigns and Traditions of Succession

Babur (1526-1530) was the first Mughal ruler who succeeded to the throne of Ferghana in 1494 when he was 12 years old. However, he had to leave this throne because of invasion by Uzbegs.

After some years, Babur seized Kabul in 1504. In 1526, he defeated the Sultan of Delhi, Ibrahim Lodi at Panipat and captured Delhi and Agra.

Mughals followed **coparcenary inheritance** custom where inheritance was divided amongst all the sons of the emperor.

Mughals did not believe in rule of **primogeniture**, where the eldest son inherited his fathers's empire.

4.3 Mughal Relations with other Rulers

The Mughal rulers campaigned against the rulers who refused to accept their authority. Sometimes, many rulers joined them voluntarily as the Mughals had become very powerful. For example, Rajputs married their daughters into Mughal families to receive high positions.

However, many rulers resisted them. For example, the Sisodiya Rajputs of Mewar refused to accept Mughal authority for a long time.

The Mughals defeated their opponents but did not humiliate them. This enabled them to extend their influence over many kings and chieftains.

For example, after defeating the Sisodiya Rajputs of Mewar, the Mughals treated them fairly by giving back their lands (*watan*) as assignments (*watan jagir*).

4.4 *Mansabdars and Jagirdars*

As the Mughal empire expanded, the Mughals recruited a large number of people to manage the empire. These included Turanis (Turkish nobles), Iranians, Indian Muslims, Afghans, Rajputs, Marathas and other groups.

Those who joined Mughal service were enrolled as *mansabdars. Mansabdar* refers to an individual who holds a **Mansab**[2], meaning a position or rank. It was a grading system used to fix rank, salary and military responsibilities.

Rank and salary was determined by a numerical value called ***zat***. The higher the *zat*, the higher was the noble's position in court and the larger his salary.

1 **Ancestry** It refers to the origin of a family.

2 **Mansab**It means an office,position or rank in Mughal administration.

The military responsibility of *mansabdar* was to maintain a required number of *sawar* or horsemen. The *mansabdar* used to get his men registered, horses branded and then received money to pay them as salary.

Mansabdars received their salaries as revenue assignments called *jagirs*. Most *mansabdars* did not actually reside in their allotted *jagirs*. They only had rights over the revenue from these assignments. The revenue was collected by their servants, while they served in some other part of the country.

In Akbar's reign, *jagirs* were carefully assessed so that their revenues were roughly equal to the salary of *mansabdars*. However, during Aurangzeb's reign, actual revenue collected was often less than the amount to be paid as salary. This was because there was a huge increase in the number of mansabdars.

These factors led to a shortage in the number of jagirs. As a result, many *jagirdars* tried to extract maximum possible revenue while they had a jagir. Aurangzeb was unable to control these developments during his region.

4.5 *Zabt* and Zamindars

The main source of Mughal income was tax collected on the produce of the peasants. In most places, peasants used to pay taxes through intermediaries headman or local chieftain. These intermediaries were termed as zamindars by the Mughals.

During Akbar's reign, tax was fixed on each crop on the basis of a survey conducted by his revenue minister **Todar Mal**. He carried out a survey of crop yields, prices and areas cultivated fora 10 years period.

Each province was divided into revenue circles with its own schedule of revenue rates for individual crops. This revenue system was known as *zabt*.

This system was prevalent only where Mughal administrators could survey and maintain accounts. It was not possible in provinces such as Gujarat and Bengal.

In some areas, the zamindars exploited the peasants and this led to rebellion. Sometimes, peasants and zamindars of the same caste rebelled against the Mughal Authority.

Akbar Nama and Ain-i Akbari

Akbar Nama is a three-volume history of Akbar's reign written by **Abul Fazl**, the courtier of Akbar. The first volume dealt with Akbar's ancestors and the second volume recorded the events of Akbar's reign.

The third volume is the Ain-i Akbari. It deals with Akbar's administration, household, army, the revenues and the geography of his empire. It also provides details about the traditions and culture of the people living in India.

Try These

1. **What do you understandd by 'Zabt'?**
2. **Who wrote 'Ain-in Akbari'?**
3. **Identify the Mughal emperor who seized power from the hands of his regent Bairam Khan.**
4. **Where were the religious discussions conducted by Akbar held?**

4.6 The Mughal Empire in the 17th Century and After

The administrative and military efficiency of the Mughal Empire led to great economic and commercial prosperity. However, poverty existed in the state and there were income inequalities.

For example, during Shah Jahan's reign, out of total 8000 *mansabdars* , 445 had the highest ranking. They received 61.5 per cent of the total revenue of the empire.

Mughal emperors and their *mansabdars* spent large part of their income on salaries and goods. This expenditure benefitted the artisans and peasants who supplied them with goods and produce. However, they had to pay high revenues and were not able to invest in the tools and supplies to increase productivity. Thus, they had to live in poverty.

The Mughal Elite including the merchants and bankers became extremely powerful in the late 17th century, through their wealth and resources.

As the authority of Mughal empire slowly declined, their servants became powerful. They established new dynasties and controlled provinces like in Awadh and Hyderabad. By the 18th century, these provinces had constituted their independent political identities.

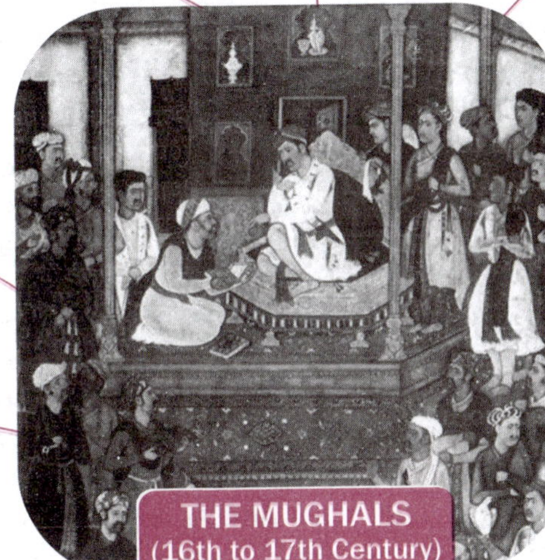

THE MUGHALS (16th to 17th Century)

Tradition of Succession

Mughals followed the custom of coparcenary inheritance or division of inheritance amongst all the sons.

The Mughals

From their mother's side they were descendants of Genghis Khan and from the father's side, they were descendant of Timur.

The Mughal Empire in the 17th Century and after

- The administrative and military efficiency of the Mughal empire led to great economic and commercial prosperity in 17th century.
- By 18th century it started decline.

Zabt and Zamindars

- Revenue Minister in Akbar reigns - Todar Mal
- Zabt-the revenue system

Mughal Military Campaigns

- Babur succeeded the throne in 1494.
- He captured Kabul in 1504.
- In 1526, he defeated Ibrahim Lodhi at Panipat and captured Delhi and Agra.

Mughal Relations with other Rulers

- Mughals campaigned against rulers who refused their authority.
- Rajputs married their daughters with Mughal to receive high position.

Mansabdars and Jagirdars

- Mansabdar was the high rank officer.
- Jagir was the revenue assignment of Mansabdars.

NCERT FOLDER

Covering Intext Questions and Exercises of NCERT

NCERT PAGE 41

Q.1 Which do you think is a fairer division of inheritance : primogeniture or coparcenary ?

Ans. Coparcenary, where wealth is equally divided among all sons, is a fairer division of inheritance than primogeniture. In coparcenary, every child is entitled to a share of the family's assets, promoting equality and merit-based distribution. Primogeniture, on the other hand, unfairly privileges the eldest son, and disregards the individual capabilities of other siblings.

NCERT PAGE 42

Q.2 Nobles with a zat of 5,000 were ranked higher than those of 1,000. In Akbar's reign, there were 29 mansabdars with a rank of 5,000 zat; by Aurangzeb's reign the number of mansabdars had increased to 79. Would this have meant more expenditure for the state?

Ans. Yes, the increase in the number of mansabdars with a rank of 5,000 zat from 29 in Akbar's reign to 79 in Aurangzeb's reign would have meant more expenditure for the state. In the Mughal empire, the zat and sawar ranks of mansabdars determined their pay, and a higher rank meant a higher salary. Therefore, with an increase in the number of high-ranking mansabdars, the state would have had to allocate more funds to meet their salaries.

NCERT PAGE 46 (LET'S IMAGINE)

Q.3 Babur and Akbar were about your age when they became rulers. Imagine you have inherited a kingdom. How would you make your kingdom stable and prosperous?

Ans. I would make my kingdom stable and prosperous by taking the following actions

- There should be equal representation of all citizens through election.
- There should be a system of spy and military power.
- Taxes should be equal and justifiable.
- Government should help each to earn their living.
- Government banks should be formed.
- Janata Darbar should be organised regularly.
- Peaceful relations with neighbour kingdoms should be maintained.

EXERCISES

Q.1 Match the Columns.

	List I	List II
A.	*Mansab*	1. Marwar
B.	Mongol	2. Uzbeg
C.	Sisodiya Rajput	3. Mewar
D.	Rathor Rajput	4. Rank
E.	Nur Jahan	5. Jahangir

Codes

	A	B	C	D	E		A	B	C	D	E
(a)	4	2	3	1	5	(b)	3	2	4	1	5
(c)	1	2	3	4	5	(d)	4	1	2	3	5

Ans. (a)

Q.2 Fill in the blanks.

(a) The five Deccan Sultanate were Berar, Khandesh, Ahmadnagar, ... and ....

(b) If *zat* determined a *mansabdar's* rank and salary, sawar indicated his ....

(c) Abul Fazl, Akbar's friend and counsellor, helped him frame the idea of .... so that he could govern a society composed of many religions, cultures and castes.

Ans. (a) Bijapur, Golconda (b) number of horses maintained (c) administration

Q.3 What were the central provinces under the control of the Mughals?

Ans. The central provinces under the control of the Mughals were Delhi, Agra, Lahore, Panipat, Mathura, Amber, Ajmer, Fatehpur Sikri, Chittor, Ranthambhore and Allahabad (Prayagraj).

Q.4 What were the relationships between the *mansabdar* and the *jagir*?

Ans. The relationship between the *manasabdars* and the jagir was that while *mansabdars* were the patrons who joined Mughal services, they received their salaries as revenue assignments called *jagir*.

Mansabdars did not actually reside in or administer their *jagir*. They only had rights to the revenue of their assignments. The revenue was collected for them by their servants, while the *mansabdars* themselves served in some other part of the country.

Q.5 What was the role of the zamindar in Mughal administration?

Ans. Zamindars played the role of intermediary between peasants and the empire.

Zamindars were powerful local chieftains appointed by the Mughal rulers. They collected taxes from the peasants and gave them to the Mughal Emperor. They had influence over their region and enjoyed power over peasants.

Q.6 How were the debates with religious scholars important in the formation of Akbar's ideas on governance?

Ans. Debates with religious scholars were important in shaping Akbar's governance ideas. By engaging in open dialogues with scholars from various faiths, Akbar tried to understand different perspectives and promote religious tolerance. These debates allowed him to appreciate the diversity of his empire and recognise the need for a more inclusive approach to governance.

Akbar's policy of Sulh-i-kul, or 'peace with all', emerged from these discussions, emphasising harmony and respect for all religions. This approach influenced his policies, such as the removal of the jizya tax on non-Muslims and the promotion of a more inclusive and just administrative system.

Q.7 Why did the Mughals emphasise their Timurid and not their Mongol descent?

Ans. The Mughals did not emphasise their Mongol descent because Mongol's especially Genghis Khan's, memory was associated with massacre of innumerable people. It was also linked with the Uzbegs, their Mongols competitors. On the other hand, the Mughals were proud of their Timurid ancestry, because Timur captured Delhi in 1398.

Q. 8 How important was the income from land revenue to the stability of the Mughal empire?

Ans. Land revenue was important to maintain the stability of the Mughal empire as the income from land revenue was the primary source of revenue for the Mughal empire. It was used to pay salaries of soldiers, fund welfare programs, build forests and other administrative expenses.

Q.9 Why was it important for the Mughals to recruit mansabdars from diverse backgrounds and not just Turanis and Iranis?

Ans. It was important for the Mughals to recruit *mansabdars* from diverse backgrounds due to various reasons such as

- To develop loyalty among different communities towards Mughals.
- To maintain social harmony in the empire.
- To recruit brave and honest leaders and soldiers in the Mughal army.

Q.10 Like the Mughal empire, India today is also made up of many social and cultural units. Does this pose a challenge to national integration?

Ans. No, this does not pose any challenge to national integration. Unity in diversity is a special feature of India. Indians may belong to different regions, cultures, castes and creed. But this does not signify that they all are different people. They are all one and are proud of being Indians. Our Constitution does not discriminate us on the basis of caste, religion and sex. There is no official religion.

At times, social conflicts emerge, but they are sorted out in an peaceful way. Whenever, there is an external threat, all Indians come together. The unity of India was seen during the freedom struggle, during external aggression where it be from Pakistan or China.

Q. 11 Peasants were vital for economy of the Mughal empire. Do you think that they are as important today? Has the gap in the income between the rich and the poor in India changed a great deal from the period of the Mughals?

Ans. Yes, peasants are important today as they were during the Mughal empire. They pay land revenue to the government which is used in various policies, grants, subsidies, projects. During the Mughal rule, all were virtually agriculturists. No other source of income was different from that of agriculture.

So, income gap between rich and poor was not as much as it is today. Now, people find more income based jobs other than agriculture. Still peasants are important today as more than 55 per cent of the population of our country is agriculturists. Agriculture and allied sectors like forestry and fisheries accounted for 13.7 per cent of the GDP.

Q. 12 The Mughal empire left its impact on the different regions of the sub-continent in a variety of ways. Find out if it had any impact in the city, village or region in which you live.

Ans. The Mughal empire left its impact on different regions of the sub-continent. But most noticeable impact can be seen in Delhi.

REVIEW EXERCISE

Including Competency Based Questions

Part I

Multiple Choice Questions (MCQs)

1. When did Timur capture Delhi?
(a) 1250 (b) 1420 (c) 1398 (d) 1320

2. Whom did Babur defeat in the Battle of Panipat?
(a) Genghis Khan (b) Safavid
(c) Timur (d) Ibrahim Lodi

3. The mother of Jahangir was the daughter of the Rajput ruler of
(a) Jodhpur (b) Jaipur (c) Amber (d) Ajmer

4. Those who joined Mughal service were enrolled as
(a) Mansabdars (b) Jagirdars
(c) Subedars (d) Muqtis

5. Abul Fazl wrote the book called
(a) Minhaj-i-Siraj (b) Siraj-e-Hind
(c) Abul Nama (d) Akbar Nama

6. Who was the revenue minister of Akbar?
(a) Todar Mal (b) Tansen (c) Abul Fazl (d) Birbal

7. What does Sulh-i-kul meant?
(a) Universal peace (b) Gender discrimination
(c) Revenue system (d) Jagir system

8. Which among the following account is given in Ain-i-Akbari about Akbar's?
(a) Religious policy (b) Ancestors
(c) Administrative policy (d) Personal views

9. Consider the following statements and identify in whose reign these conditions existed. **Competency Based**
(i) Revenue collected from jagir was often less than the salary of the mansabdar.
(ii) Peasantry was suffering tremendously.
(iii) The number of mansabdars had increased to 79.

Codes
(a) Akbar (b) Aurangzeb (c) Shah Jahan (d) Jahangir

10. Choose the correct option among the following.
I. Jagir's revenue were roughly equal to the salary of mansabdar during Aurangzeb reign.
II. Zamindars were intermediaries to collect tax from peasants.
III. Jagirs were some what like Iqtas.

Codes
(a) I and II (b) II and III
(c) Only I (d) Only III

11. Choose the incorrect option among the following. **Competency Based**
I. The Sisodiya Rajput accepted the Mughal authority when offered.
II. Shah Jahan was the son of Akbar.
III. Babur seized Kabul in 1504.

Codes
(a) I and II (b) I and III
(c) II and III (d) All I, II and III

12. Arrange the rulers given below in correct sequence.
(i) Akbar (ii) Babur
(iii) Shah Jahan (iv) Jahangir

Codes
(a) (i), (iii), (ii), (iv) (b) (ii), (i), (iii), (iv)
(c) (ii), (iii), (iv), (i) (d) (ii), (i), (iv), (iii)

13. Arrange the territories won by Babur in sequence.
(i) Ferghana (ii) Kabul
(iii) Delhi (iv) Chandani

Codes
(a) (i), (iii), (ii), (iv) (b) (ii), (i), (iv), (iii)
(c) (ii), (i), (iii), (iv) (d) (i), (ii), (iii), (iv)

Answers

1. (c) 2. (d) 3. (c) 4. (a) 5. (d)
6. (a) 7. (a) 8. (c) 9. (b) 10. (b)
11. (a) 12. (d) 13. (d)

Match the Following

1.

	List I		List II
A.	Babur	1.	Sisodiya ruler accepted Mughal authority
B.	Humayun	2.	Sulh-i-kul
C.	Jahangir	3.	Sher Khan defeated him
D.	Akbar	4.	Defeated Ibrahim Lodi

Codes

	A	B	C	D
(a)	4	3	1	2
(b)	2	3	1	4
(c)	1	2	4	3
(d)	3	1	2	4

2.

	List I		List II
A.	Genghis Khan	1.	People who join Mughal service
B.	Primogeniture	2.	Revenue Minister
C.	Mansabdar	3.	Rule of Inheritance
D.	Todar Mal	4.	Ruler of Mongol tribe
E.	Abul Fazl	5.	Akbar Nama

Codes

	A	B	C	D	E		A	B	C	D	E
(a)	4	3	1	2	5	(b)	2	3	1	4	5
(c)	1	5	2	4	3	(d)	3	1	2	5	4

Ans. 1. (a) 2. (a)

Assertion and Reason

1. **Assertion** (A) *Zabt* was revenue system introduced by Todar Mal.

   Reason (R) *Zabt* was prevalent in areas such as Gujarat and Bengal.

   Codes

   (a) Both A and R are true and R is the correct explanation of A

   (b) Both A and R are true, but R is not the correct explanation of A

   (c) A is true, but R is false

   (d) A is false, but R is true

2. **Assertion** (A) Mughals extend their influence over many kings and chieftains.

   Reason (R) Mughals treated rulers honourably who accept their authority.

   Codes

   (a) Both A and R are true and R is the correct explanation of A

   (b) Both A and R are true, but R is not the correct explanation of A

   (c) A is true, but R is false

   (d) A is false, but R is true

Ans. 1. (c) A is true, but R is false
2. (a) Both A and R are true and R is the correct explanation of A

Fill in the Blanks

1. Many Rajputs married their daughters into Mughal families in order to get ....
2. The Red Fort at Delhi was the residence of .... Emperors.
3. .... was the ruler of the Mongol tribes; China and Central Asia.
4. *Mansabdar's* rank and salary were determined by a numerical value called ....
5. The Mughals used the term zamindars to describe all ....
6. Babur seized .... in 1504.

Ans. 1. high positions 2. Mughal 3. Genghis Khan 4. zat 5. intermediaries 6. Kabul

True/False

1. Mughals were proud of their Mongol ancestors.
2. Babur was defeated at first Battle of Panipat.
3. The mother of Shah Jahan was from a Rajput family.
4. Babur established control over Agra and Delhi.
5. Cannons were first used in the 16th century warfare.

Ans. 1. False 2. False 3. True 4. True 5. True

Picture Based Questions

1. **Which Mughal emperor's court is shown in the image?**

(a) Shah Jahan (b) Babur
(c) Akbar (d) Jahangir

2. **Under whose reign, the miniature shown in image was created ?**

(a) Akbar (b) Jahangir
(c) Shah Jahan (d) Aurangzeb

Ans. 1. (c) Akbar 2. (c) Shah Jahan

Case Based Question

1. Read the passage given below and answer the following questions.

In Akbar's reign, these Jagirs were carefully assessed so that their revenues were roughly equal to the salary of the *mansabdar*. By Aurangzeb's reign, this was no longer the case and the actual revenue collected was often less than the granted sum. There was also a huge increase in the number of *mansabdars*, which meant a long wait before they received a jagir. These and other factors created a shortage in the number of *jagirs*. As a result many *jagirdars* tried to extract as much revenue as possible while they had a *jagir*.

(i) Who introduced *mansabdar* system?

(a) Babur (b) Humayun (c) Akbar (d) Aurangzeb

(ii) *Mansabdar* received their salaries as revenue assignments called

(a) *Mansab* (b) *Jagir* (c) *Zat* (d) *Iqtas*

(iii) How many *mansabdars* were there during the Akbar's reign ?

(a) 29 (b) 79 (c) 39 (d) 69

(iii) Jagir is the term used to describe ....

(a) rank (b) land

(c) property (d) salary

Ans (i) (c) Akbar (ii) (b) *Jagir*

(iii) (a) 29 (iv) (b) Land

Part II

Very Short Answer Type Questions

1. Why the rulers of the middle ages faced difficulties to rule the Indian sub-continent?

Ans. The rulers of the middle ages faced difficulties to rule the Indian sub-contincent because people of diverse backgrounds and cultures lived here.

2. Why Mughals were proud of their Timurid ancestry?

Ans. Mughals were proud of their Timurid ancestry because of their achievements like capturing Delhi in 1398.

3. Who were Uzbegs ?

Ans. Uzbegs were Mongol competitors of Timur.

4. Why was Babur forced to leave his ancestral throne?

Ans. Babur was forced to leave his ancestral throne due to the invasion of another Mongol groups, the Uzbegs.

5. Who was the founder of Mughal empire in India? Diksha

Ans. Babur was the founder of Mughal empire in India.

6. When was the first Battle of Panipat fought ? Diksha

Ans. The first battle of Panipat was fought in 1526 between Babur and Ibrahim Lodi.

7. Who defeated Ibrahim Lodi and his Afghan supporters in 1526?

Ans. Babur defeated Ibrahim Lodi and his Afghan supporters in 1526 at Panipat.

8. What do you mean by the rule of primogeniture?

Ans. Under the primogeniture system, the eldest son inherits the father's property after his death.

9. Who is a Mansabdar?

Ans. Mansabdar refers to an individual who holds a mansab i.e. a position or rank in Mughal administration.

10. What was zat?

Ans. Rank and salary of a *mansabdar* were determined by a numerical value called *zat*. The higher the *zat*, the more prestigious was the noble's position in court and the larger his salary.

11. What is the meaning of Jagir?

Ans. Mansabdars received their salaries as revenue assignments known as *Jagirs*.

12. At what age did Akbar become the emperor of the Mughal empire?

Ans. Akbar became the Mughal Empire at the age of 13.

13. What is the name of the third volume of Akbar Nama?

Ans. The name of the third volume of Akbar Nama is Ain-i-Akbari.

14. What was another name of Nur Jahan?

Ans. Mehrunnisa was the another name of Nur Jahan.

15. Where did new provinces emerge after the Mughal empire declined ? Competency Based

Ans. New provinces emerged in Awadh and Hyderabad.

Short Answer Type Questions

1. How were the Mughal emperors greater than their predecessors?

Ans. Mughal emperors were greater than their predecessors, as their predecessors believed in plunder and massacre, while Mughals believed in establishment of fair governance. Emperors like Akbar worked for peaceful coexistence of people from all religions. Mughals created a great empire in Indian sub-continent and left a political legacy.

2. How was Mughal rule established in India? How did Mughals establish relations with Rajputs.

Ans. Mughal rule was established in India after Babur defeated Sultan of Delhi, Ibrahim Lodi at the Battle of Panipat in 1526. Babur captured Delhi and Agra after his victory and laid the foundation of Mughal Empire in India.

The Mughal rulers constantly campaigned against rulers who were not ready to accept their authority. Gradually, when the Mughals became powerful, many rulers joined them willingly to prevent any attacks in future.

Many Rajputs married their daughters into Mughal families to gain high positions or offices. For example, mother of Jahangir was from a Rajput family. In this way, Mughals establish relations with Rajputs.

3. How Todar Mal organised revenue system under Akbar? **Competency Based**

Ans. Todar Mal was Akbar's revenue minister. He carried out a careful survey of crop yields, prices and areas cultivated for a 10 years period (1570-1580).

On the basis of this survey, tax was fixed on each crop in cash. Each province was divided into revenue circles with its own schedule of revenue rates for individual crops. This revenue system came to be known as *zabt*. However, this *zabt* system was present in only those areas where Mughal administrators could survey the land.

4. Describe jagirdars and their duties.

Ans. *Jagirdar* was a *mansab* (rank) under Mughal administration. He was assigned to collect revenue of the *jagir* (land) that was alloted to him. *Jagirdari* was not a hereditary post.

People could be removed from the rank if they did anything illegal. Jagirs were carefully assessed so that their revenues were roughy equal to the salary of the mansabdar.

5. Give an account of Akbar Nama and Ain-i-Akbari.

Ans. Abul Fazl wrote a three volume history of the reign of Akbar. It was titled as *Akbar Nama*.

The first volume speaks about the Akbar's ancestors, the second volume recorded the events of Akbar's reign. Ain-i-Akbari is the third volume. Ain-i-Akbari gives detail on account of Akbar's administration, household, army, the revenues and the geography of the empire. This book also provides details about the traditions and cultures of the Indian people. It also provide statistical details about things as diverse as crops, yields, prices, wages and revenues.

6. What was Sulh-i-kul and its main features?

Ans. The Sulh-i-kul meant universal peace, and it was introduced by Akbar.

Its main features were

- This idea was based on idea of tolerance which did not discriminate between people of different religions in his realm.
- This idea focussed on a system of ethics which included honesty, justice and peace. These values were universally applicable.

7. What were the main administrative reforms of Mughal Emperor, Akbar? **Diksha**

Ans. The main administrative reforms of Mughal emperor Akbar were as follows

- Akbar adopted Sher Shah's administrative system reforms. He introduced Mansabdari system for regulating army and commanders.
- He gave idea of 'Sulh-i-kul' for maintaining peace and harmony.
- He maintained cordial relations with the Rajputs.

8. "Aurangzeb was unable to control these developments and the peasantry therefore suffered tremendously." What developments are being referred to here? **Competency Based**

Ans. Peasantry suffered a lot in Aurangzeb's reign due to certain developments. Aurangzeb's reign was marked by the *jagirdari* crisis.

In Akbar's reign, *jagirs* were carefully assessed so that their revenues were roughly equal to the salary of the *mansabdar*. But in Aurangzeb's reign, the actual revenue collected was often less than the sum granted to a *mansabdar*. There was also a huge increase in the number of *mansabdars*, which resulted in delay in receiving a jagir. This created a shortage in the number of *jagirs*. As a result, many *jagirdars* tried to extract more revenue while they had a jagir.

Long Answer Type Questions

1. Who were *mansabdars*? What were their duties? Which people joined Mughal service as *mansabdars*?

Ans. The term *mansabdar* refers to an individual who holds a *mansab*, means a position or rank. It was a grading system used by the Mughals to fix rank, salary and military responsibilities.

The duties of *mansabdars* were

- Mansabdars had to maintain a specified number of Sawar or cavalrymen.
- Mansabdar had to bring his sawar for review get them registered, their horses branded and then they received money to pay them as salary.

The people who joined Mughal service as *mansabdars* included Turanis (Turkish nobles), Iranians, Indian Muslims, Afghans, Rajputs, Marathas and other groups.

2. Who were the zamindars? What duty was assigned to them? Describe about *zabt* system.

Ans. Zamindars were the rural elities through whom peasants paid their taxes. In Mughal period Zamindars was the term used to describe all intermediaries whether they were local headman of villages or powerful cheiftains.

The duty of zamindars was to collect taxes for the king in their area.

Zabt was a revenue system conducted by Todar Mal, the revenue minister of Abkar. Under this system, he carried out a survey of crop yields, and areas cultivated for a 10-year period. Tax was fixed for each crops (in cash) on the basis of this survey.

Each province was divided into revenue circles with its own schedule of revenue rates for individual crops.

3. Give a brief sketch about the Mughal empire in the 17th century and afterwards.

Ans. In the 17th century, the Mughal empire was characterised by remarkable administrative and military efficiency, promoting economic prosperity and commercial success.

International travellers highlighted the sharp income inequalities. During Shah Jahan's reign, 5.6% of total mansabdars, received 61.5% of the empire's, revenue as salaries. To meet the increased expenditure, revenue rates were increased. However, this increased revenue collection hampered the economic growth of the poorest.

By the late 17th century, as Mughal authority declined, some powerful mansabdars emerged as influential regional centres of power in Awadh and Hyderabad, eventually leading to the decline of the empire by the 18th century.

4. "This expenditure benefited the artisans and peasantry who supplied them with goods and produce". Do you think that peasants had a prosperous life during Mughal rule ? **Competency Based**

Ans. The peasants did not have a prosperous life during the Mughal rule. Their condition during Mughal rule is discussed below

- The Mughal emperors and their *mansabdars* spent a great deal of their income on buying goods produced by artisans and peasantry.
- This expenditure benefitted the artisans and peasantry but it was insignificant as compared to the amount they had to pay as tax.
- Revenue rates were increased to finance the increased expenditure of the state.
- Peasants and artisans were left with very little for investment. They lived in poverty and they could hardly consider investing in additional resources like tools and supplies to increase productivity.

Picture Based Questions

1. Look at the information and picture given below and answer the following questions.

A miniature painting (dated 1702-1712) of *Timur*, his descendants and the Mughal Emperors. Timur is in the centre and on his right is his son Miran Shah (the first Mughal Emperor Babur's great-great- grandfather) and then Abu Said (Babur's grandfather). To the left of Timur are Sultan Muhammad Mirza (Babur's great-grandfather) and Umar Shaikh (Babur's father). The Mughal emperors Babur, Akbar and Shah Jahan are the third, fourth and fifth individuals on Timur's right and on his left, in the same order are Humayun, Jahangir and Aurangzeb.

(i) Do you think this painting suggests that the Mughals claimed kingship as a birth right?

Ans. This painting truly suggests that the Mughals claimed kingship as a birthright. All the rulers were seen sitting together in a hierarchical way. The inheritance was regarded as their birthright. They showed great respect to be descendant of Timurids. All the kings showed ability to rule which they considered to be as high as the heavens.

(ii) Which area was ruled by Timur?

Ans. Timur was the ruler of Iran, Iraq and Modern-day Turkey. He died in 1404.

(iii) Which ancestry were Mughals proud of ?

Ans. Mughals were proud of their Timurid ancestry.

2. Answer the following questions in reference to the pictures below.

Picture 1

Picture 2

(i) What details are shown in the pictures?

Ans. These miniatures from Shah Jahan's reign show the figures depicting corruption in his father Jahangir's administration.

(ii) **State the two instances shown in the pictures.**

Ans. The two instances shown in the pictures are

(a) A corrupt officer receiving a bribe.

(b) A tax collector punishing a poor peasant to collect taxes.

(iii) **Both the picutures show what type of administration, a good administration or a bad administration?**

Ans. Both the pictures show bad administration or bad governance.

Case Based Questions

1. Read the passage given below and answer the following questions.

Nur Jahan's Influence in Jahangir's Court

Mehrunnisa married the Emperor Jahangir in 1611 and received the title Nur Jahan. She remained extremely loyal and supportive to the monarch. As a mark of honour, Jahangir struck silver coins bearing his own titles on one side and on the other the inscription "struck in the name of the Queen Begum, Nur Jahan."

The adjoining document is an order (*farman*) of Nur Jahan. The square seal states, "Command of her most sublime and Elevated Majesty Nur Jahan Padshah Begum." "The round seal states, "by the sun of Shah Jahangir she became as brillant as the moon; may Nur Jahan Padshah be the lady of the age."

(i) **How did Jahangir honour Nur Jahan's loyalty?**

Ans. Jahangir showed great loyalty towards Nur Jahan. He introuced silver coins bearing his own titles on one side and on the other the inscription, "struck in the name of the Queen Begum, Nur Jahan." According to historians, Empress Nur Jahan became the real power behind the throne and competently ruled on behalf of the king.

(ii) **Who succeeded Akbar as the fourth Mughal emperor ?**

Ans. Jahangir succeeded his father Akbar in 1605 as the fourth Mughal emperor.

2. Read the following information and answer the question that follows.

Sulh-i-Kul

Jahangir, Akbar's son, described his father's policy of Sulh-i-kul in the following words:

As in the wide expanse of the divine compassion there is room for all classes and the followers of all creeds, so ... in his imperial dominions, which on all sides were limited only by the sea, there was room for the professors of opposite religions, and for beliefs, good and bad, and the road to intolerance was closed. Sunnis and Shias met in one mosque and Christians and Jews in one church to pray. He consistently followed the principle of 'universal peace' (Sulh-i-kul).

(i) **How did Jahangir describe his father's policy of Sulh-i-kul? Why were roads to intolerance closed?**

Ans. Jahangir described his father, Akbar's policy of Sulh-i kul (universal peace) as a policy that was open to all religions and beliefs. He mentioned that in Akbar's empire, there was room for everyone, regardless of their faith.

He also mentioned that Akbar closed the road to intolerance, meaning that he did not allow for discrimination of people on the basis of their religion.

(ii) **Describe the religious policy of Akbar.**

Ans. Akbar believes in religious harmony and principle of universal peace. He believed there should be common belief and no hate to each other religion. He also believed in equality of every religion.

Map Based Question

1. On the map of India, mark the following areas of military campaigns under Akbar and Aurangzeb.

(a) Malwa (1561) **(b) Bengal (1574)**

(c) Bijapur (1685) **(d) Gujarat (1572)**

(e) Golconda (1687)

Ans.

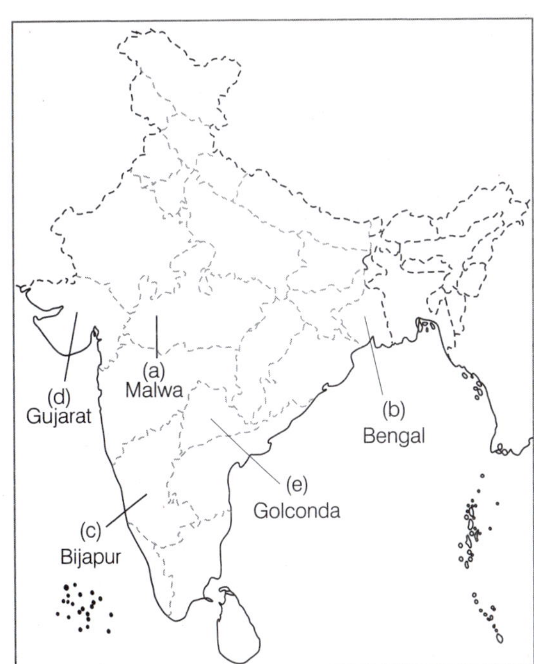

ASSESSMENT EXERCISE

Multiple Choice Questions (MCQs)

1. Which of the following areas was seized by Babur after years of wandering?
(a) Mongol (b) Kabul
(c) Central Asia (d) China

2. In which year Babur defeated Ibrahim Lodi (Sultan of Delhi)?
(a) 1504 (b)1515
(c) 1526 (d) 1530

3. Which Mughal emperor was defeated by Sher Shah Suri?
(a) Babur (b) Humayun
(c) Akbar (d) Jahangir

4. Genghis Khan was a ruler of which tribe?
(a) Turkish
(b) Mongols
(c) Huns
(d) None of the above

Subjective Questions (VSA, SA & LA)

1. Who was Abul Fazl?

2. Who were the Zamindars?

3. Where did Mughal emperors and their mansabdars spent their income?

4. How can you say that mughals did not believe in the rule of Primogeniture?

5. Why did jagirdars try to extract as much revenue as possible?

6. How taxes were imposed on each crop during Akbar's reign?

7. Write a brief note on zabt and zamindars.

8. How did debates with religious scholars influence Akbar's ideas an governance? Write about descendants of the Mughals.

9. Write about the difficulties faced by Babur and Humayun to establish their rule in India.

Tribes, Nomads and Settled Communities

CHAPTER 5

Over the centuries, important political, social and economic developments had taken place. However, social change was not the same everywhere, because different kinds of societies evolved differently. Society was divided according to the rules of **Varna** in large parts of Indian sub-continent.

These rules were prescribed by the Brahmanas. Gradually, the difference between the high and low and between the rich and poor, increased. Under the Delhi Sultans and the Mughals, this **hierarchy** between social classes grew further.

5.1 Tribal Societies

Many societies in the sub-continent did not follow the social rules and rituals prescribed by Brahmanas. They were divided into a number of unequal classes. These societies are called tribes.

Characteristics of Tribal Societies

- Members of each tribe were united by **kinship**[1] bonds. Many tribes obtained their livelihood from agriculture while some were **hunter-gatherers** or **herders**. They make full use of the natural resources of the area in which they lived.
- Some tribes were **nomadic** and moved from one place to another.
- A tribal group controlled land and pastures jointly and divided these amongst all households according to its own rules.
- The tribes lived in forests, hills, deserts and places that are difficult to reach.
- They retained their freedom and preserved their separate culture.
- The caste-based and tribal societies depended on each other for their different needs. This relationship, of conflict and dependence, caused a change gradually in both societies.

5.2 Tribal People

Tribal people did not keep any written records but they preserved rich customs and oral traditions. Historians today use these oral traditions to write tribal histories.

Tribal people were found in almost every region of the subcontinent. Some powerful tribes controlled large territories.

Some of the different tribes who belong to different regions are given below

- In Punjab, the **Khokhar** tribe was very powerful during the 13th and 14th centuries. Later the **Ghakkars** became more important. Their chief, Kamal Khan Ghakkar was made a noble (*mansabdar*) by Akbar.
- In Multan and Sind, the **Langahs** and **Arghuns** dominated extensive regions.
- The Balochis were another large and powerful tribe in the North-West. They were divided into many smaller **clans**[2] under different chiefs.
- In the Western Himalaya, the shepherd tribe of **Gaddis** lived.
- The North-Eastern part was dominated by the **Nagas**, **Ahoms** and many others.
- By 12th century, **Chero** chiefdoms emerged in many areas of present-day Jharkhand and Bihar. Raja Man Singh, Akbar's famous general, attacked and defeated the Cheros in 1591. Under Aurangzeb, Mughal forces captured many Chero fortresses and suppressed the tribe.
- The Mundas and Santhals were other important tribes in Jharkhand, Bihar, Orissa and Bengal.
- **Kolis, Berads** and other tribes lived in the Maharashtra highlands and Karnataka. The Kolis also lived in many areas of Gujarat.

1 **Kinship** It refers to the relationship between the members of the same family.
2 **Clans** It is a group of families having a common ancestor.

- **Koragas**, **Vetars**, **Maravars** and many others tribes live in the Southern region.
- The large tribe of **Bhils** lived across Western and Central India. By the late 16th century, many of them became settled agriculturists, some became zamindars and many others remained hunter-gathers.
- The **Gonds** were found in Chhattisgarh, Madhya Pradesh, Maharashtra and Andhra Pradesh.

5.3 Lives of Nomadic People

Nomadic pastoralists moved over long distances with their animals. They lived on milk and other pastoral products. They exchanged wool, ghee, etc with settled people for food, grain, utensils, etc. They bought and sold these goods as they moved from one place to another, transporting them on their animals.

Banjaras were the most important trader-nomads. Their caravan was called **tanda**. Sultan Alauddin Khalji used Banjaras to transport grain to the city markets. In his **memoirs**, Jahangir mentioned that Banjaras carried grain on their bullocks from different areas and sold in towns. They transported food grains for the Mughal army during military campaigns.

Many pastoral tribes reared and sold animals to the prosperous people. Different castes of **pedlars**[3] travelled from village to village selling ropes, reeds, straw mats and coarse sacks made by them.

5.4 Changing Society : New Castes and Hierarchies

As the economy and the needs of society grew, people with new skills were required. Smaller castes, or ***jatis***, emerged within *varnas*[4]. New castes appeared amongst the Brahmanas.

Jatis became the basis for organising society. Many tribes and social groups were taken into caste-based society and given the status of *jatis*. Specialised artisans like smiths, carpenters and masons were also recognised as separate *jatis* by the Brahmanas.

By the 11th and 12th centuries, new Rajput clans became powerful among the Kshatriyas. They belonged to different lineages such as Hunas, Chandelas, Chalukyas, etc. Some of them were tribes earlier. Gradually, they replaced the older rulers especially in rural areas.

With the support of Brahmanas, many tribes became a part of the caste system. But only the leading families could join the ruling class. A large majority joined the lower *jatis* of the caste society.

On the other hand, many tribes of Punjab, Sind and the North-West Frontier adopted Islam and refused to follow the caste system.

5.5 Gonds

They lived in a forested region called **Gondwana.** They practised **shifting cultivation**[5]. The Gond tribe was further divided into smaller clans. Each clan had its own ***rai*** (or raja).

When the power of the Delhi Sultans was declining, some large Gond kingdoms were beginning to dominate the smaller Gond chiefs.

Administration and Society

The administration of Gond kingdoms was centralised. The kingdom was divided into ***garhs***. Each *garh* was controlled by a particular Gond clan.

Garh was further divided into units of 84 villages called ***chaurasi***. The *chaurasi* was subdivided into ***barhots*** which were made up of 12 villages each.

With the emergence of large states, the equal society of Gonds got divided into unequal social classes. Brahmanas received land grants from the Gond rajas and became more powerful.

Gond chiefs wished to be recognised as Rajputs. So, **Aman Das**, the Gond raja of Garha Katanga assumed the title of Sangram Shah.

There is a mention about Gond kingdom of Garha Katanga in Akbar Nama. It was a rich state. It earned wealth by exporting elephants to other kingdoms.

In 1565, the Mughal forces under Asaf Khan attacked the Garha Katanga and defeated the Gonds. They captured the precious coins and elephants. The Gond kingdoms further became weak after the attacks of Bundelas and Marathas.

---

3 **Pedlar** It refers to a person who travels from place to place trying to sell something.

4 **Varna** It is a division of society into castes based on occupation, tradition, family backgrounds.

5 **Shifting Cultivation** It is a technique of farming in which land is cleared for cultivation (normally by fire) and then left to regenerate after a few years.

5.6 The Ahoms

The Ahoms migrated to the **Brahmaputra Valley** from present day Myanmar in the 13th century. They created a new state by suppressing the older system of *bhuiyans* (landlords).

In the 16th century, they annexed the kingdoms of Chhutiyas (1523) and Koch-Hajo (1581). They use firearms in 1530s for building a large state. By the 1660s, they also made high quality gunpowder and cannons.

Ahoms faced many invasions from the South-West. In 1662, they were defeated by the Mughals under Mir Jumla.

Administration and Society

Ahom state depended upon forced labour and those who were forced to work for the state were called ***paiks***. Each village had to send a number of *paiks* by rotation.

By the first half of the 17th century, the administration of Ahoms became centralised. Almost all adult males served in the army during war. At other times, they were engaged in building dams, irrigation systems and other public works. Ahoms also introduced new methods of rice cultivation.

Ahom society was divided into clans or ***khels***. A *khel* controlled several villages. The village community provided lands to its peasants. This land could not be taken away even by the king, without the community's consent.

Ahom society was very advanced. Land grants were given to poets and scholars, and theatre was encouraged.

Religious Beliefs and Culture

Ahoms worshipped their own tribal gods. However, during the first half of 17th century, the influence of Brahmanas increased. The king granted land to the temples and Brahmanas.

During the reign of **Sib Singh** (1714-1744), Hinduism became the main religion. But the Ahom kings did not completely give up their traditional beliefs even after adopting Hinduism.

During Ahom kingdom, important Sanskrit works were translated into the local language. Historical works known as ***buranjis*** were written first in Ahom language and then in Assamese language.

Try These

1. **Name the vast forested region where the Gonds lived.**
2. **What is the meaning of 'bhuiyans'?**
3. **Who defeated Cheros in the Mughal period?**
4. **Identify the name of the tribe that specialises in transporting grains.**

5.7 Conclusion

During the period of 16th to 18th century, considerable social change took place in the subcontinent Over a period of time, many of the tribes merged with caste-based society. However, others, rejected both the caste system and orthodox Hinduism.

Some tribes established extensive states with well organised systems of administration and became politically powerful. This led to conflict between these tribes and large kingdoms and empires.

Mind Map

Lives of Nomadic People

- They moved over long distance with their animals.
- They lived on milk and other pastoral products.
- Trader Nomads – Banjaras
- Tanda– the Caravan of Banjaras

Tribal People

- Khokhar and Ghakkars tribe in Punjab.
- Langahs and Arghuns in Multan and Sind.
- Gaddis in the Western Himalayas.
- Nagas, Ahoms in the North-Eastern part.
- Chero in Jharkhand and Bihar.
- Mundas and Santhal in Jharkhand, Bihar, Orissa and Bengal.
- Kolis and Berads in Maharashtra.
- Bhil in Western and Central India.
- Gond in Chhattisgarh, Madhya Pradesh, Maharashtra and Andhra Pradesh.

TRIBES, NOMADS AND SETTLED COMMUNITIES

Tribal Societies

- Don't follow social rules and rituals of Brahmanas
- Obtained livelihood from agriculture and hunter-gathering.
- Have own freedom and culture

New Castes and Hierarchies

- Jatis and Varnas emerged with economic development.
- The rise of Rajput clans to the position of rulers inspires tribal people to follow.

Major Tribes

Gonds

- Lived in Gondwana
- Practiced shifting cultivation
- Rose when Delhi Sultanate declined
- The Kingdom divided into garhs.
- In 1565, the Mughal force attacked and defeated the Gonds.

The Ahoms

- Migrated to Brahmaputra from Myanmar.
- They annexed to the Kingdom Chhutiyas and Koch-Hajo.
- Introduce new method in rice cultivation.
- Society divided into Khels.
- Worshipped tribal gods.
- Hinduism was the important religion.
- Buranjis-historical work first written in Ahoms language.

NCERT FOLDER

Covering Intext Questions and Exercises of NCERT

NCERT ON PAGE 57

Q.1 Discuss why the Mughals were interested in the land of the Gonds.

Ans. Mughals were interested in the lands of Gonds due to following reasons

- Garha Katanga was a rich Gond state.
- Gonds had earned huge wealth by trapping and exporting wild elephants to other kingdoms.
- Gonds were famous for their precious coins.
- Gond state was large and Mughals wanted to expand their kingdom.

NCERT ON PAGE 58

Q.2 Why do you think the Mughals tried to conquer the land of the Ahoms?

Ans. The Mughals tried to conquer the land of the Ahoms because

- The Ahoms had built a large state by subjugating Chhutiyas (1523), Kach-Hajo (1581) and other tribal areas. So, by defeating the Ahoms Mughals could establish their control over a large area.
- Mughals also wanted to suppress the upcoming threat to their kingdom and establish their supermacy over large kingdoms.

NCERT ON PAGE 59 (IMAGINE)

Q.3 You are a member of a nomadic community that shifts residence every three months. How would this change your life?

Ans. Being a member of a nomadic community that moves every three months would bring unique challenges in my life. Finding food could be difficult since we would have to adapt to different landscapes and resources. We would have to hunt, gather, or trade for what we need. Making and keeping friends might also be difficult. Life would be full of adventure and challenges.

EXERCISES

Q.1 Match the following.

List I	List II
A. Garh	1. Khel
B. Tanda	2. Chaurasi
C. Labourer	3. Caravan
D. Clan	4. Garha Katanga
E. Sib Singh	5. Ahom state
F. Durgawati	6. Paik

Codes

	A	B	C	D	E	F
(a)	2	3	6	1	5	4
(b)	6	5	4	3	2	1
(c)	1	2	3	4	5	6
(d)	2	3	4	5	1	6

Ans. (a)

Q.2 Fill in the blanks.

(a) The new castes emerging within varnas were called ....

(b) .... were historical works written by the Ahoms.

(c) The .... mentions that Garha Katanga had 70,000 villages.

(d) As tribal states became bigger and stronger, they gave land grants to .... and ....

Ans. (a) Jatis (b) Buranjis (c) Akbar Nama (d) Temples, Brahmanas

Q.3 State whether true or false.

(a) Tribal societies had rich oral traditions.

(b) There were no tribal communities in the North-Western part of the sub-continent.

(c) The Chaurasi in Gond states contained several cities.

(d) The Bhils lived in the North-Eastern part of the sub-continent.

Ans. (a) True (b) False (c) False (d) False

Q.4 What kinds of exchanges took place between nomadic pastoralists and settled agriculturists?

Ans. The nomadic pastoralists exchanged milk, wool, ghee, etc with settled agriculturists for grain, cloth, utensils and other products.

Q.5 How was the administration of the Ahom state organised?

Ans. The administration of the Ahom state was centrally organised by the first half of 17th century. The Ahom state depended upon forced labour. Those who were forced to work for the state were known as *paiks*. A census of the population was taken. Each of the village had to send a number of paiks by rotation.

People of densely populated areas were shifted to less populated areas. Ahom clans were thus broken up. Almost all adult males served in the army during war. At other time, they are involved in building dams, irrigation systems and other public works.

Ahom society was divided into class or khels, a khel controlled several villages. The peasant was given land by his village community, which even the king could not take it easily. Ahom society was very sophisticated. Poets and scholars were encouraged and given land grants.

Q.6 What changes took place in varna-based society?

Ans. The changes that took place in varna-based society were as follows

- Rules prescribed by the Brahmanas, were accepted by the rulers of large kingdoms.
- The difference between the high and low, and between the rich and the poor, increased. This further created hierarchy between social classes.
- Smaller castes or *jatis* emerged within varnas.
- New castes among the Brahmanas emerged. Specialised artisans like smiths, carpenters and masons were recognised as separate *jatis* by the Brahmanas.

Q.7 How did tribal societies change after being organised into a state ?

Ans. Tribal societies changed in the following ways after being organised into a state

- The emergence of large states changed the nature of tribal society. The equal society gradually got divided into various unequal social classes.
- Brahmanas received land grants from the Gond rajas and they became more influential.
- The Gond chiefs now wished to be recognised as Rajputs. So, Aman Das, the Gond raja of Garha Katanga assumed the title of Sangram Shah. His son Dalpat, married princess Durgawati, daughter of Salbahan, the Chandel Rajput King.

Q.8. Were the Banjaras important for the economy ?

Ans. The Banjaras were very important for the economy as they were trader-nomads and controlled trade and commerce as they played an important role in transportation of grains to the city markets.

They usually bought grain where it was cheaply available and carried it to places where it was expensive. They even transported foodgrain for the Mughal towns and during military campaigns.

Q.9 In what ways was the history of the Gonds different from that of the Ahoms? Were there any similarities?

Ans. History of the Gonds was different from the Ahom in the following ways

Gonds	Ahoms
They lived in Gondwana.	They lived in Brahmaputra valley.
They practiced shifting cultivation.	They did not practice shifting cultivation.
They did not use firearms.	They used firearms

The similarities between the history of Gonds and Ahoms were

- Both the Gonds andAhoms faced Mughals.
- Both the Gonds and Ahoms built a large kingdom.
- Both the Gonds and Ahoms granted lands to Brahmanas.

Q.10 Plot the location of the tribes mentioned in this chapter on a map. For any two, discuss whether their mode of livelihood was suited to the geography and the environment of the area where they lived.

Ans. Several tribes live in different parts of India. Some of these are shown in the map given below

The mode of livelihood of these tribes was suited to the geography and the environment of the area where they lived. For example

(i) The Khokhar tribes are from the Punjab region of Pakistan and North-Western India. They were agricultural tribes and were usually classified as Jat and Rajput. There were several sub-divisions of the Khokhar tribe, e.g., Bandial, Bhachan, Dhaulka, Ganjial, Jalap, etc. All of them were mainly dependent on their fertile land for livelihood. So, they settled in regions between Indus and Ganga.

(ii) The Gaddis are people who normally reside in the Himachal Pradesh. Their main occupation is sheepherding. They make their livelihood by rearing and selling sheep, goats, mules and horses.

They spent their winter in the low hills of Shiwalik range, grazing their flocks in forests. By April, they moved on to higher mountain meadows when the snow melted. By September, they again began their return movement.

Q.11 Find out about the present-day government policies towards tribal populations and organise a discussion about these.

Ans. The Indian government has enacted several laws to protect the interests of the tribes. Some of them are listed below

- Scheduled Tribes and Other Traditional Forest Dwellers (Recognition of Forest Rights) Act, 2006, recognises and secures the land and forest rights of tribal and forest-dwelling communities.
- Adivasi Mahila Sashaktikaran Yojana is an exclusive scheme for Scheduled Tribe women.

Q.12 Find out more about present-day nomadic pastoral groups in the sub-continent. What animals do they keep? Which are the areas frequented by the groups?

Ans. Present-day nomadic pastoral groups in the Indian sub-continent include communities like the Gujjars(or Bakarwals) and Raikas.

They primarily keep livestock, such as goats, sheep, camels and cattle.

These groups are often found in the hilly and mountainous regions of Northern India, especially in states like Jammu and Kashmir, Himachal Pradesh and Rajasthan(Raikas). They migrate seasonally to find suitable grazing lands for their animals, taking advantage of the rich pastures in higher altitudes during the summer and moving to lower places during the harsh winter.

REVIEW EXERCISE

Including Competency Based Questions

Part I

Multiple Choice Questions (MCQs)

1. On what basis was the societies divided during 11th century?
(a) Vedas (b) King (c) Varna (d) Mughals

2. Multan and Sind were dominated by which tribe?
(a) Arghuns (b) Langahs
(c) Balochis (d) Both (a) and (b)

3. Which tribe resided in Western Himalayan region?
(a) Balochis (b) Khokhar
(c) Gaddis (d) None of these

4. Which among the following tribes was called as notable trader-nomads?
(a) Bhils (b) Cheros (c) Santhals (d) Banjaras

5. The caravan of the Banjaras are called
(a) Ratha (b) Tanda (c) Burajis (d) None of these

6. Which among the following tribes was famous for shifting cultivation?
(a) Bhils (b) Gonds (c) Cheros (d) Ahoms

7. Who assumed the title of Sangram Shah?
(a) Bir Narain (b) Dal Pat
(c) Aman Das (d) Chaman Das

8. The Mughals under Mir Jumla attacked the Ahom Kingdom in
(a) 1662 (b) 1660 (c) 1720 (d) 1857

9. Who were Paiks?
(a) The landlords (b) Clan in Ahom state
(c) The forced labourers of Ahom (d) Clan in Gondwana

10. The Ahoms introduced new methods in the cultivation of which crop?
(a) Wheat (b) Rice (c) Barley (d) Maize

11. Sib Singh was an important ruler of which among the following tribes?
(a) Ahoms (b) Bhils (c) Gonds (d) Kolis

12. Under the Delhi Sultans and the Mughals, social hierarchy of society ....
(a) grew (b) remained constant
(c) decreased (d) None of these

13. The influential tribe of Punjab during the 13th and 14th century was
(a) Singhals (b) Chahamans (c) Dhillon (d) Khokhar

14. During which period, Chero chiefdoms had emerged?
(a) 11th century (b) 13th century
(c) 12th century (d) 14th century

15. The Bhils tribes are settled in
(a) Western India
(b) Western and Central India
(c) Western and Southern India
(d) Western and Northern India

16. In which region did the Rani Durgawati rule?
(a) Garha Katanga (b) Ahom
(c) Sind (d) Kolis

17. Who was Bir Narain?
(a) Ruler of Punjab (b) Son of Rani Durgawati
(c) Ruler of Multan (d) Ruler of Sind

18. **The main occupation of Gond tribes was**

(a) agriculture (b) hunting (c) pastoralism (d) weaving

19. **Identify the region or state associated with the following statement.** **Competency Based**

"The Khokhar tribe was very influential during the 13th and 14th centuries. Later, the Gakkhars became more important. Their chief, Kamal Khan Gakkhar, was made a noble (mansabdar) by Emperor Akbar".

Options

(a) Jharkhand (b) Orissa
(c) Punjab (d) Himachal Pradesh

20. **Choose the correct statement(s) among the following.** **Competency Based**

I. Rani Durgawati was the Gond queen.
II. Caravan of the Banjaras was known as Ratha.
III. *Barhots* were made up of 12 villages each.

Codes

(a) Only I (b) I and II (c) I and III (d) Only III

21. **Choose the incorrect statement(s) among the following.**

I. Bir Narain was the son of King Dalpat.
II. Mughals attacked Ahoms in 1662.
III. Gonds used firearms and cannons to built large state.

Codes

(a) Only I (b) Only II (c) Only III (d) I and II

22. **Arrange the following administrative units in top to bottom order.** **Competency Based**

I. *Garh* II. *Chaurasi*
III. *Barhot* IV. Villages

Codes

(a) II, I, III, IV (b) IV, I, II, III
(c) I, III, IV, II (d) I, II, III, IV

Answers

1. (c)	**2.** (d)	**3.** (c)	**4.** (d)	**5.** (b)
6. (b)	**7.** (c)	**8.** (a)	**9.** (c)	**10.** (b)
11. (a)	**12.** (a)	**13.** (d)	**14.** (c)	**15.** (b)
16. (a)	**17.** (b)	**18.** (a)	**19.** (c)	**20.** (c)
21. (c)	**22.** (d)			

Match the Following

1.

	List I (Tribe)		**List II** (Region)
A.	Gakkhar	1.	North-East
B,.	Balochis	2.	Punjab
C.	Gaddis	3.	Orissa
D.	Nagas	4.	Western Himalayas
E.	Santhals	5.	North-West

Codes

	A	B	C	D	E		A	B	C	D	E
(a)	2	5	4	1	3	(b)	1	3	2	4	5
(c)	3	2	1	4	5	(d)	5	4	3	2	1

2.

List I	**List II**
A. Buranjis	1. Gond society
B. Akbar Nama	2. Forced labour
C. *Chaurasi*	3. Ahoms
D. Ahom depended upon	4. Central India
E. Brahmaputra valley	5. Mentions Garha Katanga
F. Gonds	6. Historical works

Codes

	A	B	C	D	E	F		A	B	C	D	E	F
(a)	6	5	1	2	3	4	(b)	1	2	3	4	5	6
(c)	5	1	2	3	4	6	(d)	1	4	3	5	6	2

Ans. 1. (a) 2. (a)

Assertion-Reason

1. **Assertion** (A) Aman Das, Gond king of Garha Katanga, assumed the title of Sangram Shah.
Reason (R) Gond chiefs wished to be recognised as Rajputs.

Codes

(a) Both A and R are true and R is the correct explanation of A
(b) Both A and R are true, but R is not the correct explanation of A
(c) A is true, but R is false
(d) A is false, but R is true

2. **Assertion** (A) Ahoms used firearms in 1530s.
Reason (R) Ahoms settled in Kaveri valley in early 16th century.

Codes

(a) Both A and R are true and R is the correct explanation of A
(b) Both A and R are true, but R is not the correct explanation of A
(c) A is true, but R is false
(d) A is false, but R is true

Ans. 1. (a) Both A and R are true and R is the correct explanation of A
2. (c) A is true, but R is false

Fill in the Blanks

1. The forced workers in Ahom kingdom were called as .... .

2. Specialised artisans were recognised as separate jatis by the ....

3. The administration of Ahoms was ....

4. During the Mughal rule, the Balochis tribals lived in the ....

Ans. 1. paiks 2. brahmanas
3. [illegible]alised 4. North-West

True/False

1. The Khokhar tribe was influential in Punjab.
2. The Gonds were Nomadic pastoralists.
3. The Ahoms practiced shifting cultivation.
4. Garha Katanga was a poor state.
5. Sultan Alauddin Khalji used the Banjaras to transport grain to the city markets.

Ans. 1. True 2. False 3. False 4. False 5. True

Picture Based Questions

1. **The trading shown in the image is related to which tribe?**

(a) Bhils (b) Gonds (c) Banjaras (d) Koragas

2. **Carved door shown in the image found in Madhya Pradesh belongs to which tribe?**

(a) Ahoms (b) Gonds (c) Cheros (d) Bhils

Ans. 1. (c) Banjaras 2. (b) Gonds

Case Based Question

1. **Read the passage given below and answer the following questions.**

In 1565, the Mughal forces under Asaf Khan attacked Garha Katanga. A strong resistance was put up by Rani Durgawati. She was defeated and preferred to die rather than surrender. Her son, too, died fighting soon after. Garha Katanga was a rich state. It earned much wealth by trapping and exporting wild elephants to other kingdoms. When the Mughals defeated the Gonds, they captured a huge booty of precious coins and elephants. They annexed part of the kingdom and granted the rest to Chandra Shah, an uncle of Bir Narain. Despite the fall of Garha Katanga, the Gond kingdoms survived for some time. However, they became much weaker and later struggled unsuccessfully against the stronger Bundelas and Marathas."

(i) Who was the leader of Mughal forces when they attack Garha Katanga?

(a) Mir Jumla (b) Mir Jafar
(c) Asaf Khan (d) Bahadur Khan

(ii) How did Garha Katanga become rich ?

(a) By plundering nearby kingdoms.
(b) By growing commercial crops.
(c) By exporting elephants.
(d) By rearing animals.

(iii) Gonds could not survive against which powers ?

(a) Ahoms and Marathas (b) Chandels and Bundelas
(c) Bundelas and Marathas (d) Marathas and Burmeses

(iv) The annexed part of the Gond kingdom was given to whom by the Mughals?

(a) Bir Narain (b) Chandra Shah
(c) Salbahan (d) Dalpat

Ans (i) (c) Asaf Khan
(ii) (c) By exporting elephants
(iii) (c) Bundelas and Marathas
(iv) (b) Chandra Shah

Part II

Very Short Answer Type Questions

1. **What do you understand by varna?**

Ans. Varna are the rules on the basis of which society is divided. They are prescribed by the Brahmanas.

2. **Where did the tribes settle?**

Ans. The tribes settled in forests, hills, deserts and places which are difficult to reach.

3. **What do present-day historian use to write tribal histories?**

Ans. Present-day historians use oral traditions and rich customs of the tribal people to write tribal histories.

4. **What is a clan?**

Ans. A clan is a group of families or households claiming descent from a common ancestor.

5. **Who was made *mansabdar* of Punjab by Akbar?**

Ans. The Gakkhar's chief Kamal Khan Gakkhar was made *mansabdar* by Emperor Akbar.

6. **Who were the tribals of North-West India?**

Ans. The Balochis were the tribals of North-West India.

7. **Name the important tribes that lived in Orissa and Bengal.**

Ans. The Mundas and Santhals were the important tribes that lived in Orissa and Bengal.

8. Name the present-day states where the Gonds were found in great numbers.

Ans. The Gonds were found in great numbers across the present-day states of Chhattisgarh, Madhya Pradesh, Maharashtra and Andhra Pradesh.

9. Who defeated the Cheros in 1591?

Ans. The Cheros were defeated by Akbar's general Raja Man Singh in 1591.

10. When did Rajput clans become powerful?

Ans. New Rajput clans became powerful by the 11th and 12th centuries and rose to the position of rulers.

11. Mention the meaning of 'Gondwana'.

Ans. Gondwana means 'country inhabited by Gonds'.

12. Name the agricultural system practiced by most Gonds. Diksha

Ans. Shifting cultivation was practiced by most Gonds.

13. Who was the Gond raja of Garha Katanga?

Ans. Aman Das was the Gond raja of Garha Katanga.

14. Name the things which the Mughals captured by defeating the Gonds.

Ans. The Mughals captured precious coins and elephants after defeating the Gonds.

15. Where did the Ahoms migrate to?

Ans. The Ahoms migrated to the Brahmaputra valley.

16. When did the Ahoms annex the kingdoms of Chhutiyas?

Ans. The Ahoms annexed the kingdoms of Chhutiyas in 1523.

17. What are known as Buranjis?

Ans. In Ahom society, historical works are known as Buranjis which were first written in the Ahom language and then in Assamese.

18. Which tribe was very influential in Punjab during 13th and 14th century? Diksha

Ans. Khokhar tribe was very influential in Punjab during 13th and 14th century.

Short Answer Type Questions

1. Who were the tribes? Explain about their area of influence, their settlement and how they preserve their culture?

Ans. The tribes were the societies who did not follow the social rules and rituals prescribed by the Brahmanas nor were they divided into numerous unequal classes.

The area and influence of a tribe varied at different points of time. They settled away from towns and civilisation and usually lived in forests, hills, deserts and places difficult to reach. The tribes retained their freedom and preserved their separate culture in various ways.

2. How did Sultan Alauddin Khalji and Mughals use the Banjaras ? Diksha

Ans. Sultan Alauddin Khalji used the Banjaras to transport grain to the city markets.

According to Emperor Jahangir's memoirs, the Banjaras carried grain on their bullocks from different areas and sold it in towns. They transported food grain for the Mughal army during military campaigns. To supply a large army 100,000 bullocks were needed to carry grain.

3. How did Jatis become the basis for organising society ?

Ans. Jatis became the basis for organising society as many tribes and social groups were taken into caste-based society and given the status of *jatis*. Specialised artisans like smiths, carpenters and masons were also recognised as separate *jatis* by the Brahmanas.

With the support of Brahmanas, many tribes became a part of the caste system. But only the leading families could join the ruling class. A large majority joined the lower *jatis* of the caste society.

On the other hand, many tribes of Punjab, Sind and the North-West Frontier adopted Islam and refused to follow the caste system.

4. Explain the social changes that emerged among the tribal people during 11th and 12th centuries.

Ans. The social changes that emerged among the tribal people during 11th and 12th centuries were as follows

- By the 11th and 12th centuries, Rajput clans became powerful amongst some tribes. The Rajput became the rulers in different parts of India which inspired the tribal people.
- Gradually with the support of the Brahmanas, many tribes included in the caste system. But only the leading tribal families could join the ruling class. A large majority of tribes joined the lower jatis of caste society.
- Many dominant tribes of Punjab, Sind and North-West Frontier had adopted Islam to reject the orthodox Hindu casteism.

5. Write a brief note on the administrative system and society of Gond Kingdom. Diksha

Ans. The administrative system of Gonds was centralised. The kingdom was divided into garhs. Each garh was controlled by a particular Gond clan. This was further divided into units of 84 villages called *Chaurasi*. The *Chaurasi* was sub-divided into *barhots* which were made up of 12 villages each.

With the emergence of large states the equal society of Gonds got divided into unequal social classes. Brahmanas received land grants from the Gond rajas and became more powerful.

6. How can you say that Garha Katanga was a rich state? Competency Based

Ans. Garha Katanga was a rich state in the following ways

- It earned wealth by exporting elephants to other kingdoms.
- The Akbar Nama, a history of Akbar's reign, mentions that the Gond kingdom of Garha Katanga that had 70,000 villages.
- When the Mughals defeated the Gonds, they captured a huge booty of precious coins and elephants.

7. What do you know about the religion of the Ahoms?

Ans. Ahoms worshipped their own tribal gods. However, during the first half of 17th century, the influence of Brahmanas increased. The king granted land to the temples and Brahmanas.

During the reign of Sib Singh (1714-1744), Hinduism became the main religion. But the Ahom kings did not completely give up their traditional beliefs even after adopting Hinduism.

8. Write a short note on Durgawati. Diksha

Ans. Rani Durgawati was born in the family of famous Rajput Chandel Emperor Keerat Rai of Mohoba in 1524. Her father was Salbahan, the Chandel Rajput Raja. In 1542, she was married to Dalpat Shah, the eldest son of king Sangram Shah of Garha Katanga. The Chandel and Gond dynasties were allied because of this marriage.

When her son was five years old, her husband died. Rani took the reigns of the Gond Kingdom in her hand. In 1565, the Mughals under Asaf Khan attacked her kingdom. She fought bravely and died in the battlefield. Her son, too died fighting with the Mughals.

9. "The Gond chiefs now wished to be recognised as Rajputs." What circumstances led to this ? How did Gond chiefs do this? Competency Based

Ans. The emergence of large states changed the nature of Gond society. It got divided into unequal social classes. When the power of the Delhi Sultans was declining, a few large Gond kingdoms were beginning to dominate the smaller Gond chiefs. As Gonds became powerful they wished to be recognised as rajputs because the title of 'Rajput' was associated with a higher social status and prestige.

They did this by marrying their sons with Rajput princesses. For example, Gond raja of Garha Katanga's son, Dalpat, married princess Durgawati, the daughter of Chandel Rajput Raja.

Long Answer Type Questions

1. Give a brief account of tribal people found in different parts of the sub-continent. Diksha

Ans. The tribal people found in the different parts of sub-continent were

- In Punjab, the Khokhar tribe was very powerful during the 13th and 14th centuries.
- In Multan and Sind, the Langahs and Arghuns dominated extensive regions.
- The Balochis were another large and powerful tribe in the North-West.
- In the Western Himalaya, the shepherd tribe of Gaddis lived.
- The North-Eastern part was dominated by the Nagas, Ahoms and many others.
- By 12th century, Chero chiefdoms emerged in many areas of present-day Jharkhand and Bihar.
- The Mundas and Santals were other important tribes in Jharkhand, Bihar, Orissa and Bengal.
- Kolis, Berads and other tribes lived in the Maharashtra highlands and Karnataka. The Kolis also lived in many areas of Gujarat.
- Koragas, Vetars, Maravars and many others tribes live in the Southern region.
- The large tribe of Bhils lived across Western and Central India.
- The Gonds were found in Chhattisgarh, Madhya Pradesh, Maharashtra and Andhra Pradesh.

2. What were the key characteristics and social structures commonly found in tribal societies in the sub-continent?

Ans. Characteristics and social structures found in tribal societies were as follows

- Tribal societies do not follow the social rules and rituals prescribed by the Brahmanas. They are not divided into numerous unequal classes.
- Members of each tribe were united by kinship bonds.
- They obtained their livelihood from agriculture. Some were hunter-gatherers or herders. Most often they combined these activities to make full use of the natural resources of the area in which they lived.
- Some were nomadic and moved from one place to another. They moved over long distances with their animals. They lived on milk and other pastoral products.
- A tribal group controlled land and pastures jointly, and divided these amongst households according to its own rules.
- They usually lived in forests, hills, deserts and places difficult to reach.

3. How nomads and mobile people lived?

Or **How did nomads pastoralists earn their living?** Diksha

Ans. Nomadic pastoralists moved over long distances with their animals. They lived on milk and other pastoral products. They bought and sold these goods as they moved from one place to another. They carried them on the back of their animals.

The Banjaras were the most important trader nomads. Sultan Alauddin Khalji and Mughal Emperor Jahangir used the Banjaras to transport grain to the city markets.

Many pastoral tribes reared and sold animals like cattle and horses, to the prosperous people. Different castes of petty pedlars travelled from village to village and sold such as ropes, reeds, straw matting and coarse socks. Mendicants acted as wandering merchants.

4. Write a note on tribes of Gondwana.

Ans. The Gonds lived in Gondwana region, a vast forested region of central India. They practised shifting cultivation. The large Gond tribe was further divided into many smaller clans. Each of these clans had its own raja or rai. When Delhi Sultanate was declining of a few large Gond kingdoms began to dominate the smaller Gond chiefs.

The emergence of large states changed the nature of Gond society. Their equal society gradually got divided into unequal social classes. Brahmanas received land grants from the Gond rajas and became more influential. The Gond chiefs wished to be recognised as Rajputs and gain more power.

5. What were the key cultural, historical and societal features of the Ahom tribes?

Ans. The key cultural, historical and societal features of the Ahom tribes were

- The Ahoms migrated to the Brahmaputra valley from present-day Myanmar in the 13th century. They created a new state by suppressing the older system of Bhuiyans (landlords). By 1530s they had built a large state.
- Ahom state depended upon forced labour. Those forced to work for the state were called *paiks*. Each village had to send a number of *paiks* by rotation. Almost all adult males served in the army during war. Ahoms also introduced new methods of rice cultivation.
- Ahom society was divided into clans or khels. A khel controlled several villages.The peasant was given land by his village community.
- Ahoms worshipped their own tribal gods. Although, Hinduism became the predominant religion but the Ahom kings did not completely give up their traditional beliefs even after adopting Hinduism.
- Poets and scholars were given land grants in the Ahom society and theatre was encouraged. Important Sanskrit works were translated into the local language.

6. "The emergence of states is closely related to social change amongst tribal people." What social changes emerged in tribal societies? **Competency Based**

Ans. The social changes that emerged among the tribal people were as follows

- With growing needs of the society people with new skills were required. Smaller castes, or jatis, emerged within varnas. New castes appeared amongst the Brahmanas.
- Many tribes and social groups were taken into caste-based society and given the status of jatis. Specialised artisans like smiths, carpenters and masons were also recognised as separate jatis by the Brahmanas. Jatis, became the basis for organising society.
- With the support of the Brahmanas, many tribes merged into the caste system. But only the leading tribal families could join the ruling class. While others had to join the lower jatis of caste society.
- Many dominant tribes of Punjab, Sind and the North-West Frontier adopted Islam. They avoided being part of the unequal caste system. The unequal social order, prescribed by orthodox Hinduism, was not accepted in these areas.

Picture Based Questions

1. What is being depicted in the image given below?

Ans. The image shows Bhils hunting deer at night. Bhils are spread across Western and Central India. Bhils lived in deep dense forest because they were hunters and gatherers. By the late 16th century, many of them became settled agriculturists and even zamindars. However, many Bhil clans remained hunter-gatherers.

2. Look at the picture given below and answer the following questions.

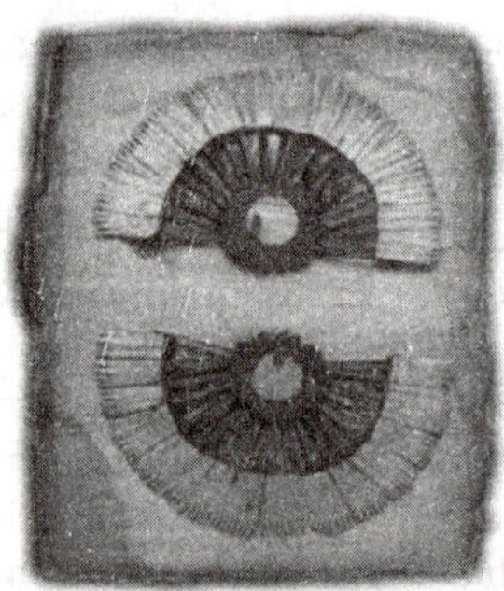

(i) This ornament belongs to which tribe?

Ans. This ear ornament belongs to Koboi Naga tribe, Manipur.

(ii) What is unique in this type of jewellery ?

Ans. This ornament is unique as it seems to be made using products derived from nature. Feathers, bark and wool may have been used to make such ornaments so that they are light in weight.

Case Based Question

1. Read the following information and answer the question that follows.

The Banjaras

Peter Mundy, an English trader who came to India during the early 17th century, has described the Banjaras.

In the morning, we met a tanda of Banjaras with 14,000 oxen. They were all laden with grains such as wheat and rice. These Banjaras carry their household, wives and children, along with them.

One tanda consists of many families. Their way of life is similar to that of carriers who continuously travel from place to place. They own their oxen. They are sometimes hired by merchants, but most commonly they are themselves merchants. They buy grain where it is cheaply available and carry it to places where it is dearer. From there, they again reload their oxen with anything that can be profitably sold in other places. In a tanda, there may be as many as 6 or 7 hundred persons.

They do not travel more than 6 or 7 miles a day that, too, in the cool weather. After unloading their oxen, they turn them free to graze as there is enough land here and no one there to forbid them.

(i) Find out how grain is transported from villages to cities at present. In what ways is this similar to or different from the ways in which the Banjaras functioned?

Ans. At present, the peasants produce food grains in the villages. They themselves carry the grains in auto rickshaw or mini trucks to the nearby town.

In many ways, the present peasants are different from the former Banjaras. Now, we have motor operated mode of transport which replaced the oxen or camels. Banjaras are not travelling in tanda or groups. They are replaced by small merchants of near by villages or towns.

(ii) Who used Banjaras for transporting foodgrains for military army?

Ans. Emperor Jahangir mentioned in his memoir that Banjaras carried food grains for Mughal army during military campaigns.

Map Based Question

1. On a physical map of the sub-continent, locate following tribes

(i) Ahoms (ii) Nagas (iii) Vetars (iv) Gonds (v) Kolis (vi) Balochis (vii) Koragas (viii) Maravars (ix) Cheros

Ans.

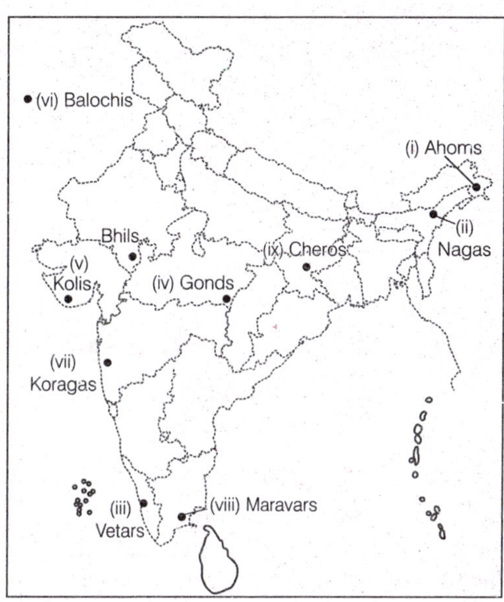

ASSESSMENT EXERCISE

Multiple Choice Questions (MCQs)

1. Which of the following tribes were used to transport grain to the city market by Sultan Alauddin Khalji?
(a) Gonds (b) Banjaras (c) Khokhar (d) Langahs

2. Which of the Mughal ruler defeated Ahom Kingdom?
(a) Mir Jumla (b) Akbar
(c) Jahangir (d) Mir Qasim

3. Aman Das, the Gond raja of Garha Katanga assumed the title of
(a) Aman Shah (b) Abhijeet
(c) Sangram Shah (d) Toran Shah

4. In Ahom state, landlords were called by which name?
(a) Khel (b) Buranji (c) Tanda (d) Bhuiyans

Subjecitve Questions (VSA, SA & LA)

5. Mention any one characteristics of tribal societies.

6. Name the tribe which was very influential during 13th and 14th centuries.

7. What was the main occupation of the Gond tribes?

8. What were the religious and cultural beliefs of Ahom?

9. Mention any four tribes who belong to different regions.

10. What do you mean by deliberations of Jati?

11. What were the administrative set-up and changes in the Gond society?

12. Which kinds of threats were faced by the Ahom?

13. What do you mean by tribes? Mention the characteristics of tribal societies.

14. Contemporary historians and travellers give very few information about the different tribes. Discuss the tribes who belong to different regions.

15. Explain the varnas system of India.

Devotional Paths to the Divine

CHAPTER 6

In 8th century, the various kinds of Bhakti and Sufi movements have emerged that led to the intense devotion and love for God. These introduced expressing love and devotion for God by performing rituals of worship or singing *bhajans*, *kirtans* or *qawwalis*, or even repeating the name of God in silence.

6.1 The Idea of a Supreme God

Before large kingdoms emerged, different groups of people worshipped their own gods and goddesses.

New ideas began to develop with the growth of towns, trade and empires. These new ideas were

- All living things pass through countless cycles of birth and rebirth performing good and bad deeds.
- All human beings are not equal even at birth. It was believed that social privileges came from birth in a 'noble' or a 'high' caste family .

Many people who were worried with these ideas followed the teachings of the Buddha or the Jainas to overcome social differences and break the cycle of rebirth through personal effort.

Other people were attracted to the idea of a Supreme God who could free humans from such bondage if worshipped with devotion (or *bhakti*). This idea of the ***Bhagavadgita***, became popular in the early centuries of the Common Era.

Lord Shiva, Vishnu and Goddess Durga came to be worshipped as supreme deities through elaborate rituals. The gods and goddesses worshipped in different areas also came to be identified with Shiva, Vishnu or Durga.

Methods of worship recommended in the Puranas were introduced to the local **cults**[1]. According to the Puranas, devotees from any caste could receive the grace of God. This idea of bhakti was even adopted by Buddhists and Jainas.

6.2 A New Kind of Bhakti in South India

From the **7th to 9th** centuries, new religious movements emerged which were led by the **Nayanars** (saints devoted to Lord Shiva) and **Alvars** (saints devoted to Lord Vishnu).

These saints came from all castes including those considered as **untouchables** like the Pulaiyar and the Panars.

They criticised the ideas of bhakti of the Buddhists and Jainas and advocated intense love of Shiva or Vishnu for achieving **salvation**[2].

They emphasised on the ideals of love and heroism mentioned in the **Sangam literature** and blended them with the values of bhakti. Sangam literature is the earliest example of Tamil literature, composed during the early centuries of the Common Era.

The Nayanars and Alvars went from place to place and composed poems in praise of the deities worshipped in the villages they visited.

Between the 10th and 12th centuries, the Chola and Pandya kings built large temples around many of the shrines visited by the saint-poets. This strengthened the links between the bhakti tradition and temple worship.

Apart from these, **hagiographies** or religious biographies of the Alvars and Nayanars were also composed.

1 Cult It refers to a type of religion or religious group, especially one that is considered unusual.

2 Salvation It refers to the state of being saved from harm, risk, etc.

Nayanars and Alvars

There were 63 Nayanars, who belonged to different caste backgrounds, such as potters, untouchable workers, peasants, hunters, soldiers, Brahmanas and chiefs. The popular among them were **Appar**, **Sambandar**, **Sundarar** and **Manikkavasagar**. **Tevaram** and **Tiruvacakam** are the two sets of compilations of Nayanars' songs.

There were 12 Alvars, who belonged to equally divergent backgrounds. The popular among them were **Periyalvar**, his daughter **Andal**, **Tondaradippodi Alvar** and **Nammalvar**. Their songs were compiled in the **Divya Prabandham**.

6.3 Philosophy and Bhakti

Shankara

He was born in Kerala in the 8th century. He was an advocate of doctrine of **Advaita** according to which both the individual soul and the Supreme God (**the Ultimate Reality**) are united.

He taught that Brahman is the Ultimate Reality who is formless and without any attributes.

He considered the world to be an illusion or *maya*. He advocated abandonment of the world and adoption of the path of knowledge to understand the true nature of Brahman and achieve salvation.

Ramanuja

He was born in Tamil Nadu in the 11th century. He was strongly influenced by the Alvars.

According to him, the best means of achieving salvation was through intense devotion to Vishnu. Vishnu helps the devotee to achieve the pleasure of union with him.

He advocated the doctrine of **Vishishtadvaita** according to which the soul maintains its separate existence, even after uniting with God.

Basavanna

He along with his companions like **Allama Prabhu** and **Akkamahadevi** initiated the Virashaiva movement. This movement began in Karnataka in the mid-12th century.

They argued strongly for the equality of all human beings, and criticised Brahmanical ideas about caste and the treatment of women. They were also against all forms of ritual and idol worship.

Try These

1. **Who advocated the doctrine of oneness of the individual soul and the Supreme God ?**
2. **Alvars were devoted to which God ?**
3. **What was the best way to attain salvation according to Ramanuja?**
4. **Identify the earliest form of Tamil literature.**

6.4 Bhakti Movement in the Deccan

From the 13th to the 17th centuries, there were many saint-poets in Maharashtra. They composed songs in simple Marathi which continues to inspire people.

The most importants saints among them were Dnyaneshwar (Gyaneshwar), Namdev, Eknath, Tukaram, Sakhubai and the family of Chokhamela, who belonged to the untouchable Mahar caste.

These saint poets focused on the **Vitthala** (a form of Vishnu) in Pandharpur, and the belief of a personal god residing in the hearts of all people.

They rejected all forms of **ritualism**[3] and social differences based on birth. They also rejected the idea of **renunciation**[4], and preferred to live with their families and earning their livelihood like any other person.

They insisted that the true bhakti is sharing the pain of others. According to the famous Gujarati saint **Narsi Mehta**, the saint poets of Maharashtra were Vaishnavas who understand the pain of others.

6.5 Nathpanthis, Siddhas and Yogis

They criticised the rituals and other aspects of traditional religion, and the social order using simple and logical arguments.

They believed in renunciating the world which means leaving all material desires. According to them, salvation can be achieved through meditation on the Ultimate Reality which is formless. Uniting with this Ultimate Reality was gaining salvation.

They advocated intense training of the mind and body through practices like yogasanas, breathing exercises and meditation.

These groups became particularly popular among low castes. Their criticism of traditional religion created the basis for the development of devotional religion, which became a popular movement in Northern India.

---

3 **Ritualism** It refers to the regular observance or practice of a ritual.
4 **Renunciation** It refers to an act of abandoning or sacrificing something.

6.6 Islam and Sufism

Sufis were **Muslim mystics** who rejected outward religiosity. They emphasised love and devotion to God, and compassion towards all fellow human beings.

The Sufis and the saints had many similarities as they were believed to have adopted many ideas of each other.

Islam promoted strict **monotheism** or submission to one God. In the 8th and 9th centuries, religious scholars developed different aspects of the **Holy Law** (Shariat) and philosophy of Islam. When Islam had become more complex, Sufis provided an additional dimension that favoured a more personal devotion to God.

The Sufis often rejected the elaborate rituals and codes of behaviour demanded by Muslim religious scholars.

The Sufis also composed poems expressing their feelings, and a rich literature in prose, including **anecdotes**[5] and **fables**[6].

Famous Sufi Saints and Emergence of Silsilas

Some great Sufis of Central Asia were Ghazzali, Rumi and Sadi. They developed detailed methods of training using ***zikr*** (chanting of a name or sacred formula), *Sama* (singing), ***raqs*** (dancing), discussion of **parables**, breath control, etc under the guidance of a master or *pir*.

This led to the emergence of the *silsilas*, a spiritual **genealogy**[7] of Sufi teachers. Each of them followed a slightly different method (*tariqa*) of instruction and ritual practice.

The **Chishti *silsila*** was the most influential spiritual order. It included many teachers like **Khwaja Muinuddin Chishti** of Ajmer, **Qutbuddin Bakhtiar Kaki** of Delhi, **Baba Farid** of Punjab, **Khwaja Nizamuddin Auliya** of Delhi and **Bandanawaz Gisudaraz** of Gulbarga.

Sufism in India

A large number of Sufis from Central Asia settled in Hindustan from the 11th century onwards. Many Sufi centres were developed all over the subcontinent during the period of Delhi Sultanate.

The Sufi masters organised their assemblies in their *khanqahs* or **hospices**. Many devotees belonging to the members of the royalty and nobility, and ordinary people gathered in these khanqahs to discuss spiritual matters, get the blessings of the saints and attend the music and dance sessions.

People believed that the Sufi masters have miraculous powers that could relieve them from their illnesses and troubles. The tomb or *dargah* of a Sufi saint became a place of pilgrimage.

6.7 New Religious Developments in North India

Bhakti movements emerged in North India in the period after 13th century. During this period, Islam, Brahmanical Hinduism, Sufism, various elements of bhakti, and the Nathpanths, Siddhas and Yogis influenced one another.

Following bhakti saints emerged during this period

Tulsidas

- He conceived God in the form of Rama.
- He composed the ***Ramcharitmanas*** in Awadhi language which is used in Eastern Uttar Pradesh.

Surdas

- He was an intense devotee of Krishna.
- His poems are compiled in ***Sursagara, Surasaravali*** and ***Sahitya Lahari***.

Shankaradeva

- He was a saint from Assam in the late 15th century.
- He was devoted to Vishnu, and composed poems and plays in Assamese language.
- He began setting up ***namghars*** or houses of recitation and prayer.

Mirabai

- She was a Rajput princess married into the royal family of Mewar in the 16th century.
- She was a disciple of ***Ravidas*** (a saint from a caste considered as untouchable) and a devotee of Krishna.
- Her songs openly challenged the norms of the upper castes and became popular in Rajasthan and Gujarat.

Kabir

- He was one of the most influential saints who belonged to the period of 15th-16th centuries.
- He was brought up in a Muslim family of weavers (*julahas*) in Benares (Varanasi). His collection of verses is called ***sakhis*** and ***pads***. They are preserved in the *Guru Granth Sahib, Panch Vani* and *Bijak*.

5 **Anecdote** It refers to a short interesting story about a real person or event.
6 **Fable** It refers to a short story that teaches a lesson (or moral) and often has animals as main characters.
7 **Genealogy** It refers to the study of family origins and history.

- He wrote in a form of spoken Hindi but sometimes used difficult language. He had both Hindus and Muslims followers.
- His teachings rejected the following traditions
  - All forms of external worship of both Brahmanical Hinduism and Islam
  - The pre-eminence of the priestly classes
  - The caste system
- Kabir believed in a formless Supreme God and advocated that bhakti or devotion is the only path to salvation.

Baba Guru Nanak

- Guru Nanak (1469-1539) was born at Talwandi (Nankana Sahib in Pakistan). He established a centre at Kartarpur on the river Ravi, known as **Dera Baba Nanak**.
- He arranged common kitchen (langar), in which his followers ate together irrespective of their former creed, caste or gender.
- He created a sacred place known as **dharmsal**. It is now known as Gurdwara.
- He emphasised the importance of the worship of one God. He insisted that caste, creed or gender was irrelevant for attaining liberation. His idea of liberation was living with a strong sense of social commitment.
- He himself used the terms *nam*, *dan* and *isnan* for the essence of his teaching, which actually meant right worship, welfare of others and purity of conduct.
- His teachings are remembered as *nam-japna*, *kirt-karna* and *vandchhakna*, which also underline the importance of right belief and worship, honest living and helping others.
- In 1539, he appointed one of his followers as his successor, before his death. His name was **Lehna** who later came to be known as **Guru Angad**.

Compilation of Guru Granth Sahib

Guru Angad compiled the compositions of Baba Guru Nanak. He also added his own compositions in it in a new script known as **Gurmukhi**.

The three successors of Guru Angad also wrote under the name of 'Nanak' and all of their compositions were compiled by Guru Arjan in 1604.

The writings of other figures like Shaikh Farid, Sant Kabir, Bhagat Namdev and Guru Tegh Bahadur were also added to this compilation.

In 1706, this compilation was authenticated by Guru Tegh Bahadur's son and successor, Guru Gobind Singh. It is now known as **Guru Granth Sahib**, the holy scripture of the Sikhs.

Followers of Baba Guru Nanak and Spread of Sikhism

The number of Baba Guru Nanak's followers increased through the sixteenth century under his successors. They belonged to a number of castes but traders, agriculturists, artisans and craftsmen predominated.

By the beginning of the 17th century, the town of **Ramdaspur** (Amritsar) had developed around the central Gurdwara called **Harmandar Sahib** (Golden Temple). Historians refer to the early 17th-century Sikh community as 'a state within the state'.

The Mughal emperor Jahangir regarded Sikh people as a threat. In 1606, he ordered the execution of Guru Arjan.

The Sikh movement began to develop under the institution of the Khalsa by Guru Gobind Singh in 1699. The community of the Sikhs, called the **Khalsa Panth**, became a political entity.

Try These

1. **Name some sufi saints of Central Asia.**
2. **What was the old name of Amritsar ?**
3. **Which language was used by Shankaradeva?**
4. **What is the name of Tulsidas' composition?**

Mind Map

DEVOTIONAL PATHS TO THE DIVINE

Philosophy and Bhakti

- **Shankara** Advocated the doctrine of Advaita.
- **Ramanuja** Advocated the doctrine of Vishishtadvaita.
- **Basavanna** Initiated the Virashaiva movement along with his companions.

Bhakti Movement in the Deccan

The saint poets Dnyaneshwar, Namdev, Eknath, Tukaram, Sakhubai and the family of Chokhamela focused on the Vitthala (a form of Vishnu).

Islam and Sufism

Famous Sufi Saints and Emergence of Silsilas

- Sufis of Central Asia were Gazzali, Rumi and Sadi.
- Chishti silsila was the most influential spiritual order.

Sufism in India

The tomb or dargah of a Sufi saint became a place of pilgrimage.

A New Kind of Bhakti in South India

- New religious movements emerged led by the Nayanars and Alvars.
- **Nayanars** – Saints devoted to Shiva.
- **Alvars** – Saints devoted to Vishnu.

Nathpanthis, Siddhas and Yogis

Advocated intense training of the mind and body through practices like Yogasanas, breathing exercises and meditation.

The idea of Supreme God

- People started doing special rituals to worship Shiva, Vishnu and Durga.
- Idea of Supreme God got emerged to end cycle of births and rebirths.

New Religious Developments in North India

Tulsidas

- Conceived God in the form of Rama.
- Composed the Ramcharitmanas in Awadhi language.

Mirabai

- Was a disciple of Ravidas.
- Devotee of Krishna.

Kabir

Believed in a formless supreme God.

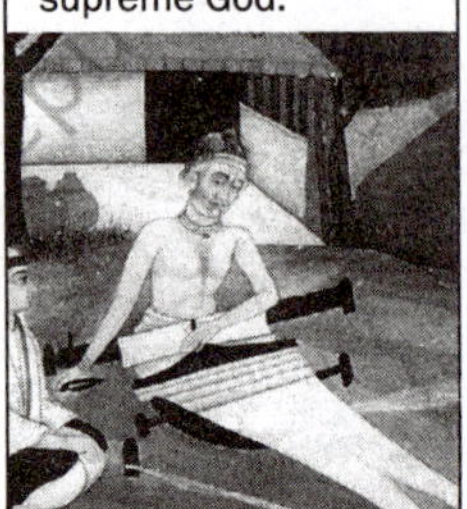

Baba Guru Nanak

- Created a sacred place known as Dharamsal, now known as Gurudwara.
- Emphasised the importance of the worship of one God.

Shankaradeva

- Devoted to Vishnu
- Set up namghars or houses of recitation.

Surdas

- Intense devotee of Krishna.
- His poems are compiled in Sursagara, Surasaravali and Sahitya Lahari.

NCERT FOLDER

Covering Intext Questions and Exercises of NCERT

NCERT PAGE 62

Q.1 You can observe this process of local myths and legends receiving wider acceptance even today. Can you find some examples around you?

Ans. Many local myths and legends have been receiving wider acceptance even today. Some notable amongst them are

- India is a land of snake charmers and black magic. India have been facing this myth even before there was any temple. But this myth does not define India.
- Indians believed to have bad luck, if black cat crosses their way. This myth is gaining ground even among the literate classes of society.
- Indians don't eat anything sweet or milk while leaving for a journey. They instead can take curd. This myth is still much prevalent.

NCERT PAGE 64

Q.2 Try and find out more about the ideas of Shankara or Ramanuja.

Ans. The ideas of Shankara and Ramanuja were as follows

Shankara He was known for the idea of Advaita Vedanta. He gave the theory of Advaita which is based on the texts like upanishads, the Bhagavadgita and the Brahma Sutras.

Advaita refers to the identity of the true self, Atman, which is pure consciousness and highest reality, Brahman, which is also pure consciousness. Followers seek liberation by acquiring Vidya of the identity of Atman and Brahman. He established four Ashramas in four corners of India.

Ramanuja He was called as the radiant one, born in Tamil Nadu. His intelligence and ability to understand highly complex philosophical points were legendary. He advocated Vishishtadvaita School. He treated all people equal without considering their castes. He encouraged temples to open their doors to everyone irrespective of caste or position.

NCERT (PAGE 76) IMAGINE

Q.3 You are attending a meeting where a saint is discussing the caste system. Relate the conversation.

Ans. In such a meeting, a saint would likely emphasise that everyone, regardless of their birth or caste, is equal in the eyes of the divine. The saint would argue that it's one's actions and devotion that matter, not their social background. They might encourage people to follow the path of love and devotion to God, beyond societal divisions. The saint's message would promote unity, equality, and the idea that spirituality is a personal journey open to all.

EXERCISES

Q.1 Match the following.

	List I	List II
A.	The Buddha	1. Namghar
B	Shankaradeva	2. Worship of Vishnu
C.	Nizamuddin Auliya	3. Questioned social differences
D.	Nayanars	4. Sufi saint
E.	Alvars	5. Worship of Shiva

Codes

	A	B	C	D	E		A	B	C	D	E
(a)	3	1	4	5	2	(b)	4	3	1	2	5
(c)	1	2	3	4	5	(d)	5	1	2	3	4

Ans. (a)

Q.2 Fill in the blanks.

(a) Shankara was an advocate of ....

(b) Ramanuja was influenced by the ....

(c) ......, ... and ...... were advocates of Virashaivism.

(d) .... was an important centre of the Bhakti tradition in Maharashtra.

Ans. (a) Advaita

(b) Alvars

(c) Basavanna, Allama Prabhu, Akkamahadevi

(d) Vitthala temple

Q.3 Describe the beliefs and practices of the Nathpanths, Siddhas and Yogis.

Ans. Nathpanths, Siddhas and Yogis criticised the rituals, social order and other aspects of conventional religion using logical arguments.

They advocated renunciation of the world. For them, the path to salvation was meditation on the formless Ultimate Reality and the realisation of unity with it. To achieve this, they recommend intense training of the mind and body through practices like yogasanas, breathing exercises and meditation. These groups became particularly popular among low castes. Their criticism of conventional religion was a reason for devotional religion to become a popular in Northern India.

Q. 4 What were the major ideas expressed by Kabir? How did he express these?

Ans. The major idea expressed in Kabir's teachings was rejection of major religious traditions. He criticised all forms of external worship of both Brahmanical Hinduism and Islam, the supremacy of the priestly classes and the caste system.

Kabir believed in a formless Supreme God and preached that the only path to salvation was through bhakti or devotion. Kabir had both Hindus and Muslims followers.

He expressed these ideas through verses composed in spoken Hindi. They were easily understood by ordinary people. His compositions were collected and preserved in the Guru Granth Sahib, Panch Vani and Bijak.

Q.5 What were the major belief and practices of Sufis?

Ans. The following were the major beliefs and practices of Sufis

- Sufis emphasised love and devotion to God, and compassion towards all fellow human beings.
- The Sufis often rejected the elaborate rituals and codes of behaviour demanded by Muslim religious scholars.
- The Sufis also composed poems expressing their feelings, and a rich literature in prose, including anecdotes and fables.

Q.6 Why do you think many teachers rejected prevalent religious beliefs and practices?

Ans. Many teachers rejected prevalent religious beliefs and practices because they believed in a direct and personal connection with the divine. They felt that the rigid caste system and complex rituals had created divisions and inequalities in society.

Bhakti teachers emphasised love and devotion to God, teaching that it was the most important aspect of one's faith. They wanted to make religion accessible to everyone, regardless of their social status, and to promote an inclusive approach to spirituality. They aimed to promote equality, and offer direct connection to the divine. His vast collection of verses is called sakhis and pads.

Q. 7 What were the major teachings of Baba Guru Nanak?

Ans. The major teachings of Guru Nanak were

- Guru Nanak emphasised the importance of the worship of one God. He insisted that caste, creed or gender was irrelevant for attaining liberation.
- His idea of liberation was living with a strong sense of social commitment.
- He also used the terms *nam*, *dan* and *isnan* for the essence of his teachings, which actually meant right worship, welfare of others and purity of conduct.
- He gave importance to right belief and worship, honest living and helping others. He promoted the idea of equality.

Q.8 For either the Virashaivas or the saints of Maharashtra, discuss their attitude towards caste.

Ans. The attitude of Virashaivas or the saints of Maharashtra towards caste was that they were against Brahmanical ideas about caste and the treatment of women. They believed in the equality of all human beings.

Moreover, they believed that bhakti means sharing other's pains. They wished a society where people could live in harmony without any feelings of high and low, rich and poor.

Q. 9 Why do you think ordinary people preserved the memory of Mirabai?

Ans. I think ordinary people preserved the memory of Mirabai because

- Though, she was a Rajput princess married into the royal family of Mewar, she had no interest in worldly affairs. Mirabai was devoted to Krishna and composed many innumerable bhajans expressing her intense devotion.
- Her devotion to her deity was supreme. She lived a simple life with ordinary people.
- Her songs openly challenged the norms of the upper caste and became popular with the masses in Rajasthan and Gujarat.

Q.10 Find out whether in your neighbourhood there are any dargahs, gurudwaras or temple associated with saints of the bhakti tradition. Visit one of these and describe what you see and hear.

Ans. Do it yourself.

Q.11 For any of the saint-poets whose compositions have been included in this chapter, find out more about their works, noting down other poems. Find out whether these are sung, how they are sung, and what the poets wrote about.

Ans. Compositions of many saint-poets have been included in the chapter. Basavanna was a philosopher-saint from Karnataka. He is known for his Vachanas, a form of devotional poetry. Around 1,600 Basavanna's *Vachanas* have been published.

His poems are sung, typically in the form of bhajans or devotional songs, accompanied by musical instruments during religious gatherings. Basavanna's works emphasise devotion to Lord Shiva and address issues of social inequality, caste discrimination and spiritual equality.

Q.12 There are several saint-poets whose names have been mentioned but their works have not been included in the chapter.

Find out more about the language in which they composed, whether their compositions were sung and what their compositions were about.

Ans. Information about the composition of some of the saint-poets are

- **Ramanuja** He wrote his works in the Sanskrit language. His main compositions were about the philosophy of Vishishtadvaita, which means 'qualified non-dualism'.
- **Basavanna** He wrote his devotional works known as '*Vachanas*' in the Kannada language. His compositions primarily revolved around themes of spiritual equality, social justice and devotion to the Shiva.
- **Namdev** He wrote his devotional compositions in the Marathi language. His works mainly focused on devotion to Lord Vithoba, a form of Lord Krishna and his love for the divine.
- **Al-Ghazzali** He was a renowned Islamic scholar, wrote in the Arabic language.He emphasised on Sufism, a mystical form of Islam, promoting the inner journey towards God through personal spiritual experience and devotion.

REVIEW EXERCISE

Including Competency Based Questions

Part I

Multiple Choice Questions (MCQs)

1. Vitthala is a form of

(a) Shiva (b) Vishnu
(c) Krishna (d) Ganesh

2. Which diety was worshipped by Nayanar saints of South India ? Diksha

(a) Lord Shiva (b) Lord Brahma
(c) Lord Krishna (d) Lord Vishnu

3. Why Nayanars and Alvars went from place to place?

(a) For composing exquisite poems
(b) For composing devotional songs
(c) For composing epics
(d) For composing religious texts

4. Ramanuja was born in

(a) Kerala (b) Tamil Nadu
(c) Sri lanka (d) Bombay

5. Muslim scholars developed a holy law called as

(a) Sufiyat (b) Silsilas (c) Shariat (d) *Zikr*

6. The Sufi masters held their assemblies in their

(a) *dargahs* (b) *gulbarga*
(c) *khanqahs* (d) *tariqa*

7. Who was Kabir ? Diksha

(a) Nirguna Saint (b) Sagun Saint
(c) Adiguru (d) Sufi Saint

8. Identify the Bhakti saint from the statements given below. Competency Based

(i) He was an advocate of Advaita doctrine.
(ii) He taught that Brahman, the only or Ultimate Reality, was formless and without any attributes.
(iii) He considered the world to be an illusion or maya, and preached renunciation of the world.

Codes

(a) Ramanuja (b) Basavanna's
(c) Shankara (d) Sant Tukaram

9. Identify the Bhakti Saint from the information given below.

(i) He rejected all orthodox religions.
(ii) His ideas are collected in verses called sakhis and pads.
(iii) He settled in or near the city of Benaras.

Codes

(a) Surdas (b) Guru Nanak
(c) Tulsidas (d) Kabir

10. Choose the correct statement(s) from the following.

I. Tulsidas accepted existing beliefs and practices.
II. Jalaluddin Rumi was a 13th century Sufi poet from Afghanistan.

Codes

(a) Only I (b) Only II
(c) Both I and II (d) None of these

11. Choose the incorrect statement(s) from the following.

I. Mirabai was a Rajput princess married into the royal family of Mewar.
II. Most of the saints work were composed in Sanskrit.
III. Saint Kabir was born in Brahman family.

Codes

(a) Only II (b) I and II
(c) II and III (d) None of these

12. **Arrange the follwoing Sikh Gurus in correct sequence.**

I. Guru Nanak II. Guru Ram Das
III. Guru Angad IV. Guru Amar Das
V. Guru Arjan

Codes

(a) I, II, III, IV, V (b) I, III, IV, II, V
(c) II, V, I, III, IV (d) V, I, II, III, IV

13. **Arrange the following saints in the chronological order of their period of influence.**

I. Basavanna's II. Guru Nanak Dev
III. Manikkavasagar IV. Namdev

Codes

(a) III, II, IV, I (b) I, III, IV, II
(c) III, I, IV, II (d) I, II, III, IV

Answers

1. (b) **2.** (a) **3.** (a) **4.** (b) **5.** (c)
6. (c) **7.** (a) **8.** (c) **9.** (d) **10.** (a)
11. (c) **12.** (b) **13.** (b)

Match the Following

1.

List I	List II
A. Social privileges came from	1. Set of compilation of Alvar's songs
B. Namghars	2. Successor of Guru Nanak
C. Break the cycle of rebirth by personal effort	3. Noble family
D. Divya Prabandham	4. Buddhas and Jainas
E. Guru Angad	5. Houses of recitation and prayer

Codes

	A	B	C	D	E		A	B	C	D	E
(a)	3	5	4	1	2	(b)	3	4	2	5	1
(c)	4	1	2	5	3	(d)	2	5	3	4	1

2.

List I	List II
A. Baba Farid	1. Assam
B. Bandanawaz Gisudaraz	2. Delhi
C. Shankaradeva	3. Gulbarga
D. Guru Nanak	4. Punjab
E. Qutbuddin Bakhtiar Kaki	5. Kartarpur

Codes

	A	B	C	D	E		A	B	C	D	E
(a)	4	3	1	5	2	(b)	3	4	2	5	1
(c)	5	1	2	3	4	(d)	2	3	4	1	5

Ans. 1. (a) 2. (a)

Assertion-Reason

1. **Assertion** (A) Sursagara, Surasaravali and Sahitya are the compositions of Surdas.

Reason (R) Surdas was an ardent devotee of Rama.

Codes

(a) Both A and R are true and R is the correct explanation of A
(b) Both A and R are true, but R is not the correct explanation of A
(c) A is true, but R is false
(d) A is false, but R is true

2. **Assertion** (A) The Sufis often rejected the elaborate rituals and codes of behaviour demanded by Muslim religious scholars.

Reason (R) Sufis developed methods of training using zikr, sama, raqs, etc.

Codes

(a) Both A and R are true and R is the correct explanation of A
(b) Both A and R are true, but R is not the correct explanation of A
(c) A is true, but R is false
(d) A is false, but R is true

Ans. 1. (c) A is true, but R is false
2. (a) Both A and R are true and R is the correct explanation of A

Fill in the Blanks

1. Buddha and Jainas taught that it was possible to overcome social differences and break the cycle of rebirth through ....

2. From 7th to 9th centuries saw the emergence of new religious movements, led by the Nayanars and ....

3. According to Shankara, renunciation of the world was the path to attain ....

4. According to Ramanuja, the best means of attaining salvation was through intense devotion to ....

5. .... argued strongly for the equality of all human beings.

6. A genealogy of Sufi teachers is called as ....

Ans. 1. personal effort 2. Alvars
3. salvation 4. Vishnu
5. Virashaivas 6. silsilas

True/False

1. Mirabai became a disciple of Ravidas.
2. Ghazzali was a great Sufi saint of Central Asia.
3. Saint Janeshwara rewrote Gita in Marathi.
4. Adi Granth is the other name of Guru Granth Sahib.
5. Nayanars and Alvars developed new kind of Bhakti in North India.
6. There were 63 Nayanars in all.

Ans. 1. True 2. True 3. False
4. True 5. False 6. True

Picture Based Questions

1. **The picture shown below is a part of which religious book?**

(a) Ramcharitmanas (b) Bhagavadgita
(c) Rigveda (d) Ramayana

2. **In the given picture, followers of 16th century Bhakti Saint Chaintanyadeva are engaged in ecstatic dancing and singing. Where did he belong to?**

(a) Bengal (b) Assam
(c) Delhi (d) Punjab

Ans. 1. (b) Bhagavadgita 2. (a) Bengal

Case Based Question

1. **Read the passage given below and answer the following questions.**

Some of them like Kabir and Baba Guru Nanak rejected all orthodox religions. Other like Tulsidas and Surdas accepted existing beliefs and practices but wanted to make these accessible to all. Tulisdas conceived of God in the form of Rama. Tulsidas's composition, the Ramcharitmanas, written in Awadhi (a language used in Eastern Uttar Pradesh), is important both as an expression of his devotion and as a literacy work. Surdas was an ardent devotee of Krishna. His compositions, compiled in the Sursagara, Surasaravali and Sahitya Lahari, express his devotion. Also contemporary was Shankaradeva of Assam who emphasised devotion of Vishnu, and composed poems and plays in Assamese.

(i) Which composition, written in Awadhi, is considered important as an expression of devotion and as a literary work?
(a) Ramcharitmanas (b) Sursagara
(c) Sahitya Lahari (d) Surasaravali

(ii) Which work is not associated with expressing the devotion of Surdas?
(a) Ramcharitmanas
(b) Sursagara
(c) Sahitya Lahari
(d) Surasaravali

(iii) Which poet from Assam emphasised devotion to Vishnu?
(a) Kabir
(b) Tulsidas
(c) Shankaradeva (d) Guru Nanak

(iv) According to the passage, who rejected all orthodox religions?
(a) Kabir (b) Guru Nanak
(c) Tulsidas (d) Both (a) and (b)

Ans. (i) (a) Ramcharitmanas
(ii) (a) Ramcharitmanas
(iii) (c) Shankaradeva
(iv) (d) Both (a) and (b)

Part II

Very Short Answer Type Questions

1. **How many Alvars were there?**

Ans. There were 12 Alvars.

2. **Who were the Pulaiyar and the Panar?**

Ans. 'Pulaiyar and Panar' were the Hindus who were considered as untouchables.

3. **Name the two notable saints of Maharashtra.**

Ans. Notable saints of Maharashtra were Namdev and Tukaram.

4. Who were Sufis?

Ans. Sufis were Muslim mystics who saw the world in a different way than that of others.

5. Khwaja Muinuddin Chishti belonged to which silsila? Diksha

Ans. Khwaja Muinuddin Chishti belonged to Chishti Silsila in India.

6. Who composed Ramcharitmanas ?

Ans. Tulsidas composed the Ramcharitmanas.

7. What are Namghars?

Ans. Namghars are houses of recitation and prayer.

8. Who was Mirabai ? Diksha

Ans. Mirabai was a Rajput princess married into the royal family of Mewar in the 16th century. She was a disciple of Ravidas.

9. What do you mean by langar?

Ans. Langar refers to common kitchen where people from all backgrounds eat.

10. What is Guru Granth Sahib?

Ans. Guru Granth Sahib is the holy scripture of the Sikhs.

11. Who compiled the compositions of Guru Nanak?

Ans. Guru Angad compiled the compositions of Guru Nanak.

12 Guru Gobind Singh was associated with which institution?

Ans. Guru Gobind Singh was associated with the 'institution of Khalsa'.

Short Answer Type Questions

1. What new ideas were developed after the emergence of large kingdoms?

Ans. New ideas that were developed after the emergence of large kingdoms were

- All living things pass through countless cycles of birth and rebirth performing good and bad deeds.
- All human beings are not equal even at birth. It was believed that social privileges came from birth in a 'noble' or a 'high' caste family .

2. "The Vishva Hindu Parishad (VHP) on Thursday demanded the *'Bhagavadgita'* be declared the national book of India and its teaching-learning made compulsory across all levels of education in the country to stop the eroding of values". Competency Based

(i) Which idea is advocated in the *Bhagavadgita*?

Ans. *Bhagavadgita* advocated the idea of a Supreme God who could relieve humans from bondage and problems if approached with devotion (or bhakti).

(ii) Why do you think *Bhagavadgita* should be made compulsory in education?

Ans. Bhagavadgita should be made compulsory in education because it is believed that promoting the *Bhagavadgita's* teachings will help instil moral and ethical values in the younger generation. It is seen as a way to preserve and propagate the philosophical and spiritual wisdom contained in this ancient Hindu scripture.

3. Who were the Nayanars and Alvars?

Ans. The Nayanars were saints devoted to Shiva and Alvars were devoted to Vishnu. There were 63 Nayanars, who belonged to different caste backgrounds, such as potters, untouchable workers, peasants, hunters, soldiers, Brahmanas and chiefs. The popular among them were Appar, Sambandar, Sundarar and Manikkavasagar. Tevaram and Tiruvacakam are the two sets of compilations of Nayanars' songs.

There were 12 Alvars, who belonged to equally divergent backgrounds. The popular among them were Periyalvar, his daughter Andal, Tondaradippodi Alvar and Nammalvar. Their songs were compiled in the Divya Prabandham.

4. Who was Ramanuja? What were the main points of his preachings?

Ans. Ramanuja was a bhakti saint. He was born in Tamil Nadu in the 11th century. He was deeply influenced by the Alvars.

The main points of his preachings were

- He taught people to attain salvation by showing devotion to Vishnu.
- He proposed the doctrine of Vishishtadvaita or qualified oneness.

5. Who initiated the Virashaiva movement? Explain its ideas.

Ans. Basavanna along with his companions like Allama Prabhu and Akkamahadevi initiated the Virashaiva movement. This movement began in Karnataka in the mid-12th century.

They argued strongly for the equality of all human beings, and criticised Brahmanical ideas about caste and the treatment of women. They were also against all forms of ritual and idol worship.

6. What were the beliefs of Nathpanthis, Siddhas and Yogis?

Ans. The beliefs of Nathpanthis, Siddhas and Yogis were

- They criticised the rituals and other aspects of traditional religion, and the social order using simple and logical arguments.

- They advocated renunciation of the world. According to them, meditation on the formless Ultimate Reality and the realisation of writing with it is the path for achieving salvation.
- They advocated intense training of the mind and body through practices like yogasanas, breathing exercises and meditation.

7. Write a short note on Khanqahs.

Ans. *Khanqahs* were houses of rest for travellers especially the one kept by a religious order. Sufi masters usually held their assemblies here.

Devotees of various descriptions including members of the royalty, nobility and ordinary people gathered here to discuss spiritual matters, sought blessings of the saints and attend music and dance sessions.

8. Who were the followers of Baba Guru Nanak?

Ans. Baba Guru Nanak had a large number of followers. They belonged to different castes but traders, agriculturists, artisans and craftsmen predominated. He always asked his followers to be households and should adopt productive and useful occupations. They were also expected to contribute to the general funds of the community of followers.

Long Answer Type Questions

1. A blogger is writing about Bhakti movement and searching key points in the movement. Discuss the key elements that makes Bhakti movement so sustainable in the 15th century. Competency Based

Ans. Bhakti movement become popular in 15th century due to the following reasons

- There were several foreign invasions during this period which led to the cultural and religious interactions.
- Bhakti saints spread the idea of equality of all human being before God irrespective of caste, creed or gender.
- Bhakti movement discarded the caste system which gave hope and dignity to marginalised communities.
- Bhakti saints spread their teaching in common language which was known to all.
- Bhakti saints give importance to love and devotion to God. They discard complex rituals of religious. Even poor sections of the society could now be part of religious practices.
- Bhakti saints expressed their ideas in poems, verses and songs which were sung by devotees and led to spread of these ideas.

2. From 13th to 17th centuries, there were many saint-poets in Maharashtra? Explain about them and their beliefs. Competency Based

Ans. From the 13th to the 17th centuries, there were many saint-poets in Maharashtra. They composed songs in simple Marathi which continue to inspire people. The most importants saints among them were Dnyaneshwar (Gyaneshwar), Namdev, Eknath, Tukaram, Sakhubai and the family of Chokhamela, who belonged to the untouchable Mahar caste.

These saint poets focused on the Vitthala (a form of Vishnu) in Pandharpur, and the belief of a personal god residing in the hearts of all people. They rejected all forms of ritualism and social differences based on birth. They also rejected the idea of renunciation, and preferred to live with their families and earning their livelihood like any other person. They insisted that the true bhakti is sharing the pain of others.

3. Write a brief note on new religious developments in North India.

Ans. A new idea of Bhakti movement emerged in North India in the period after 13th century. During this period, Islam, Brahmanical Hinduism, Sufism, various elements of bhakti, and the Nathpanths, Siddhas and Yogis influenced one another.

Some of the bhakti saints that emerged during this period were

- **Tulsidas** He conceived God in the form of Rama. He composed the *Ramcharitmanas* in Awadhi language which is used in Eastern Uttar Pradesh.
- **Surdas** He was an intense devotee of Krishna. His poems are compiled in *Sursagara*, *Surasaravali* and *Sahitya Lahari*.
- **Shankaradeva** He was a saint from Assam in the late 15th century. He was devoted to Vishnu, and composed poems and plays in Assamese language. He began setting up namghars or houses of recitation and prayer.
- **Mirabai** She was a Rajput princess married into the royal family of Mewar in the 16th century. She was a disciple of Ravidas (a saint from a caste considered as untouchable) and a devotee of Krishna. Her songs openly challenged the norms of the upper castes and became popular in Rajasthan and Gujarat.

4. Describe the teachings of Saint Kabir. Diksha

Ans. Saint Kabir was one of the influential saints of the 15th-16th century. His teachings are an integral part of Bhakti movement. These were

- Kabir's teachings were based on a complete, rejection of the major religious traditions.
- He ridiculed all forms of external worship of both Brahmanical Hinduism and Islam.
- He rejected pre-eminence of the priestly classes and the caste system.

- He believed in a formless Supreme God.
- He preached that only path to salvation was through bhakti or devotion.
- He spread his spritual and philosophical teachings through his verses in poetic manner. He composed in spoken Hindi language.

Picture Based Questions

1. What does the image tell us about the inclusiveness of Sufism?

Ans. The image tells us that Sufism is a diverse and inclusive tradition that welcomes people from all religions.

The people in the image are all dressed in different types of clothing, which suggests that Sufism does not require people to conform to a particular dress code or religion. The fact that the people in the image are visiting a Sufi shrine suggests that they shared devotion to Sufism irrespective of their religion.

2. What information can be acquired about the lifestyle of Saints according to this image?

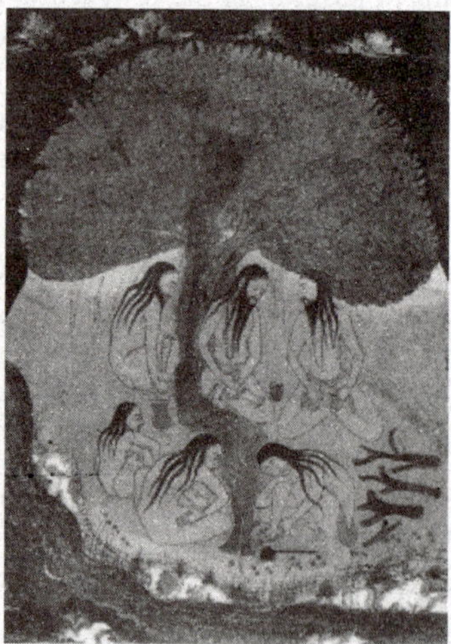

Ans. According to the image, the saints have a simple lifestyle. They are not wearing any elaborate clothing or jewellery, and they are not surrounded by any material assets. The ascetics in the image are gathered around a fire, which is a simple and basic source of heat and light. This suggests that they are satisfied with the simple things in life.

Case Based Questions

1. Read the following extract and answer the question that follows.

The Devotee and the Lord

by (Manikkavasagar)

Into my vile body of flesh
You came, as though it were a temple of gold,
And soothed me, wholly and saved me,
O Lord of Grace, O Gem most Pure,
Sorrow and birth, death and illusion
You took from me, and set me free.
O Bliss! O Light! I have taken refuge in You,
And never can I be parted from You.

How does the poet describe his relationship with the deity?

Ans. In this poem, the poet, Manikkavasagar describes his relationship with the deity as close and loving.The poet finds immense joy and light in this connection and believes, he has taken refuge in the deity forever, meaning he feels he can never be separated from the divine presence.

2. Read the following extract and answer the question that follows.

Virashaiva Vachanas

These are vachanas or sayings attributed to Basavanna:

The rich,
Will make temples for Shiva.
What shall I,
A poor man,
Do?
My legs are pillars,
The body the shrine,
The head a cupola
Of gold.
Listen, O Lord of the meeting rivers,
Things standing shall fall,
But the moving ever shall stay.

What is the temple that Basavanna is offering to God?

Ans. The temple that Basavanna is offering to God is not a traditional physical structure made of bricks and cement. In his *vachana*, Basavanna conveys that he, as a poor man, cannot afford to build grand temples for Lord Shiva, but he offers something far more valuable. He describes his own body as the temple, with his legs as pillars, his body as the shrine, and his head as a cupola of gold. This symbolises that true devotion and worship can take place within oneself.

3. Read the following extract and answer the question that follows.

Questioning the Social Order

Abhang by Sant Tukaram:
He who identifies
with the battered and the beaten
Mark him as a saint
For God is with him

He holds
Every forsaken man
Close to his heart
He treats
A slave
As his own son

Says Tuka
I won't be tired
to repeat again
Such a man
Is God
In person.

Abhang by Chokhamela's son:
You made us low caste,
Why don't you face that fact, Great Lord?
Our whole life – left-over food to eat.
You should be ashamed of this.
You have eaten in our home.
How can you deny it?
Chokha's (son) Karmamela asks
Why did you give me life?

Discuss the ideas about the social order expressed in these compositions.

Ans. Tukaram and Chokhamela's son expressed different ideas about the social orders. Their ideas are as follows

- **Tukaram** Tukaram, through his Abhang, talks about how someone, who sees themselves as oppressed or mistreated, can find God within themselves. He emphasises that those who seek truth and God, are especially close to experiencing the presence of God.
- **Chokhamela's Son** He expresses his discomfort and deprivation to God in his Abhang. He questioned why God made some people low caste and why there is inequality. He compared life to leftover food, suggesting that they have to live with the bitterness of being considered low-born.

He urged God to remember that everyone, including those of low caste, is equal in his eyes. If people devoted to God can't understand this equality, it would have been better not to be given life.

4. Read the following extract and answer the question that follows.

Beyond the Rana's palace

This is a song composed by Mirabai:
Ranaji, I have left your norms of shame,
and false decorum of the princely life.
I have left your town.
And yet Rana why have you kept up enmity against me?
Rana you gave me a cup of poison.
I drank it laughing.
Rana I will not be destroyed by you.
And yet Rana why have you kept up
enmity against me?

Why do you think Mirabai left the Rana's palace?

Ans. Mirabai left Rana's palace because she chose to abandon the luxuries of the princely life, which included shame and false decorum. She felt a deep calling towards her devotion to Lord Krishna and wanted to lead a life focused on her spiritual path rather than the worldly life of a princess.

5. Read the following extract and answer the question as follows.

In search of the True Lord

Here is a composition of Kabir:
O Allah-Ram present in all living beings
Have mercy on your servants, O Lord!
Why bump your head on the ground,
Why bathe your body in water?

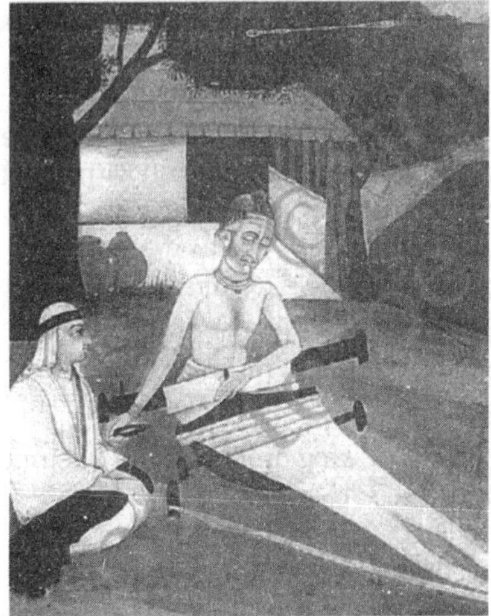

You kill and you call yourself "humble"
But your vices you conceal.
Twenty-four times the Brahmana keeps the *ekadasi* fast
While the Qazi observes the *Ramzan*
Tell me why does he set aside the eleven months

To seek spiritual fruit in the twelfth?
Hari dwells in the East, they say
And Allah resides in the West,
Search for him in your heart, in the heart of your heart;
There he dwells, Rahim-Ram.

In what ways are the ideas in this poem similar to or different from those of Basavanna and Jalaluddin Rumi?

Ans. The ideas in above composition of Kabir are similar to Jalaluddin Rumi and Basavanna's in the following ways

- Jalaluddin Rumi, the great Sufi poet from Iran, wrote about the God's place is in the heart of human beings. He went to all the holy places of different religions but according to him, there was no sign of God anywhere except his place of residing in the heart of his followers. This belief is similar to Kabir's composition.
- Basavanna says that his legs are pillars of temple, his body the shrine of God and the head as a cupola (a roof in the form of a dome in Buddhist Stupas) made up of gold. He further says that true devotion and worship takes place within onself. This belief is similar to Kabir's composition.

Map Based Question

1. In the given map, some states associated with great saints are marked. Name the saint that belong to each of the following states.

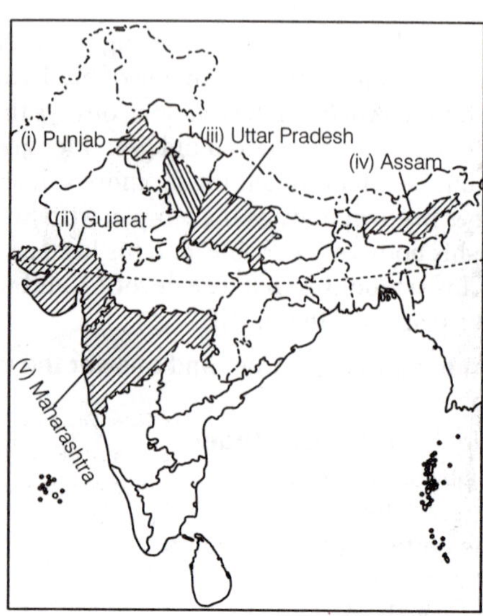

Ans. (i) Baba Guru Nanak was born at Talwandi (Nankana Sahib in Pakistan). Harmandir Sahib (Golden temple) in Ramdaspur (Amritsar), Punjab is the most important pilgrimage site of Sikhs.

(ii) Narsi Mehta was a Gujarati saint. Mirabai's songs were popular in Rajasthan and Gujarat.

(iii) Surdas belonged to Uttar Pradesh. He wrote in Braj language.

(iv) Shankaradeva of Assam emphasised devotion to Vishnu, and composed poems and plays in Assamese.

(v) Namdev, Eknath and Tukaram were saint points from Maharashtra.

ASSESSMENT EXERCISE

Multiple Choice Questions (MCQs)

1. The idea of a Supreme God who could deliver humans from such bondage if approached with devotion is advocated in the
(a) Mahabharata (b) Ramayana
(c) Bhagavadgita (c) Puranas

2. Which of the following is devoted to Vishnu?
(a) Nayanars (b) Alvars
(c) Sangams (d) Pulaiyars

3. Which of the following propound the doctrine of Vishishtadvaita?
(a) Ramanuja (b) Shankara
(c) Mirabai (d) Tukaram

4. What was the name of holy law developed by Muslim Scholar?
(a) Khanqah
(b) Shariat
(c) Dharmsal
(d) None of the above

Subjective Questions (VSA, SA & LA)

1. The Sufis rejected which kind of religiosity and emphasised on what?

2. What do you mean by Siddhacharas?

3. Who was the main promoter of Chishti Silsila?

4. Who was Shankaradeva?

5. Mention any three different teachings and beliefs?

6. What do you mean by doctrine of Vishishtadvaita and Virashaiva?

7. How did the Sufism in India expand?

8. What were the major teachings of Kabir?

9. Who were the Sufis? Discuss their major teachings and literatures.

10. The period after the 13th century saw a new wave of the Bhakti movement in North India. Mention any four leaders of these movement and their practices.

11. How did Sikhism expand in the Mughal period?

The Making of Regional Cultures

CHAPTER 7

The most common way to describe people is in terms of the language they speak. For example, when a person is referred to as a Tamil or an Odia, this usually means that he or she speaks Tamil or Odia and lives in Tamil Nadu or Odisha. Sometimes food, clothes, poetry, dance, music and painting are also associated with these identities.

Regional cultures today are a result of a complex processes of intermixing of local traditions with ideas from other parts of the sub-continent.

7.1 The Cheras and the Development of Malayalam

The Chera kingdom of **Mahodayapuram** was established in the 9th century in the South-Western part of Indian peninsula (present-day Kerala).

The rulers of Chera Kingdom introduced the Malayalam language and script in their inscriptions. It was the earliest example of the use of a regional language in official records in the subcontinent.

Apart from Malayalam, the Cheras also applied Sanskritic traditions. For example,

- The temple theatre of Kerala borrowed stories from the Sanskrit epics.
- The first literary works in Malayalam, were directly influenced by Sanskrit.
- A 14th-century text, the **Lilatilakam** refers to the two languages, Sanskrit and the regional language. It deals with grammar and poetics and was composed in **Manipravalam** (literally meaning diamonds and corals).

7.2 Rules and Religious Traditions : The Jagannatha Cult

In some regions, regional cultures grew around religious traditions e.g. the cult of Jagannatha at Puri, Orissa. Even today, the local tribal people make the wooden image of the deity, which suggests that the deity was originally a local god, who was later identified with Vishnu.

In the 12th century, **Anantavarman**, ruler of the Ganga dynasty, erected a temple for Purushottama Jagannatha at Puri.

In 1230, king **Anangabhima III** dedicated his kingdom to the deity and proclaimed himself as the 'deputy' of the god.

As the temple gained importance as a centre of pilgrimage, its authority in social and political matters also increased.

The Mughals, the Marathas and the English East India Company who conquered Orissa, attempted to gain control over the temple. They felt that this would make their rule acceptable to the local people.

7.3 The Rajputs and Traditions of Heroism

In 19th century, the region that constituted most of the present-day Rajasthan, was called **Rajputana** by the British. This might be due to the reason that this area was inhabited only by Rajputs.

However, there were several groups who identify themselves as Rajputs in many areas of Northern and Central India, and several people other than Rajputs live in Rajasthan.

The Rajputs are often recognised for their contribution to the distinctive culture of Rajasthan. The cultural traditions were closely linked with the ideals and aspirations of rulers.

From about 8th century, most of the present-day state of Rajasthan was ruled by various Rajput families, e.g. **Prithviraj Chauhan** was one such ruler.

The Rajput rulers admired the ideal of the hero who fought courageously, who often choose death on the battlefield rather than defeat.

Stories about Rajput heroes were recorded in poems and songs, which were recited by specially trained **minstrels.**

Ordinary people were attracted by these stories which often depicted dramatic situations and emotions like loyalty, friendship, love, valour, anger, etc.

Sometimes women were also depicted in these stories like stories about the practice of *sati*, or the **sacrifice** of widows on the funeral pyre of their husbands.

7.4 The Story of *Kathak*

Kathak is a dance form associated with several parts of North India. It involves intricate and rapid footwork, elaborate costumes, and the enactment of stories. The term Kathak is derived from the word 'katha', which means story.

The Kathaks were originally a caste of story-tellers in temples of North India, who performed with gestures and songs.

In the 15th and 16th centuries, Kathak began to develop into a distinct mode of dance with the spread of the bhakti movement.

The folk plays called ***rasa lila*** in which the legends of Radha-Krishna were enacted, combined folk dance with the basic gestures of the kathak story-tellers.

Under the Mughal emperors and their nobles, Kathak was performed in the court and developed into a dance form with a distinctive style. Later, it developed in two traditions or **gharanas**, one in the courts of Rajasthan (Jaipur) and the other in Lucknow.

Under the patronage of **Wajid Ali Shah**, the last Nawab of Awadh, Kathak grew into a major art form. It spread to Punjab, Haryana, Jammu and Kashmir, Bihar and Madhya Pradesh by the end of 19th century. Most of the British administrators in the 19th and 20th centuries did not like Kathak, like many other cultural practices.

However, it continued to be performed by courtesans. It was recognised as one of six **classical** forms of dance in the country after independence.

KNOWLEDGE PLUS Dance forms, other than Kathak, which are recognised as classical at present are **Bharatanatyam** (Tamil Nadu), **Kathakali** (Kerala), **Odissi** (Odisha), **Kuchipudi** (Andhra Pradesh) and **Manipuri** (Manipur).

Try These

1. **Who established the kingdom at Mahodayapuram?**
2. **Who proclaimed himself as the deputy of god?**
3. **Identify the text that was written in 14th century and deals with grammar and poetics.**
4. **Who built the Jagannath temple?**

7.5 The Tradition of Miniatures

Miniatures are small-sized paintings, generally done in water colour on cloth or paper. The earliest miniatures were made on palm leaves or wood. Some of the most beautiful miniatures are found in Jaina texts in Western India.

The Mughal emperors **Akbar**, **Jahangir** and **Shah Jahan** patronised highly skilled painters mainly illustrated manuscripts containing historical accounts and poetry. These portrayed court scenes, scenes of battle or hunting, and other aspects of social life. They were often exchanged as gifts.

With the decline of the Mughal Empire, many painters shifted to the courts of the emerging regional states. Thus, Mughal artistic preferences influenced the regional courts of the Deccan and the Rajput courts of Rajasthan. However, they also retained and developed their distinctive characteristics.

Portraits[1] of rulers, court scenes, themes from mythology and poetry were depicted in miniature paintings of regions such as Mewar, Jodhpur, Bundi, Kota and Kishangarh.

By the late 17th century, **Basohli style** of miniature painting developed in regions of Himalayan foothills which is a bold and intense style. The most popular text to be painted here was **Bhanudatta's *Rasamanjari.***

In 1739, Nadir Shah's invasion and the conquest of Delhi resulted in the migration of Mughal artists to the hills where they founded the Kangra school of painting.

By the mid-18th century, the Kangra artists developed a new style after getting inspired from the Vaishnavite traditions. This new style of Kangra painting is characterised by using soft colours including cool blues and greens, and a lyrical presentation of themes.

1 **Portrait** It refers to a picture, painting or photograph of a person.

7.6 Bengal : The Growth of a Regional Language

In Bengal, **Bengali** is recognised as a language which is derived from Sanskrit. However, according to early Sanskrit texts (mid-1st millennium BCE), the people of Bengal did not speak Sanskritic languages.

From the 4th-3rd centuries BCE, commercial ties between Bengal and Magadha, may have led to the growing influence of Sanskrit.

Over the period of time, there were many linguistic and cultural influence on Bengal.

These were

- During the 4th century, the Gupta rulers established political control over North Bengal and began to settle Brahmanas in this area. Thus, the linguistic and cultural influence from the mid-Ganga valley became stronger.
- In the 7th century the **Chinese traveller Xuan Zang** observed that languages related to Sanskrit were in use all over Bengal.
- From the 8th century, Bengal became the centre of a regional kingdom under the Palas. Between the 14th and 16th centuries. Bengal was ruled by independent rulers.
- In 1586, when Akbar conquered Bengal, Persian was used as the language of administration, but Bengali developed as a regional language.
- By the 15th century, the Bengali group of **dialects**[2] were united by a common literary language which was based on the spoken language of the Western part of the region (now known as West Bengal).

Thus, Bengali passed through several stages of evolution. A wide range of non-Sanskrit words, derived from tribal languages, Persian, and European languages, have been included in modern Bengali.

Bengali Literature

Early Bengali literature is divided into two categories

(i) **Bengali Literature Influenced by Sanskrit** It includes translations of the Sanskrit epics, the **Mangalakavyas**[3] and bhakti literature such as the biographies of Chaitanyadeva, the leader of the Vaishnava Bhakti Movement. They are easier to date, as several manuscripts have been found.

(ii) **Bengali Literature Independent of Sanskrit** It includes Nath literature, such as the songs of Maynamati and Gopichandra, stories related to worship of Dharma Thakur, and fairy tales, folk tales and **ballads**[4].

They were circulated orally and cannot be accurately dated. They were popular in Eastern Bengal, where the influence of Brahmanas was relatively weak.

7.7 Pirs and Temples

From the 16th century, many people began to migrate from the less fertile Western Bengal to the forested areas of South-Eastern Bengal.

They cleared forests and brought the land under rice cultivation. Gradually, these new communities of peasants merged with local communities of **fisherfolk** and shifting **cultivators** (often tribals).

During this period, Mughal rule was established in Bengal with the capital at Dhaka. Officials and functionaries mostly set-up ***mosques*** on the lands they received. These served as centres for religious transformation in these areas.

The early settlers wanted some order and assurance in the unstable conditions of the new settlements. These were provided by community leaders, who functioned as teachers and adjudicators. They were believed to have supernatural powers and are known as ***Pirs***.

Pirs included saints and other religious personalities, various Hindu and Buddhist deities and even **animistic** spirits tradition. They became very popular in Bengal.

Temples in Bengal

From the late 15th century, temple-building began in Bengal and reached its peak in 19th century. The temples and other religious structures were often built by individuals or groups who tried to demonstrate their power and devotion.

Simple brick and terracotta temples in Bengal were built with the support of low social groups, such as the **Kolu** (oil pressers) and the **Kansari** (bell metal workers).

2 **Dialect** It refers to sub-division of a particular spoken language.
3 **Mangalakavyas** These refer to poems dealing with local deities.
4 **Ballad** It refers to a long poem or song that tells a story.

The social and economic position of these groups improved with the coming of the European trading companies.

When local deities, gained the recognition of the Brahmanas, their images began to be placed in temples which were earlier placed in thatched huts in villages.

The temples began to copy the **double-roofed** (*dochala*) or **four-roofed** (*chauchala*) structure of the thatched huts. This led to the evolution of the typical Bengali style in temple architecture.

Temples were usually built on a square platform. The interior was relatively plain, but the outer walls of many temples were decorated with paintings, ornamental tiles or terracotta tablets, e.g. temples in Vishnupur in the Bankura district of West Bengal.

7.8 Fish as Food

Traditional food habits are generally based on locally available items of food.

Bengal is a **riverine plain**[5] which produces plenty of rice and fish. Thus, these items are part of food of even poor Bengalis'.

Fishing has always been an important occupation and Bengali literature contains several references to fish. The walls of temples and *viharas* (Buddhist monasteries) depict scenes related to fishes.

Brahmins were not allowed to eat non-vegetarian food, but the popularity of fish in the local diet made the Brahmanical authorities to reduce this restriction for the Bengal Brahmanas. The ***Brihaddharma Purana,*** 13th Century Sanskrit text permitted the local Brahmanas to eat certain varieties of fish.

Try These

1. **Under whose patronage Kathak developed as a dance form?**
2. **What was the cultural practice disfavoured by British administrators?**
3. **This tradition inspired the Kangra paintings due to which it developed into miniature painting. Identify the tradition.**
4. **Who wrote the book 'Rasamanjari'?**

5 **Riverine Plain** It refers to a flat or gently sloping land area that is formed by the deposition of sediments carried by a river.

THE MAKING OF REGIONAL CULTURES

Bengal

Fish as Food

- Fish is a popular item in the local diet.
- The Brihaddharma Purana, permitted the local Brahmanas to eat fish.

Pirs and Temples

- Pirs were community leaders who functioned as teachers and adjudicators and had supernatural powers.
- Simple brick and terracotta temples were built in Bengal.

The Growth of a Regional Language

Bengali language derived from Sanskrit is spoken in Bengal.

Bengali Literature Influenced by Sanskrit

Includes translations of the Sanskrit epics, the Mangalakavyas and bhakti literature such as the biographies of Chaitanyadeva.

Bengali Literature Independent of Sanskrit

Includes Nath literature, such as the songs of Maynamati and Gopichandra, stories related to worship of Dharma Thakur and fairy tales, folk tales and ballads.

The Rajputs and Traditions of Heroism

- Stories about Rajput heroes were recorded in poems and songs.
- Prithviraj Chauhan was one of the greatest Rajput ruler.

The Cheras and the development of Malayalam

- The Chera kingdom of Mahodayapuram was established in the 9th century.
- Rulers of Chera Kingdom introduced the Malayalam language.

Rules and Religious Traditions : The Jagannath Cult

- In 12th century, Anantavarman, ruler of the Ganga dynasty built a temple for Purushotamma Jagannatha at Puri.
- In 1230, King Anangabhima III, dedicated his kingdom to the deity.

The Tradition of Miniatures

- Small sized paintings done in water colour on cloth or paper.
- Some beautiful miniatures are found in Jaina texts in Western India.

The Story of Kathak

- Kathak is derived from the word 'Katha' meaning story.
- Initially performed in the court and later developed into dance form.

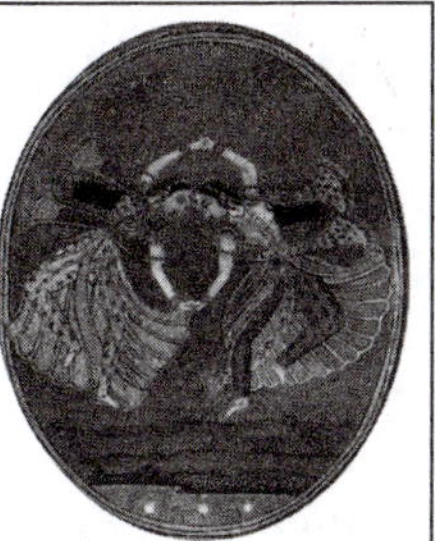

NCERT FOLDER

Covering Intext Questions and Exercises of NCERT

NCERT PAGE 79-80

Q.1 Find out how many states have been created in the last 10 years. Is each of these states a region?

Ans. In the last 10 years only one state, Telangana has been created. It was separated from Andhra Pradesh in 2014.

Yes, Telangana can be considered as a region.

Q.2 Find out when the languages you speak at home were first used for writing.

Ans. I speak Hindi at home. Hindi was first used for writing in the 7th to 8th centuries CE. During this period, Hindi, or its parent languages, were used in the form of inscriptions and poetic compositions.

The language evolved over time, and Old Hindi (also known as Apabhramsa) gradually transitioned into the modern forms of Hindi and other North Indian languages.

The use of Devanagari script for writing Hindi also became prominent during this evolution.

NCERT PAGE 83

Q.3 Find out whether there are traditions of heroes/ heroines in your town or village. What are the qualities associated with them? In what ways are these similar to or different from the heroic ideals of the Rajputs?

Ans. I am from Delhi and Panna Lal is one of the unsung heroes from Delhi. He was a prominent freedom fighter

who dedicated his life to India's struggle for independence. For his active involvement in the Quit India Movement, Panna Lal was arrested by the British authorities and was jailed for two years.

The qualities associated with him are similar to those of Rajputs, courage, loyalty, anger and love for country.

NCERT PAGE 89-90

Q.4 Why do you think the second category of texts was not written down?

Ans. The second category of Bengali texts was not written down because they were part of an oral tradition that was passed down through generations by word of mouth. In Eastern Bengal where these texts were popular, the influence of Brahmanas was relatively weak and thus less people knew how to write.

Q.5 Compare the temple shown in this chapter with that in chapter 2.

Ans. The Temple of Gangaikondacholapuram shown in chapter 2 built during the Chola dynasty, showcases Dravidian architecture with a tall pyramid-shaped tower. It is dedicated to Lord Shiva.

In contrast, the Jagannatha Puri Temple shown in this chapter has a curved tower. It is devoted to Lord Jagannatha and is famous for its annual Rath Yatra festival.

NCERT PAGE 92 (LET'S IMAGINE)

Q.6 You are a Rajput prince. How would you like your story to be told?

Ans. I would want my story of bravery and courage to be told through written texts. I will get the stories translated to all possible regional languages and then send them to various regions. I would also get some stories engraved on the walls of my palace. My story should inspire future generations to carry forward the legacy of valour, loyalty and compassion.

EXERCISES

Q.1 Match the following.

	List I		List II
A.	Anantavarman	1.	Kerala
B.	Jagannatha	2.	Bengal
C.	Mahodayapuram	3.	Orissa
D.	Lilatilakam	4.	Kangra
E.	Mangalakavya	5.	Puri
F.	Miniature	6.	Kerala

Codes

	A	B	C	D	E	F
(a)	3	5	1	6	2	4
(b)	5	1	6	2	4	3
(c)	4	5	1	3	2	6
(d)	3	5	6	2	4	1

Ans. (a) (3), (b) (5), (c) (1), (d) (6), (e) (2), (f) (4)

Q.2 What is Manipravalam? Name a book written in that language.

Ans. Manipravalam is a language consisting of Sanskrit and the regional language (Malayalam). A 14th century text the 'Lilatilakam' is written in Manipravalam.

Q.3 Who were the major patrons of Kathak?

Ans. The major patrons of Kathak were the Mughal Emperors and the Nawabs of Lucknow, especially Wajid Ali Shah.

Q.4 What are the important architectural features of the temples of Bengal?

Ans. The important architectural features of the temples of Bengal are

- The temples started to copy the double-roofed or four-roofed structure of the thatched huts.
- A complex temple structure was built, four triangular roofs were placed on the four walls that converged on a curved line or a point.
- The temples were usually built on a square platform.
- The interior of temple was relatively plain, but the outer walls of many temples were decorated with paintings, ornamental tiles or terracotta tablets.

Q.5 Why did minstrels proclaim the achievements of heroes?

Ans. Minstrels proclaimed the achievements of heroes to inspire the ruling class and ordinary population. Ordinary people were also attracted by these stories.

Minstrels used to recite poems and songs which depicted the stories of Rajputs which have great emotions, loyalties, friendship, love, valour, anger, etc.

Q.6 Why do we know much more about the cultural practices of rulers than about those of ordinary people?

Ans. We know more about the cultural practices of rulers because they had the resources to document their lives through art, architecture and written records. Rulers built grand palaces, commissioned artworks, and chronicled their achievements. Ordinary people did not have such resources, thus they left little information about themselves. Additionally, historians focused on recording the lives of powerful figures.

Q.7 Why did conquerors try to control the temple of Jagannatha at Puri?

Ans. The conquerors tried to control the temple of Jagannatha at Puri as it was a centre of pilgrimage. It had great authority that out they in social and political matters. The temple had huge wealth, collected from offerings. They felt that this would make their rule acceptable to the local people.

Q.8 Why were the temples built in Bengal?

Ans. Bengal witnessed temple-building on a large-scale in the 15th century. Temples and other religious structures were often built by powerful individuals or groups to demonstrate their power and show their devotion.

When the social and economic position of people improved, they constructed temples to demonstrate their status.

Q.9 Describe the most important features of the culture of your region, focusing on buildings, performing arts and paintings.

Ans. I belong to Delhi. Delhi's culture is a blend of history and modernity. Majestic buildings like the Red Fort and Qutub Minar tell stories of ancient empires, while India Gate depicts modern architecture.

Delhi's culture embraces religious diversity, celebrates all festivals with joy, and enjoys a delicious mix of cuisines. Thus, Delhi has a mixed culture.

Q.10 Do you use different languages for (a) speaking (b) reading (c) writing? Find out about one major composition in language that you use and discuss why you find it interesting.

Ans. No, I use Hindi and English for speaking, reading and writing.

One major composition in Hindi language is 'Ramcharitamanas' written by Tulsidas. I find it interesting because it teaches us the duties of a son, brother, wife, husband and a father.

Q.11 Choose one state each from North, West, South, East and Central India. For each of these, prepare a list of foods that are commonly consumed, highlighting any differences and similarities that you notice.

Ans.

States	Foods	Differences/Similarities
North-Haryana	Dal, Chapatis	Vegetarian
West-Gujarat	Khakra, Dhokla	Vegetarian
South-Kerala	Rice, Sambhar, Fish	Vegetarian and Non-vegetarian
East-West Bengal	Rice and Fish	Vegetarian and Non-vegetarian
Central - Madhya Pradesh	Dal, Chapatis	Vegetarian

Q.12 Choose another set of five states from each of these regions and prepare a list of clothes that are generally worn by women and men in each. Discuss your findings.

Ans.

States	Clothes (Men)	Clothes (Woman)
North-Punjab	Lungi, Kurta and Head gear (Pagri)	Salwar and Kameez
West-Rajasthan	Dhoti, Kurta	Lehanga, Saree, Blouse
East-Orissa	Dhoti, Kurta	Saree and Blouse
South-Tamil Nadu	Kameez and Lungi	Saree and Blouse
Central-Chhattisgarh	Kameez, Dhoti/ Pant, Trousers	Saree and Blouse

REVIEW EXERCISE

Including Competency Based Questions

Part I

Multiple Choice Questions (MCQs)

1. **The Cheras drew inspiration from the**
(a) Hinduistic traditions
(b) Sanskritic traditions
(c) Vedic traditions
(d) Religious traditions

2. **What does Manipravalam literally means?**
(a) sea and gold (b) corals and sand
(c) diamonds and corals (d) gold and silver

3. **The first literary work in Malayalam dated to about**
(a) 10th century (b) 11th century
(c) 12th century (d) 13th century

4. **Where is Jagannatha temple situated?**
(a) Puri (Odisha)
(b) Varanasi (Uttar Pradesh)
(c) Rameshwaram (Tamil Nadu)
(d) Patna (Bihar)

5. **Who proclaimed himself as deputy of God?**
(a) King Anangabhima (b) King Anantavarma
(c) Sankara (d) Ramanuja

6. **Stories about Rajput heroes were recorded in**
(a) manuscripts
(b) poems and songs
(c) texts
(d) songs and theatres

7. **Which of the following is not a classical dance?**
(a) Bhangra (b) Kuchipudi
(c) Odissi (d) Bharatnatyam

8. **Kathakali is a classical dance of which state?**
(a) Kerala (b) Tamil Nadu
(c) Karnataka (d) Andhra Pradesh

9. **What do 'miniatures' refer to?**
(a) Big-size wall photos
(b) Big-size paintings
(c) Small-sized paintings
(d) Small-sized wall photos

10. **The earliest miniatures were written on**
(a) art paper (b) silk
(c) bark of the tree (d) palm leaves

11. **When was Nadir Shah invaded Delhi?**
(a) 1735 (b) 1736
(c) 1737 (d) 1739

12. **What is Basohli?**
(a) Portrait-type painting
(b) Bold and intense style of miniature painting
(c) Tribal community
(d) One type of tree

13. **Which of the following is the language of 13th century of Brihaddharma Purana of Bengal?**
(a) Pali text (b) Sanskrit text
(c) Malayalam text (d) Hindi text

14. **An important occupation of Bengal had been**
(a) paintings (b) agriculture
(c) animal rearing (d) fishing

15. **What are Viharas?**
(a) Educational Institutions
(b) Buddhist monastries
(c) Tourist places
(d) Health centres

16. **Identify the correct option that describes about the painting given below.** Competency Based

I. The source of inspiration was Vaishnavite traditions.

II. There was use of soft colours like cool blue and green.

III. Ordinary men and women also painted on walls floors, etc.

Codes
(a) Mughal Painting (b) Madhubani Painting
(c) Magadha Painting (d) Kangra Painting

17. **Read the following statements and identify the correct answer.** Competency Based

I. They were circulated orally and cannot be precisely dated.

II. They were popular where the influence of Brahmanas was weak.

III. Included stories concerning the worship of Dharma Thakur, and fairy tales, folk tales and ballads.

Codes
(a) Malayalam text Lilatilakam
(b) Bengali text dependent on Sanskrit
(c) Bengali text independent of Sanskrit
(d) Sanskrit text Brihaddharma Purana

18. **Choose the correct statement(s) from the following.**

I. King Anangabhima III dedicated his kingdom to Jagannatha. **Competency Based**

II. Wajid Ali Shah was the first Nawab of Awadh.

III. Kuchipudi is the classical dance form of Andhra Pradesh.

Codes

(a) I and II (b) II and III
(c) I and III (d) All of these

19. **Choose the incorrect statement(s) from the following.**

I. Nadir Shah invaded Delhi in 1739.

II. Chaitanyadeva was the leader of the Shiva focused Bhakti movement.

III. The Chera kingdom of Mahodayapuram was established in the late 13th century.

Codes

(a) Only I (b) Only III
(c) I and II (d) II and III

20. **Arrange the following in chronological order of their occurrences.**

I. Nadir Shah's invasion of Delhi

II. Akbar's conquest of Bengal

III. Development of Basohli style of painting

Codes

(a) II, I, III (b) III, I, II
(c) II, III, I (d) I, II, III

Answers

1. (b)	**2.** (c)	**3.** (c)	**4.** (a)	**5.** (a)
6. (b)	**7.** (a)	**8.** (a)	**9.** (c)	**10.** (d)
11. (d)	**12.** (b)	**13.** (b)	**14.** (d)	**15.** (b)
16. (d)	**17.** (c)	**18.** (c)	**19.** (d)	**20.** (c)

Match the Following

1.

List I (Dances)	List II (State)
A. Kuchipudi	1. North India
B. Bharatanatyam	2. Andhra Pradesh
C. Odissi	3. Kerala
D. Kathakali	4. Tamil Nadu
E. Kathak	5. Odisha

Codes

	A	B	C	D	E		A	B	C	D	E
(a)	2	4	5	3	1	(b)	5	4	3	2	1
(c)	1	2	3	4	5	(d)	1	2	4	3	5

2.

List I	List II
A. Mahodayapuram	1. Cause for conflicts
B. Malayalam	2. Rasa lila
C. 14th century text	3. Kerala
D. Woman	4. The Chera kingdom
E. Folk plays	6. Lilatilakam

Codes

	A	B	C	D	E		A	B	C	D	E
(a)	4	3	5	1	2	(b)	2	3	1	4	5
(c)	1	2	3	4	5	(d)	4	5	3	2	1

Ans. 1. (a) 2. (a)

Assertion-Reason

1. **Assertion** (A) Kathak development in two traditions or gharanas i.e. Jaipur and Lucknow.
Reason (R) Kathak was favoured and encouraged by most British administrators in the 19th century.

Codes

(a) Both A and R are true and R is the correct explanation of A
(b) Both A and R are true, but R is not the correct explanation of A
(c) A is true, but R is false
(d) A is false, but R is true

2. **Assertion** (A) Terracotta plaques on the walls of temples and viharas depict scenes of fish being dressed and taken to the market in baskets.
Reason (R) Traditional food habits are generally based on locally available items of food.

Codes

(a) Both A and R are true and R is the correct explanation of A
(b) Both A and R are true, but R is not the correct explanation of A
(c) A is true, but R is false
(d) A is false, but R is true

Ans. 1. (c) A is true, but R is false
2. (b) Both A and R are true, but R is not the correct explanation of A

Fill in the Blanks

1. The language spoken in the Chera kingdom of Mahodayapuram was ....

2. The famous temple of Jagannatha is dedicated to lord ....

3. The major patrons of Kathak were ....

4. Chera kingdom got established in ....

Ans. 1. Malayalam 2. Vishnu
4. Mughals 4. 9th century

True/False

1. Anangabhima III dedicated his kingdom to the deity.
2. All those who conquered Orissa, attempted to gain control over the temple.
3. Sati was performed by women who were unable to marry.
4. Wajid Ali Shah, the last Nawab of Awadh patronised Kathak.
5. Fish was an important food in Central India.

Ans. 1. True 2. True 3. False
4. True 5. False

Picture Based Questions

1. **The image shown below is of dance class in Laskhmana temple. Where is Lakshmana temple located ?**

(a) Madhya Pradesh (b) Uttar Pradesh
(c) Andhra Pradesh (d) Himachal Pradesh

2. **The image of Krishna with gopis, terracotta plaque is shown below from the Shyamaraya temple. Where is it located?**

(a) Karnataka (b) Odisha
(c) West Bengal (d) Andhra Pradesh

Ans. 1. (a) Madhya Pradesh
2. (c) West Bengal

Case Based Question

1. **Read the passage given below and answer the following questions.**

When the decline of the Mughal Empire, many painters moved out to the courts of the emerging regional states. As a result, Mughal artistic tastes influenced the regional courts of the Deccan and the Rajput courts of Rajasthan. At the same time, they retained and developed their distinctive characteristics. Portraits of rulers and court scenes came to painted, following the Mughal example. Besides, themes from mythology and poetry were depicted at centres such as Mewar, Jodhpur, Bundi, Kota and Kishangarh.

(i) **Which style of miniature painting was developed in Himalayan foothills ?**
(a) Mural (b) Pahari
(c) Tribal (d) Basohli

(ii) **Who promoted miniature painting during their reign ?**
(a) Akbar
(b) Jahangir
(c) Shah Jahan
(d) All of the above

(iii) **What was/were painted in miniature painting ?**
(a) Court scenes
(b) Scenes of battle
(c) Portraits
(d) All of the above

(iv) **Which famous text was painted in the area of Himachal Pradesh ?**
(a) Rasamanjari (b) Guru Gobind
(c) Kiratarjuniya (d) Ravanavadha

Ans (i) (d) Basohli (ii) (d) All of these
(iii) (d) All of these (iv) (a) Rasamanjari

Part II

Very Short Answer Type Questions

1. **Who introduced Malayalam language and script in their inscriptions?**

Ans. The rulers of Chera kingdom (Kerala) introduced the Malayalam language and script in their inscriptions.

2. **From which languages words were taken in Bengali language?**

Ans. In Bengali languages words were taken from Sanskrit and non-Sanskrit languages like tribal languages, Persian and European languages.

3. Whom did Anangabhima III dedicate his kingdom to?

Ans. King Anangabhima III dedicated his kingdom to Purushottama Jagannatha.

4. Who was Anantavarman?

Ans. Anantavarman was one of the most important rulers of the Ganga dynasty of Orissa in the 12th century.

5. What was called Rajputana by the British?

Ans. The region that constitutes most of the present-day Rajasthan was called Rajputana by the British.

6. Who were the Kathaks?

Ans. The Kathaks were originally a caste of storytellers in temples of North India.

7. Where did Kathak developed?

Ans. Kathak developed in the courts of Rajasthan and Lucknow.

8. Under whose patronage did Kathak grow into a major art form?

Ans. Kathak grew into a major art form under the patronage of Wajid Ali Shah, the last Nawab of Awadh.

9. What distinguished Kangra painting from the other paintings?

Ans. Kangra painting is distinguished from other paintings as it is marked by use of delicate lines, soft colours and depiction of Radha-Krishna themes. Its lyrical and detailed style sets it apart from other traditional Indian paintings.

10. How were miniatures used in earlier times?

Ans. In earlier times, miniature paintings were often exchanged as gifts between the emperor and his close associates.

11. Who was the last Nawab of Awadh?

Ans. The last Nawab of Awadh was Wajid Ali Shah.

12. What were the Mangalakavyas?

Ans. The Mangalakavyas were auspicious poems, dealing with local deities.

13. Who were *pirs*?

Ans. Pirs were saints or Sufis and other religions personalities who had the courage to go against colonisers, soldiers, various Hindu and Buddhist deities and even animistic spirits.

14. Who gave patronage to dancers in their royal court ? Diksha

Ans. The Mughals gave patronage dancers in their royal court.

15. Which language is considered to be the regional language of Bengal province? Diksha

Ans. Bengali language is considered to be the regional language of Bengal province.

16. What permitted the local Brahmans of Bengal to eat certain varieties of fish?

Ans. The Brihaddharma Purana, a 13th century Sanskrit text from Bengal, permitted the local Brahmans to eat certain varieties of fish.

Short Answer Type Questions

1. How did regional cultures evolve?

Ans. Regional cultures evolved by intermixing local traditions with other fresh ideas from different parts of the sub-continent. Different traditions can be unique to certain areas, while some are similar across regions.

Some traditions come from older practices in a specific area but transform into new forms in other regions. Thus, this blending of different cultures gives rise to regional cultures.

2. How did the Cheras draw upon Sanskritic traditions?

Ans. The Cheras drew upon Sanskritic traditions in the following ways

- The temple theatre of Kerala borrowed stories from the Sanskrit epics.
- The first literary works in Malayalam, are directly influenced by Sanskrit.
- A 14th-century text, the **Lilatilakam** refers to the two languages, Sanskrit and the regional language. It deals with grammar and poetics and was composed in **Manipravalam** (literally meaning diamonds and corals).

3. Explain about the stories of Rajput heroes. How women are depicted in these stories?

Ans. Stories about Rajput heroes were recorded in poems and songs, which were recited by specially trained minstrels. Ordinary people were attracted by these stories which often depicted dramatic situations and emotions like loyalty, friendship, love, valour, anger, etc.

Various stories about Rajput heroes depict women as the cause for any conflict, as men fought with one another to either win or protect the women. Women are also depicted as following their heroic husbands in both life and death. Practice of Sati was prevalent, so those who followed the heroic ideal often had to pay for it with their lives.

4. What are miniatures? What themes were depicted in miniatures?

Ans. Miniatures are small-sized paintings, generally done in water colour on cloth or paper. The earliest miniatures were made on palm leaves or wood. Some of the most beautiful miniatures are found in Jaina texts in Western India.

The themes depicted in miniatures include court scenes, scenes of battle or hunting, and other aspects of social life.

5. **Who were the pirs? What was their position in the society?**

Ans. Pirs were spiritual leaders who believed to have supernatural powers. They also functions as teachers and adjudicators. When early settlers in Bengal sought some order and assurance in the unstable conditions of the new settlements, *pirs* favoured them and gave them full moral support.

Pirs had respected position in the society. The cult of pirs became very popular and their shrines can be found everywhere in Bengal.

6. **"In the comparatively more complex four-roofed structure, four triangular roofs placed on the four walls move up to converge on a curved line or a point." What is being referred to in the statement given ? Explain.** **Competency Based**

Ans. The statement refers to temple architecture in Bengal .

The temples in Bengal began to copy the double-roofed (dochala) or four-roofed (chauchala) structure of the thatched huts. This led to the evolution of the typical Bengali style in temple architecture.

Temples were usually built on a square platform. The interior was relatively plain, but the outer walls of many temples were decorated with paintings, ornamental tiles or terracotta tablets, e.g. temples in Vishnupur in the Bankura district of West Bengal.

7. **What role does fish play in Bengal's society?**

Ans. Fish plays an important role in economic and cultural aspect of Bengal's society. Bengal is a riverine plain which produces plenty of fish. Fishing has always been an important occupation and Bengali literature contains several references to fish.

The terracotta plaques on the walls of temples and viharas depict scenes of fish being dressed and taken to the nearby market in baskets.

Long Answer Type Questions

1. **How did regional cultures grow around religious traditions?**

Ans. Regional cultures grew around religious traditions as people expressed their beliefs through art, music and rituals. Temples were centres of all cultural activities.

The best example of this process is the cult of Jagannatha (a name for Vishnu) at Puri, Odisha. Anantavarman, constructed a temple for Purushottama Jagannatha at Puri. In 1230, king Anangabhima III dedicated his kingdom to the deity. He proclaimed himself as the 'Deputy' of the God. With the temple gaining importance as a centre of pilgrimage, its authority in social and political matters also increased.

Those rulers who conquered Odisha, like the Mughals, the Marathas and the English East India Company, attempted to gain control over the temple. They felt that this would make their rule acceptable to local people.

2. **Give an account of the development of Kathak as a dance form.**

A scholar is writing an article on Kathak. Discuss how Kathak was originated. Also elaborate the development of Kathak as a dance form. **Competency Based**

Ans. The term Kathak is derived from 'katha', a word used in Sanskrit and other languages for story. The Kathaks were originally a caste of story- tellers in temples of North India, who performed with gestures and songs.

In the 15th and 16th century, Kathak began evolving into a distinct mode of dance with the spread of bhakti movement. Kathak underwent significant transformation during the Mughal period. Kathak was started performing in the court of emperors and their nobles, where it acquired its present features and emerged as a form of dance.

It developed into two gharanas or traditions, one in the courts of Rajasthan (Jaipur) and other in Lucknow. It grew into a major art form under the patronage of Wajid Ali Shah (the last Nawab of Awadh).

In the third quarter of the 19th century, Kathak was well established in Punjab, Haryana, Jammu and Kashmir, Bihar and Madhya Pradesh.

Although, Kathak was not favoured by British administrators, it survived and continued to be performed by courtesans. It was recoginsed as one of the six classical dances in India after independence.

3. **Describe the development of temples in Bengal.**

Ans. The following points explain the development of temples in the Bengal region

- The temples and various other religious structures were often built by individuals or groups who were becoming powerful to demonstrate their power and proclaim their piety as well.
- Many of the modest brick and terracotta temples in Bengal were built with the support of several 'low' social groups, like Kolu (oil pressers) and the Kansari (bell metal workers).
- When local deities gained the recognition of the Brahmanas, their images began to be honoured in temples.
- The temples began to copy the double roofed or four roofed thatched huts.

- Temples were built on raised square platforms. Outer walls were decorated with paintings, ornamental tiles or terrocotta tablets. Vishnupur in the Bankura district of West Bengal has a remarkable set of temples decorated with terracotta reliefs.

4. Bengali passed through several stages of evolution? Explain.

Ans. Bengali passed through several stages of evolution due to many linguistic and cultural influence on Bengal. These were

- During the 4th century, the Gupta rulers established political control over North Bengal and began to settle Brahmanas in this area. Thus, the linguistic and cultural influence from the mid-Ganga valley became stronger.
- In the 7th century the Chinese traveller Xuan Zang observed that languages related to Sanskrit were in use all over Bengal.
- From the 8th century, Bengal became the centre of a regional kingdom under the Palas. Between the 14th and 16th centuries. Bengal was ruled by independent rulers.
- In 1586, when Akbar conquered Bengal, Persian was used as the language of administration, but Bengali developed as a regional language.
- By the 15th century, the Bengali group of dialects were united by a common literary language which was based on the spoken language of the Western part of the region (now known as West Bengal).

Picture Based Questions

1. Observe the following image and answer the questions that follow.

(i) Which deities are shown in the image ?

Ans. Deities Balabhadra, Subhadra and Jagannatha are shown in the image.

(ii) In which temple these deities are worshipped today ?

Ans. These deities are worshipped in Jagannatha Temple at Puri, Odisha.

2. Observe the following image and answer the question that follow.

(i) Identify the style of painting and the theme depicted in the image.

Ans. This is Kangra style of miniature painting. The theme depicted in the image is of Krishna, Radha and her companions.

(ii) Where did this style of painting develop?

Ans. This style of painting developed in the foothills of Himalayas around present-day state of Himachal Pradesh.

Case Based Question

1. Read the following passage and answer the question that follows.

'Classical' dances

The question of defining any art form as 'classical' is often quite complicated. Do we define something as classical if it deals with a religious theme?

Or do we consider it classical because it appears to require a great deal of skill acquired through long years of training? Or is it classical because it is performed according to rules that are laid down and variations are not encouraged?

These are questions we need to think about. It is worth remembering that many dance forms that are classified as 'folk' also share several of the characteristics considered typical of 'classical' forms. So, while the use of the term 'classical' may suggest that these forms are superior, this need not always be literally true.

Other dance forms that are recognised as classical at present are

Bharatanatyam (Tamil Nadu)
Kathakali (Kerala)
Odissi (Odisha)
Kuchipudi (Andhra Pradesh)
Manipuri (Manipur)

(i) **Find out more about any one of these dance forms.**

Ans. Bharatanatyam (Tamil Nadu) dance form is among the leading dance forms of India. It emerged 19-20th century with the efforts of Sadir, the art of temple dancers called Devadasis. It was described in the treatise.

The word Bharatanatyam combines, 'Bhavam' meaning expression, 'ragam' meaning music, 'thalam' meaning rhythm and 'Natyam' meaning dance.

Tamil, Telugu, Kannada and Sanskrit are traditionally used in the music of Bharatanatyam.

(ii) **Name the classical dance of North India.**

Ans. Kathak is the classical dance of North India.

Map Based Question

1. Locate the following on the political map of India .

(i) State where Jagannatha Temple is located.

(ii) State called Rajputana by the British.

(iii) State where Malayalam is spoken.

(iv) State which has Bharatanatyam as classical dance form.

Ans.

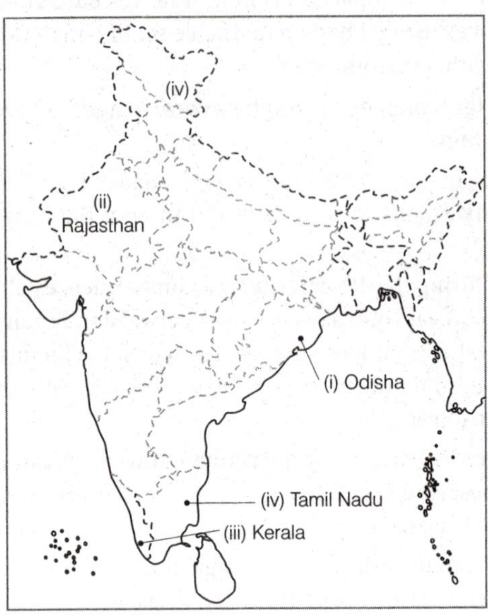

ASSESSMENT EXERCISE

Multiple Choice Questions (MCQs)

1. In which of the following Indian languages, Lilatilakam was written?

(a) Sanskrit (b) Kannad
(c) Malayalam (d) Bengali

2. The legends of Radha-Krishna were enacted in folk plays called

(a) Ram-leela (b) Rasa-lila
(c) Kathak (d) Jogan

3. Which of the following in Mughal period called Pirs?

(a) Religious head (b) Teacher and adjudicators
(c) Saints (d) The Emperor

4. Which of the following is called Kansari?

(a) Double roofed structure
(b) Bell metal work
(c) Oil pressers community of the Hindus
(d) Traditional food

Subjective Questions (VSA, SA & LA)

1. What do you mean by the Lilatilakam?

2. What do you understand by the portraits?

3. Mention a feature of Kangra school of painting.

4. 'Kathak developed into a distinct mode of dance in 15th and 16th centuries with the spread of the Bhakti Movement.' What were the patronage of Kathak?

5. What were the linguistic and cultural influences on the language?

6. Briefly describe the *pirs*.

7. Why are fish and rice most important food in Bengal?

8. The Rajput rulers cherished the ideal of the hero who fought courageously. What were their heroic folklore?

9. Discuss the regions which attracted the miniature paintings.

10. What are the differences between Bharatanatyam and Kathak?

Eighteenth-Century Political Formations

CHAPTER 8

The political conditions massively changed the face of India in a relatively short period during the 18th century. The Mughal Empire started to decline due to several reasons like weak and inefficient rulers after Aurangzeb, etc. This led to control of Rajputs, Sikhs and Marathas over states like Rajasthan, Punjab, Gujarat, etc. The Jats also consolidated their power during this period.

8.1 The Crisis in Mughal Empire and the Later Mughals

At the end of the 17th century, the Mughal Empire started facing a variety of crises. These were caused by a number of factors as follows

- Emperor Aurangzeb had used up the military and financial resources of his empire by fighting a long war in the Deccan. Under his successors, the efficiency of the administration broke down.

  The offices of revenue and military administration (*diwani* and *faujdari*) were mostly controlled by nobles appointed as governors (*subadars*).

  This gave them extraordinary political, economic and military powers over vast regions of the Mughal Empire. As Governors gained more control over provinces, the revenue reaching to the capital decreased.
- In many parts of Northern and Western India, there were rebellions of the peasants and zamindars. These revolts were sometimes caused due to increasing taxes while sometimes the powerful chieftains rebelled to strengthen their own positions.

  These groups were able to capture the economic resources of the region to strengthen their positions.
- The later Mughals were unable to stop the gradual transfer of power into the hands of provincial Governors, local chieftains and other groups.
- The ruler of Iran, **Nadir Shah,** attacked Delhi in 1739 and looted vast wealth. It was followed by a series of invasion by five raids by the Afghan ruler **Ahmad Shah Abdali** who invaded North India five times between 1748 and 1761.
- The empire was further weakened by competition amongst different groups of nobles. They were divided into two major groups, the **Iranis** and **Turanis.**

  The later Mughal emperors were controlled by either of these two groups for a long time. The Mughal emperors, Farrukh Siyar (1713-1719) and Alamgir II (1754-1759) were killed and Ahmad Shah (1748-1754) and Shah Alam II (1759-1816) were blinded by their nobles.

With the decline in the authority of the Mughal emperors, the governors, *subadars*, and the great zamindars strengthen their position in different regions such as Awadh, Bengal and Hyderabad.

8.2 The Rajputs

Many Rajput kings, particularly kings of Amber and Jodhpur, had served under the Mughals. In exchange, they were given freedom to control their *watan jagirs.*

Raja Ajit Singh of Jodhpur and **Sawai Raja Jai Singh** of Amber were the Governors of Gujarat and Malwa respectively.

These rulers tried to extend their control over nearby regions. Ajit Singh conquered Nagaur while Jai Singh captured large parts of Bundi.

Sawai Raja Jai Singh founded his new capital at Jaipur and was given the *subadari* of Agra in 1722.

However, their further expansion was prevented by the Maratha campaigns into Rajasthan from the 1740s.

Fortifications by Rajputs

Many Rajput chieftains built a number of forts on hill tops which became the centres of power. With extensive **fortifications**[1], these large structures included urban centres, palaces, temples, trading centres, water harvesting structures and other buildings.

For example, the **Chittorgarh Fort** contained many water bodies varying from *talabs* (ponds) to *kundis* (wells), *baolis* (stepwells), etc.

8.3 The Sikhs

During the 17th century, the Sikhs were organised into a political community which helped in regional state-building in the Punjab.

Guru Gobind Singh fought several battles against the Rajput and Mughal rulers, before and after the institution of the Khalsa in 1699.

After his death in 1708, the Khalsa revolted against the Mughals under the leadership of **Banda Bahadur** and declared their independent rule in the name of Guru Nanak and Guru Gobind Singh.

They established their own administration between the Sutlej and the Jamuna. However, Banda Bahadur was captured in 1715 and executed in 1716.

In 18th century, the Sikhs organised themselves into **jathas**[2] and *misls*. Their combined forces were known as grand army (*dal khalsa*). They used to meet at Amritsar at the time of Baisakhi and Diwali to take collective actions called **resolutions of Guru gurmatas**[3].

A system called ***rakhi*** was introduced to protect cultivators on the payment of a tax of 20 per cent of the produce.

Guru Gobind Singh had inspired the *Khalsa* with the belief that their destiny was to rule. They were able to resist the Mughal Governors and then to Ahmad Shah Abdali who had captured the province of Punjab and the Sarkar of Sirhind from the Mughals.

The Khalsa declared their independent rule again by making striking their own coin in 1765. In the late 18th century, the Sikh territories extended from the Indus to the Jamuna but they were divided under different rulers. In 1799, **Maharaja Ranjit Singh** reunited these groups and established his capital at Lahore.

Try These

1. **Who established the independent state of Jats?**
2. **What was sardeshmukhi?**
3. **Identify the Persian ruler who raided India for the first time.**
4. **What was the collective name given to the whole army of the 'misls'?**

8.4 The Marathas

The Maratha kingdom was carved out by Shivaji (1627-1680) with the support of powerful warrior families of **deshmukhs**.

The groups of highly mobile, peasant-pastoralists (kunbis) were the backbone of the Maratha army, which were used by Shivaji to challenge the Mughals. After Shivaji's death a family of Chitpavan Brahmanas gained power who were Shivaji's successors as **Peshwa** (principal master). **Poona** became the capital of the Maratha kingdom.

Under the Peshwas, the Marathas developed a very successful military organisation. The Maratha empire expanded between 1720 and 1761. Malwa and Gujarat were captured from the Mughals by the 1720s.

By the 1730s, the Maratha king was recognised as the Maratha's overlord of the Deccan peninsula. He had the right to levy **chauth**[4] and **sardeshmukhi**[5] in the entire region.

After raiding Delhi in 1737, the Marathas had built authority over Rajasthan and the Punjab in the North; Bengal and Odisha in the East; Karnataka and the Tamil and Telugu countries in the South. These were not formally included in the Maratha empire, but they were made to pay tribute to the empire.

The expansion by Marathas brought enormous resources but it made other rulers opposed to the Marathas. As a result, they did not support the Marathas during the **Third Battle of Panipat** in 1761.

1 **Fortification** It refers to a defensive wall built to strengthen a place against attack.
2 **Jathas** These refer to military bands under Sikhs.
3 **Gurmatas** These refer to resolutions of the Guru.
4 **Chauth** It was an annual tax nominally levied at 25% on produce.
5 **Sardeshmukhi** It was an additional 10% tax levied upon the collected 'Chauth'.

Administration under Marathas

The Marathas developed an effective administrative system. The Maratha chiefs (*sardars*) like Sindhia of Gwalior, Gaekwad of Baroda and Bhonsle of Nagpur built powerful armies by the resources raised through revenue demand, encouraging agriculture and reviving trade.

The cities like Ujjain under Sindhia and Indore under Holkar functioned as important commercial and cultural centres. New trade routes emerged within the areas controlled by the Marathas.

The silk produced in the **Chanderi** found a new outlet in Poona, the Maratha capital. **Burhanpur**, which was earlier involved in the trade between Agra and Surat, expanded to include Poona and Nagpur in the South and Lucknow and Allahabad in the East. Most Maratha cities were prosperous and important commercial centres.

8.5 The Jats

The Jats consolidated their power during the late 17th and 18th centuries. Under the leadership of **Churaman**, they acquired control over territories to the west of the city of Delhi, and by the 1680s, they dominated the region between the cities of Delhi and Agra.

The Jats were prosperous agriculturists, and towns like **Panipat** and **Ballabhgarh** became their important trading centres.

Under **Suraj Mal**, the kingdom of Bharatpur emerged as a strong state. His son **Jawahir Shah** hired soldiers from Marathas and Sikhs to fight against the Mughals. The **Bharatpur** fort was built by Suraj Mal in a traditional style.

The Jats built a garden palace at Dig, combining the architectural styles of Amber and Agra. Its buildings were based on architectural forms prevalent during Shah Jahan's rule.

EIGHTEENTH-CENTURY POLITICAL FORMATIONS

The Crisis in the Mughal Empire and the Later Mughals

- Emperor Aurangzeb used up the military and financial resources.
- Later Mughals were unable to stop the transfer of power into the hands of provincial governors.
- Nadir Shah attacked Delhi in 1739.
- Ahmad Shah Abdali invaded North India between 1748 and 1761.

The Jats

- The Jats consolidated their power during late 17th and 18th centuries.
- Churaman acquired control over territories to the West of Delhi.
- In 1680s, jats dominated the region between the cities of Delhi and Agra.
- Under Suraj Mal, the kingdomof Bharatpur emerged as a strong state.

The Rajputs

- Rajput kings had given freedom to control their watan Jagirs.
- Raja Ajit Singh of Jodhpur and Sawai Raja Jai Singh of Amber were Governors of Gujarat and Malwa, respectively.

The Sikhs

- Khalsa was institutionalised in 1699.
- Guru Gobind Singh fought against the Rajputs and Mughals.
- The Khalsa revolt rose against Mughal authority under Banda Bahadur, after Guru Gobind Singh.
- In 18th century, the Sikhs organised themselves into jathas and misls.
- In 1799, Maharaja Ranjit Singh established his capital at Lahore.

The Marathas

- The Maratha kingdom was carved out by Shivaji (1627-1680) with the support of Deshmukhs.
- After Shivaji's death, Peshwas established Poona as the capital of Maratha kingdom.
- The Maratha empire expanded between 1720 and 1761.
- By 1730s, the Marathas levied Chauth and Sardeshmukhi in the entire region.
- Third Battle of Panipat was fought in 1761.

NCERT FOLDER

Covering Intext Questions and Exercises of NCERT

NCERT PAGE 95

Q.1 See chapter - 4 Table 1. Which group of people challenged Mughal authority for the longest time in Aurangzeb's reign?

Ans. In Aurangzeb's time, the Rajputs and the Marathas challenged Mughal authority for the longest time. Mughal intervention in the internal politics of Rajput kingdoms led to the rebellion of Marwar. Initially, Mughal campaign against Shivaji was successful, but later Shivaji started his campaigns against the Mughals till his death.

NCERT PAGE 100

Q.2 What is the Khalsa? Do you recall reading about it in Chapter 6?

Ans. Khalsa is a significant concept of Sikhism. The Sikh movement began to get politicised in the 17th century after the execution of Guru Arjan. It led to the development of institution of the Khalsa by Guru Gobind Singh in 1699. Khalsa Panth became a political group.

Q.3 You are a ruler of an eighteenth-century kingdom. Tell us about the steps you would take to make your position strong in your province, and what opposition or problems you might face while doing so.

Ans. If I would be an eighteenth-century ruler of a kingdom, then to strengthen my rule, I would focus on fair governance, improving agriculture and promoting trade. I would build alliances with neighbouring rulers and maintain a well-trained army to protect myself from growing powers like Marathas and Sikhs.

However, challenges may arise from rebels rivalries, and external threats. Managing the economy, ensuring justice, and increasing loyalty among subjects would be crucial.

Balancing power and addressing the concerns of different groups would be key to overcoming opposition and creating a stable kingdom.

EXERCISES

Q.1 State whether true or false.

(a) Nadir Shah invaded Bengal.

(b) Sawai Raja Jai Singh was the ruler of Indore.

(c) Guru Gobind Singh was the 10th Guru of the Sikhs.

(d) Poona became the capital of the Marathas in the 18th century.

Ans. (a) False (b) False (c) True (d) True

Q.2 How were the Sikhs organised in the 18th century?

Ans. In the 18th century, the Sikhs organised themselves into a number of bands called Jathas and later on misls.

The Sikh under the Khalsa declared their sovereign rule and their territories in the late 18th century extended from the Indus to the Jamuna. Maharaja Ranjit Singh reunited the divided groups of Sikhs and established his capital at Lahore in 1799.

Q.3 Why did the Marathas want to expand beyond the Deccan?

Ans. Marathas wanted to expand beyond the Deccan because of the following reasons

- They wanted to reduce the authority of the Mughal Empire.
- They wanted to be recognised as the overlord of the entire Deccan Plateau.
- They wanted to have the right to collect chauth and sardeshmukhi in the entire region.

Q.4 Do you think merchants and bankers today have the kind of influence they had in the 18th century?

Ans. During the 18th century, merchants and bankers were more influential than today. They used to provide loans at higher interest rates but people had no other option as there were no formal banking institutions during that time. But now, with the spread of education, people prefer banks which provide loans and other financial assistance at reasonable rates.

Q.5 Did any of the kingdoms mentioned in this chapter develop in your state? If so, in what way do you think life in the state would have been different in the 18th century from what it is in the 21st century?

Ans. Yes, I am from Uttar Pradesh and the Awadh kingdom developed in my state. Life in the state during that time would have been very different from the 21st century. In the 18th century, people's lifestyles were simpler, with agriculture being a primary occupation. There were no modern facilities, and society was structured differently. The ruling Nawabs governed with a different system than the present government.

Today, Uttar Pradesh has evolved with technological advancements, urbanisation and a different government structure.

Q.6 Collect popular tales about rulers from any one of the following groups of people.

The Rajput, Jats, Sikhs or Marathas.

Ans. I have collected tales about Maratha ruler Chhatrapati Shivaji . He was a brave Maratha ruler. Legends tell of his childhood courage, once he bravely escaped from the hold of the Mughal Emperor Aurangzeb in the Agra Fort.

Shivaji pretended to be a servant and cleverly fooled his enemies with a plan. He was excellent at using guerilla warfare, which helped him build the Maratha empire.

REVIEW EXERCISE

Including Competency Based Questions

Part I

Multiple Choice Questions (MCQs)

1. When did the third Battle of Panipat take place?
(a) 1760 (b) 1761 (c) 1762 (d) 1763

2. In which of the following years Aurangzeb died?
(a) 1700 (b)1710 (c) 1707 (d) 1725

3. Mughal Emperors kept a check on their powerful
(a) *jotedars* (b) *jagirdars*
(c) *mansabdars* (d) *faujdars*

4. Peasants and Zamindari rebellions are caused by the pressures of
(a) exploitation of tillers (b) exploitation of Zamindars
(c) mounting prices of goods (d) mounting taxes

5. Nadir Shah sacked and plundered the city of Delhi in
(a) 1735 (b)1738 (c)1739 (d)1737

6. Dal Khalsa was set up in 1699 by
(a) Guru Har Kishan (b) Guru Gobind Singh
(c) Guru Tegh Bahadur (d) Guru Nanak Singh

7. Ahmad Shah Abdali had seized the rich province of the
(a) Awadh and Hyderabad (b) Bengal and Orissa
(c) Punjab and Sirhind (d) Amber and Nagpur

8. Where did Maharaja Ranjit Singh establish his capital?
(a) Ludhiana (b) Amritsar
(c) Lahore (d) Chandigarh

9. In which year, Marathas were defeated by Ahmad Shah Abdali in Panipat ?
(a) 1761 (b)1762 (c)1785 (d)1765

10. What were the powerful warrior families of Maratha kingdom known as?
(a) Kunbis (b) Deshmukhs
(c) Peshwas (d) Sardars

11. After the death of Shivaji, Peshwa took control of the Maratha kingdom. Their capital was
(a) Punjab (b) Awadh (c) Bombay (d) Poona

12. Which provinces were seized by Marathas from Mughals?
(a) Malwa and Gujarat (b) Agra and Delhi
(c) Awadh and Hyderabad (d) Bengal and Orissa

13. Chauth was the .... of the land revenue.
(a) 10% (b) 25% (c) 50% (d) 20%

14. Maratha chief Gaekwad belonged to
(a) Gwalior (b) Baroda (c) Malwa (d) Nagpur

15. The Jats consolidated their power during which period?
(a) Late 17th and 18th centuries
(b) Late 18th and 19th centuries
(c) Late 19th and 20th centuries
(d) Late 16th and 17th centuries

16. Panipat and Ballabhgarh became important trading centres under the domination of the
(a) Jats (b) Marathas (c) Sikhs (d) Rajputs

17. Identify the personality about whom the statements are given below. Competency Based
(i) He was the Governor of Malwa.
(ii) He commissioned five astronomical observatories at Delhi, Jaipur, Ujjain, Mathura and Varanasi.
(iii) He constructed the city of Jaipur.

Codes
(a) Raja Ajit Singh (b) Raja Jai Singh
(c) Raja Bhanu Singh (d) Raja Ram Singh

18. Choose the correct statement(s) from the given below. Competency Based
I. Farrukh Siyar and Alamgir II were assassinated by their nobles.
II. Raja Ajit Singh was the Governor of Malwa.
III. Rakhi was system of offering protection of cultivators on payment of a tax of 20 per cent of the produce.

Codes
(a) Only I (b) I and II (c) I and III (d) Only III

19. Arrange the following Mughal Emperor in the correct sequence of succession. **Competency Based**

I. Alamgir II   II. Shah Alam II
III. Ahmad Shah   IV. Farrukh Siyar

Codes
(a) I, II, III, IV   (b) I, II, III, IV
(c) III, IV, II, I   (d) IV, III, I, II

20. Arrange the following events in chronological order.

I. Raja Jai Singh was given the *subadari* of Agra.
II. Institution of the Khalsa.
III. Maharaja Ranjit Singh established his capital at Lahore.
IV. Nadir Shah plundered Delhi.

Codes
(a) I, IV, III, II   (b) II, I, IV, III
(c) IV, III, II, I   (d) III, I, IV, II

Answers

1. (b)	**2.** (c)	**3.** (c)	**4.** (d)	**5.** (c)
6. (b)	**7.** (c)	**8.** (c)	**9.** (a)	**10.** (b)
11. (d)	**12.** (a)	**13.** (b)	**14.** (b)	**15.** (a)
16. (a)	**17.** (b)	**18.** (c)	**19.** (d)	**20.** (b)

Match the Following

1.

List I	List II
A. Third Battle of Panipat	1. Invaded North India
B. Nobles appointed as	2. Assassinated by his nobles
C. Nadir Shah	3. Fought by Marathas
D. Ahmad Shah Abdali	4. Governors (Subadars)
E. Alamgir II	5. Delhi

Codes

	A	B	C	D	E		A	B	C	D	E
(a)	3	4	5	1	2	(b)	1	2	3	4	5
(c)	3	1	2	5	4	(d)	4	5	3	1	2

2.

List I	List II
A. Chitpavan Brahmanas	1. Gwalior
B. Sindhia	2. Baroda
C. Khalsa	3. Jodhpur
D. Raja Ajit Singh	4. Peshwa
E. Gaekwad	5. Punjab

Codes

	A	B	C	D	E		A	B	C	D	E
(a)	4	1	5	3	2	(b)	1	2	3	4	5
(c)	3	1	2	5	4	(d)	4	5	3	1	2

Ans. 1. (a) 2. (a)

Assertion-Reason

1. Assertion (A) Governors of large provinces, subadars and zamindars consolidated their authority in different parts of the sub-continent.

Reason (R) Aurangzeb gradually shifted political and economic authority into the hands of provincial governers and local chieftains.

Codes
(a) Both A and R are true and R is the correct explanation of A
(b) Both A and R are true, but R is not the correct explanation of A
(c) A is true, but R is false
(d) A is false, but R is true

2. Assertion (A) Maratha king was recognised as the overland of the Deccan Peninsula by the 1730s.

Reason (R) The silk produced in the Chanderi region found a new outlet in Poona.

Codes
(a) Both A and R are true and R is the correct explanation of A
(b) Both A and R are true, but R is not the correct explanation of A
(c) A is true, but R is false
(d) A is false, but R is true

Ans. 1. (a) Both A and R are true and R is the correct explanation of A
2. (b) Both A and R are true, but R is not the correct explanation of A

Fill in the Blanks

1. The Mughal Emperors after .... were unable to arrest the gradual shifting of political and economic authority in the hands of provincial governors.

2. Ahmad Shah Abdali, invaded.................. five times between 1748 and 1761.

3. Later Mughals were puppets in the hands of ... .

4. ....had inspired the Khalsa with the belief that their destiny was to rule.

Ans. 1. Aurangzeb   2. North India
3. Iranis and Turanis   4. Guru Gobind Singh

True/False

1. The Coromandel coast in the East were checked by the British.

2. Influential Rajput families claimed the *subadari* of the rich provinces of Gujarat and Malwa.

3. Mughal emperor Shah Alam II was blinded by his nobles.

4. Mehrangarh Fort is located at Jaipur.

Ans. 1. True   2. True   4. True   5. False

Picture Based Questions

1. The image shown below is portrait of Nadir Shah. In which century did he rule?

(a) 15th century (b) 16th century
(c) 17th century (d) 18th century

2. Mughal ruler Farrukh Siyar is shown in the picture below. What was the reign period for Farrukh Siyar?

(a) 1713-1719 (b) 1754-1759
(c) 1748-1754 (d) 1759-1816

Ans. 1. (d) 18th century
2. (a) 1713-1719

Case Based Question

1. Read the given passage and answer the following questions.

Guru Gobind Singh had inspired the Khalsa with the belief that their destiny was to rule (raj karega Khalsa). Their well-knit organisation enabled them to put up a successful resistance to the Mughal governors first and then to Ahmad Shah Abdali who had seized the rich province of the Punjab and the Sarkar of Sirhind from the Mughals. The Khalsa declared their sovereign rule by striking their own coin again in 1765. Significantly, this coin bore the same inscription as the one on the orders issued by the Khalsa in the time of Banda Bahadur.

(i) What was the term given to the bands in which Sikhs organised themselves ?

(a) Rakhi (b) Khalsa (c) Deshmukhs (d) Jathas

(ii) In which of the following years Guru Gobind Singh died ?

(a) 1708 (b) 1716
(c) 1699 (d) 1715

(iii) Who reunited Sikhs groups again and established Sikh empire in 1799?

(a) Banda Bahadur (b) Hiza Singh Dogra
(c) Maharaja Ranjit Singh (d) Guru Gobind Singh

(iv) According to Guru Govind Singh, what was the primary objective of the Khalsa?

(a) Cultural preservation (b) Economic prosperity
(c) Political rule (d) Social reform

Ans. (i) (d) Jathas (ii) (a) 1708
(iii) (c) Maharaja Ranjit Singh (iv) (c) Political rule

Part II

Very Short Answer Type Questions

1. Name the two major groups or factions of nobles of later Mughal period.

Ans. Nobles were divided into two major groups or factions, the Iranis and Turanis (nobles of Turkish descent) at later Mughal period.

2. Who held the governorship of Gujarat?

Ans. The governorship of Gujarat was held by Raja Ajit Singh of Jodhpur.

3. Name the Rajput leader who founded his new capital at Jaipur.

Ans. Sawai Raja Jai Singh founded his new capital at Jaipur.

4. Into how many Misls were the Sikh provinces of Punjab divided ? Diksha

Ans. The Sikh provinces of Punjab were divided into twelve Misls.

5. How Sikhs organised themselves?

Ans. The Sikhs organised themselves into a number of bands called Jathas and later on misls.

6. How Guru Gobind Singh had inspired the Khalsa?

Ans. Guru Gobind Singh had inspired the Khalsa with the belief that their destiny was to rule (Raj *Karega Khalsa*).

7. Why was a system called *rakhi* introduced?

Ans. The system of *rakhi* was introduced by the Sikhs to protect the cultivators on the payment of a tax of 20 per cent of the produce.

8. Who took over as the leader of the Sikhs after Guru Gobind Singh?

Ans. Banda Bahadur took over as the leader of the Sikh after Guru Gobind Singh.

9. What was the extent of Sikh territories?

Ans. The Sikh territories extended from the Indus to the Jamuna in the late 18th century.

10. Which were the territories of Maratha in the East?

Ans. Maratha rule extended in the East of India upto Bengal and Odisha.

11. Name the three states that were carved out of the old Mughal provinces in the 18th century.

Ans. Awadh, Bengal and Hyderabad were the three states that were carved out of the old Mughal provinces in the 18th century.

12. Under whose patronage the city of Ujjain expanded?

Ans. The city of Ujjain was expanded under Sindhia's (Gwalior) patronage.

13. Where did the Jats began to dominate by 1680's?

Ans. The Jats began to dominate by 1680's between the two imperial cities of Delhi and Agra.

14. Under whose leadership the Jats became powerful?

Ans. The Jats became powerful under the leadership of Churaman.

15. Under whom did Bharatpur emerge as a strong state?

Ans. Under Suraj Mal, the kingdom of Bharatpur emerged as a strong state.

16. Where did the Jats build an elaborate garden palace?

Ans. Jats build an elaborate garden palace at Dig, Rajasthan combining the styles of Amber and Agra.

Short Answer Type Questions

1. How did the nobles gain their control over the Mughals?

Ans. Nobles gained control over the Mughals as later Mughal rulers were weak. Nobles were divided into the Iranis and Turanis, competing for power. These factions manipulated later Mughal emperors like puppets. The nobles' rivalry weakened the empire, leading to a series of assassinations and cruel acts against emperors.

Notably, Farrukh Siyar and Alamgir II were murdered, while Ahmad Shah and Shah Alam II were blinded by their own nobles. The nobles' influence and control over the Mughal emperors ultimately resulted in a state of turmoil and decline of the Mughal empire.

2. Describe the impact of foreign invasion upon Delhi.

Ans. Foreign invasion impacted Delhi in the following ways

- The ruler of Iran, Nadir Shah, plundered the city of Delhi in 1739 and took away immense amount of wealth. The Mughal treasury was looted.
- Delhi turned into a deserted place. The wealthy became beggars. Chaos spread everywhere. Those who wore stylish clothes went naked and those owned property were homeless.
- The new city, i.e. Shahjahanabad turned into ruins. Nadir Shah also attacked the old quarters of the city and destroyed it completely.

3. Many Rajputs, particularly those belonging to Amber and Jodhpur, had served under the Mughals with distinction. **Competency Based**

(i) Who held the governorship of Malwa and Gujarat?

Ans. Sawai Raja Jai Singh of Amber and Raja Ajit Singh of Jodhpur held the governorship of Malwa and Gujarat respectively.

(ii) Why Rajput kings served under the Mughals ?

Ans. Rajput kings served under the Mughals with distinction. In exchange, they were permitted to enjoy autonomy in their *watan Jagirs*.

4. What do you mean by fortification? Explain about the fortifications by Rajputs.

Ans. Fortification refers to a defensive wall built to strengthen a place against attack. Many Rajput chieftains built a number of forts on hill tops which became the centres of power. With extensive fortifications, these large structures included urban centres, palaces, temples, trading centres, water harvesting structures and other buildings.

For example, the Chittorgarh fort contained many water bodies varying fromtalabs (ponds) to kundis (wells), baolis (stepwells), etc.

5. The Marathas developed an effective administrative system? Justify the statement.

Ans. The Marathas developed an effective administrative system. The Maratha chiefs (sardars) like Sindhia of Gwalior, Gaekwad of Baroda and Bhonsle of Nagpur built powerful armies by the resources raised through revenue demand, encouraging agriculture and reviving trade.

The cities like Ujjain under Sindhia and Indore under Holkar functioned as important commercial and cultural centres. New trade routes emerged within the areas controlled by the Marathas.

6. Who were the Jats? Explain how Jats consolidated their kingdom?

Ans Jats were prosperous agriculturists. They acquired territories situated to the West of the city of Delhi under their leader Churaman.

The power of the Jats reached its peak under Suraj Mal who consolidated the Jat kingdom at Bharatpur during 1756-1763. Bharatpur Fort was built by Jats in a fairly traditional style. They dominated the region between two imperial cities Delhi and Agra.

Long Answer Type Questions

1. A Research Institute has been given the task to understand the condition of later Mughals in the 18th century. Competency Based

Discuss the key factors that led to the crisis of the Mughal empire.

Ans. The key factors that led to the crisis of the Mughal Empire were

- Emperor Aurangzeb had used up the military and financial resources of his empire by fighting a long war in the Deccan. Under his successors, the efficiency of the administration broke down.
- In many parts of Northern and Western India, there were rebellions of the peasants and zamindars. These revolts were sometimes caused due to increasing taxes while sometimes the powerful chieftains rebelled to strengthen their own positions.
- The later Mughals were unable to stop the gradual transfer of power into the hands of provincial Governors, local chieftains and other groups.
- The ruler of Iran, Nadir Shah, attacked Delhi in 1739 and looted vast wealth. It was followed by a series of invasion by five raids by the Afghan ruler Ahmad Shah Abdali who invaded North India five times between 1748 and 1761.
- The empire was further weakened by competition amongst different groups of nobles. They were divided into two major groups, the Iranis and Turanis. The later Mughal emperors were controlled by either of these two groups for a long time.

2. How the Sikhs consolidated their power during 17th to 18th century?

Ans. During the 17th century, the Sikhs were organised into a political community which helped in regional state-building in the Punjab. Guru Gobind Singh fought several battles against the Rajput and Mughal rulers, before and after the institution of the Khalsa in 1699.

After his death in 1708, the Khalsa revolted against the Mughals under the leadership of Banda Bahadur and declared their independent rule in the name of Guru Nanak and Guru Gobind Singh. They established their own administration between the Sutlej and the Jamuna. However, Banda Bahadur was captured in 1715 and executed in 1716.

In 18th century, the Sikhs organised themselves into Jathas and Misls. Their combined forces were known as grand army (Dal Khalsa). The Khalsa declared their independent rule again by striking their own coin in 1765.

In the late 18th century, the Sikh territories extended from the Indus to the Jamuna but they were divided under different rulers. In 1799, Maharaja Ranjit Singh reunited these groups and established his capital.

3. How Marathas carved out a stable kingdom in India?

Ans. Marathas under the leadership of Shivaji (1627-1680) carved out a stable kingdom with the support of powerful warrior families (*deshmukhs*).

The backbone of Maratha army were Kuntis, a group of highly mobile peasant-pastoralists. Shivaji used these forces to challenge the Mughals in the peninsula.

Marathas developed a very successful military organisation under the Peshwas. Maratha King was recognised as the overload of the entire Deccan Peninsula.

Declining Mughal Empire also provided opportunity to expand Marathas in the North India. They raised Delhi in 1737 and expanded in Rajasthan and Punjab in North, into Bengal and Orissa in the East, and into Karnataka and the Tamil and Telugu countries in the South. These regions paid tribute to the Marathas. Along with military campaigns, the Marathas also developed an effective administrative system to stablise their kingdom.

Picture Based Question

1. Look at the image given below and answer the questions that follow.

(i) Identify the fort shown in the image.

Ans. This is Chittorgarh Fort of Rajasthan.

(ii) What is the locational and architectural significance of this fort ?

Ans. This fort is located on a hilltop.

The Chittorgarh Fort contains many water bodies varying from *talabs* (ponds) to *kundis* (wells), *baolis* (stepwells), etc. With extensive fortifications, these majestic structures housed urban centres, palaces, temples, trading centres, water harvesting structures and other buildings.

Case Based Question

1. **Read the given passage and answer the questions that follow.**

"The great lords are helpless and impoverished. Their peasants raise two crops a year, but their lords see nothing of either, and their agents on the spot are virtual prisoners in the peasants' hands, like a peasant kept in his creditor's house until he can pay his debt. So complete is the collapse of all order and administration that though the peasant reaps a harvest of gold, his lord does not see so much as a wisp of straw. How then can the lord keep the armed force he should? How can he pay the soldiers who should go before him when he goes out, or the horsemen who should ride behind him?"

(i) **Why are the great lords portrayed as helpless and impoverished in the passage?**

Ans. The great lords are in helpless and impoverished condition because, despite their peasants yielding two crops a year, they receive no share. This may be because of corruption on the part of agents or breakdown of the feudal system.

(ii) **How does the collapse of order and administration affect the lords' ability to manage armies and support soldiers amid peasant's prosperity?**

Ans. The collapse of order makes it challenging for the lords to sustain armed forces, as they lack the resources. Despite the peasant's prospering, the lords don't benefit from the harvest, leading to a disruption in traditional sources of income for maintaining military forces.

Map Based Question

1. **(i) In the map of India, mark the territory under British control during the mid-18th Century.**

(ii) Also mark external boundary of Mughal empire, 1700.

Ans.

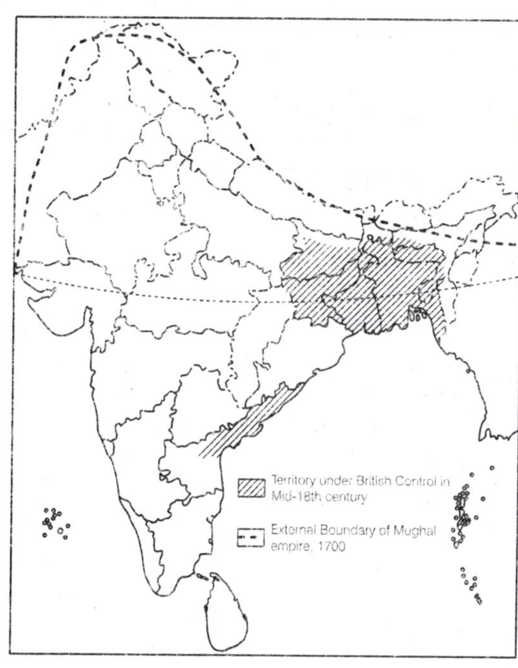

ASSESSMENT EXERCISE

Multiple Choice Questions (MCQs)

1. Peasants and Zamindar rebelled in many parts of Northern India because of
   (a) increasing power (b) mounting taxes
   (c) armed forces (d) Both (a) and (b)
2. Who were the watan jagirs?
   (a) State under the Mughals (b) Governors
   (c) Mughal authority (d) Economic authority
3. Which of the following was the founder of Hyderabad state?
   (a) Guru Tegh Bahadur (b) Nadir Shah
   (c) Ahmad Shah Abdali (d) Nizam-ul-Mulk Asaf Jah
4. The state of Hyderabad was constantly engaged in struggle against independent Telugu warrior chiefs
   (a) Jotedars (b) Nayakas
   (c) Mansabdars (d) Jagirdar

Subjective Questions (VSA, SA & LA)

1. Who was appointed as Subadar of Awadh in 1722?
2. How did Subadar of Awadh region reduced Mughal influence?
3. When did entire body of Dal Khalsa used to meet at Amritsar?
4. How did Khalsa declared their sovereign rule?
5. Why Aurangzeb had depleted the military?
6. 'Other rulers did not help the Marathas during the third Battle of Panipat in 1761'. Discuss the reasons.
7. Write in brief about the Jats.
8. Write about Sikh territories in the late eighteenth century.
9. Write about the factors which were responsible for downfall of later Mughals.
10. Discuss in brief about division of Mughal states of eighteenth century.
11. 'The state of Hyderabad was constantly engaged in a struggle against the Marathas'. Explain.

CHAPTER 1

Environment

Environment is everything that is around us. It can be living or non-living things and includes physical, chemical and other natural forces. Balance in nature is maintained by the interaction between biotic components with that of abiotic components. In this chapter, we will learn about natural environment and it's different domains, biotic and abiotic components, ecosystem and human environment.

Environment is a basic life support system that provides air to breathe, water to drink, food to eat and the land to live. The word 'environment' comes from the French word ***environer/environner***, meaning **neighbourhood**. The place, people, things and nature that surround any living organism is called environment. It is a combination of natural and **human-made**[1] phenomena.

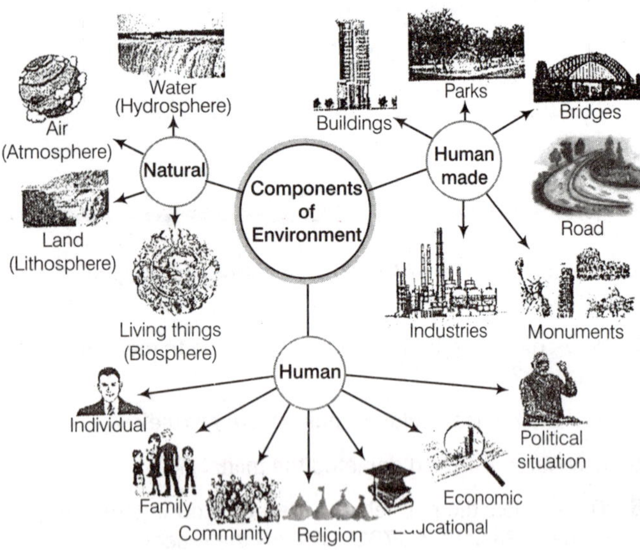

• Components of Environment

Both humans and environment are interrelated. Thus, a perfect balance is necessary between natural and human environment.

1.1 Natural Environment

It refers to both **biotic** and **abiotic** conditions existing on the Earth which are as follows

- **Biotic Environment** It includes all the living organisms in the world. For example, plants and animals.
- **Abiotic Environment** It includes every non-living thing. For example, land, water and air.

Domains of Natural Environment

There are four domains of natural environment. These are lithosphere, hydrosphere, atmosphere and biosphere.

1. Lithosphere

The lithosphere is the **solid crust**[2] or **hard top layer** of the Earth. It is made up of rocks and minerals and covered by a thin layer of soil.

Lithosphere is an irregular surface with various landforms like mountains, plateaus, plains and valleys. These landforms can be found over the **continents**[3] and also on the ocean floors. The lithosphere provides us land for forests, **grasslands**[4], agriculture and human settlements. It is also a source of valuable minerals.

2. Hydrosphere

The hydrosphere is the **domain of water**. It includes various sources of water and water bodies like rivers, lakes, seas, oceans, etc. It is essential for the survival of all living organisms on the Earth.

1 **Human-made** When humans change natural environment for their survival according to their need, it is called man-made environment.
2 **Solid Crust** It is the hard top layer of the Earth.
3 **Continent** It is a huge landmass surrounded by water.
4 **Grasslands** Grassland is a large area of open land covered with wild grass.

3. Atmosphere

The atmosphere is the **thin layer of air** surrounding the Earth. The **gravitational force**[5] of the Earth holds the atmosphere around it.

It protects us from harmful rays and extreme heat of the Sun. The atmosphere consists of a number of gases, dust and water vapour. The changes in the atmosphere influence Earth's **weather**[6] and **climate**[7].

4. Biosphere

The biosphere or the **living world** consists of all living organisms, including both plant and animal kingdoms. It is a narrow zone on the earth where land, water and air interact with each other to support life.

KNOWLEDGE PLUS **World Environment Day** is celebrated on 5th June each year to raise awareness about environmental issues and promote environmental protection.

Ecosystem

The relation between the living organisms as well as the relation between organisms and their surroundings, form an ecosystem.

In other words, ecosystem is formed by the interaction of all living organisms with each other and with the physical and chemical factors of the environment in which they live. All these are linked by transfer of energy and material.

The ecosystem could be large like rainforests, deserts and oceans or it could be small like lakes or ponds.

1.2 Human Environment

Human beings interact with the environment and modify it according to their need.

Early humans adapted themselves to the natural surroundings. They lived simple lives and fulfilled their requirements from the natural surroundings.

Over time humans learn new ways to use and change their environment. They learn to grow crops, domesticate animals and lead a settled life.

Later, different developments took place like

- The wheel was invented.
- Surplus food was produced.
- **Barter system**[8] emerged, trade started and commerce developed.
- Large scale production was made possible by Industrial Revolution.
- Transportation became faster, and communication became easier and speedy across the world by information revolution.

---

5 **Gravitational Force** It is the force of attraction between all masses in the universe.
6 **Weather** It reflects short term condition of atmosphere.
7 **Climate** It is the variation of weather at a given place for a specified interval of time.
8 **Barter system** It is a trade in which goods are exchanged without the use of money.

ENVIRONMENT

Natural Environment
- Consists of land, water, air, plants and animals

Elements

Biotic
- Living organism e.g. plants and animals

Abiotic
- Non living element e.g. land

Ecosystem
- It is the interaction within all living organism and their surrounding.

Human Environment
- It is the interaction between human and environment.
- Different development occurs like
  - Barter System
  - Industrial Revolution
  - Transportation and Communication

Domains of Environment

Lithosphere
- Hard top layer of the Earth
- Irregular surface with various landforms like mountains, plateaus, etc.
- Provides land for forests, grasslands, agriculture and human settlements.

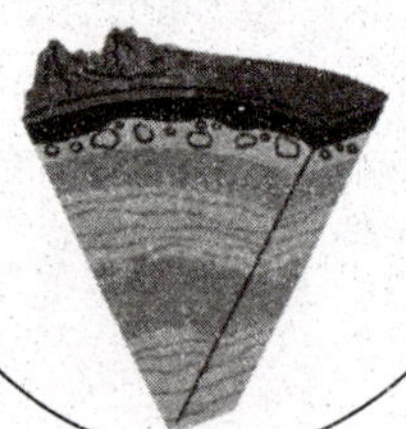

Hydrosphere
- Various sources of water and water bodies present on the Earth
- Essential for survival of all living organisms on the Earth.

Atmosphere
- Thin layer of air surrounding the Earth.
- Protects from harmful rays and extreme heat of the Sun.
- Consists of many gases like carbon dioxide and oxygen, dust and water vapour.

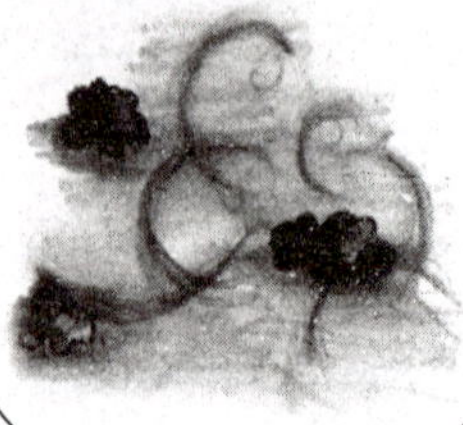

Biosphere
- Narrow zone on the Earth where land, water and air interact with each other to support life.
- Consists of all living organisms, including plant and animal kingdoms.

NCERT FOLDER

Covering Intext Questions and Exercises of NCERT

NCERT ON PAGE 1

Q.1 How do human beings modify natural environment?

Ans. Human beings modify natural environment by building factories, cutting trees, making dams, inventing objects like cars and air conditioners which pollute the air, rivers and contribute to climate change.

NCERT ON PAGE 3

Q.2 Look at your surroundings. Make a list of uses that the land in your neighbourhood is being put to.

Ans. Land is used for various purposes, including agriculture, places of worship, institutions, industries and parks in my neighbourhood.

Q.3 Where does the water you use in your home and school come from? Make a list of different uses of water in our daily life. Have you seen anyone wasting water? How?

Ans. Water for homes and schools comes from the following sources

- **Municipal Supply** In urban areas, water is usually supplied by municipal authorities through pipelines. It is sourced from rivers, lakes or reservoirs. Municipal authorities treated the water to make it safe for consumption and then distributed to households and schools.
- **Tube Wells and Hand Pumps** In some rural and urban areas, groundwater is accessed through tube wells and hand pumps.
- **Rainwater Harvesting** Some homes and schools collect rainwater during the monsoon season to meet their water needs.
- **Tanker Supply** In some areas with limited access to piped water, water tankers may deliver water to homes and schools.

Different uses of water in our daily life include

- **Drinking and Cooking** Water is essential for human survival and is used for drinking and cooking.
- **Bathing and Personal Hygiene** Water is used for bathing, washing hands and other personal hygiene activities.
- **Cleaning** Water is used for cleaning dishes, clothes, and living spaces.

I have often seen people leaving the tap open when not in use, or spoiling excessive water while watering the plants and giving bath to the animals.

NCERT ON PAGE 5

Q.4 Talk to some elderly person in your neighbourhood and collect information about

- The trees in his/ her neighbourhood when he/ she was your age.
- The indoor games he/she played.
- His/her favourite fruit at your age.
- How did they make themselves comfortable during hot summers and cold winters? Display your answers on a wall/bulletin board.

Ans. Trees in their neighbourhood were Neem, Peepal, Sheesham, etc.

The indoor games they used to play during their youth were Table Tennis, Chess and Carrom Board.

Their favourite fruits were guava, mango, apple, etc.

During hot summers, they used to sit under the shade of trees and use fans for cooling. To stay comfortable during cold winters, they preferred to sit in the sun for warmth during the day and use charcoal fires at night.

EXERCISES

Q.1 Answer the following questions.

(i) What is an ecosystem?

Ans. Ecosystem is the relation between the living organisms as well as the relation between organisms and their surroundings.

(ii) What do you mean by natural environment?

Ans. Natural environment refers to both biotic (for example, plants and animals) and abiotic (for example, land, water and air) conditions existing on the Earth.

(iii) Which are the major components of the environment.

Ans. The environment consists of three main components

- Natural components including land, water, air and living organisms.
- Human-made components include buildings, parks, bridges, roads, monuments and industries.
- Human components, such as individuals, religions, political situations, family, education, community and the economy.

(iv) Give four examples of human made environment.

Ans. Four examples of the human-made environment are buildings, parks, bridges and roads.

(v) **What is lithosphere?**

Ans. The lithosphere refers to the outermost solid crust or hard top layer of the earth. It is primarily composed of rocks and minerals and covered by a thin layer of soil.

(vi) **Which are the two major components of biotic environment?**

Ans. The two major components of the biotic environment are plants and animals.

(vii) **What is biosphere?**

Ans. The biosphere is a narrow zone of the earth where land, water and air interact to support life. It includes all the living organisms and their interactions within the earth's ecosystems.

Q.2 Tick the correct answer.

(i) Which is not a natural ecosystem?
(a) Desert (b) Aquarium (c) Forest

(ii) Which is not a component of human environment?
(a) Land (b) Religion (c) Community

(iii) Which is a human made environment?
(a) Mountain (b) Sea (c) Road

(iv) Which is a threat to environment?
(a) Growing plant (b) Growing population
(c) Growing crops

Ans. (i) (b) Aquarium (ii) (a) Land
(iii) (c) Road (iv) (b) Growing population

Q.3 Match the following.

	List I		List II
A.	Biosphere	1.	Blanket of air which surrounds the Earth
B.	Atmosphere	2.	Domain of water
C.	Hydrosphere	3.	Gravitational force of the earth
D.	Environment	4.	Our surroundings
		5.	Narrow zone where land water and air interact
		6.	Relation between the organisms and their surroundings

Ans. (a) A-5, B-1, C-2, D-4

Q.4 Give Reasons

(a) **Man modifies his environment.**

Ans. Man modifies his environment to meet his needs and adapt to natural surroundings. For example, clearing forests to grow crops is a way of modifying the environment.

(b) **Plants and animals depend on each other.**

Ans. Plants release oxygen that animals need to breathe, and animals produce carbon dioxide, which plants use for photosynthesis. Thus, plants and animals depend on each other and this interdependence ensures their mutual survival.

REVIEW EXERCISE

Including Competency Based Questions

PART I

Multiple Choice Questions (MCQs)

1. **What does the word 'environment' originate from?**
(a) German (b) English
(c) French (d) Spanish

2. **Which of the following is not a component of the natural environment?**
(a) Biotic environment (b) Abiotic environment
(c) Human-made environment (d) Lithosphere

3. **Which one of these is a part of natural environment?** Diksha
(a) School (b) Tree
(c) Road (d) House

4. **Which of the following is a part of the lithosphere?**
(a) Rivers (b) Oceans
(c) Mountains (d) Atmosphere

5. **What does the hydrosphere include?**
(a) Plateaus (b) Grasslands
(c) Rivers (d) Human settlements

6. **Which force holds the atmosphere around the Earth?**
(a) Gravitational force (b) Electromagnetic force
(c) Magnetic force (d) Atmospheric force

7. **Which domain of the natural environment is primarily responsible for supporting life on the earth, as it includes all living organisms, both plant and animal kingdoms, and is referred to as the 'living world'?**
(a) Hydrosphere (b) Atmosphere
(c) Lithosphere (d) Biosphere

8. **Which is the domain of living things?** Diksha
(a) Atmosphere (b) Hydrosphere
(c) Biosphere (d) Lithosphere

9. When is World Environment Day celebrated?

(a) 1st January (b) 5th June
(c) 10th December (d) 22nd April

10. What made communication easier and speedy across the world? Diksha

(a) Green Revolution (b) Information Revolution
(c) Glorious Revolution (d) White Revolution

11. What economic system is characterised by the exchange of goods and services directly between parties without the involvement of money, often relying on mutual agreement of value and necessity for trade? Competency Based

(a) Commodity money
(b) The Barter system
(c) A system of international trade
(d) An economic system based on virtual currency

12. It describes a complex and interconnected community of living organisms including plants, animals and micro-organisms, interacting with one another and their physical surroundings, forming a dynamic and self-sustaining system. Identify the term. Competency Based

(a) Biosphere (b) Atmosphere
(c) An Ecosystem (d) Hydrospehre

13. Which of the following best characterises the concept of the human environment, representing the result of human activities and their interactions with the surrounding world, shaping the landscape to meet their evolving needs and desires? Competency Based

(a) The environment that humans cannot modify
(b) The natural environment untouched by humans
(c) The environment created by human interactions with their surroundings
(d) The environment outside the biosphere

14. Deforestation in the Amazon rainforest has led to the loss of habitat for numerous plant and animal species. Which of the following actions is most aligned with environmental conservation and the principles of the biosphere? Competency Based

(a) Implementing sustainable logging practices to continue deforestation while minimising harm to the ecosystem.
(b) Halting all deforestation activities in the Amazon rainforest to protect its biodiversity.
(c) Expanding deforestation to create space for agriculture and human settlements.
(d) Encouraging increased deforestation to boost the global timber industry.

15. As urbanisation in a coastal city continues to grow rapidly, large areas of mangrove forests are being cleared to make way for infrastructure development. What is the most likely environmental consequence of this trend in the near future?

(a) Increased biodiversity within the coastal region.
(b) Enhanced protection from coastal erosion and storm surges.
(c) Decreased habitat for various plant and animal species.
(d) Improved air quality in the urban areas.

16. Nasir, a 35-year-old farmer in a rural area, struggles to support his family on a small piece of arable land. He faces challenges due to changing weather patterns and the limited opportunities in his community.

Accordingly, which development objective would be the most crucial for improving Nasir and his family's well-being? Competency Based

(a) Promoting sustainable agricultural practices to increase crop yield
(b) Reducing air pollution in Nasir's region to improve air quality
(c) Establishing a community-based healthcare center for better medical access
(d) Creating more recreational facilities in the village for leisure activities

17. Identify the correct option that describes the type of environment given below.

(i) It is world of non-living elements.
(ii) Its examples are land and water.
(iii) It does not include plants.

Options

(a) Biotic (b) Abiotic (c) Man-made (d) Natural

18. Choose the correct statement(s) from the following.

I. The lithosphere is the solid crust or hard top layer of the Earth, consisting of rocks and minerals, and it provides land for various purposes.
II. The hydrosphere includes rivers, lakes, seas, oceans, and is vital for the survival of all living organisms on Earth.
III. The atmosphere is a thin layer of air held in place by the gravitational force of the Earth, protecting us from harmful rays and regulating Earth's weather and climate.

Codes

(a) I and II (b) Only I
(c) I and III (d) All of these

19. Choose the incorrect statement from the following.

I. Early humans were adapted to natural surroundings leading a simple life.
II. Lithosphere is thin layer of air that surrounds the earth.
III. Environment is combination of natural and human made phenomena.

Codes

(a) Only I (b) Only II
(c) Only III (d) None of these

Answers

1. (c)	2. (c)	3. (b)	4. (c)	5. (c)
6. (a)	7. (d)	8. (c)	9. (b)	10. (b)
11. (b)	12. (c)	13. (c)	14. (b)	15. (c)
16. (a)	17. (b)	18. (d)	19. (b)	

Match the Following

1.

List I	List II
A. Lithosphere	1. Protective air layer
B. Hydrosphere	2. Domain of water
C. Atmosphere	3. Earth's solid surface
D. Biosphere	4. Zone where life occurs

Codes

	A	B	C	D		A	B	C	D
(a)	1	3	2	4	(b)	3	2	1	4
(c)	1	4	3	2	(d)	1	2	4	3

2.

List I	List II
A. Natural Environment	1. Trade without money
B. Human Environment	2. Community of living and non-living elements
C. Ecosystem	3. Created by human interactions with surroundings
D. Barter System	4. Surroundings with natural elements and living organisms

Codes

	A	B	C	D		A	B	C	D
(a)	1	3	4	2	(b)	4	3	2	1
(c)	2	3	4	1	(d)	1	2	4	3

Ans. 1. (b) 2. (c)

Assertion-Reason

1. **Assertion** (A) The biosphere is also referred to as the 'living world.'

   Reason (R) Biosphere is the outermost solid surface of the Earth.

   Codes

   (a) Both the A and the R are true, and is the correct explanation of A
   (b) Both A and R are true, but R is not the correct explanation of R
   (c) A is true, but R is false
   (d) A is false, but R is true

2. **Assertion** (A) The human environment has evolved over time, driven by changing needs and innovations of human societies.

   Reason (R) Early humans initially adapted to their natural surroundings, but as their needs grew, they developed new technologies, such as agriculture, the wheel and the barter system.

   Codes

   (a) Both the A and the R are true, and is the correct explanation of A
   (b) Both A and R are true, but R is not the correct explanation of R
   (c) A is true, but R is false
   (d) A is false, but R is true

Ans. 1. (c) A is true, but R is false
2. (a) Both the A and the R are true, and is the correct explanation of A

Fill in the Blanks

1. .... is the solid crust or the hard top layer of the Earth.
2. Human beings modify .... according to their needs.
3. The gravitational force of the Earth holds the .... around it.
4. Trading of goods through exchange of goods is called ....
5. Environment is French word meaning ....

Ans. 1. Lithosphere 2. natural environment
3. atmosphere 4. barter system
5. neighbourhood

True/False

1. The natural environment includes both living and non-living elements.
2. The lithosphere comprises of various landforms like mountains, plateaus, plains and valleys.
3. The hydrosphere encompasses the domain of water on the Earth, including rivers, lakes, seas and oceans, and is not essential for the survival of living organisms.
4. The atmosphere, made up of gases like CO_2, O_2, and water vapour, plays a role in protecting the Earth from harmful rays and maintaining its climate.

Ans. 1. True 2. True
3. False 4. True

Picture Based Question

1. **In the given image people are exchanging goods without the use of money. What was this system called?**

(a) Gift system (b) Trade system
(c) Exchange system (d) Barter system

Ans. (d) Barter system

Case Based Question

1. **Read the passage given below and answer the questions that follow.**

In this bustling urban environment, a community of people resides in an area surrounded by high-rise buildings, busy streets, and various human-made structures, comprising what is commonly referred to as a "human-made environment". Over the years, they've witnessed substantial changes in their surroundings as the city has evolved. These changes may include increased urban development, technological advancements, and a higher population density. This urban community's environment is characterised by its vibrant, fast-paced lifestyle, the presence of various amenities and services, and a significant human influence on the landscape. It exemplifies how human interaction with the environment can lead to the development and transformation of urban spaces.

(i) **In what type of environment do the people in urban community primarily reside?**
(a) Biotic
(b) Abiotic
(c) Human-made
(d) Natural

(ii) **As the city has evolved, what could be one significant change that the community might have observed in their environment?**
(a) A decrease in pollution
(b) An increase in natural green spaces
(c) More urban development
(d) Decreased population

(iii) **What is the key characteristic of the environment in this urban community?**
(a) Presence of forests and wildlife
(b) Limited human influence
(c) High population density and human-made structures
(d) Absence of technological advancements

(iv) **What best describes the environment of the urban community surrounded by high-rise buildings and busy streets?**
(a) A natural environment with minimal human influence.
(b) A rural environment with a focus on agriculture and farming.
(c) A human-made environment shaped by urban development.
(d) An untouched wilderness with no human presence.

Ans. (i) (c) Human-made
(ii) (c) More urban development
(iii) (c) High population density and human-made structures
(iv) (c) A human-made environment shaped by urban development.

PART II

Very Short Answer Type Questions

1. **What is the meaning of the word 'environment', and why is it important?**

Ans. The word 'environment' comes from the French word 'environer,' meaning 'neighbourhood,' and it includes all surroundings that affect living organisms. It is important for supporting life and maintaining ecological balance.

2. **What are the four domains of the natural environment?**

Ans. The four domains of the natural environment are lithosphere (Earth's solid surface), hydrosphere (water bodies), atmosphere (protective air layer) and biosphere (the realm of living organisms).

3. **What constitutes an ecosystem? Give examples**

Ans. An ecosystem constitute the relationship between the biotic and abiotic components and with their environment. For example, oceans, lakes, rivers, mountains, deserts, forests, grasslands.

4. What is the primary purpose of World Environment Day? Competency Based

Ans. The primary purpose of World Environment Day is to raise awareness about environmental issues and promote environmental protection.

Short Answers Type Questions

1. What is the composition of the lithosphere? Also mention its characteristics and purpose.

Ans. The lithosphere is the solid crust or hard top layer of the Earth. It is made up of rocks and minerals and covered by a thin layer of soil.

The lithosphere is characterised by diverse landforms, including mountains, plateaus, plains, valleys, and more.

Lithosphere serves various purposes, such as providing land for forests, grasslands, agriculture, human settlements, and is a source of mineral wealth.

2. What is atmosphere? What the role of the atmosphere?

Ans. The atmosphere is a thin layer of air enveloping the Earth. The roles of atmosphere are as follows

The atmosphere acts as a protective shield. It protects us from harmful solar radiation and extreme heat from the Sun.

Atmosphere consists of a mixture of gases, dust particles, and water vapour. Changes within the atmosphere result in changes in weather and climate patterns.

3. Why should we protect our environment? Diksha

Ans. The protection of our environment is very important because it provides the necessary conditions for life, such as clean air, fresh water and food resources.

Moreover, the environment plays a crucial role in regulating global climate and weather patterns and acts as a natural defense against natural disasters.

4. How did early humans initially adapt to their natural surroundings and learn new ways to change their environment?

Ans. Early humans adapted themselves to the natural surroundings. They lived simple lives and fulfilled their requirements from the natural surroundings.

Over time humans learnt new ways to use and change their environment. They learnt to grow crops, domesticate animals and lead a settled life.

5. "Humans transition from a barter system to a trade and commerce system". Justify the statement. Competency Based

Ans. The shift from a barter system to a trade and commerce system was driven by the Industrial Revolution. With the coming up of mass production, there was a need for markets to exchange goods efficiently. As human requirements increased, a structured system of trade and commerce became essential as it enable goods to be readily available.

Long Answer Type Questions

1. Describe the various domains of the environment.

Ans. The environment consists of several distinct domains, each with its unique characteristics. These are discussed below

(i) **Lithosphere** The lithosphere is the solid crust or hard top layer of the Earth. It is made up of rocks and minerals and covered by a thin layer of soil.

(ii) **Hydrosphere** The hydrosphere is the domain of water. It includes various sources of water and water bodies like rivers, lakes, seas, oceans, etc.

(iii) **Atmosphere** The atmosphere is the thin layer of air surrounding the Earth. The gravitational force of the Earth holds the atmosphere around it. It protects us from harmful rays and excessive heat from the Sun.

(iv) **Biosphere** The biosphere or the living world consists of all living organisms, including both plant and animal kingdoms. It is a narrow zone on the Earth where land, water and air interact with each other to support life.

2. How have human beings adapted to their environment to meet their needs? Diksha

Ans. Human beings have adapted to their environment and modified it to meet their needs in the following ways

- Early humans led simple lives and were dependent on the natural environment for their requirements. They constructed shelters suitable for their environment, from huts and igloos to high-rise apartments as the population grew.
- Gradually, humans learned to grow crops, domesticate animals and engage in fishing to secure a stable food supply, adapting their practices to local soil and weather conditions.
- The invention of the wheel and the development of tools and machinery allowed for efficient resource utilisation and the emergence of a trade and commerce system.

- The Industrial Revolution brought about mass production, further enhancing the availability of goods.
- Advancements in transportation, from horse-riding to airplanes, facilitated the movement of people and goods.
- Innovations in information and communication technology, such as internet, have made information accessible to people worldwide.

3. "Ecosystem is formed by the interaction of all living organisms with each other and with the physical and chemical factors of the environment in which they live."

Explain about ecosystem and give reason why the balance between the interactions in ecosystem is crucial. **Competency Based**

Ans. An ecosystem is a complex system where all living organisms interact with one another and with the physical and chemical factors of their environment. This interaction involves the exchange of both energy and materials.

In simpler terms, an ecosystem is like a community of plants and animals living together in a particular place, and connected by shared resources and influencing each other's lives. The ecosystem could be large like rainforests, deserts and oceans or it could be small like lakes or ponds.

The balance of these interactions is crucial for the health and sustainability of the ecosystem, as any disturbance can have significant effects on the organisms and their environment.

Picture Based Question

1. Look at the picture given below and answer the following questions.

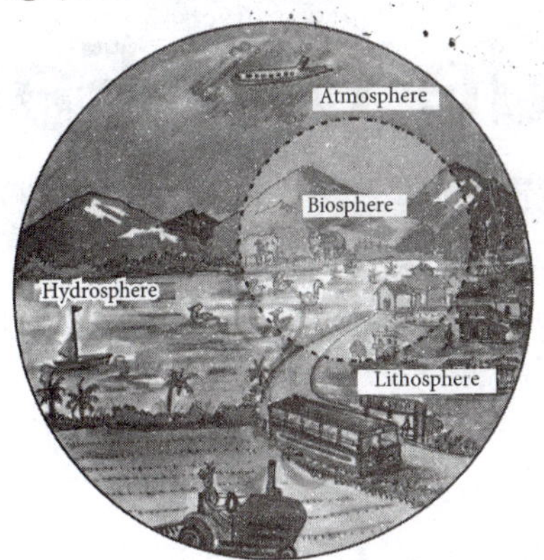

(i) Explain the interactions between the domain of natural environment for a balanced ecosystem.

Ans. In the image, the biosphere is represented by diverse plant and animal life, the lithosphere by the landforms, the hydrosphere by bodies of water and the atmosphere by the sky. Interactions among these components create a balanced ecosystem.

(ii) How do human activities affect this harmony in the picture?

Ans. Human activities, such as deforestation or pollution, can disrupt this hermony, e.g. deforestation harms the biosphere, affecting the balance of nature. Human actions play a crucial role in preserving or disturbing nature's harmony.

ASSESSMENT EXERCISE

Multiple Choice Questions (MCQs)

1. Which of the following is not an example of Biotic component?
   (a) Plants
   (b) Animals
   (c) Lands
   (d) Human
2. Which of the following is not a component of Lithosphere?
   (a) Rock (b) Minerals
   (c) Soil (d) Air
3. Living organism is the main constituent of which of the following domains?
   (a) Lithosphere
   (b) Atmosphere
   (c) Biosphere
   (d) Hydrosphere

Subjective Questions (VSA, SA & LA)

1. What are the components of hydrosphere?
2. Write a note about the constituents of atmosphere.
3. What are the consequences of the changes in atmospheric conditions?
4. How can we say that atmosphere plays an essential role in the sustenance of life?
5. What are factors of natural environment? Differentiate them.
6. What are the different landforms of lithosphere?
7. What are different steps of human development?
8. Explain different types of life support provided by the environment.
9. Human beings must learn to live and use their environment in sustainable ways. Explain the above statement.

Inside Our Earth

CHAPTER 2

The Earth is a dynamic planet. It is constantly undergoing changes from inside and outside. Both interior and exterior of the Earth consists of different types of rocks and minerals. In this chapter, we will discuss about the interior of Earth and the various rocks and minerals found in it.

2.1 Interior of the Earth

The Earth is made up of several **concentric** layers with one inside another just like an **onion**. The radius of the Earth is 6371 Kms.

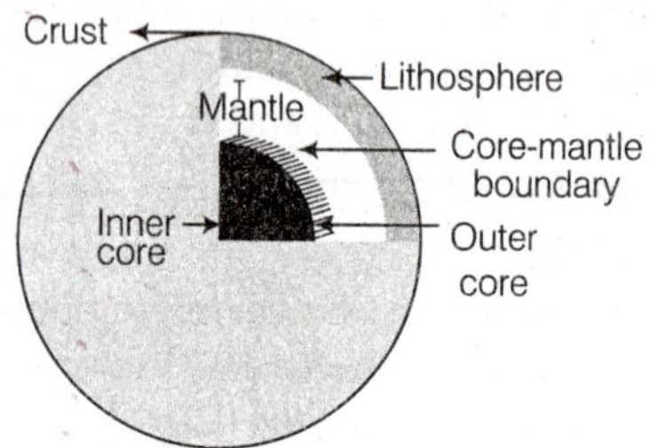

• Interior of the Earth

There are three layers of the Earth. These are

(i) **Crust** The uppermost layer over the Earth's surface is called the crust. It is the **thinnest** of all the layers. It is about 35 km on the continental masses and only 5 km on the ocean floors.

Continental mass mainly consists of Silica and Alumina thus it is called **SiAl** (Si-Silica and Al-Alumina).

The oceanic crust mainly consists of Silica and Magnesium, thus it is called **SiMa** (Si-Silica and Ma-Magnesium). The crust forms only 1 per cent of the volume of the Earth.

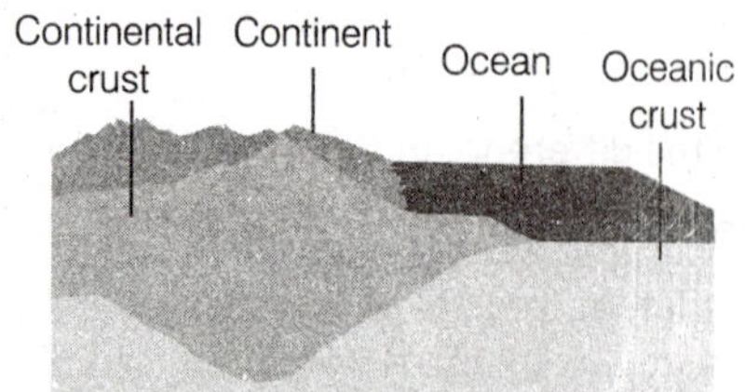

• Continental Crust and Oceanic Crust

(ii) **Mantle** It lies just below the crust and extends upto a depth of 2900 km below the crust. The mantle forms 84 per cent of the volume of the Earth.

(iii) **Core** The inner most layer of the Earth is called core. It has a radius of about 3500 km. It is made up of Nickel and Iron, thus it is called **NiFe** (Ni-Nickel and Fe-Ferrous i.e iron).

The central core has very high temperature and pressure. The core forms 15 per cent of the volume of the Earth.

KNOWLEDGE PLUS A person has to dig a hole 6000 km deep on the ocean floor to reach to the centre of the Earth.

2.2 Rocks and Minerals

The Earth's crust is made up of various types of rocks. Rocks are made up of different types of minerals. The rocks and minerals are discussed below

Rocks

Any natural mass of mineral matter that makes up the Earth's crust is called a **rock**. Rocks can be of different colour, size and texture.

There are three major types of rocks which are discussed below

1. Igneous Rocks

These rocks are formed when the molten **magma**[1] cools, and becomes solid. These are also called **primary rocks.** There are two types of **igneous**[2] rocks which are given below.

(i) **Intrusive Igneous Rocks** These rocks are formed when the molten magma cools down deep inside the Earth's crust and becomes solid. Since, they cool down slowly, they form large grains.

1 **Magma** It is molten rock present in the Earth's crust.
2 **Igneous** It is derived from Latin word 'Ignis' meaning 'fire'.

Granite is an example of intrusive igneous rock. It is used as grinding stones for preparing paste/powder of spices and grains.

(ii) **Extrusive Igneous Rocks** These rocks are formed when molten **lava**[3] coming on the Earth's surface rapidly cools down and becomes solid.

They have a very fine grained structure, e.g. basalt. The **Deccan plateau** is an example of basalt rocks.

2. Sedimentary Rocks

When the rocks rolled down, crack and hit each other, they are broken into small fragments or particles which are called **sediments**.

When these loose sediments are transported and deposited by wind, water, etc, they are compressed and hardened to form layers of rocks that are called **sedimentary**[4] rocks. For example, sandstone is made from grains of sand.

Sedimentary rocks may contain **fossils**[5] of dead plants, animals and other micro-organisms.

3. Metamorphic Rocks

When igneous and sedimentary rocks undergo great heat and pressure, they are changed into **metamorphic**[6] rocks. For example, clay changes into slate and limestone into marble.

Uses of Rocks

Rocks are very useful. The hard rocks are used for making roads, houses and buildings.

These are also used in many games like seven stones (pitthoo), hop-scotch (stapu/kit kit) and five stones (gitti).

Rock Cycle

One type of rock changes to another type under certain conditions in a cyclic manner. This process of transformation of the rock from one to another is called rock cycle.

The process of transformation in rock cycle is given below

- When the molten magma cools, it solidifies to become igneous rocks.
- When igneous rocks are broken down into small particles, they are transported and deposited to form sedimentary rocks.
- When the igneous and sedimentary rocks undergo heat and pressure, they change into **metamorphic** rocks.
- The metamorphic rocks which are still under great heat and pressure, melt down to form molten magma. This molten magma again can cool down and solidify into igneous rocks.

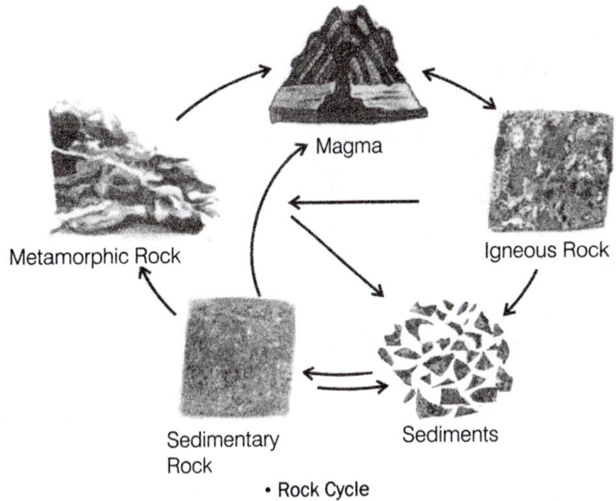

• Rock Cycle

Minerals

The naturally occurring substances which have certain physical properties and definite chemical composition are called minerals.

Minerals are used in industries (iron, aluminium, gold, uranium, etc), in medicine, in fertilisers, and as fuels like coal, natural gas and petroleum.

KNOWLEDGE PLUS The oil mine in South Africa is the **deepest mine** in the world.

---

3 **Lava** It is red molten magma coming out from the interior of the Earth on its surface.
4 **Sedimentary** It is derived from Latin word 'sedimentum' meaning 'settle down'.
5 **Fossils** They are remains of the dead plants and animals trapped in the layers of rocks.
6 **Metamorphic** It is derived from Greek word 'metamorphose' meaning 'change of form'.

INSIDE OUR EARTH

Minerals

Substances having certain physical properties and chemical composition, e.g. coal, natural gas, petroleum.

Interior of the Earth

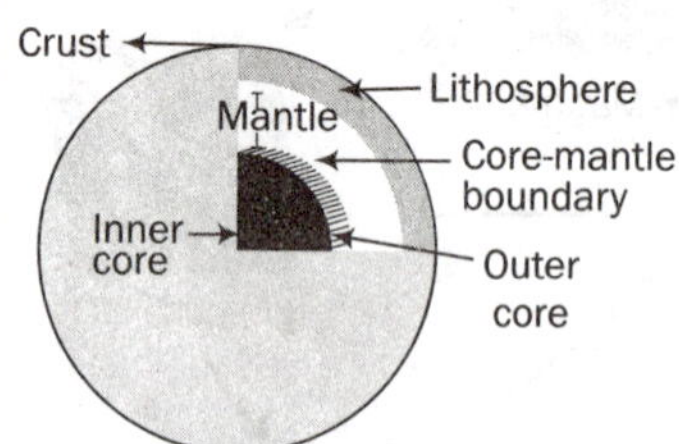

Mantle

- The layer below the crust, depth 2900 km below the crust.

Core

- The innermost layer of the Earth.
- **Depth** 3500 km
- **Composition** – NiFe (Ni-Nickel and Fe-Ferrous i.e. iron)

Crust

- Outermost layer of Earth surface.
- **Depth** 35 km on the continental masses and 5 km on the ocean floors continental mass.
- **Composition**–SiAl (Si-Silica and Alumina)
- **Oceanic crust**–SiMa (Si-Silica and Ma-Magnesium)

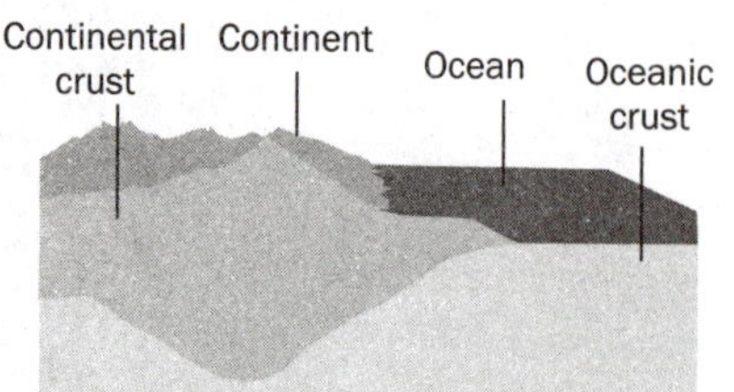

Rocks

- Any natural mass of mineral matter that makes up the Earth crust.

Rockcycle

- One type of rock changes to another type under certain conditions in a cyclic manner.

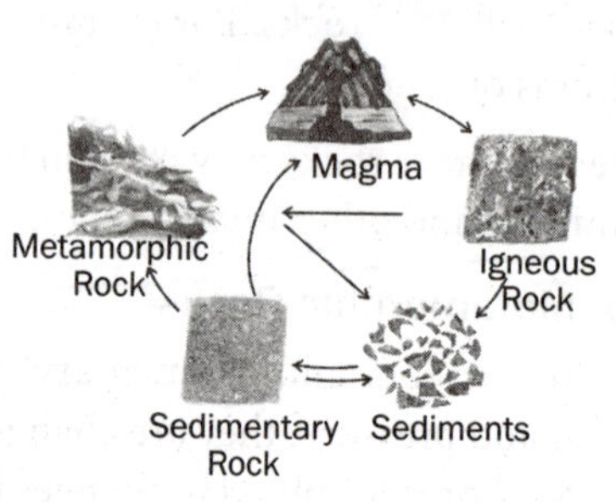

Types of Rocks

Igneous

- Formed when molten magma cools down and become solid.

Intrusive

Formed when molten magma cools down and solid inside the Earth crust. e.g. granite.

Extrusive

Formed when molten magma comes out on Earth surface and cools down and become solid, e.g. basalt.

Sedimentary

- Formed when looses sediments are compressed and hardened, e.g. sandstone.
- May contain fossils of dead plants, animals and other micro-organisms.

Metamorphic

- Formed when igneous and sedimentary rocks are under great heat and pressure e.g. limestone changes into marble.

NCERT FOLDER

Covering Intext Questions and Exercises of NCERT

NCERT ON PAGE 9-10

Q.1 Collect pictures of some monuments and find out which are the rocks used to build them.

Ans. The three pictures collected are

(a) The Taj Mahal which is made up of white marble.
(b) The Red Fort which is made up of red sandstone.
(c) The Humayun tomb which is made up of red sandstone.

Q.2 What are the minerals found in your state? Collect some samples to show in your class.

Ans. The minerals found in my state are coal, silica, limestone, clay, etc.

EXERCISES

Q.1 Answer the following questions.

(i) What are the three layers of the Earth?

Ans. Crust, mantle and core are the three layers of the Earth.

(ii) What is a rock?

Ans. Any natural mass of mineral matter that makes up the Earth's crust is called a rock.

(iii) Name three types of rocks.

Ans. The three major types of rocks are igneous rocks, sedimentary rocks and metamorphic rocks.

(iv) How are extrusive and intrusive rocks formed?

Ans. Extrusive igneous rocks are formed when molten lave coming on the Earth is surface rapidly cools down and becomes solid, e.g. basalt.

Intrusive igneous rocks are formed when the molten magma cools down deep inside the Earth's crust and becomes solid, e.g. granite.

(v) What do you mean by a rock cycle?

Ans. The process of transformation of the rock from one type to another in a cyclic manner, under certain conditions in is known as the rock cycle.

(vi) What are the uses of rocks?

Ans. Rocks are very useful to us. The hard rocks are used for making roads, houses and buildings.

(vii) What are metamorphic rocks?

Ans. When igneous and sedimentary rocks undergo great heat and pressure, they are changed into metamorphic rocks. For example, clay changes into slate and limestone into marble.

Q.2 Tick the correct answer.

(i) The rock which is made up of molten magma is
(a) igneous (b) sedimentary (c) metamorphic

(ii) The innermost layer of the Earth is
(a) crust (b) core (c) mantle

(iii) Gold, petroleum and coal are examples of
(a) rocks (b) minerals (c) fossils

(iv) Rocks which contain fossils are
(a) sedimentary rocks (b) metamorphic rocks
(c) igneous rocks

(v) The thinnest layer of the Earth is
(a) crust (b) mantle (c) core

Ans. (i) (a), (ii) (b), (iii) (b), (iv) (a), (v) (a)

Q.3 Match the following.

	List - I	List II
A.	Core	1. Earth's surface
B.	Minerals	2. Used for roads and buildings
C.	Rocks	3. Made of Silica and Alumina
D.	Clay	4. Has definite chemical composition
E.	SiAl	5. Innermost layer
		6. Changes into slate
		7. Process of transformation of the rock

Ans. A-5, B-4, C–1, D–6, E–3

Q.4 Give reasons

(a) We cannot go to the centre of the Earth.

Ans. We cannot go to the centre of the Earth as to reach the centre is not possible because one will have to dig a hole 6000 km deep in the ocean. Also, it has very high temperature and pressure.

(b) Sedimentary rocks are formed from sediments.

Ans. Sedimentary rocks are formed from sediments as when the rocks rolled down, crack and hit each other, they are broken into small fragments or particles called sediments. When these loose sediments are transported and deposited by wind, water, etc, they are compressed and hardened to form layers of rocks called sedimentary rocks.

(c) Limestone changes into marble.

Ans. Limestone which changes into marble when it undergoes great heat and pressure.

REVIEW EXERCISE

Including Competency Based Questions

Part I

Multiple Choice Questions (MCQs)

1. What is the radius of the Earth?

(a) 8371 km (b) 5371 km
(c) 4371 km (d) 6371 km

2. What is the primary composition of the continental crust?

(a) Silica and Alumina (SiAl)
(b) Silica and Magnesium (SiMa)
(c) Nickel and Iron (NiFe)
(d) Granite and Basalt

3. Name the minerals found in the oceanic crust. Diksha

(a) Silica and Aluminium
(b) Silica and Sodium
(c) Silica and Magnesium
(d) Silica and Sulphur

4. Which layer of the Earth forms 84 per cent of its volume and is located just beneath the crust?

(a) Crust (b) Mantle
(c) Core (d) Rock layer

5. What are the three major types of rocks found on Earth's crust?

(a) Primary rocks, Secondary Rocks, Tertiary rocks
(b) Igneous rocks, Sedimentary rocks, Metamorphic rocks
(c) Granite, Sandstone, Marble
(d) Magma rocks, Sediment rocks, Core rocks

6. Which type of igneous rock forms when molten magma cools deep inside the Earth's crust?

(a) Basalt
(b) Extrusive igneous rock
(c) Granite
(d) Sedimentary rock

7. The Earth's crust is composed of various types of rocks, including igneous, sedimentary and metamorphic rocks. These rocks undergo a continuous cycle of transformation. Given this information, which of the following statements is most accurate regarding the significance of the rock cycle? Competency Based

(a) The rock cycle helps us understand the formation of rocks, but does not have any practical implications.
(b) The rock cycle is essential for geological research, but has no relevance to everyday life.
(c) The rock cycle has significant practical applications, such as the source of construction materials and the study of Earth's history.
(d) The rock cycle is merely a theoretical concept and does not affect any real-world processes.

8. Laxmi, a geology enthusiast, is exploring a region with diverse rock formations. As she uncovers the secrets of the Earth's interior, which process in the rock cycle is she most likely to witness? Competency Based

(a) Observing the growth of new minerals on the Earth's surface.
(b) Documenting the cooling and solidification of molten magma.
(c) Studying the transport and deposition of small rock fragments by natural forces.
(d) Analysing the melting and reformation of rocks due to high heat and pressure.

9. What is the process called when metamorphic rocks melt and become molten magma, which later cools and solidifies into igneous rocks?

(a) Sedimentation (b) Rock transformation
(c) The rock cycle (d) Plate tectonics

10. Shubham, a resident from Pune, Maharashtra observed the increasing construction of buildings and infrastructure, many hard rocks are being used for road and building construction. What is the most likely consequence of this extensive use of hard rocks in construction in the near future? Competency Based

(a) Increased seismic activity in the region
(b) Soil erosion and degradation
(c) Enhanced availability of groundwater
(d) Depletion of natural rock resources

11. Identify the correct option that describes the type of rock given below.

(i) These rocks have a very fine grained structure.
(ii) These rocks are formed when lava comes out on Earth's surface and rapidly cools down and becomes solid.
(iii) Basalt is an example of these rocks.

Options

(a) Sedimentary rocks (b) Intrusive igneous rocks
(c) Extrusive igneous rocks (d) Metamorphic rocks.

12. **Identify the correct option that describes the type of which rock given below.** **Competency Based**

(i) They are formed, when the molten magma cools and becomes solid.

(ii) They are also known as 'primary rocks'.

(iii) There are two types of igneous rocks–intrusive rocks and extrusive rocks.

Options

(a) Sedimentary rocks (b) Metamorphic rocks
(c) Igneous rocks (d) None of the above

13. **Choose the correct statement(s) from the following.**

I. The deepest mine in the world is in South America.

II. The main mineral constituents of the continental mass are silica and magnesium.

III. Earth's structure can be divided into three main layers.

Codes

(a) Only I (b) I and III
(c) Only III (d) I, II and III

14. **Choose the incorrect statement(s) from the following.**

I. Crust is just beneath the mantle.

II. Metamorphic rocks contain fossils of plants.

III. The radius of the Earth is 8500 km.

Codes

(a) I and II (b) II and III
(c) Only II (d) I, II and III

Answers

1. (d) **2.** (a) **3.** (c) **4.** (b) **5.** (b)
6. (c) **7.** (c) **8.** (d) **9.** (c) **10.** (d)
11. (c) **12.** (c) **13.** (c) **14.** (d)

Match the Following

1.

List I	List II
A. Intrusive igneous rock	1. Forms large grains
B. Sedimentary rock	2. Made from grains of sand and contains fossils
C. Metamorphic rock	3. Changes due to great heat and pressure
D. Exposed to high heat	4. Forms from molten magma cooling rapidly

Codes

	A	B	C	D		A	B	C	D
(a)	4	3	1	2	(b)	2	1	3	4
(c)	4	2	3	1	(d)	4	1	3	2

2.

	List I		List II
A.	Earth's crust	1.	Forms the thinnest layer of the Earth's surface
B.	Mantle	2.	Extends up to 2900 km below the crust
C.	Core	3.	Made up of Nickel and Iron (NiFe)

Codes

	A	B	C		A	B	C
(a)	1	2	3	(b)	3	1	2
(c)	3	2	1	(d)	2	3	1

Ans. 1. (c) 2. (a)

Assertion-Reason

1. **Assertion** (A) The Earth's mantle constitutes the majority of its volume.

Reason (R) The mantle forms 84 per cent of the Earth's volume.

Codes

(a) Both A and R are true and R is the correct explanation of A
(b) Both A and R are true, but R is not the correct explanation of A
(c) A is true, but R is false
(d) A is false, but R is true

2. **Assertion** (A) Granite is an example of an extensive igneous rock with large grains.

Reason (R) Intrusive igneous rocks cool down slowly deep inside the Earth's crust, allowing for the formation of large grains.

Codes

(a) Both A and R are true and R is the correct explanation of A
(b) Both A and R are true, but R is not the correct explanation of A
(c) A is true, but R is false
(d) A is false, but R is true

Ans. 1. (a) Both A and R are true and R is the correct explanation of A

2. (d) A is false, but R is true

Fill in the Blanks

1. The deepest mine in the world is in ....

2. The crust forms only .... per cent of the volume of the Earth.

3. The remains of the dead plants and animals trapped in the layers of rocks are called ....

4. The Red Fort is made of ....

Ans. 1. South Africa 2. 1
3. fossils 4. red sandstone

True/False

1. The Deccan plateau is an example of intrusive igneous rocks.
2. Sedimentary rocks are formed from the cooling of molten magma.
3. Metamorphic rocks can be created from both igneous and sedimentary rocks through exposure to heat and pressure.
4. The process of transformation of rocks from one type to another is known as 'rock cycle'.

Ans. 1. False 2. False 3. True 4. True

Picture Based Questions

1. Image given below is of layer of continental and oceanic crust. What is height of oceanic crust?

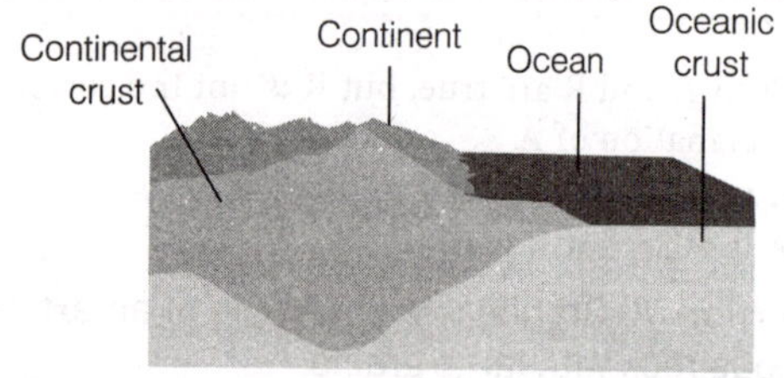

(a) 5 km (b) 15 km (c) 25 km (d) 35 km

2. The image given below is of rock cycle. Which rock is formed when high pressure and heat are applied on rocks?

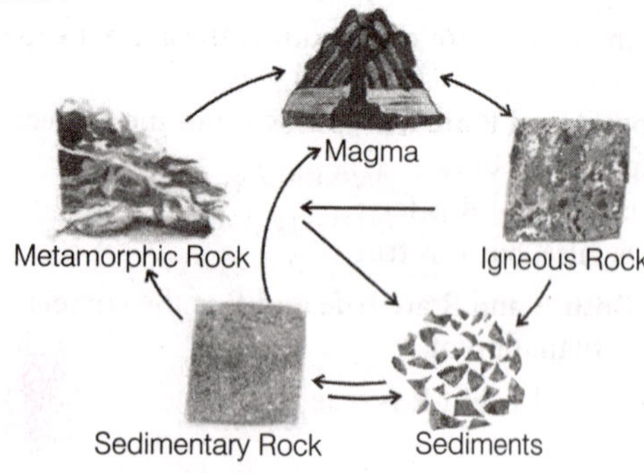

(a) Intrusive igneous rock
(b) Extrusive igneous rock
(c) Metamorphic rock
(d) Sedimentary rock

Ans. 1. (a) 5 km
2. (c) Metamorphic rock

Case Based Question

1. Read the passage given below and answer the following question.

Rocks are made up of different minerals. Minerals are naturally occurring substances which have certain physical properties and definite chemical composition. Minerals are very important to human kind. Some are used as fuels. For example, coal, natural gas and petroleum. They are also used in industries– iron, aluminium, gold, uranium, etc. in medicine, in fertilisers, etc.

(i) What are rocks primarily composed of?
(a) Organic materials (b) Minerals
(c) Gases (d) Water

(ii) Which of the following is not a characteristic of minerals?
(a) Crystalline structure
(b) Specific physical properties
(c) Naturally occurring
(d) Variable chemical composition

(iii) Which of the following minerals is used as fuel?
(a) Coal (b) Iron
(c) Mica (d) Gypsum

(iv) Which of the following is an example of industries in which minerals like iron, aluminium commonly are used?
(a) Agriculture
(b) Textiles
(c) Healthcare
(d) Automobiles

Ans. (i) (b) Minerals
(ii) (d) Variable chemical composition.
(iii) (a) Coal
(iv) (d) Automobiles

Part II

Very Short Answer Type Questions

1. What is the primary composition of the Earth's continental crust?

Ans. The continental crust is primarily composed of Silica and Alumina, giving it the name SiAl.

2. What are the two major constituents of the oceanic crust?

Ans. The two major constituents of the oceanic crust are Silica and Magnesium, making it SiMa.

3. How deep does the mantle extend below the Earth's crust?

Ans. The mantle extends to a depth of 2900 kilometers below the Earth's crust.

4. What are fossils?

Ans. Fossils are the remains of the dead plants and animals trapped in the layers of rocks.

5. Which type of igneous rock has a fine-grained structure and is an example of the Deccan plateau's rock composition? **Competency Based**

Ans. Basalt is an extrusive igneous rock which has a fine-grained structure and it is an example of the Deccan plateau's rock composition.

6. What are sediments?

Ans. Sediments are the small fragments or particles which are formed when rocks roll down, crack and hit each other.

7. What processes forms sedimentary rocks from small fragmented rocks transported and deposited by natural forces? **Competency Based**

Ans. The processes of compression and hardening of loose sediments forms sedimentary rocks from small fragmented rocks transported and deposited by wind, water and other natural forces.

8. What type of rocks can metamorphic rocks form from due to heat and pressure?

Ans. Metamorphic rocks can form from both igneous and sedimentary due to high heat and pressure.

9. What is the primary use of hard rocks in construction?

Ans. Hard rocks are commonly used in the construction of roads, houses, and buildings due to their durability and strength.

Short Answer Type Questions

1. Differentiate between igneous and metamorphic rocks.

Ans. The differences between igneous and metamorphic rocks are as follows

Igneous rocks	Metamorphic rocks
They are formed, when the molten magma cools and becomes solid.	They are formed due to great heat and pressure over igneous and sedimentary rocks.
For example, basalt and granite	For example, clay changes into slate and limestone into marble.

2. Name the types of igneous rocks and write one difference. **Diksha**

Ans The two types of igneous rocks are extrusive and intrusive igneous rocks.

A difference between the extrusive and intrusive igneous rocks is that extrusive igneous rocks are formed when molten lave coming on the Earth's surface rapidly cools down and becomes solid.

On the other hand, intrusive igneous rocks are formed when the molten magma cools down deep inside the Earth's crust and becomes solid.

3. "Rocks roll down, crack, and hit each other and are broken down into small fragments. These smaller particles are called sediments. These sediments are transported and deposited by wind, water, etc." **Competency Based**

How are sediments formed, and what processes are involved in their transportation and deposition?

Ans. Sediments are formed when rocks roll down, crack, and hit each other, breaking into small fragments. They are then transported and deposited by various natural agents such as wind and water. This process of sediment formation, transportation and deposition plays a crucial role in the formation of sedimentary rocks and the Earth's geological history.

4. What are minerals? How are they useful for mankind?

Ans. Minerals are naturally occurring substances which have certain physical properties and definite chemical composition.

Minerals are very important to humankind. Some are used as fuels. e.g. coal, natural gas and petroleum. They are also used in industries (iron, aluminium, gold, uranium, etc), in medicines, in fertilisers, etc.

5. Differentiate between rocks and minerals. **Competency Based**

Ans. Differences between rocks and minerals are

Rock	Minerals
They are an aggregate of minerals.	They are naturally occurring substance.
They do not have a definite chemical composition.	They have a definite chemical composition.
Rocks have wide range of physical properties such as colour, texture and size.	Minerals have certain physical properties such as hardness, crystal shape lustre.

Long Answer Type Questions

1. What are the primary differences between crust, mantle and core? Also, discuss about the composition of continental crust and oceanic crust.

Ans. The difference between crust, mantle and core are

Crust	Mantle	Core
It is the uppermost layer of the Earth.	It lies just below the crust.	It is the inner most layer of the Earth.
It is the thinnest layer and extend about 35 km on the continental masses and only 5 km on the ocean floors.	It extends upto a depth of 2900 km below the crust.	It has a radius of about 3500 km.
The crust forms only 1% of the volume of the Earth.	The mantle forms 84% of the volume of the Earth.	The core forms 15% of the volume of the Earth.

Continental mass mainly consists of Silica and Alumina mineral constituents, thus it is called sIaL (Si-Silica and Al-Alumina).

The oceanic crust mainly consists of Silica and Magnesium, thus it is called sImA (Si-Silica and Ma-Magnesium).

2. Discuss the various types of rocks in detail.

Ans. The various types of rocks are discussed below

- **Igneous Rocks** These rocks are formed when the molten magma cools, and becomes solid. These are also called primary rocks. There are two types of igneous rocks which are intrusive igneous rocks and extrusive igneous rocks.
- **Sedimentary Rocks** When the rocks roll down crack and hit each other, they are broken into small fragments or particles which are called sediments. When these loose sediments are transported and deposited by wind, water, etc, they are compressed and hardened to form layers of rocks that are called sedimentary rocks.
- **Metamorphic Rocks** When igneous and sedimentary rocks undergo great heat and pressure, they are changed into metamorphic rocks.

3. Give Brief about the rock cycle and process of transformation in rock cycle.

Or **"Rocks changes into another type under certain conditions in a cyclic manner". Explain this stater** Diksha

Ans. Rocks changes into another type under certain conditions in a cyclic manner. The process of transformation in rock cycle is given below

- When the molten magma cools, it solidifies to become igneous rocks.
- When igneous rocks are broken down into small particles, they are transported and deposited to form sedimentary rocks.
- When the igneous and sedimentary rocks undergo heat and pressure, they change into metamorphic rocks.
- The metamorphic rocks when are still under great heat and pressure, melt down to form molten magma. This molten magma again can cool down and solidify into igneous rocks.

Picture Based Question

1. Look at the picture given below and answer the questions that follow.

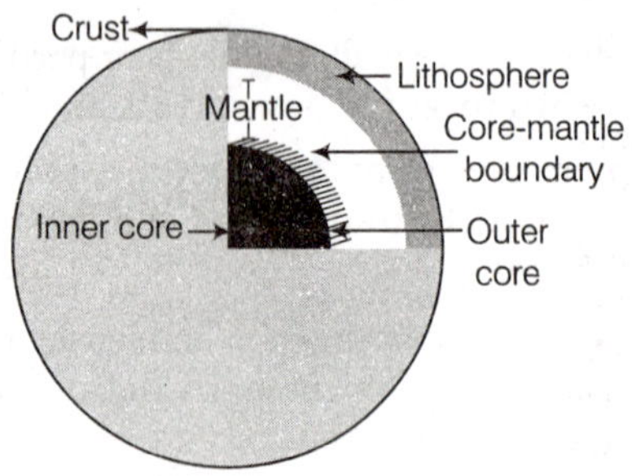

(i) Which layer of atmosphere is the thinnest among all?

Ans. Crust is the thinnest of all the layers.

(ii) What is the thickness of the Earth's crust?

Ans. The thickness of the crust varies, with it being about 35 km thick on continental land masses and only 5 km thick beneath the ocean floors.

(iii) Which layer experiences extremely high temperature and pressure conditions?

Ans. Core experiences extremely high temperatures and pressure conditions.

Case Based Question

1. Read the passage given below and answer the following questions.

The Earth's crust is made up of various types of rocks. There are three types of rocks i.e. igneous, sedimentary and metamorphic rocks. Any natural mass of mineral matter that makes up the crust is called rocks. Minerals are naturally occurring substances which have certain physical properties and definite chemical composition. Minerals are very important to humankind. Some are used as fuels.

For example, coal, natural gas and petroleum. They are also used in industries–iron, aluminium, gold, uranium, etc, in medicine, in fertilisers, etc.

(i) **What role do rocks play in supporting various industries? Give examples of minerals that are crucial for industrial uses.**

Ans. Rocks support the industries by providing essential minerals such as aluminium, gold, iron and uranium. These minerals play crucial roles in manufacturing as well as energy production.

(ii) **In addition to fuel, where are minerals such as iron, aluminium, gold and uranium, commonly used?**

Ans. In addition to fuel, the minerals such as iron, aluminium, uranium and gold, are used in making of medicines and fertilisers.

ASSESSMENT EXERCISE

Multiple Choice Questions (MCQs)

1. What is the thickness of the Earth's crust on continental mass?

(a) 35 km (b) 5 km
(c) 2 km (d) 30 km

2. Core is made-up of

(a) Silica-Alumina
(b) Silica-Magnesium
(c) Nickel-Iron
(d) Iron-Magnesium

3. Which of the following factors is responsible for the formation of metamorphic rocks?

(a) Heat
(b) Pressure
(c) Heat and Pressure
(d) Chemically

Subjective Questions (VSA, SA & LA)

1. What are the different layers of Earth?

2. Why igneous rocks are also known as primary rocks?

3. Why different types of rocks may vary in colour, size and texture?

4. Differentiate between intrusive and extrusive igneous rocks.

5. Write about the composition of different layers of Earth and its extension.

6. Explain the process of formation of sedimentary rocks and its example.

7. Briefly explain about

(a) SiAl (b) SiMa (c) NiFe

8. What are the uses of different types of rocks and minerals?

CHAPTER 3

Our Changing Earth

The outermost solid surface of the Earth is called lithosphere. The lithosphere is broken into a number of plates known as the lithospheric plates. The movement of these plates causes changes on the surface of the Earth.

These plates are moving very slowly (a few millimetres each year) because of the movement of the molten magma inside the Earth. The molten magma moves in a circular manner.

3.1 Evolution of Landforms

The evolution of various landforms are caused due to two types of Earth movements which are divided on the basis of the forces. These are

- **Endogenic forces** The forces which act in the interior of the Earth are called **endogenic**[1] forces.

  Endogenic forces sometimes produce sudden movements and sometimes slow movements. Sudden movements like earthquakes and volcanoes cause mass destruction over the surface of the Earth.
- **Exogenic forces** The forces that work on the surface of the Earth are called as **exogenic**[2] forces.

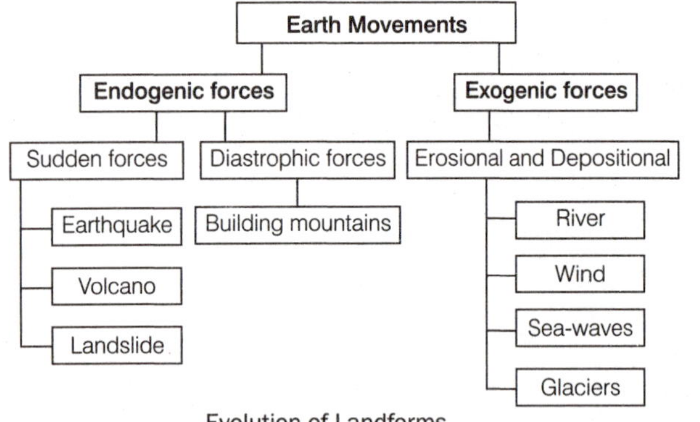

Evolution of Landforms

Volcano

A volcano is a **vent**[3] in the Earth's crust through which molten material erupts suddenly.

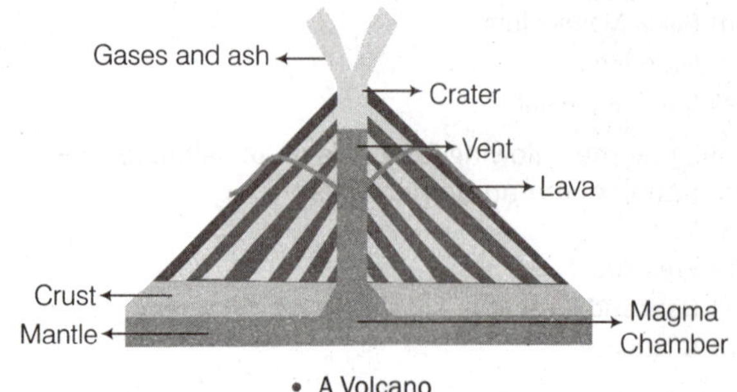

• A Volcano

Earthquake

Earthquakes are the vibration of the Earth's surface caused by the movements of the **lithospheric plates**[4]. These vibrations can travel all around the Earth.

The place in the crust where the movement starts is called the **focus**. The place on the surface above the focus is called the **epicentre**.

Vibrations travel outwards from the epicentre as waves. Greatest damage is usually observed near the epicentre and the strength of the earthquake decreases away from the centre.

There are three types of earthquake waves

(i) **P waves** or longitudinal waves

(ii) **S waves** or transverse waves

(iii) **L waves** or surface waves

Earthquakes are measured using a machine called **Seismograph**, and their magnitude is measured on the **Richter Scale**.

1 **Endogenic** It means inside origin (endo means inside and genic means origin).

2 **Exogenic** It means outside origin (exo means outside and genic means origin).

3 **Vent** A fissure or opening in the Earth's crust through which molten lava and gases erupt.

4 **Lithospheric Plates** These consists of several large and some small, rigid, irregularly-shaped plates (slabs) in the Earth's crust, which carry continents and the ocean floor.

KNOWLEDGE PLUS Earthquakes with a magnitude of 2.0 or less can be felt only a little while an earthquake over 5.0 can cause damage like falling of things. An Earthquake with a magnitude of 6.0 or higher is considered very strong, and an earthquake with a magnitude of 7.0 is classified as a major earthquake.

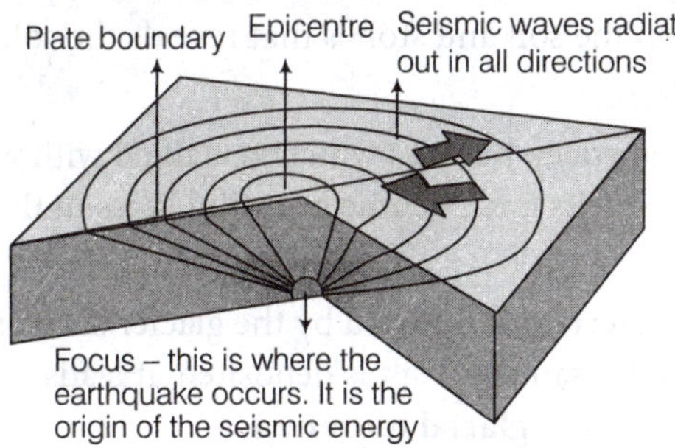

• Origin of an Earthquake

Preparedness for Earthquake

Earthquakes cannot be predicted, however their impact can certainly be minimised, by preparing for it in advance.

Some common earthquake prediction methods adopted locally by people include studying animal behaviour, for example, fish in the ponds get agitated, snakes come to the surface, etc.

Some measures that can be adopted for minimising the damage from an earthquake are

- **Choosing a safe spot** like under a kitchen counter, table or desk, against an inside corner or wall.
- **Staying away** from fire places, areas around chimneys, windows that shatter including mirrors and picture frames.
- **Being prepared** by spreading awareness amongst friends and family members.

3.1 Major Landforms

The landscape is being continuously worn away or eroded by two processes which are given below

(i) **Weathering** It is the breaking up of the rocks on the Earth's surface.

(ii) **Erosion** It is the wearing away of the landscape by different agents like water, wind and ice.

The eroded material is transported by water, wind, etc and is later deposited.

This process of erosion and deposition create various landforms on the Earth's surface.

Work of a River

The running water in the river erodes the landscape, through which various landforms are formed. The following landforms are created by the work of river

- **Waterfall** When the river fall down suddenly at steep angle over very hard rocks or down a steep valley side, it forms a **waterfall.**
- **Meander** It is a large bend formed by twisting and turning of the river, while it enters the plain.
- **Ox-bow Lake** With the continuous erosion and deposition along the sides of the meander, the ends of the meander loop come closer. When the meander loop cuts-off from the river, it forms a cut-off lake, which is called an ox-box lake.
- **Flood Plains** When the river overflows its banks, it leads to the flooding of the neighbouring areas. During this flooding, the river deposits layers of fine soil and other material (sediments) along its banks. This leads to the formation of a flat fertile which is called flood plain.
- **Levees** The raised banks of the rivers formed due to their overflow are called levees.

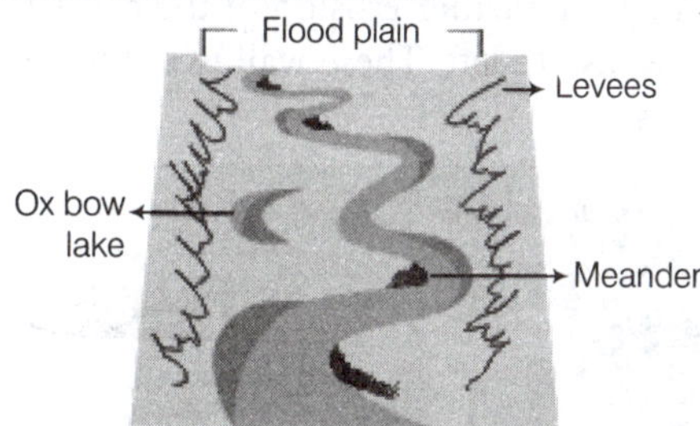

• Features made by a River in a Flood Plain

- **Distributaries** When the river approaches the sea, the speed of the flowing water decreases and the river begins to break up into a number of streams which are called distributaries.
- **Delta** After distributaries of a river are formed, the river becomes so slow that it begins to deposit its load. As a result, each distributary forms its own mouth and the collection of sediments from all these distributaries forms a delta.

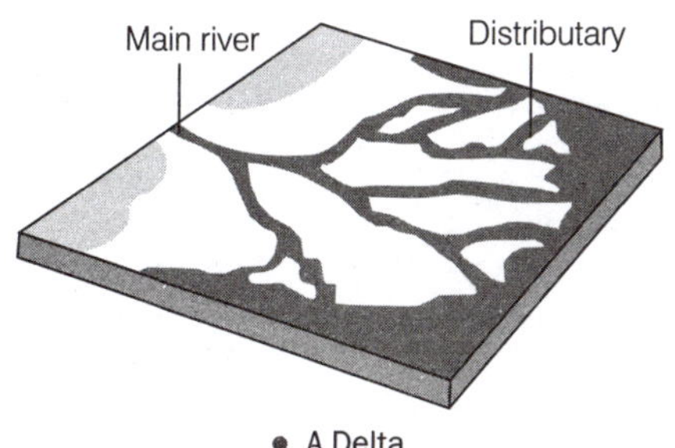

• A Delta

Waterfalls in the World

In the world, there are many small waterfalls. The **highest waterfall** is **Angel Falls** in Venezuela, South America.

Other notable waterfalls include Niagara Falls, situated on the border between Canada and the USA in North America, and Victoria Falls, located on the borders of Zambia and Zimbabwe in Africa.

Work of Sea Waves

The erosion and **deposition**[5] of the sea waves create coastal landforms. The following landforms are created by the work of sea waves

- **Sea Caves** When the sea waves continuously strike at the rocks, cracks are developed in the rocks which become larger and wider over time. This leads to the formation of hollow like caves which are called sea caves.
- **Sea Arches** These are formed when **sea cavities** or sea caves become bigger and only the roof of the caves is left.
- **Stacks** When the further erosion of the caves breaks its roof, only walls are left. These wall like features are called stacks.

• Features made by Sea Waves

- **Sea Cliff** The steep rocky coast rising almost vertically above sea water is called sea cliff.
- **Beaches** These are formed when sea waves deposit sediments along the shores.

Work of Ice

Glaciers are rivers of ice which erode the landscape by tearing down the soil and stones that reveals the solid rock below.

Glaciers create deep hollows which gets filled with water when the ice melts and become beautiful lakes in the mountains.

When the material transported by the glacier such as rocks (big and small), sand and silt is deposited, it leads to the formation of **glacial moraines**.

Work of Wind

Wind is an active agent of erosion and deposition in the deserts. The following landforms are created by the work of wind

- **Mushroom Rocks** These are the rocks found in deserts in the shape of a mushroom. These rocks have narrower base and wider top because the winds erode the lower section of the rock more than the upper part.
- **Sand Dunes** When the wind blows, it lifts and transports sand from one place to another. When it stops blowing, the sand falls and gets deposited in low hill-like structures. These are called sand dunes.
- **Loess** When the grains of sand are very fine and light, the wind can carry it over very long distances. When such sand is deposited in large areas, it is called oess. For example, large deposits of loess are found in China.

5 Deposition It refers to the larying down of sediment carried by wind, flowing water, sea or ice.

OUR CHANGING EARTH

Earth Movement

Endogenic Forces
Forces acting in the interior of the Earth

- **Diastrophic forces**
  - Building Mountains
- **Sudden forces**
  - **Landslide**
  - **Volcano**
    An opening in the Earth's crust through which molten material erupts suddenly

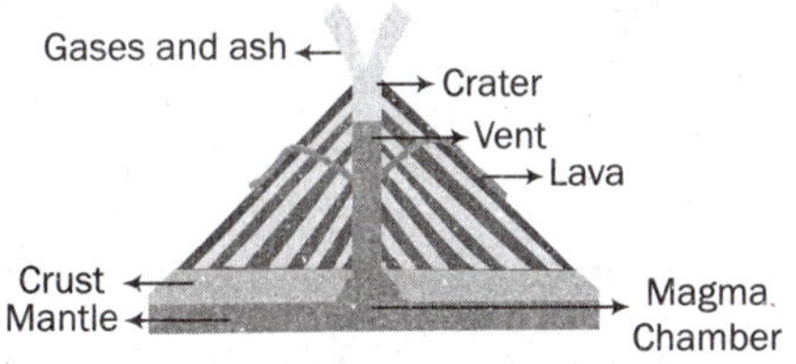

    Gases and ash
    Crater
    Vent
    Lava
    Crust
    Mantle
    Magma Chamber
  - **Earthquake**
    Vibration of the Earth's surface caused by the movements of the lithospheric plates

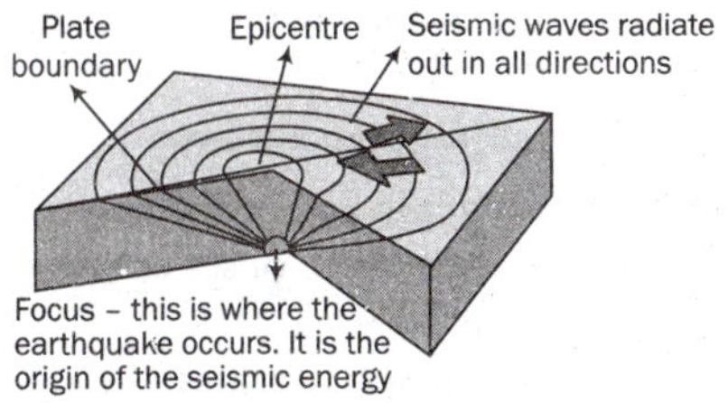

    Plate boundary
    Epicentre
    Seismic waves radiate out in all directions
    Focus – this is where the earthquake occurs. It is the origin of the seismic energy

    - **Types of Earthquake Wave**
      - P waves (Longitudinal waves)
      - S waves (Transverse wave)
      - L waves (Surface waves)

Exogenic Forces
Forces acting on the surface of the Earth

- **Weathering**
  Breaking up of the rocks on the Earth's surface
- **Erosional and Depositional Landforms**
  - **River**
    Landforms formed waterfall, meanders, ox-bow lake, flood plain, leaves, delta.

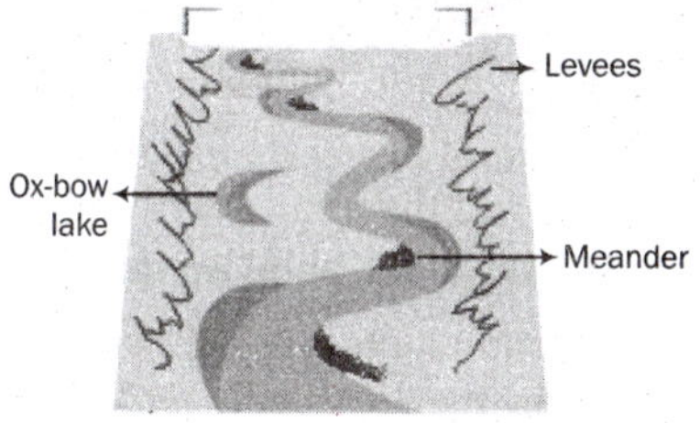

    Levees
    Ox-bow lake
    Meander
  - **Glaciers**
    Landforms formed glacial moraines
  - **Wind**
    Landforms formed : mushroom rocks, sand dunes, loess
  - **Sea Waves**
    Landforms formed : sea caves, sea arches, stacks, sea cliff

    Stack
    Sea arch
    Sea cave

NCERT FOLDER

Covering Intext Questions and Exercises of NCERT

NCERT ON PAGE 16

Q.1 Find out the names of a few rivers of the world that form a delta.

Ans. Name of some rivers that form a delta are Ganga, Amazon, Nile, Salwin, Indus , Narmada and Mississippi river.

EXERCISES

Q.1 Answer the following questions.

(a) Why do the plates move?

Ans. The plates are moving because of the movement of molten magma inside the Earth.

(b) What are exogenic and endogenic forces?

Ans. Endogenic forces are those forces which act in the interior of the Earth. Exogenic forces are those forces that work on the surface of the Earth.

(c) What is erosion?

Ans. Erosion is the wearing away of the landscape by different agents like water, wind and ice.

(d) How are flood plains formed?

Ans. Flood plains are formed by the deposition of fine soil and other materials through floods.

(e) What are sand dunes?

Ans. Sand dunes are hill-like structures which are formed by the deposition of blowing wind in deserts.

(f) How are beaches formed?

Ans. Beaches are formed by the deposition of sediments along the sea shores through the sea waves.

(g) What are ox-bow lakes?

Ans. An ox-bow lake is a cut-off lake formed due to cut-off of a meander loop.

Q.2 Tick the correct answer.

1. Which is not an erosional feature of sea waves?
   (a) Cliff (b) Beach (c) Sea cave
2. The depositional feature of a glacier is ....
   (a) flood plain (b) beach (c) moraine
3. Which is caused by the sudden movements of the Earth?
   (a) Earthquake (b) Folding (c) Flood plain
4. Mushroom rocks are found in ....
   (a) deserts (b) river valleys (c) glaciers
5. Ox-bow lakes are found in ....
   (a) glaciers (b) river valleys (c) deserts

Ans. 1–(b), 2–(c), 3–(a), 4–(a), 5–(b)

Q.3 Match the following.

List I	List II
A. Glacier	1. Sea shore
B. Meanders	2. Mushroom rock
C. Beach	3. River of ice
D. Sand dunes	4. Rivers
E. Waterfall	5. Vibrations of Earth
F. Earthquake	6. Sea cliff
	7. Hard bed rock
	8. Deserts

Ans. A–3, B–6 , C–1, D–8, E–4, F–5

Q.4 Give reasons.

(a) Some rocks have a shape of a mushroom.

Ans. In deserts, rocks are in the shape of a mushroom due to active agent of erosion and deposition by winds. Winds erode the lower section of the rock more than the upper part. Therefore, such rocks have narrower base and wider top.

(b) Flood plains are very fertile.

Ans. Flood plains are fertile because rivers deposit layers of fine soil and sediments along the plains during flooding.

(c) Sea caves are turned into stacks.

Ans. Sea caves are turned into stacks due to erosion by the sea waves that break the roof of sea arches which was formed from sea caves.

(d) Buildings collapse due to earthquakes.

Ans. Most of the time building collapse due to the vibration of the earthquakes as they have structural weakness and inadequate earthquake-resistant designs.

NCERT ON PAGE 19

Q.1 For Fun

Solve the crossword puzzle with the help of given clues.

Across

2. Loop like the bend of river
4. Solid form of water
7. Moving mass of ice
9. Sudden descent of water in the bed of a river
11. Natural cavity on weak rocks formed by action of waves
12. Embankment on a river that keeps it in its channel
13. Large body of sea water
14. Dry area where sand dunes are found
15. Small hill of sand caused by the action of the wind
16. Flat plain formed by river deposits during time of blood

Down

1. Rise and fall of water caused by friction of wind on water surface
3. Flow of water in a channel
5. Steep perpendicular face of a rock along a sea coast
6. Debris of boulder and coarse material carried by glacier
8. Crescent shaped lake formed by a meandering river
10. Fine sand deposited by the action of the wind
13. Isolated mass of rising steep rock near a coastline
14. Alluvial tracts of land formed by the river deposits at the mouth of a river.

Ans. Across

2. Meander 4. Ice 7. Glacier
9. Waterfall 11. Cave 12. Levee
13. Sea 4. Desert 15. Sand dune
16. Flood plain

Down

1. Tide 3. River 5. Cliff
6. Moraine 8. Ox-bow lake 10. Loess
13. Stack 14. Delta

2. Observe the photographs given below. These are various features made by a river. Identify them and also tell whether they are erosional or depositional or landforms formed by both.

Photograph	Name of the Feature	Type (Erosional , Depositional or Both)
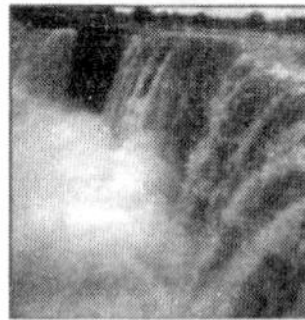		
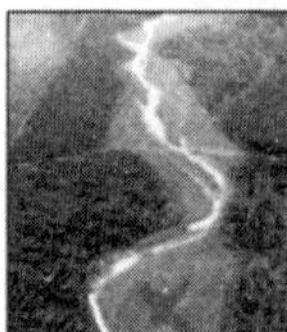		

Ans.

Photograph	Name	Type
1st Photograph	Waterfall	Erosional and
2nd Photograph	Meander	Erosional and depositional
3rd Photograph	Flood plain	Depositional

REVIEW EXERCISE

Including Competency Based Questions

PART I

Multiple Choice Questions (MCQs)

1. What is the main cause of the movement of lithospheric plates?

(a) Erosion (b) Wind
(c) Molten Magma (d) Glaciers

2. Which type of forces act in the interior of the Earth?

(a) Exogenic forces (b) Wind forces
(c) Endogenic forces (d) Oceanic forces

3. Which of the following is not caused by endogenic forces?

(a) Volcano (b) Earthquake
(c) Weathering (d) Magma chamber

4. Rakesh, a student of 7th class is observing a river flowing through a hilly region. The river is actively eroding the landscape. Which type of forces is primarily responsible for this? Competency Based

(a) Exogenic forces (b) Endogenic forces
(c) Atmospheric forces (d) Cosmic forces

5. What are the three types of earthquake waves?

(a) X waves, Y waves, Z waves
(b) Primary waves, Secondary waves, Tertiary waves
(c) P waves, S waves, L waves
(d) Tectonic waves, Surface waves, Subsurface waves

6. Which of the following is not a common earthquake prediction method, adopted by local people ? Diksha

(a) Abnormal animal behaviour
(b) Fish in the ponds get agitated
(c) Snakes come to the surface
(d) Children start crying

7. The place from where the movement of earthquake originates is known as .... Diksha

(a) vent (b) epicentre (c) focus (d) crater

8. What is the instrument used to measure earthquakes, and how is their magnitude assessed?

(a) Thermometer; on the Beaufort Scale
(b) Barometer; by the Mercalli Intensity Scale
(c) Seismograph; on the Richter Scale
(d) Wind vane; by the Fujita Scale

9. The most significant, recent earthquakes affecting Morocco were in 1994, 2004 and 2016, with magnitudes ranging between 6.0 and 6.3. These occured in the most seismically active region in Morocco and also in the Western Mediterranean region.

Source Live Science

Which scale is used to measure the magnitude of earthquake? Competency Based

(a) Likert Scale (b) Nominal Scale
(c) Richter Scale (d) Thurtstone Scale

10. What was the magnitude of the earthquake in Richter scale that hit Bhuj on 26th January 2001? Diksha

(a) 6.9 (b) 5.0 (c) 2.0 (d) 4.9

11. Madhusudan, 24 year young student belongs to the coastal area of Kerala state. His area is famous for clean beaches but it is most famous for natural sea caves and sea arches. Accordingly, which geological process is most responsible for the formation of sea caves, sea arches, and sea stacks along the coastline? Competency Based

(a) Glacial erosion (b) River deposition
(c) Wind erosion (d) Sea wave erosion

12. Which of the following coastal landforms is formed by the continuous striking of sea waves at the rocks over time?

(a) Sea caves (b) Glacial moraines
(c) Mushroom rocks (d) Levees

13. The sea waves deposit sediments along the shore forming are .... Diksha

(a) beaches (b) moraines
(c) sea caves (d) meanders

14. Moraines are the deposition features formed by .... Diksha

(a) glaciers (b) rivers
(c) wind (d) sea

15. Choose the correct statements from the following.

I. There are two types of earthquake waves.
II. Endogenic forces are internal forces.
III. The place in the crust where the movement starts is called the epicentre.

Codes

(a) Only I (b) Only II (c) II and III (d) I, II and III

16. Choose the incorrect statements from the following.

I. P waves are also called the longitudinal waves.
II. The strength of the earthquake increases away from the centre.
III. The magnitude of earthquake is measured by Vernier scale.

Codes

(a) Only I (b) Only II (c) II and III (d) I and II

17. **Identify the correct option that describes the type of term given below.** **Competency Based Ques.**

(i) It continuously strike at the rocks.

(ii) It deposits sediments along the shores forming beaches

(iii) It's erosion and deposition gives rise to coastal landforms.

Options

(a) Waterfall (b) Meander

(c) Sea cave (d) Glacial moraine

Answers

1. (c)	**2.** (c)	**3.** (c)	**4.** (a)	**5.** (c)
6. (d)	**7.** (c)	**8.** (c)	**9.** (c)	**10.** (a)
11. (d)	**12.** (a)	**13.** (a)	**14.** (a)	**15.** (b)
16. (c)	**17.** (c)			

Match the Following

1.

List I (Landforms)	List II (Description)
A. Waterfall	1. Hollow like caves formed by sea wave striking rocks
B. Meander	2. Large bend formed by twisting and turning of a river
C. Flood plain	3. Flat-fertile plain formed by the deposition of sediments
D. Sea caves	4. Low hill-like structures formed by wind deposition
E. Mushroom rocks	5. Formed when a river tumbles at a steep angle over hard rocks

Codes

	A	B	C	D	E		A	B	C	D	E
(a)	5	1	2	3	4	(b)	4	1	2	3	5
(c)	5	2	3	1	4	(d)	5	4	3	2	1

2.

List I	List II
A. Sudden forces	1. Vibration
B. Earthquake	2. River of ice
C. Glacier	3. Desert
D. Mushroom rocks	4. landslides
E. Ox-bow lakes	5. River Valley

Codes

	A	B	C	D	E		A	B	C	D	E
(a)	5	1	2	4	3	(b)	1	2	3	4	5
(c)	4	1	2	3	5	(d)	5	4	3	2	1

Ans. 1. (c) 2. (c)

Assertion-Reason

1. **Assertion** (A) The lithosphere is divided into several plates, and their movement is caused by the circulation of molten magma within the Earth.

Reason (R) The movement of molten magma within the Earth creates forces known as endogenic and exogenic forces, which lead to the creation of landforms and natural phenomena.

Codes

(a) Both A and R are true and R is the correct explanation of A

(b) Both A and R are true, but R is not the correct explanation of A

(c) A is true, but R is false

(d) A is false, but R is true

2. **Assertion** (A) Glaciers does not create deep hollows in their path and form picturesque mountain lakes as they push soil and stones aside.

Reason (R) Glacial moraines are formed when material transported by glaciers is deposited, leading to the creation of various landforms.

Codes

(a) Both A and R are true and R is the correct explanation of A

(b) Both A and R are true, but R is not the correct explanation of A

(c) A is true, but R is false

(d) A is false, but R is true

Ans. 1. (a) Both A and R are true and R is the correct explanation of A

2. (d) A is false, but R is true

Fill in the Blanks

1. The lithosphere is broken into a number of plates known as the ....

2. The Earth movements are divided on the basis of the .... which cause them.

3. A .... is a vent (opening) in the Earth's crust through which molten material erupts suddenly.

4. The place on the surface above the focus is called the ....

5. An .... is measured with a machine called a seismograph.

Ans. 1. lithospheric plates 2. forces

3. volcano 4. epicentre

5. earthquake

True/False

1. The lithosphere is divided into plates due to the movement of molten magma inside the Earth.
2. Endogenic forces primarily cause slow, gradual movements and are responsible for landforms like earthquakes and volcanoes.
3. The Richter scale is used to measure the intensity of earthquakes, and a magnitude of 2.0 or less is considered very strong.
4. Rivers can create landforms such as waterfalls, meanders, flood plains and levees through erosion and deposition.
5. Glaciers erode the landscape by revealing the underlying solid rock and the material transported by glaciers can lead to the formation of glacial moraines.

Ans. 1. True 2. False 3. False 4. True 5. True

Picture Based Questions

1. **The image given below is of a glacier. What are called deposits when material carried by the glacier gets deposited?**

(a) Stacks (b) Moraines
(c) Delta (d) Loess

2. **As shown in image given below river break upto streams, what is known as collection of sediments from all streams mouths?**

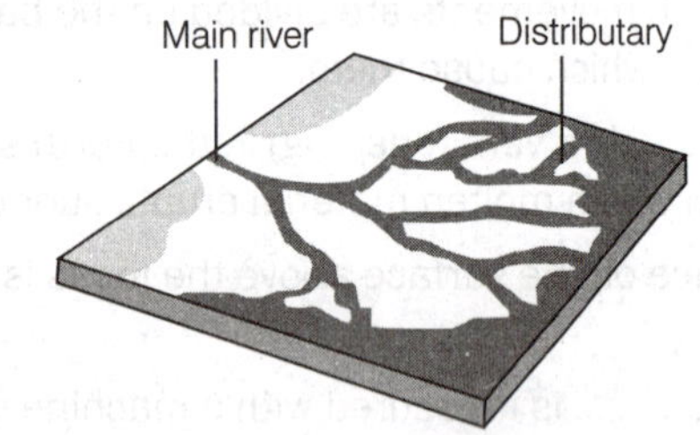

(a) Delta (b) Arches
(c) Moraines (d) Dunes

Ans. 1. (b) Moraines 2. (a) Delta

Case Based Question

1. **Read the passage given below and answer the following questions.**

The running water in the river erodes the landscape. When the river tumbles at steep angle over very hard rocks or down a steep valley side it forms a waterfall. As the river enters the plain it twists and turns forming large bends known as meanders. Due to continuous erosion and deposition along the sides of the meander, the ends of the meander loop come closer and closer. In due course of time, the meander loop cuts off from the river and forms a cut-off lake, also called an ox-bow lake. At times the river overflows its banks. This leads to the flooding of the neighbouring areas. As it floods, it deposits layers of fine soil and other material called sediments along its banks.

This leads to the formation of a flat fertile floodplain. The raised banks are called levees. As the river approaches the sea, the speed of the flowing water decreases and the river begins to break up into a number of streams called distributaries. The river becomes so slow that it begins to deposit its load. Each distributary forms its own mouth. The collection of sediments from all the mouths forms a delta.

(i) **What is formed when a river tumbles at a steep angle over hard rocks or down a steep valley side?**
(a) Floodplain (b) Meander
(c) Waterfall (d) Levee

(ii) **What is the term for large bends in a river formed as it enters the plain and twists and turns?**
(a) Levee (b) Delta
(c) Meander (d) Sediment

(iii) **What is the result of continuous erosion and deposition along the sides of a meander loop?**
(a) Formation of a waterfall
(b) Creation of an ox-bow lake
(c) Flooding of neighbouring areas
(d) Development of levees

(iv) **What is the term for the flat, fertile plain formed by the deposition of fine soil and sediments during river flooding?**
(a) Delta (b) Floodplain
(c) Meander (d) Distributary

Ans. (i) (c) Waterfall
(ii) (c) Meander
(iii) (b) Creation of an ox-bow lake
(iv) (b) Floodplain

PART II

Very Short Answer Type Questions

1. What do you understand by volcano?

Ans. A volcano is a vent or opening in the Earth's crust through which molten material erupts suddenly.

2. What are the three types of earthquake waves?

Ans. The three types of earthquake waves are P waves (longitudinal waves), S waves (transverse waves), and L waves (surface waves).

3. What is the focus and epicenter of an earthquake?

Ans. The focus is the point in the Earth's crust where the earthquake's movement starts, and the epicenter is the point on the Earth's surface directly above the focus.

4. How are earthquakes measured, and what is the Richter scale used for?

Ans. Earthquakes are measured using a seismograph, and the Richter scale is used to assess their magnitude.

5. What is the highest waterfall in the world, and where is it located?

Ans. The highest waterfall in the world is Angel Falls, located in Venezuela, South America.

6. What landforms are created by the work of sea waves ?

Ans. Coastal landforms created by sea waves include sea caves, sea arches, stacks, sea cliffs, and beaches.

7. What do you understand by delta?

Ans. After distributaries of a river are formed, the river becomes so slow that it begins to deposit its load. As a result, each distributary forms its own mouth and the collection of sediments from all these distributaries forms a delta.

Short Answer Type Questions

1. Explain about the Earth movements on the surface of the Earth.

Ans. The movement of lithospheric movement led to changes over the surface of the Earth. The plates are moving very slowly (a few millimetres each year) because of the movement of the molten magma inside the Earth.

There are two types of Earth movements which are divided on the basis of the forces. These are

- **Endogenic forces** The forces which act in the interior of the Earth are called endogenic forces.
- **Exogenic forces** The forces that work on the surface of the Earth are called as exogenic forces.

2. What are endogenic forces, and how do they affect the Earth's surface?

Ans. Endogenic forces are geological forces that originate from within the Earth's interior.

These forces lead to various dynamic processes, including earthquakes and volcanic eruptions. Earthquakes occur due to the sudden release of energy along faults in the Earth's crust, resulting in the shaking of the Earth's surface.

Volcanic eruptions are caused by the upward movement of molten magma from the Earth's mantle, leading to the formation of volcanic vents.

Endogenic forces play a crucial role in shaping the Earth's surface by creating landforms, impacting landscapes and, at times, causing widespread destruction.

3. Define earthquake. What are some common earthquake prediction methods?

Ans. Earthquakes are the vibration of the Earth's surface caused by the movements of the lithospheric plates. These vibrations can travel all around the Earth.

Some common earthquake prediction methods adopted locally by people include studying animal behaviour, for example, fish in the ponds get agitated, snakes come to the surface, etc.

4. How is the magnitude of earthquake is measured? Mention the damage cause by an earthquake on the basis of its magnitude.

Ans. The magnitude of earthquake is measured on the Richter Scale.

Earthquakes with a magnitude of 2.0 or less can be felt only a little while an earthquake over 5.0 can cause damage like falling of things.

An Earthquake with a magnitude of 6.0 or higher is considered very strong, and an earthquake with a magnitude of 7.0 is classified as a major earthquake.

5. Explain the term weathering, erosion and deposition. Diksha

Ans. **Weathering** is the process of breaking down rocks on the Earth's surface.

Erosion is the wearing away of the landscape by agents such as water, wind and ice. It involves the transport of eroded material.

Deposition refers to the laying down of sediment carried by wind, flowing water, sea or ice.

6. How an ox-bow lake is formed?

Ans. With the continuous erosion and deposition along the sides of the meander, the ends of the meander loop come closer. When the meander loop cuts-off from the river, it forms a cut-off lake, which is called an ox-box lake.

7. How do glaciers contribute to the formation of landforms, and what are glacial moraines?

Ans. Glaciers are rivers of ice which erode the landscape by tearing down the soil and stones that reveals the solid rock below.

Glaciers create deep hollows which gets filled with water when the ice melts and become beautiful lakes in the mountains.

When the material transported by the glacier such as rocks (big and small), sand and silt is deposited, it leads to the formation of glacial moraines.

Long Answer Type Questions

1. What is the difference between endogenic and exogenic forces of nature? Give one example of each. Diksha

Ans. The difference between endogenic and exogenic forces is given below

Endogenic forces	Exogenic forces
Endogenic forces act in the interior of the Earth.	Exogenic forces act on the surface of the Earth.
It leads to creation of geological structures like mountains, volcano etc.	It modifies Earth's surface features by breaking down and reshaping existing structures.
Example of endogenic forces movement of tectonic plates.	Example of exogenic forces is erosion of river valley.

2. Explain the work of river as an agent of denudation. Diksha

Ans. The work of river as an agent of denudation led to the formation of various landforms which are given below. The following points explain the erosional work of river

- **Waterfall** When the river fall down suddenly at steep angle over very hard rocks or down a steep valley side, it forms a waterfall.
- **Meander** It is a large bend formed by twisting and turning of the river, while it enters the plain.
- **Ox-bow Lake** With the continuous erosion and deposition along the sides of the meander, the ends of the meander loop come closer. When the meander loop cuts-off from the river, it forms a cut-off lake, which is called an ox-box lake.
- **Flood Plains** When the river overflows its banks, it leads to the flooding of the neighbouring areas. During this flooding, the river deposits layers of fine soil and other material (sediments) along its banks. This leads to the formation of a flat fertile which is called flood plain.
- **Levees** The raised banks of the rivers formed due to their overflow are called levees.

3. "The erosion and deposition of the sea waves gives rise to coastal landforms". Justify the statement? Competency Based

Ans. The erosion and deposition of the sea waves gives rise to coastal landforms.

The following landforms are created by the work of sea waves

- **Sea Caves** When the sea waves continuously strike at the rocks, cracks are developed in the rocks which become larger and wider over time. This led to the formation of hollow like caves which are called sea caves.
- **Sea Arches** These are formed when sea cavities or sea caves become bigger and bigger and only the roof of the caves is left.
- **Stacks** When the further erosion of the caves breaks its roof, only walls are left. These wall like features are called stacks.
- **Sea Cliff** The steep rocky coast rising almost vertically above sea water is called sea cliff.
- **Beaches** These are formed when sea waves deposit sediments along the shores.

4. How does wind shape desert landscapes, and what are some of the landforms created by wind erosion and deposition?

Ans. Wind plays a significant role in shaping desert landscapes through erosion and deposition processes.

The following landforms are created by the work of wind

- **Mushroom Rocks** These are the rocks found in deserts in the shape of a mushroom. These rocks have narrower base and wider top because the winds erode the lower section of the rock more than the upper part.
- **Sand Dunes** When the wind blows, it lifts and transports sand from one place to another. When it stops blowing, the sand falls and gets deposited in low hill-like structures. These are called sand dunes.
- **Loess** When the grains of sand are very fine and light, the wind can carry it over very long distances. When such sand is deposited in large areas, it is called loess. For example, large deposits of loess are found in China.

5. News editor is working an article on awareness about earthquake. Give some major part on earthquakes preparedness that should be included. Competency Based

Ans. Earthquakes cannot be predicted, however their impact can certainly be minimised, by preparing for it in advance.

Some measures that can be adopted for minimising the damage from an earthquake are

- Choosing a safe spot to take like under a kitchen counter, table or desk, against an inside corner or wall.
- Staying away from fire places, areas around chimneys, windows that shatter including mirrors and picture frames.
- Being prepared by spreading awareness amongst friends and family members.

Picture Based Question

1. Look at the picture given below and answer the questions that follow.

(i) Where is Niagara Falls situated?

Ans. Niagara Falls is situated at the border between Canada and the United States.

(ii) How a waterfall is formed?

Ans. When the river fall down suddenly at steep angle over very hard rocks or down a steep valley side, it forms a waterfall.

Case Based Question

1. Read the passage given below and answer the following questions.

In deserts you can see rocks in the shape of a mushroom, commonly called mushroom rocks.

Winds erode the lower section of the rock more than the upper part. Therefore, such rocks have narrower base and wider top. When the wind blows, it lifts and transports sand from one place to another. When it stops blowing the sand falls and gets deposited in low hill-like structures. These are called sand dunes. When the grains of sand are very fine and light, the wind can carry it over very long distances. When such sand is deposited in large areas, it is called loess. Large deposits of loess is found in China.

(i) Define the characteristics of mushroom rocks based on the process of their formation.

Ans. Mushroom rocks are significant in desert landscapes due to the differential erosion caused by wind, resulting in a distinctive shape with a narrow base and a wider top.

(ii) What is the relationship between wind driven deposition, and the formation of hill-like structures in deserts, as described in the passage?

Ans. Wind activity lifts and transport sand, and when the wind stops blowing, the sand falls and gets deposited in low hill-like structures, forming sand dunes. There is an interplay between wind and the creation of these landforms.

ASSESSMENT EXERCISE

Multiple Choice Questions (MCQs)

1. Which of the following is the opening in the Earth crust through which molten lava erupts?

(a) Crater (b) Vent (c) Chamber (d) Focus

2. Which of the following landforms are formed due to twisting and turning of the river?

(a) Ox-bow (b) Trench (c) Levees (d) Meander

3. Which of the following is the fastest earthquake wave?

(a) P wave (b) S wave
(c) L wave (d) Surface wave

4. Which one of the following waves can pass through all solid, liquid and gas?

(a) P waves or longitudinal waves
(b) S waves or transverse waves
(c) L waves or surface waves
(d) None of the above

Subjective Questions (VSA, SA & LA)

1. What are the two different types of Earth's movements?

2. Explain about weathering of the Earth's surface.

3. Name different types of landforms formed due to flow of river.

4. Explain the different type of earthquake waves?

5. Differentiate between epicentre and focus.

6. What are the landforms created by sea waves?

7. Glaciers and rivers of the ice also erode the landscape. Define moraines in this aspect.

8. Landforms are created by weathering and erosion. Explain.

9. Write about mushroom rocks, sand dunes and loess.

Air

CHAPTER 4

The atmosphere is a huge blanket of air that surrounds the Earth. All living beings on the Earth depend on the atmosphere for their survival. It provides us the air we breathe and protects us from the harmful effects of the Sun's rays.

Without this blanket of protection, we would be burnt alive by the heat of the Sun during day and get frozen during night. So, this makes the temperature on the Earth liveable.

4.1 Composition of the Atmosphere

Atmosphere is a mixture of various gases. It mainly consists of nitrogen (78%), oxygen (21%), argon (0.93%), carbon dioxide (0.03%), and other gases (0.04%) like helium, ozone and hydrogen. Apart from these gases, tiny dust particles are also present in the air.

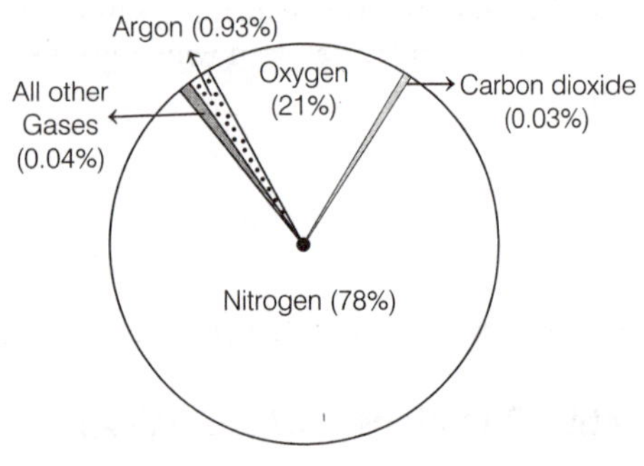

• Constituents of Air

Nitrogen

It is the **most abundant** gas in the air. Humans inhale and exhale a certain amount of nitrogen as they breathe.

Nitrogen is very important for survival of plants. They cannot take nitrogen directly from the air.

Bacteria that live in the soil and roots of some plants take nitrogen from the air and change its form so that plants can use it.

Oxygen

It is the second most abundant gas in the air. Humans and animals take oxygen from the air as they breathe.

Green plants produce oxygen during **photosynthesis**[1]. Thus, oxygen content remains constant in the air. This balance gets disturbed if trees are cut.

Carbon Dioxide

It is another important gas in the atmosphere. Green plants use carbon dioxide to make their food and release oxygen.

Humans or animals also release carbon dioxide. The carbon dioxide released by them seems to be equal to the amount used by plants, which creates a perfect balance.

However, this balance is disturbed by burning of fuels such as coal and oil which add high quantity of carbon dioxide into the atmosphere each year. Consequently, Earth's climate and weather are badly affected by this increasing amount of carbon dioxide.

Carbon dioxide released in the atmosphere is called a **greenhouse gas**[2] as it creates a greenhouse effect by trapping the heat radiated from the Earth. Without carbon dioxide, the Earth would have been too cold to live in.

1 **Photosynthesis** It is the process by which green plants turn carbon dioxide and water into food using energy from sunlight.

2 **Greenhouse Gas** It is a gas in atmosphere that absorbs and emits radiation within the thermal infrared range.

However, when its level in the atmosphere increases due to factory smoke or car fumes, the heat retained increases the temperature of the Earth. This is called **global warming**[3].

This rise in temperature causes the **snow**[4] in coldest parts of the world to melt. As a result the sea level rises, causing floods in the coastal areas.

KNOWLEDGE PLUS When air gets heated, it expands and becomes lighter, causing it to rise upwards. In contrast, cold air is denser and heavier, so it tends to sink down. When hot air rises, cold air from the surrounding area rushes there to fill in the gap. In this way, air circulation takes place.

4.2 Structure of the Atmosphere

The atmosphere is divided into five layers starting from the Earth's surface. These are Troposphere, Stratosphere, Mesosphere, Thermosphere and Exosphere. These are discussed below

(i) **Troposphere** It is the most important layer of the atmosphere. The air we breathe exists here. Its average height is 13 km.

Almost all the weather phenomena like rainfall, snow, **sleet**[5], fog and **hail**[6] occur in this layer.

(ii) **Stratosphere** It lies above the troposphere which extends up to a height of 50 km.

This layer is almost free from clouds and associated weather phenomenon, which makes ideal conditions for flying aeroplanes.

One important feature of stratosphere is that it contains a layer of **ozone gas**.

(iii) **Mesosphere** It is the third layer of the atmosphere which lies above the stratosphere. It extends up to the height of 80 km. **Meteorites** burn up in this layer on entering from the space.

(iv) **Thermosphere** In this layer, temperature rises very rapidly with increasing height. **Ionosphere** is a part of this layer. It extends between 80-400 km.

This layer helps in radio transmission. In fact, radio waves transmitted from the Earth are reflected back to the Earth by this layer.

(v) **Exosphere** It is the **uppermost layer** of the atmosphere. It has very thin air and light gases like helium and hydrogen float into the space from here.

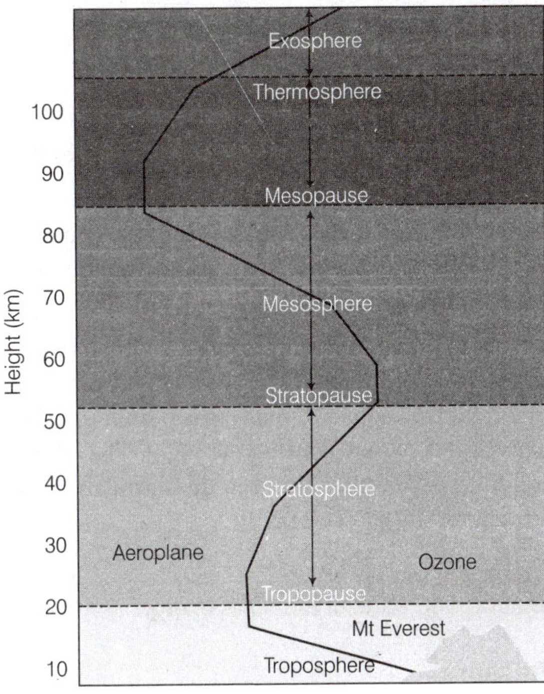

• Layers of the Atmosphere

Try These

1. What is the percentage of nitrogen in the atmosphere?
2. During which process, green plants produce oxygen?
3. Which layer of atmosphere is almost free from clouds and associated weather phenomenon?
4. Name the uppermost layer of the atmosphere.

Weather and Climate

The hour-to-hour and day to day condition of the atmosphere is known as weather. Weather is not same everywhere.

Climate refers to the average weather condition of a place for a long period of time.

3 **Global Warming** It is the increase of the Earth's average surface temperature due to the effect of greenhouse gases, such as carbon dioxide emissions which trap heat that would otherwise escape from Earth.

4 **Snow** It is precipitation falling from clouds in the form of ice crystals.

5 **Sleet** It is partially melted snow (or a mixture of rain and snow).

6 **Hail** It is the precipitation in the form of small ice particles.

Temperature

The degree of hotness and coldness of the air is known as temperature.

The temperature of the atmosphere changes not only between day and night but also from season to season. Summers are hotter than winters.

Degree Celsius (°c) is the standard unit of measuring temperature. It was invented by **Anders Celsius.**

Insolation is the incoming solar energy captured by the Earth which is an important factor that influences the distribution of temperature.

The amount of insolation decreases from the equator towards the poles. Therefore, the temperature decreases in the same manner.

It has been observed that temperature in cities is much higher than that of village. The concrete and metals in buildings and the asphalt of roads gets heated up during the day. This heat is released during the night. The crowded high rise buildings of the cities also trap the warm air. Thus, temperature of the cities rises.

KNOWLEDGE PLUS The Earth receives only 1 in 2,000,000,000 parts of the Sun's energy.

Air Pressure

The pressure exerted by the weight of air on the Earth's surface is called air pressure.

The air pressure is highest at sea level and decreases with height. Horizontally the distribution of air pressure is influenced by temperature of air at a given place.

Low pressure areas are created in areas where temperature is high, the air gets heated and rises. It is associated with cloudy skies and wet weather.

High pressure areas are created in areas where temperature is low and the air is cold. Heavy air sinks and creates a high pressure area. It is associated with clear and sunny skies.

The air always moves from high pressure areas to low pressure areas. The air puts a pressure on human bodies with great force. However, human beings don't feel it because the air puts pressure from all directions and human body exerts a counter pressure.

KNOWLEDGE PLUS There is no air and air pressure on the Moon. Thus, astronauts have to wear special protective space suits filled with air when they go to the Moon. If they did not wear these space suits, the counter pressure exerted by the body of the astronauts would make the blood vessels burst.

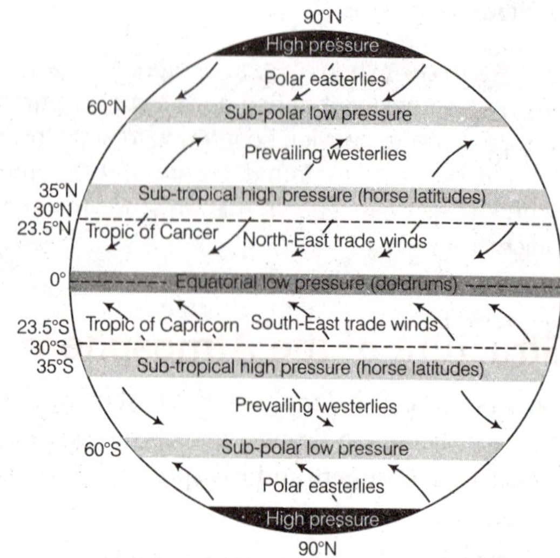

Major Pressure Belts and Wind System

Wind

The movement of air from high pressure area to low pressure areas is called wind. Winds can be broadly divided into three types i.e. Permanent winds , Seasonal winds and Local winds. These are discussed below

(i) **Permanent Winds** The **trade winds**[7], Westerlies and Easterlies are the permanent winds. They blow constantly throughout the year in a particular direction.

(ii) **Seasonal Winds** These winds change their direction in different seasons. For example, monsoons in India.

(iii) **Local Winds** These winds blow only during a particular period of the day or year in a small area. For example, **land** and **sea breeze**, loo, etc.

A wind is named after the direction from which it blows, e.g. the wind blowing from the West is called **Westerly**.

7 **Trade winds** They are the winds that blow towards the equator from the North-East in the Northern Hemisphere and South-East in the Southern Hemisphere.

Cyclone : Nature's Fury

Odisha, located on India's Eastern seacoast, is prone to cyclones[8] originating in the Bay of Bengal.

In 17th-18th October 1999, a cyclone hit five districts of Odisha.

On 25th October, 1999, the cyclone originated in the Gulf of Thailand, near East of Port Blair, gradually moved in a North-Westward direction. It intensified into a supercyclone and hit the area between Erasama and Balikuda in Odisha on 29th October.

The main factors contributing to the damage were

- Strong winds with speeds of up to 260 km/h lasting over 36 hours
- Heavy rainfall for three consecutive days
- Tidal surge

Damage caused by the cyclone are as follows

- The high velocity winds by the cyclone uprooted trees, damaged houses especially Kutcha houses.
- Roof tops of several industrial sheds and other houses were blown away.
- Power supply and telecom lines snapped completely.
- Heavy rains led to flooding of major rivers of Odisha.
- The high tidal wave raised suddenly and caused massive damage to standing crops. In addition to this, a large number of livestock was killed.
- Due to salinisation caused by tidal surge, large tract of agricultural land have turned infertile and large tracts of sal, teak and bamboo plantations were destroyed.

Moisture

When water evaporates from land and different water bodies, it becomes water vapour or moisture. **Humidity** is the amount of moisture in the air.

When the air is full of water vapour, it is called a **humid day**. When the air gets warmer, its capacity to hold the water vapour increases and so it becomes more and more humid.

When the water vapour rises, it condenses causing formation of droplets of water. The masses of such water droplets are **clouds**.

When these droplets of water become too heavy to float in air, then they come down as **precipitation**. Precipitation that comes down to the Earth in liquid form is called **rain**. Other forms of precipitation are **snow**, **sleet** and **hail**.

Most of the ground water comes from rainwater. When trees on hill sides are cut, rainwater flows down the bare mountains and can cause flooding of low lying areas.

Rainfall is very important for the survival of plants and animals. It brings fresh water to the Earth's surface. If rainfall is less, then water scarcity and drought occur, while if rainfall is more, then floods take place.

There are three types of rainfall on the basis of mechanism i.e. the **convectional rainfall**[9], the **orographic rainfall**[10] and the **cyclonic rainfall**[11].

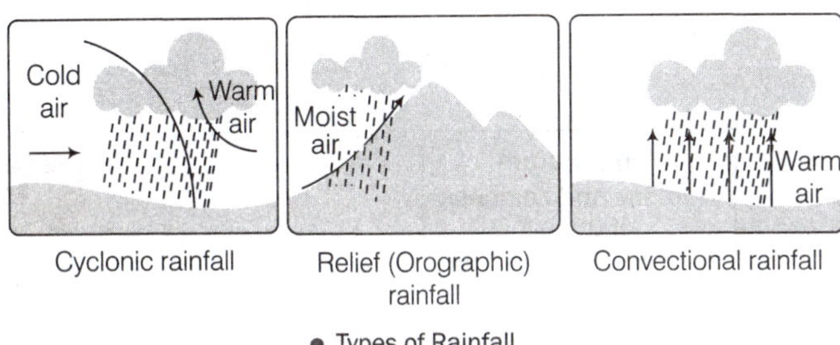

Cyclonic rainfall | Relief (Orographic) rainfall | Convectional rainfall

● Types of Rainfall

Weather Instruments

Thermometer It is a device that measures temperature or a temperature gradient using a variety of different principles.

Barometer It is a scientific instrument used in meteorology to measure atmospheric pressure.

Rain Gauge It is a type of instrument used by meteorologists and hydrologists to gather and measure the amount of liquid precipitation over a set period of time.

Wind Vane It is an instrument for showing the direction of the wind.

Try These

1. **Who invented the standard unit for measuring temperature?**
2. **Which pressure areas are associated with clear and sunny skies?**
3. **Loo is an example of which type of wind?**
4. **Where does most of the ground water come from?**

---

8 Cyclone It is a large scale of air mass that rotate around a center where the air pressure is very low. It usually forms over warm ocean water and moves toward land.

9 Convectional rainfall It occurs when the warm air deflected from a landform rises and forms rain clouds.

10 Orographic rainfall It is the rain which is produced by the lifting of moist air over a mountain.

11 Cyclonic rainfall It occurs where air masses meet and form a front (a weather system).

AIR

Weather
Hour to hour or day to day condition

Climate
Average weather condition of a place for a long period of time

Temperature
Hotness and coldness of the air

Atmosphere
Huge blanket of air surrounds the Earth

Composition
- **Nitrogen** (78%)
- **Oxygen** (21%)
- **Argon** (0.93%)
- **Carbon dioxide** (0.03%)
- **Other gases** (Helium, ozone and hydrogen) (0.04%)

Structure
- **Troposphere** (Average height 13 km)
- **Stratosphere** (Extends upto 50 km)
- **Mesosphere** (Extend upto 80 km)
- **Thermosphere** (Extend between 80-400 km)
- **Exosphere** (Uppermost layer)

Air Pressure
Weight of air on the Earth's surface
Types of air pressure area

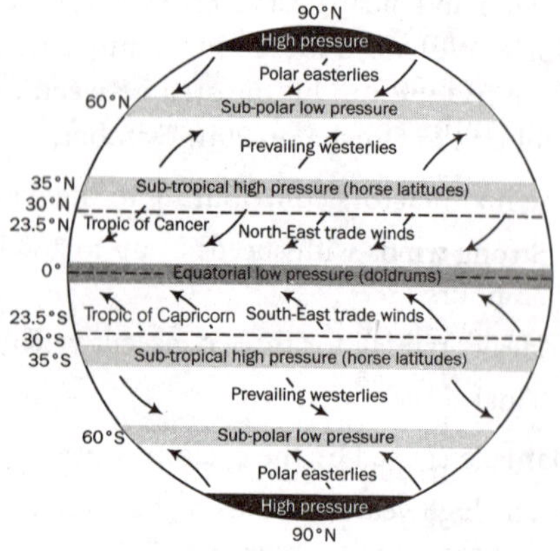

90°N
High pressure
Polar easterlies
60°N
Sub-polar low pressure
Prevailing westerlies
35°N
30°N
Sub-tropical high pressure (horse latitudes)
23.5°N
Tropic of Cancer
North-East trade winds
0°
Equatorial low pressure (doldrums)
23.5°S
Tropic of Capricorn
South-East trade winds
30°S
35°S
Sub-tropical high pressure (horse latitudes)
Prevailing westerlies
60°S
Sub-polar low pressure
Polar easterlies
High pressure
90°N

Low Pressure Area
Created where temperature is high

High Pressure Area
Created where temperature is low

Winds
Movement of air from high to low pressure area

Permanent Winds
Trade wind, Westerlies and Easterlies

Seasonal Winds
Monsoon wind in India

Local Winds
Land and sea breeze, Loo

Moisture
Water evaporated from land and water bodies

Humidity
The amount of moisture in the air

Precipitation
When droplets of water became heavy to float in the air, come down as precipitation

Types of Precipitation
- Rain
- Snow
- Sleet
- Hail

Warm air

Convectional rainfall

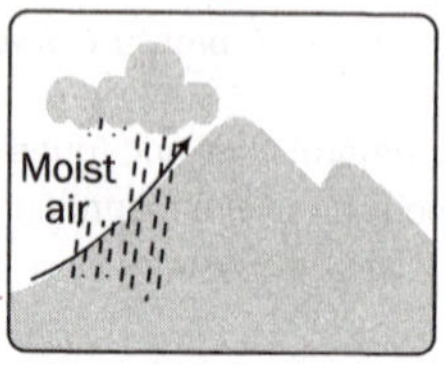

Moist air

Relief (Orographic) rainfall

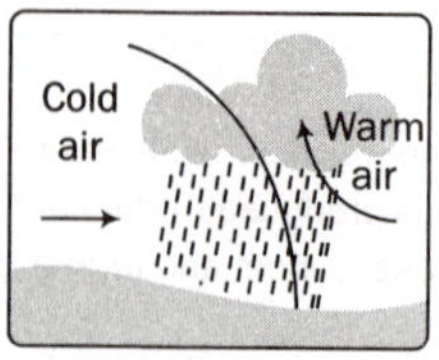

Cold air
Warm air

Cyclonic rainfall

NCERT FOLDER

Covering Intext Questions and Exercises of NCERT

NCERT ON PAGE 23

Q.1 For ten days note down weather report from a local newspaper and observe the changes occurring in the weather.

Ans. Do it yourself.

EXERCISES

Q.1 Answer the following questions.

(i) What is atmosphere?

Ans. The atmosphere is a huge blanket of air that surrounds the Earth.

(ii) Which two gases make the bulk of the atmosphere?

Ans. Nitrogen and oxygen are the gases which make the bulk of the atmosphere.

(iii) Which gas creates greenhouse effect in the atmosphere?

Ans. Carbon dioxide gas creates greenhouse effect in the atmosphere.

(iv) What is weather?

Ans. Weather is the hour-to-hour and day to day condition of the atmosphere.

(v) Name the three types of rainfall.

Ans. Three types of rainfall are the convectional rainfall, the orographic rainfall and the cyclonic rainfall

(vi) What is air pressure?

Ans. Air pressure is the pressure exerted by the weight of air on the Earth's surface.

Q.2 Choose the correct answer.

(i) Which of the following gases protects us from harmful Sun rays?

(a) Carbon dioxide (b) Nitrogen (c) Ozone

(ii) The most important layer of the atmosphere is

(a) Troposphere (b) Thermosphere
(c) Mesosphere

(iii) Which of the following layers of the atmosphere is free from clouds?

(a) Troposphere (b) Stratosphere
(c) Mesosphere

(iv) As we go up the layers of the atmosphere, the pressure

(a) increases (b) decreases
(c) Remains the same

(v) When precipitation comes down to the Earth in the liquid form, it is called

(a) cloud (b) rain (c) snow

Ans. 1. (c), 2. (a), 3. (b), 4. (b), 5. (b)

Q.3 Match the following.

List I	List II
A. Trade Winds	1. Incoming solar energy
B. Loo	2. Seasonal wind
C. Monsoon	3. Horizontal movement of air
D. Wind	4. Permanent wind
	5. Local wind

Ans. A–4, B–5, C–2, D–3

Q.4 Give reasons.

(a) Wet clothes take longer time to dry on a humid day.

Ans. Humid day is full of moisture and evaporation is very slow which makes wet clothes to take longer time to dry.

(b) Amount of insolation decreases from equator towards poles.

Ans. Insolation decreases from equator towards poles because the solar radiation received gradually decreases as one moves from equator towards poles.

Q.5 For Fun

(i) Solve this Crossword Puzzle with the help of given clues

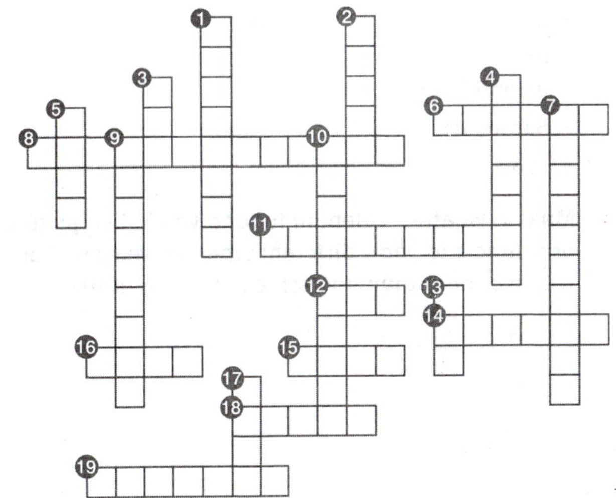

Across

6. An Indian tree having extraordinary quality of providing oxygen round the clock
8. Gas present in atmosphere occupying only 0.03% by volume
11. Outermost layer of atmosphere
12. Mixture of many gases
14. Life giving gas
15. Air in motion
16. An Indian tree valued highly for medicinal properties
18. Gas protecting us from harmful Sun rays
19. Low pressure area

Down

1. Amount of water vapour in air
2. Condensation of water vapours around dust particles in atmosphere
3. Example of local wind blowing in summer in Northern India
4. Short term changes in atmosphere
5. Precipitation in liquid form
7. Blanket of air around the Earth
9. Instrument to measure pressure
10. Incoming solar radiation
13. Reduces visibility in winters
17. It is .... time when Sun is overhead

Ans. Across

6. Peepal
8. Carbon dioxide
11. Exosphere
12. Air
15. Wind
14. Oxygen
16. Neem
18. Ozone
19. Cyclone

Down

1. Humidity
2. Cloud
3. Loo
4. Weather
5. Rain
7. Atmosphere
9. Barometer
10. Insolation
13. Fog
17. Noon

Q.6 **Make a weather calendar for one week. Use pictures or symbols to show different types of weather. You can use more than one symbol in a day. If the weather changes. For example, the Sun comes out when rain stops. An example is given below**

Day	Weather
1.	Sunny day
2.	
3.	
4.	
5.	
6.	
7.	

Ans.

Day	Weather
1.	Sunny day
2.	Cloudy day
3.	Rainy day
4.	Partially cloudy day
5.	Clean day
6.	Stormy day
7.	Calm day

REVIEW EXERCISE

Including Competency Based Questions

PART I

Multiple Choice Questions (MCQs)

1. What is the most abundant gas in Earth's atmosphere?

(a) Oxygen (b) Nitrogen
(c) Carbon dioxide (d) Helium

2. Which gas is essential for photosynthesis and is utilised by green plants during this process?

(a) Oxygen (b) Nitrogen
(c) Carbon dioxide (d) Helium

3. Which layer of the atmosphere is almost free from clouds and ideal for flying aeroplanes?

(a) Troposphere (b) Stratosphere
(c) Mesosphere (d) Thermosphere

4. Rita, a student of 7th class, see a aeroplane flying in the sky. She asked her friend in which layer does aeroplane 'fly' in atmosphere. What is the correct answer?

(a) Troposphere (b) Mesosphere
(c) Stratosphere (d) Ionosphere

5. What is the standard unit of measuring temperature?

(a) Fahrenheit (b) Kelvin
(c) Celsius (d) None of these

6. What instrument is used to measure atmospheric pressure?

(a) Thermometer (b) Barometer
(c) Rain Gauge (d) Wind Vane

7. The movement of air from high-pressure areas to low-pressure areas is called

(a) temperature (b) insolation
(c) wind (d) air pressure

8. What term refers to the increase in Earth's average surface temperature due to greenhouse gas emissions?

(a) Global cooling (b) Climate change
(c) Global warming (d) Atmospheric pressure

9. A recent report from the Yale Programme on Climate Change Communication and C Voter International reveals that a large majority of the Indian public, specifically 82%, are either alarmed or concerned about global warming.

Source Times of India

Should reports on global warming be taken into account by the government?

(a) Yes, global warming is happening, government should make plans to tackle it.
(b) Yes, global warming is going to happen in future, government should make policy for it.
(c) No, global warming is only politically motivated issue.
(d) No, there is no impact of global warming, it is hypothetical concept.

10. Which type of rainfall is produced when moist air is lifted over a mountain?

(a) Convectional rainfall (b) Orographic rainfall
(c) Cyclonic rainfall (d) Acid rain

11. Identify the layer with the help of information given below.

I. It extends upto a height of 50 km.
II. It contains a layer of ozone gas.
III. It is almost free from clouds and other weather phenomenon.

Codes

(a) Troposphere (b) Stratosphere
(c) Mesosphere (d) Thermosphere

12. Choose the correct statement(s) from the following.

I. Oxygen is the most abundant gas in the air.
II. Carbon dioxide is produced by green plants.
III. Barometer is an instrument to measure temperature.

Codes

(a) Only II (c) II and III
(b) I and II (d) None of these

13. Choose the incorrect statement(s) from the following.

I. There is no air on the Moon.
II. Air always moves from low pressure area to high pressure area.
III. Monsoons in India are example of seasonal winds.

Codes

(a) I and II (b) Only II
(c) II and III (d) None of these

14. **Arrange the following layers of atmosphere in correct sequence.**

(i) Thermosphere (ii) Troposphere
(iii) Exosphere (iv) Stratosphere
(v) Mesosphere

Codes

(a) (i), (iii), (iv), (ii), (v) (b) (v), (i), (iv), (ii), (iii)
(c) (ii), (iv), (v), (i), (iii) (d) (iv), (v), (ii), (iii), (i)

Answers

1. (b)	**2.** (c)	**3.** (b)	**4.** (a)	**5.** (c)
6. (b)	**7.** (c)	**8.** (c)	**9.** (a)	**10.** (b)
11. (b)	**12.** (d)	**13.** (b)	**14.** (c)	

Match the Following

1.

List I (Atmospheric Layer)	List II (Characteristic Features)
A. Troposphere	1. Contains the ozone layer
B. Stratosphere	2. Where meteorites burn up
C. Mesosphere	3. Weather phenomena like rainfall and snow occur
D. Thermosphere	4. Rapid increase in temperature with height

Codes

	A	B	C	D		A	B	C	D
(a)	3	1	2	4	(b)	1	2	3	4
(c)	4	3	2	1	(d)	4	1	2	3

2.

List I (Type of rainfall)	List II (Explanations)
A. Convectional rainfall	1. Occurs when moist air rises over a mountain
B. Orographic rainfall	2. Caused by warm air deflecting from a landform and forming rain clouds
C. Cyclonic rainfall	3. Results from the meeting of air masses forming a 'front'

Codes

	A	B	C		A	B	C
(a)	2	1	3	(b)	1	2	3
(c)	3	2	1	(d)	1	3	2

Ans. 1. (a) 2. (a)

Assertion-Reason

1. **Assertion** (A) The atmosphere is divided into five layers, including the troposphere and stratosphere.

Reason (R) The troposphere is where most weather phenomena occur, while the stratosphere contains a layer of ozone gas.

Codes

(a) Both A and R are true and R is the correct explanation of A
(b) Both A and R are true, but R is not the correct explanation of A
(c) A is true, but R is false
(d) A is false, but R is true

2. **Assertion** (A) Global warming is primarily caused by an increase in the level of carbon dioxide in the atmosphere due to human activities.

Reason (R) Lower levels of carbon dioxide act as a greenhouse gas, trapping heat and leading to rising temperatures on Earth.

Codes

(a) Both A and R are true and R is the correct explanation of A
(b) Both A and R are true, but R is not the correct explanation of A
(c) A is true, but R is false
(d) A is false, but R is true

Ans. 1. (b) Both A and R are true, but R is not the correct explanation of A
2. (c) A is true, but R is false

Fill in the Blanks

1. Carbon dioxide in atmosphere creates a .... effect by trapping the heat radiated from the Earth.

2. One important feature of stratosphere is that it contains a layer of ....

3. The uppermost layer of the atmosphere is known as ....

4. The standard unit of measuring temperature is ....

Ans. 1. greenhouse 2. ozone gas
3. exosphere 4. Degree Celsius

True/False

1. The atmosphere primarily consists of nitrogen, oxygen and carbon dioxide.

2. The stratosphere is the layer of the atmosphere where all weather phenomena occur.

3. Climate refers to the hour-to-hour, day-to-day condition of the atmosphere.

4. Convectional rainfall occurs when moist air is lifted over a mountain, leading to the formation of rain clouds.

5. Cyclonic rainfall occurs when warm and cold air masses meet and form a 'front.'

Ans. 1. True 2. False
3. False 4. True
5. True

Picture Based Question

1. **The picture given below shows the layers of atmosphere.**

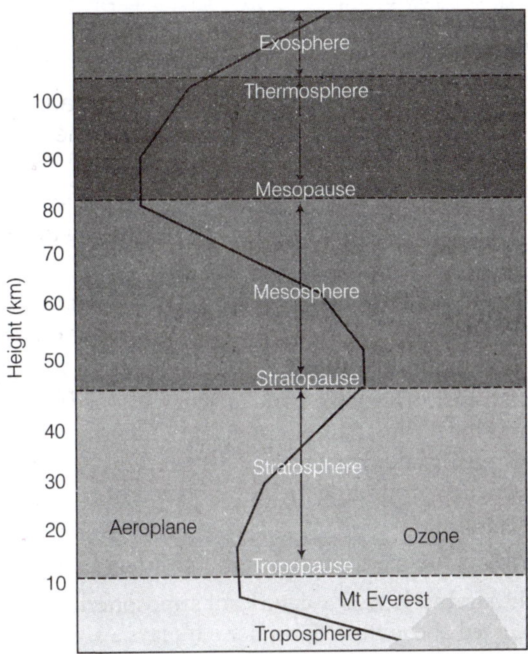

Which of the following layers of atmosphere protect us from harmful effect of the Sun rays?

(a) Stratosphere (b) Mesosphere
(c) Thermosphere (d) Exosphere

Ans. (a)

Case Based Question

1. **Read the passage given below and answer the following questions.**

Air pressure is defined as the pressure exerted by the weight of air on the Earth's surface. As we go up the layers of atmosphere, the pressure falls rapidly. The air pressure is highest at sea level and decreases with height. Horizontally the distribution of air pressure is influenced by temperature of air at a given place. In areas where temperature is high, the air gets heated and rises. This creates a low-pressure area. Low pressure is associated with cloudy skies and wet weather. In areas having lower temperature, the air is cold. It is therefore heavy. Heavy air sinks and creates a high pressure area. High pressure is associated with clear and sunny skies. The air always moves from high pressure areas to low pressure areas.

(i) **Which of the following factor influences the horizontal distribution of air pressure, as mentioned in the passage?**
(a) Altitude changes
(b) Atmospheric layers
(c) Temperature variations
(d) Wind patterns

(ii) **How is formation of a low-pressure area related to the temperature of the air in a given location?**
(a) High temperatures leads to low pressure
(b) Low temperatures create low pressure
(c) High temperatures result in high pressure
(d) Low temperatures cause high pressure

(iii) **In which atmospheric layer does air pressure fall rapidly with increasing height?**
(a) Stratosphere (b) Troposphere
(c) Mesosphere (d) Thermosphere

(iv) **What weather condition is associated with a low-pressure area, according to the passage?**
(a) Stormy weather
(b) Clear and sunny skies
(c) Overcast conditions
(d) Intense precipitation

Ans. 1. (c) Temperature variations
2. (a) High temperatures leads to low pressure
3. (b) Troposphere
4. (b) Clear and sunny skies

PART II

Very Short Answer Type Questions

1. **What is the atmosphere and why is it essential for life on Earth?**

Ans. The atmosphere is a huge blanket of air that surrounds the Earth. It is essential as it provides us the air we breathe and protects us from the harmful effects of the Sun's rays.

2. **What are the main components of Earth's atmosphere?**

Ans. Earth's atmosphere mainly consists of nitrogen (78%), oxygen (21%) and argon (0.93%), carbon dioxide (0.03%), and other gases (0.04%) like helium, ozone and hydrogen.

3. **How do plants obtain nitrogen from the atmosphere?** Competency Based

Ans. Bacteria in the soil and plant roots convert atmospheric nitrogen into a form that plants can use for their growth.

4. **What gas do humans and animals take from the atmosphere as they breathe?**

Ans. Humans and animals take oxygen from the atmosphere during respiration.

5. What role does carbon dioxide play in the atmosphere?

Ans. Carbon dioxide is important for plants to make their food through photosynthesis.

6. What is meant by greenhouse effect? Diksha

Ans. The greenhouse effect is the process through which heat is trapped near the surface of the Earth by substances known as greenhouse gases.

7. How does an increase in atmospheric carbon dioxide lead to global warming? Competency Based

Ans. When the level in of carbon dioxide in the atmosphere increases due to factory smoke or car fumes, the heat retained increases the temperature of the Earth and it leads to global warming.

8. Name the five layers of the Earth's surface.

Ans. The five layers of the Earth's surface are Troposphere, Stratosphere, Mesosphere, Thermosphere and Exosphere.

9. In which atmospheric layer do almost all weather phenomena occur?

Ans. Most weather events, such as rain, snow and hail, take place in the troposphere, the lowest layer of the atmosphere.

10. Where do meteorites burn up when entering Earth's atmosphere?

Ans. Meteorites burn up in the mesosphere, when entering Earth's atmosphere.

11. How does the thermosphere contribute to radio transmission?

Ans. The thermosphere, which extends from 80 to 400 km contribute to radio transmission by reflecting radio waves back to Earth.

12. What is the uppermost layer of Earth's atmosphere and what gases are present there?

Ans. The uppermost layer of the Earth's atmosphere is the exosphere, which contains very thin air and light gases like helium and hydrogen.

13. How do weather and climate differ?

Ans. The hour-to-hour and day to day condition of the atmosphere is known as weather. On the other hand, climate refers to the average weather condition of a place for a long period of time.

14. What is meant by insolation? Diksha

Ans. Insolation is the incoming solar energy intercepted by the Earth which influences the distribution of temperature.

15. Where can we find highest air pressure?

Ans. We can find highest air pressure at sea level.

16. What are the three types of winds, and give an example of each.

Ans. The three types of winds are permanent winds (e.g., trade winds), seasonal winds (e.g., monsoons) and local winds (e.g., land and sea breezes).

17. What caused the devastating supercyclone in Odisha in 1999?

Ans. The devastating supercyclone in Odisha in 1999 was caused by strong winds, heavy rainfall, and a tidal surge, resulting in extensive damage and loss of life.

Short Answer Type Questions

1. How do bacteria help plants in using nitrogen?

Ans. Plants cannot directly absorb nitrogen from the air, but certain soil bacteria residing in plant roots and soil transform atmospheric nitrogen into a usable form for plants. This microbial process, known as nitrogen fixation, enables plants to access essential nutrients, promoting their growth and overall survival.

2. What is the significance of the stratosphere?

Ans. The stratosphere is a significant atmospheric layer situated above the troposphere. It plays a significant role in safeguarding life on Earth with its ozone layer, which shields us from harmful solar radiation.
Its stability, absence of weather disruptions, makes it ideal for flying airplanes enabling safe and efficient air travel.

3. What is air pressure, and how does it change with altitude?

Ans. Air pressure is the force exerted by the atmosphere on the Earth's surface.

Air pressure is highest at sea level, gradually decreasing as altitude increases. This change is due to the varying weight of the air column above. Low pressure areas occur where air is heated and rises, while high pressure areas result from colder, denser air sinking. This pressure difference drives wind and weather patterns.

4. What causes low-pressure areas and which type of weather is associated with them?

Ans. Low-pressure areas develop when air is heated, causing it to rise. This rising air creates a region of lower atmospheric pressure. In these areas, weather conditions typically involve cloudy skies and wet conditions, characteried by precipitation such as rain.

Low-pressure systems are associated with stormy and unsettled weather patterns, making them an important factor in the development of various weather phenomenon.

5. Explain wind and its movement between high and low-pressure areas.

Ans. Wind is the result of air moving from regions of high air pressure to low air pressure.

High pressure is associated with cooler, denser air, while low pressure is connected to warmer, lighter air. The temperature and air pressure variations cause air to move. This movement of air is what we call 'wind', and it plays a crucial role in shaping weather patterns and climate.

6. Discuss humidity and its relation to the formation of clouds and precipitation. **Competency Based**

Ans. Humidity refers to the presence of water vapour in the air. As air rises and cools, the water vapour within it condenses to form clouds. When these water droplets gather and become heavy, they fall as precipitation, such as rain.

Humidity plays an important role in the formation of clouds and the subsequent occurrence of various forms of precipitation, impacting weather patterns and the distribution of water resources.

7. In what way nature balance our lives? How this balance would be disturbed?

Ans. Nature maintains a balance in our lives by providing essential elements like oxygen through photosynthesis by green plants. This balance would be disturbed by deforestation and reducing the number of green plants due to which the oxygen levels in the atmosphere would decrease, affecting our ability to breathe and causing environmental imbalances.

8. Green plants use carbon dioxide to make their food and release oxygen. Humans or animals release carbon dioxide. The amount of carbon dioxide released by humans or animals seems to be equal to the amount used by the plants which make a perfect balance. However, the balance is upset by burning of fuels, such as coal and oil. They add billions of tons of carbon dioxide into the atmosphere each year. As a result, the increased volume of carbon dioxide is affecting the Earth's weather and climate. **Competency Based**

(i) What disrupts the balance between carbon dioxide production and absorption in the atmosphere?

Ans. The balance between carbon dioxide production and absorption in the atmosphere is disrupted by the burning of fuels like oil and coal, which release billions of tons of carbon dioxide each year.

(ii) How does the increased volume of carbon dioxide in the atmosphere impact the Earth's weather and climate?

Ans. The increased volume of carbon dioxide is affecting the Earth's weather and climate by contributing to global warming.

Long Answer Type Questions

1. Atmosphere is a mixture of various gases. Discuss the composition of atmosphere.

Ans. Atmosphere is a mixture of various gases. It mainly consists of nitrogen (78%), oxygen (21%) and argon (0.93%), carbon dioxide (0.03%), helium, ozone and hydrogen. Apart from these gases, tiny dust particles are also present in the air. Some of the gases in the atmosphere are discussed below

- **Nitrogen** It is the most abundent gas in the air. Humans inhale and exhale a certain amount of nitrogen as they breathe. Nitrogen is very important for survival of plants. They cannot take nitrogen directly from the air.
- **Oxygen** It is the second most abundent gas in the air. Humans and animals take oxygen from the air as they breathe. Green plants produce oxygen during photosynthesis. Thus, oxygen content remains constant in the air.
- **Carbon Dioxide** It is another important gas in the atmosphere. Green plants use carbon dioxide to make their food and release oxygen. Humans or animals also release carbon dioxide. The carbon dioxide released by then seems to be equal to the amount used by plants, which create a perfect balance.

2. Explain the structure of atmosphere. **Diskha**

Ans. The atmosphere is divided into five layers starting from the Earth's surface. These are Troposphere, Stratosphere, Mesosphere, Thermosphere and Exosphere. These are discussed below

(i) **Troposphere** It is the most important layer of the atmosphere. The air we breathe exists here. Its average height is 13 km.

(ii) **Stratosphere** It lies above the troposphere which extends up to a height of 50 km. This layer is almost free from clouds and associated weather phenomenon, which makes ideal conditions for flying aeroplanes.

(iii) **Mesosphere** It is the third layer of the atmosphere which lies above the stratosphere. It extends up to the height of 80 km. Meteorites burn up in this layer on entering from the space.

(iv) **Thermosphere** In this layer, temperature rises very rapidly with increasing height. Ionosphere is a part of this layer. It extends between 80-400 km.

(v) **Exosphere** It is the uppermost layer of the atmosphere. It has very thin air and light gases like helium and hydrogen float into the space from here.

3. The air pressure is highest at sea level and decreases with height. Describe air pressure. Diksha

Ans. Air Pressure is defined as the pressure exerted by the weight of air on the Earth's surface.

The air pressure is highest at sea level and decreases with height. Horizontally the distribution of air pressure is influenced by temperature of air at a given place.

Low pressure areas are created in areas where temperature is high, the air gets heated and rises. It is associated with cloudy skies and wet weather.

High pressure areas are created in areas where temperature is low and the air is cold. Heavy air sinks and creates a high pressure area. It is associated with clear and sunny skies.

The air always moves from high pressure areas to low pressure areas. The air puts a pressure on human bodies with a great force. However, human beings don't feel it because the air put pressure from all directions and human body exerts a counter pressure.

4. Rohan was observing the winds blow during the afternoon while he was returning from school. He thought about the different types of winds that blow in a year. Explain the types of winds. Competency Based

Ans. The movement of air from high pressure area to low pressure areas is called wind. Winds can be broadly divided into three types i.e. Permanent winds , Seasonal winds, Local winds. These are discussed below

(i) **Permanent Winds** The trade winds, Westerlies and Easterlies are the permanent winds. These blow constantly throughout the year in a particular direction.

(ii) **Seasonal Winds** These winds change their direction in different seasons. For example, monsoons in India.

(iii) **Local Winds** These winds blow only during a particular period of the day or year in a small area. For example, land and sea breeze, loo, etc.

5. Differentiate between weather and temperature.

Ans. The differences between weather and temperature are

Aspect	Weather	Temperature
Definition	The hour-to-hour and day to day condition of the atmosphere is known as weather.	The degree of hotness or coldness of the air.
Variability	Highly variable, changes frequently.	Varies between day and night and across seasons.
Measurement Unit	Not measured in degrees; described qualitatively (e.g., sunny, rainy, cloudy).	Measured in degrees Celsius (°C) or Fahrenheit (°F).
Influence on Climate	Weather events contribute to short-term variations but do not determine long-term climate.	Temperature is one of the factors that influences long-term climate patterns.
Timespan	Short-term, refers to day-to-day conditions.	Long-term, describes conditions over seasons and years.
Example	Rain, snow, fog, hail, etc.	20°C on a summer day, -5°C during a cold winter night.

6. Moisture in the air at any time is known as humidity. Discuss moisture and precipitation.

Ans. Moisture in the air at any time is known as humidity.

When water evaporates from land and different water bodies, it becomes water vapour or moisture. Humidity is the amount of moisture in the air.

When the air is full of water vapour, it is called humid. When the air gets warmer, its capacity to hold the water vapour increases and so it becomes more and more humid.

When the water vapour rises, it condenses causing the formation of droplets of water. The masses of such water droplets are clouds.

When these droplets of water become too heavy to float in air, they come down as precipitation. Precipitation that comes down to the Earth in liquid form is called rain. Other forms of precipitation are snow, sleat and hail.

Picture Based Question

1. Look at the picture given below and answer the following questions.

(i) Is global warming a serious issue in today's world? Why

Ans. Yes, global warming is a serious issues of contemporary world.

Due to global warming, temperature on Earth is increasing. If it is not controlled, a day will come when all ice caps will melt and everything will get submerged into water.

(ii) **In the above newspaper cutting, state one reason for global warming.**

Ans. Over burning of fuels like coal and oil causes global warming.

(iii) **What is according to you, a way out of global warming?**

Ans. According to me, a way out of global warming involves using the bio-fuels and practising the plantation.

Case Based Question

1. Read the passage given below and answer the following questions.

Carbon dioxide released in the atmosphere creates a green house effect by trapping the heat radiated from the Earth. It is therefore called a greenhouse gas and without it the Earth would have been too cold to live in. However, when its level in the atmosphere increases due to factory smoke or car fumes, the heat retained increases the temperature of the Earth. This is called global warming. This rise in temperature causes the snow in coldest parts of the world to melt. As a result the sea level rises, causing floods in the coastal areas. There may be drastic changes in the climate of a place leading to extinction of some plants and animals in the long run.

(i) **How does global warming, caused by increased carbon dioxide levels, leading to potential ecological disruptions?**

Ans. Global warming induced by elevated carbon dioxide levels accelerates the melting of snow in colder regions. This, in turn, raises sea levels, causing coastal floods and drastic climate changes, impacting the survival of various plant and animal species.

(ii) **What role does carbon dioxide play in maintaining Earth's temperature, and how does it achieve this?**

Ans. Carbon dioxide functions as a greenhouse gas, trapping heat radiated from the Earth. Its presence prevents extreme cold, making the planet habitable. It maintains an intricate balance for a suitable living environment.

ASSESSMENT EXERCISE

Multiple Choice Questions (MCQs)

1. Which one of the following gases is used as fire extinguishers?
(a) Oxygen
(b) Nitrogen
(c) Carbon dioxide
(d) Ozone

2. Which one of the following layers is the theatre of all the weather phenomena?
(a) Troposphere
(b) Stratosphere
(c) Mesosphere
(d) Exosphere

3. Which of the following layers is the outermost in the atmosphere?
(a) Thermosphere
(b) Exosphere
(c) Mesosphere
(d) Troposphere

4. High pressure area is associated with which of the following?
(a) Cloudy skies (b) Wet weather
(c) Clear and sunny skies (d) None of these

Subjective Questions (VSA, SA & LA)

1. What protect us from harmful effects of the Sun's ultraviolet rays?

2. What are the causes and effects of greenhouse gases?

3. What are the different layers of the atmosphere?

4. How can you say that carbon dioxide is useful for plants and animals?

5. Why stratosphere is the ideal layer for flying aeroplanes?

6. Explain about the process of insolation.

7. Explain the factors that affect weather and climate.

8. What are the causes due to which temperature in cities rises? Explain any two.

CHAPTER 5

Water

Water is essential for life. Three-fourth of the Earth's surface is covered by water. Freshwater constitutes only a small part of it. In this chapter, we will learn about the process of water cycle, the various sources of saline and freshwater and the movements that occur in oceans, namely, waves, tides and currents.

Our Earth is like a **terrarium**[1] as the same water that existed centuries ago still exists today.

The major sources of fresh water are the rivers, ponds, springs and glaciers. The ocean bodies and the seas contain salty or saline water because they contain large amount of dissolved salts.

Most of the salt is sodium chloride or the common table salt that we eat.

The Sun's heat causes **evaporation**[2] of water into vapour. When the water vapour cools down, it condenses and forms clouds. Clouds may fall on the land or sea in the form of rain, snow or sleet.

The process by which water changes its form and circulates between ocean, atmosphere and land is known as the **water cycle**.

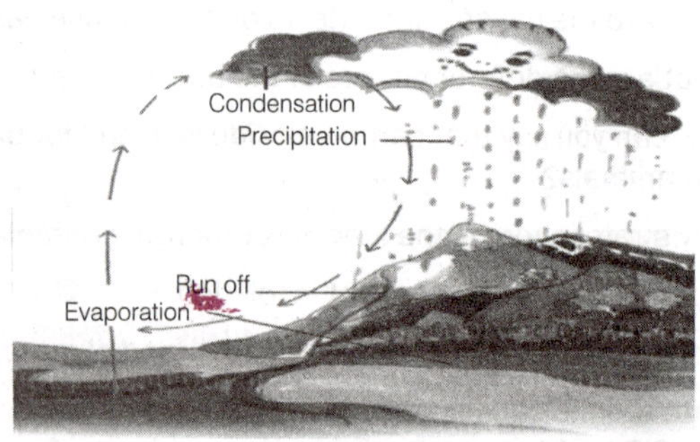

• Water Cycle

KNOWLEDGE PLUS Salinity is the amount of salt in grams present in 1000 grams of water. The average salinity of the oceans is 35 parts per thousand.

Dead sea in Israel has salinity of 340 grams per litre of water. Swimmers can float in it because the increased salt content makes it dense.

5.1 Distribution of Water Bodies

The **three-fourth** surface of the earth is covered with water. The distribution of this water in percentage is given below

- 97.3% of total water is saline or salty in oceans and seas.
- Only 3% of total water on the earth is freshwater. This freshwater can be found in ice-caps (2.0%), ground water (0.68%) fresh water lakes (0.009%) inland seas and salt lakes (0.009%), atmosphere (0.0019%) and rivers (0.0001%).

KNOWLEDGE PLUS 22nd March is celebrated as **World Water Day** to raise awareness about the conservation of fresh water in different ways.

5.2 Ocean Circulation

Ponds and lakes have calm water whereas ocean water keeps moving continuously. These movements in the oceans can be broadly categorised as **waves**, **tides** and **currents**.

Waves

When the water on the surface of the ocean rises and falls alternately, they are called waves.

Waves are formed when wind blows at high speed across the ocean surface. The size of the waves depend on the winds. The stronger the wind blows, the bigger the wave becomes.

During a storm, the winds blowing at very high speed form huge waves. These waves may cause huge destruction.

An earthquake, a volcanic eruption or underwater landslides can shift large amounts of ocean water.

1 **Terrarium** It is an artificial enclosure for keeping small house plants.
2 **Evaporation** It refers to the process of becoming a vapour.

As a result **tsunami**[3] is formed which is a huge tidal wave that can be as high as 15 m. The largest tsunami ever measured was 150 m high.

Tsunami is a Japanese word that means **harbour waves** as the harbours get destroyed whenever the tsunami comes. Tsunami waves travel at a speed of more than 700 km per hour.

Tsunami of 2004

A devastating tsunami occurred in the Indian Ocean on 26th December, 2004. This tsunami was the result of the earthquake close to the Western boundary of Sumatra with the magnitude 9.0.

The **Indira Point** in the Andaman and Nicobar Islands got submerged after this tsunami. The worst-hit areas in India included the coastal regions of Andhra Pradesh, Tamil Nadu, Kerala, Puducherry and the Andaman and Nicobar Islands.

Tides

The rhythmic rise and fall of ocean water twice in a day is called a tide.

When water covers much of the shore by rising to its highest level, it is called **high tide**. When water falls to its lowest level and moves away from the shore, it is called low tide.

Tides are caused by the strong gravitational pull applied by the Sun and the Moon on the Earth's surface.

The rise and fall of water due to tides is being used to generate electricity in some places.

Tides can be broadly categorised as follows

- **Spring Tides** During the full Moon and new Moon days when the Sun, the Moon and the Earth are in the same line, highest tides occur. These tides are called spring tides.

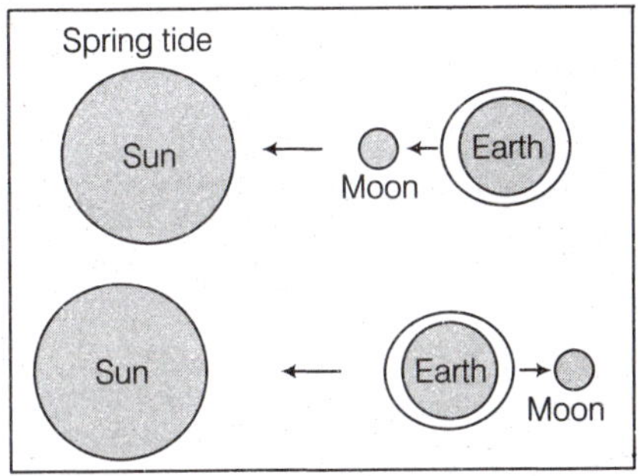

- **Neap Tides** When the moon is in its first and last quarter, the ocean waters are drawn in diagonally opposite directions by the gravitational pull of the Sun and the Moon, and results in low tides. These tides are called neap tides.

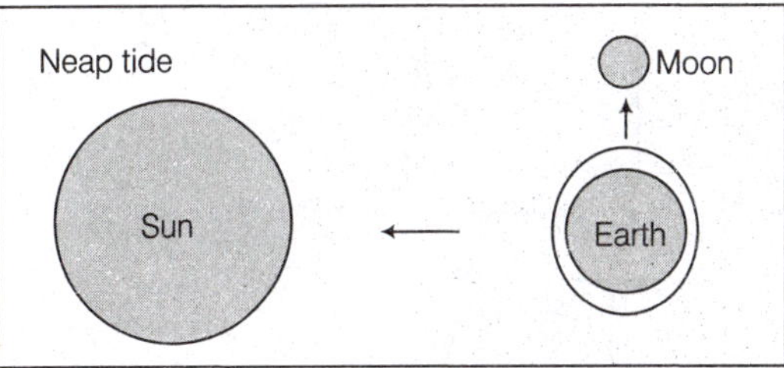

High Tides

When the water of the Earth closer to the moon gets pulled under the influence of the moon's gravitational force, high tides are caused.

High tides help in navigation. They raise the water level close to the shores which helps the ships to arrive at the harbour more easily. The high tides also help in fishing as more fish come closer to the shore during high tides.

Ocean Currents

Ocean currents are streams of water flowing constantly on the surface of the ocean in definite directions. The ocean current influences the temperature conditions of the area.

Ocean currents may be **warm** or **cold** as follows

- **Warm Ocean Currents** They originate near the equator and move towards the poles. The **Gulf Stream** is a warm current. Warm currents bring about warm temperature over land surface.
- **Cold Ocean Currents** They carry water from polar or higher latitudes to tropical or lower latitudes. The **Labrador** current is cold current.

The areas where the warm and cold currents meet provide the best fishing grounds of the world. For example, seas around Japan and the Eastern coast of. North America.

3 **Tsunami** It is a huge tidal wave.

The areas where the warm and cold currents meet, also experience foggy weather. Thus, navigation in such areas becomes difficult.

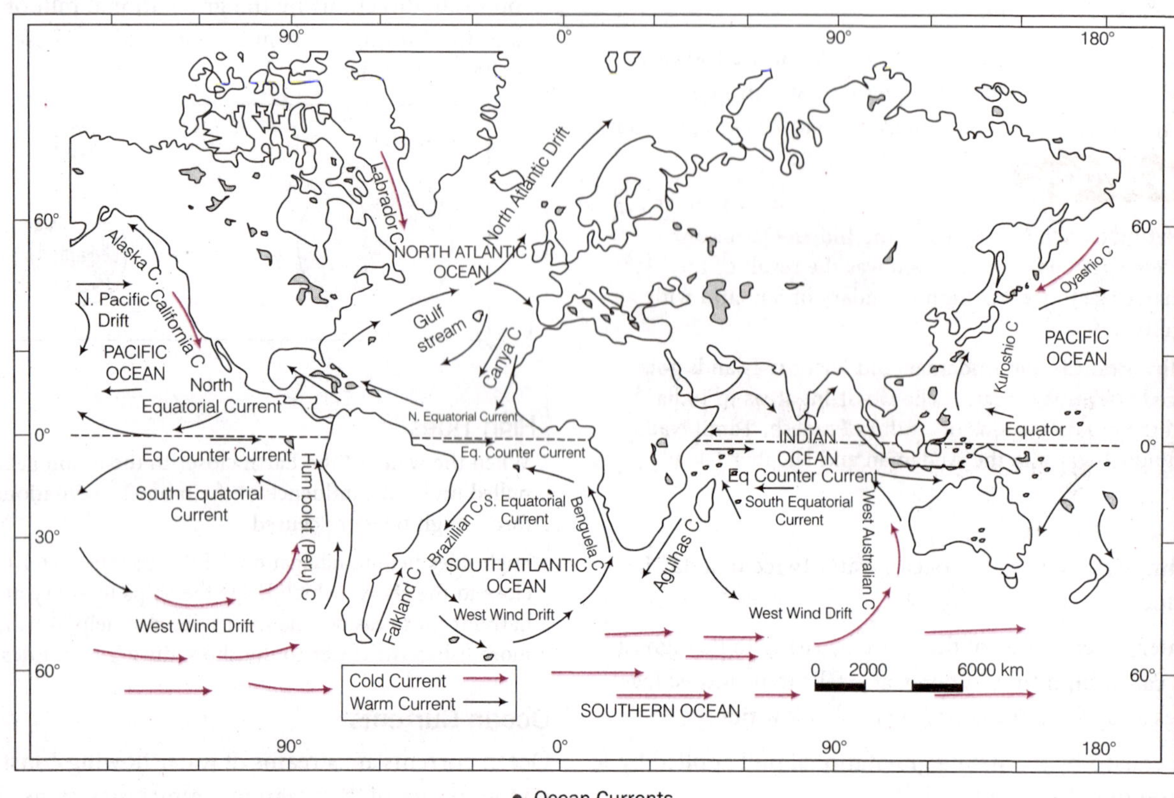

• Ocean Currents

WATER

Water Cycle

Circulation of water between ocean, atmosphere and land

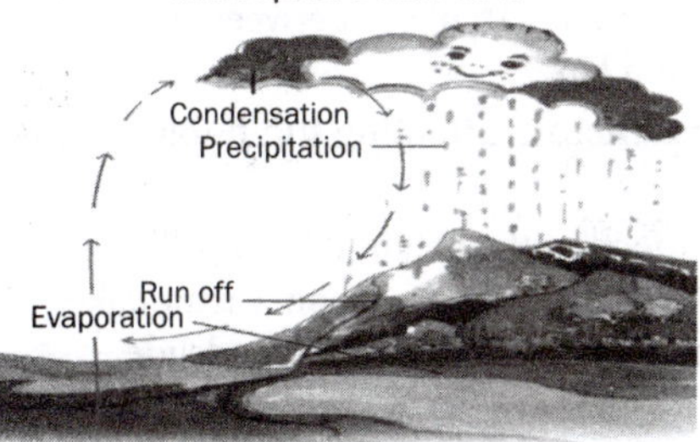

Distribution of Water

Covered 3/4th surface of the Earth

- Oceans – 97.3% Saline water
- Ice caps – 02.0%
- Ground water – 0.68%
- Fresh water lakes – 0.009%
- Inland seas and salt lakes – 0.009%
- Atmosphere – 0.0019%
- Rivers – 0.0001%

Ocean Circulation

Waves

Rise and fall of water on the surface of ocean

Tides

Rhythmic rise and fall on ocean water twice in a day

Ocean Current

- Streams of water flowing constantly on the ocean surface in definite directions
- Influences the temperature conditions of the area.

Types of Tides

Spring Tide

Occur when Sun, Moon and Earth are in the same line during the full Moon and new Moon days

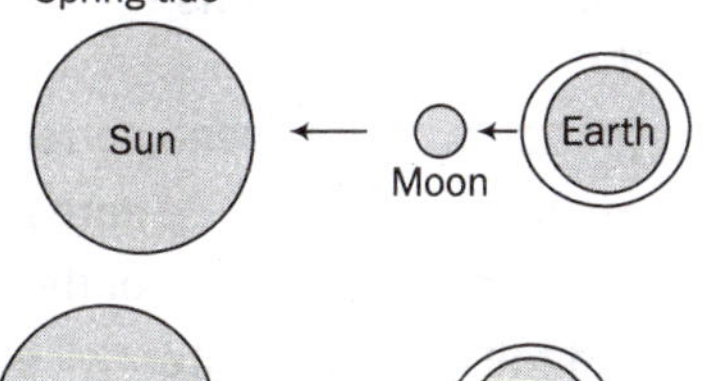

Neap tide

Low tides which occur when Moon is in its first and last quarter and the ocean water are drawn diagonally in opposite direction by gravitation force of Moon and Sun

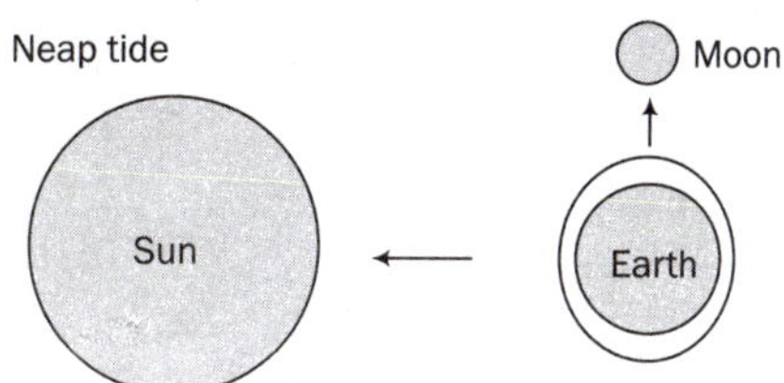

Types of Ocean Currents

Warm Ocean Current

Originate near the equator and move towards the poles, e.g. Gulf Stream

Cold Ocean Current

Carry water from polar or higher latitudes to tropical or lower latitudes, e.g. Labrador

NCERT FOLDER

Covering Intext Questions and Exercises of NCERT

NCERT ON PAGE 30

Q.1 Where does the water of puddles go?

Ans. The water of puddles drains into the ground, evaporates or absorbed by the air.

NCERT ON PAGE 32

Q.2 Why do so many countries face water scarcity?

Ans. Due to the following reasons, some countries face water scarcity

- Some countries are rocky and arid.
- Some do not have much rainfall.
- Some are desert areas.
- Most of the water is polluted.
- Excessive use of water has depleted water resources.

NCERT ON PAGE 33

Q.3 Why is water important for us?

Ans. Water is important for us because it is the basis of our lives. Life cannot be imagined without the presence of water. Water is used for a variety of purposes which includes washing, cooking, drinking and watering plant, etc.

Q.4 Suggest some ways in which water can be conserved

(a) in your home

(b) in your school

Ans. Some ways in which water can be conserved are

(a) Ways to conserve water in home

- Turn the tap off while brushing the teeth and washing our hands.
- Using a watering can to water the garden
- Use bucket instead of shower to bath
- Fix leaking pipe

(b) Ways to conserve water in school

- Practising rainwater harvesting
- Create awareness among students for water conservation
- Repair the leaking pipes

EXERCISES

Q.1 Is all water on the Earth available to us?

Ans. No, only 3% is fresh water. Its 0.3% is available to us.

Q.2 Answer the following questions.

(a) What is precipitation?

Ans. Precipitation is defined as the falling of moisture on the Earth in the form of rain, snow, hail, sleet or mist

(b) What is water cycle?

Ans. Water cycle is the process by which water continually changes its form and circulates between oceans, atmosphere and land.

(c) What are the factors affecting the height of the waves?

Ans. The factors affecting the height of waves are wind, gravitational pull of Sun and Moon, earthquake, volcanic eruption and under water landslide.

(d) Which factors affect the movement of ocean water?

Ans. The factors which affect the movement of ocean water are temperature, winds, gravitational pull of the Sun, the Earth and the Moon.

(e) What are tides and how are they caused?

Ans. The rhythmic rise and fall of ocean water twice in a day is called a tide. They are caused by strong gravitational pull exerted by the Sun and the Moon on the Earth's surface.

(f) What are ocean currents?

Ans. Ocean currents are streams of water flowing constantly on the ocean surface in definite directions which may be warm or cold.

Q.3 Give reasons

(a) Ocean water is salty.

Ans. The water of the oceans is salty because it contains large amount of dissolved salt.

(b) The quality of water is deteriorating.

Ans. The quality of water is deteriorating because water is not used judiciously and also industrial effluents and untreated water of industries get mixed into streams and rivers.

Q.4 Tick the correct answer.

1. The process by which water continually changes its form and circulates between oceans, atmosphere and land

(a) water cycle (b) tides (c) ocean currents

2. Generally, the warm ocean currents originate near

(a) pole (b) equator (c) None of these

3. The rhythmic rise and fall of ocean water twice in a day is called

(a) tide (b) ocean current (c) wave

A. (a) 2. (b) 3. (a)

Q.5 Match the following.

List I	List II
A. Caspian Sea	1. Largest lake
B. Tide	2. Periodic rise and fall of water
C. Tsunami	3. Strong setsmic waves
D. Ocean currents	4. Streams of water moving along definite paths
	5. Water cycle

Ans. A-1 , B–2, C-3, D-4

Q.6 For Fun

(i) The name of one river is hidden in each of the sentences below. Spot it.

Example Mandira, Vijayalakshmi and Surinder are my best friends

Ans. Ravi

(a) The snake charmer's busted, stables where horses are housed, and the piles of wood, all caught fire accidentally.
(**Hint:** Another name for River Brahmputra)

Ans. Teesta

(b) The conference manager put pad, material for reading and a pencil for each participant.
(**Hint:** A distributary on the Ganga-Brahmputra delta)

Ans. Padma

(c) Either jealousy or anger cause a person's fall (**Hint:** Name of a juicy fruit!)

Ans. Orange

(d) Bhavani germinated the seeds in a pot
(**Hint:** Look for her in West Africa)

Ans. Niger

(e) "I am a zonal champion now" declared the excited athlete.
(**Hint:** The river that has the biggest basin in the world)

Ans. Amazon

(f) The tiffin box rolled down and all the food fell in dusty potholes.
(**Hint:** Rises in India and journeys through Pakistan)

Ans. Indus

(g) Malini leaned against the pole when she felt that she was going to faint.
(**Hint:** Her delta in Egypt is famous)

Ans. Nile

(h) Samantha mesmerised everybody with her magic tricks. (**Hint:** London is situated on her estuary)

Ans. Thames

(i) "In this neighbourhood, please don't yell! Owners of these houses like to have peace". Warned my father when we moved into our new flat".
(**Hint:** colour!)

Ans. Yelllow

(j) 'Write the following words, Marc!' "On", "go", "in"........ said the teacher to the little boy in KG Class. (**Hint:** Rhymes with 'bongo')

Ans. Congo

(ii) With the help of an atlas, draw each river which you discovered in for fun (i), on an outline map of the world.

Ans. Do it yourself.

REVIEW EXERCISE

Including Competency Based Questions

PART I

Multiple Choice Questions (MCQs)

1. What is the primary source of fresh water on Earth?

(a) Oceans (b) Rivers
(c) Ponds (d) Springs

2. What is the main component of salt in ocean water?

(a) Magnesium chloride (b) Sodium chloride (table salt)
(c) Calcium sulfate (d) Potassium iodide

3. How much of the Earth's surface is covered by water?

(a) 25% (b) 50% (c) 75% (d) 97.3%

4. Rohan, a student of class 7th, is making a list of fresh water sources. Which one of the following is not a fresh water source? Competency Based

(a) Rivers (b) Ground water
(c) Ice-caps (d) Oceans

water stress for at least one month annually. This figure might escalate to nearly 60% by the year 2050".

Source : NDTV World. **Competency Based**

How much per cent of fresh water is stored in ice-caps?

(a) 1% (b) 2% (c) 3% (d) 4%

6. What are the major movements in oceans categorised as?

(a) Waves, tides and rivers
(b) Waves, tides and currents
(c) Waves, storms and earthquakes
(d) Tides, tsunamis and whirlpools

7. What causes the formation of waves in the ocean?

(a) Earthquakes (b) Volcanic eruptions
(c) Underwater landslides
(d) Winds scraping across the ocean surface

8. What is a tsunami?

(a) A type of wave generated by the Moon's gravity
(b) A tidal wave caused by the Sun's gravitational pull
(c) A large and destructive ocean wave caused by seismic activity
(d) A calm and gentle ocean current

9. What was the cause of the devastating tsunami in the Indian Ocean on 26th December, 2004?

(a) A volcanic eruption (b) An underwater landslide
(c) A massive earthquake (d) A solar eclipse

10. What causes tides in the oceans?

(a) Earth's rotation
(b) Gravitational pull of the Sun and the Moon
(c) Wind patterns
(d) Earth's magnetic field

11. How do high tides near the shore benefit navigation and power generation? **Competency Based**

(a) They help ships arrive at harbors more easily.
(b) They cause strong underwater currents.
(c) They are used to generate electricity.
(d) They make fishing more productive.

12. Salinity refers to amount of salt present in .... grams of water. **Diksha**

(a) 10 (b) 1000 (c) 100 (d) 10000

13. Choose the correct statement(s) from the following.

I. The Labrador Ocean current is cold current.
II. Low tides enables fisherman to get a plentiful catch.
III. The area where a warm and cold current meet is good for navigation.

Codes

(a) I and II (b) Only I (c) Only II (d) I and III

14. Choose the incorrect statement from the following.

I. Our Earth is like a terrarium.
II. There is only 30% of water on Earth is fresh water.
III. 22nd March is celebrated as World Water Day.

Codes

(a) Only I (b) Only II
(c) Only III (d) None of these

15. Identify the correct option about which given statements are true. **Competency Based**

I. It is also called spring tides.
II. It helps in navigation.
III. It is used to generate electricity in some places.

Codes

(a) Low tides (b) Cold current
(c) High tides (d) Warm current

Answers

1. (b)	2. (b)	3. (c)	4. (d)	5. (b)
6. (b)	7. (d)	8. (c)	9. (c)	10. (b)
11. (a)	12. (b)	13. (b)	14. (b)	15. (c)

Match the Following

1.

List I	List II
A. Labrador current	1. Cold current
B. Gulf Stream	2. Warm current
C. Fishing ground	3. Japan and North America

Codes

	A	B	C		A	B	C
(a)	2	1	3	(b)	3	1	2
(c)	1	2	3	(d)	2	3	1

2.

List I	List II
A. Condensation	1. Changing from a gaseous to a liquid or solid state
B. Evaporation	2. The falling of moisture on Earth in the form of rain, snow, hail, sleet, or mist
C. Precipitation	3. The process of becoming a vapour
D. Terrarium	4. An artificial enclosure for keeping small house plants

Codes

	A	B	C	D		A	B	C	D
(a)	4	3	2	1	(b)	1	3	2	4
(c)	1	2	4	3	(d)	1	2	3	4

Ans. 1. (c) 2. (b)

Assertion-Reason

1. Assertion (A) Tides occur due to the gravitational pull of the Sun and the Moon on the Earth's surface.

Reason (R) The rhythmic rise and fall of ocean water twice in a day is called a tide, and it is caused by the strong gravitational pull exerted by celestial bodies like the Sun and the Moon.

Codes

(a) Both A and R are true and R is the correct explanation of A

(b) Both A and R are true, but R is not the correct explanation of A

(c) A is true, but R is false

(d) A is false, but R is true

2. **Assertion** (A) The tsunami of 2004 was triggered by a massive earthquake near Sumatra's western boundary.

Reason (R) The earthquake had a magnitude of 4.0 on the Richter scale and was caused by the Indian plate going under the Burma plate, leading to a sudden shift in the sea floor.

Codes

(a) Both A and R are true and R is the correct explanation of A

(b) Both A and R are true, but R is not the correct explanation of A

(c) A is true, but R is false

(d) A is false, but R is true

Ans. 1. (a) Both A and R are true and R is the correct explanation of A

2. (c) A is true, but R is false

Fill in the Blanks

1. The Sun's heat causes evaporation of water into ....
2. The process by which water continually changes its form and circulates between oceans, atmosphere and .... is known as the water cycle.
3. Dead sea in Israel has salinity of .... grams per litre of water.
4. Waves are formed when winds scrape across ....
5. The strong gravitational pull exerted by .... and the Moon on the Earth's surface causes the tides.

Ans. 1.vapour 2. land 3. 340 4. the ocean surface 5. the Sun

True/False

1. The Earth's surface is covered by three-fourths of water.
2. The majority of the water on Earth is saline or salty, found in oceans and seas.
3. Waves are primarily caused by the gravitational pull of the Sun and the Moon.
4. Tsunamis can be caused by events such as earthquakes, volcanic eruptions, or underwater landslides.
5. Warm ocean currents generally originate near the poles and move towards the equator.

Ans. 1. True 2. True 3. False 4. True 5. False

Picture Based Questions

1. A wave flown is shown in the image.

What is the primary cause of the tsunami wave depicted in the image?

(a) Strong winds (b) Underwater earthquake
(c) Volcanic eruption (d) Tidal forces

2. The image shows the position of Sun, Moon and Earth during a tide. In which direction ocean waters get drawn by gravitational pull in low tide?

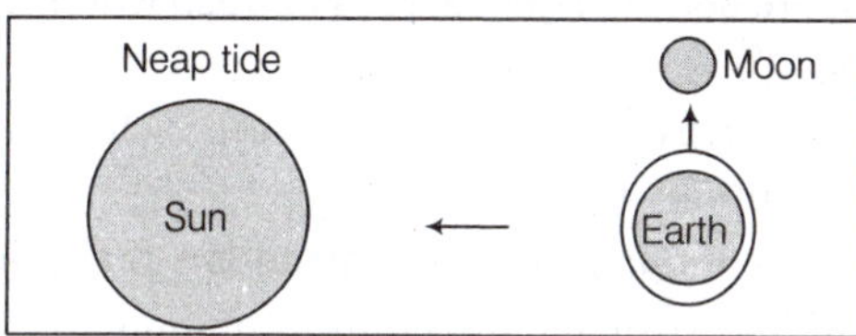

(a) Parallel (b) Same direction
(c) Diagonally opposite (d) Perpendicular

Ans. 1. (b) Underwater earthquake 2. (c) Diagonally opposite

Case Based Question

1. Read the passage given below and answer the following questions.

The rhythmic rise and fall of ocean water twice in a day is called a tide. It is high tide when water covers much of the shore by rising to its highest level. It is low tide when water falls to its lowest level and recedes from the shore.The strong gravitational pull exerted by the Sun and the Moon on the Earth's surface causes the tides. The water of the Earth closer to the Moon gets pulled under the influence of the Moon's gravitational force and causes high tide. During the full moon and new moon days, the Sun, the Moon and the Earth are in the same line and the tides are highest. These tides are called spring tides. But when the Moon is in its first and last quarter, the ocean waters get drawn in diagonally opposite directions by the gravitational pull of Sun and Moon resulting in low tides.

(i) What causes the rhythmic rise and fall of ocean water, known as tides?

(a) Winds scraping across the ocean surface
(b) Earth's rotation on its axis
(c) Gravitational pull of the Sun and the Moon
(d) Underwater volcanic eruptions

(ii) What characterises neap tides?

(a) High tides with maximum water coverage
(b) Low tides with minimal water coverage
(c) Tides occurring during the first and last quarter of the Moon
(d) Tides caused by volcanic eruptions

(iii) Spring tides occur during which of the following?

(a) Half Moon (b) Full Moon
(c) Quarter Moon (d) None of these

(iv) How tides are helpful to us?

(a) They help in navigation (b) They help in fishing
(c) They help to raise their water level close to shores.
(d) All of the above

Ans. (i) (c) Gravitational pull of the Sun and the Moon

(ii) (c) Tides occurring during the first and last quarter of the Moon

(iii) (b) Full Moon

(iv) (d) All of the above

PART II

Very Short Answer Type Questions

1. What percentage of Earth's water is saline and found in oceans and seas?

Ans. 97.3% of Earth's water is saline and is found in oceans and seas.

2. What are some major sources of fresh water on Earth?

Ans. Major sources of fresh water on Earth include rivers, ponds, springs and glaciers.

3. What event can trigger the formation of tsunamis?

Ans. Events like earthquakes, volcanic eruptions, or underwater landslides can trigger the formation of tsunamis.

4. What does the term tsunami mean in Japanese?

Ans. The term tsunami in Japanese means harbour waves.

5. What is the general movement of warm ocean currents?

Ans. Warm ocean currents generally move from the equator toward the poles.

6. Give an example of a cold current.

Ans. An example of a cold ocean current is the Labrador current.

7. What is the average salinity of the Earth's oceans?

Ans. The average salinity of the Earth's oceans is 35 parts per thousand.

8. Which ocean current is an example of a warm current?

Ans. An example of a warm ocean current is the Gulf Stream.

9. What is the unique feature of the Dead Sea in Israel that allows swimmers to float?

Ans. The unique feature of the Dead Sea in Israel is its high salinity of 340 grams per liter, which makes swimmers float on its surface.

10. What process involves changing from a gaseous to a liquid or solid state?

Ans. The process that involves changing from a gaseous to a liquid or solid state is condensation.

Short Answer Type Questions

1. Briefly explain the importance of water.

Ans. Water is essential for all life on Earth. It plays an important role in the survival of living beings. It is also used in various daily activities, from household chores to industrial processes.

The scarcity of water can lead to numerous problems, and its absence would be devastating for all living organisms. Therefore, water is a precious natural resource that must be conserved to ensure the well-being of both humans and the environment.

2. Water cycle is a natural process in which water continuously change its form. Explain water cycle. Competency Based

Ans. The water cycle, also known as the hydrologic cycle, is a natural process in which water continuously changes its form and circulates between the oceans, atmosphere and land.

It begins with the Sun's heat causing the evaporation of water from oceans, lakes and rivers. This water vapour rises into the atmosphere, cools, and condenses to form clouds. Subsequently, the condensed water droplets fall back to Earth as precipitation, which can take the form of rain, snow, or sleet. This cycle is essential for maintaining the Earth's water balance and sustaining life.

3. What are waves? How they are caused. Diksha

Ans. Waves are a phenomena wherein the water in the surface of the ocean rises and falls alternately.

Waves are primarily caused by the scraping of winds across the ocean surface, with stronger winds leading to larger waves. Storms, high-speed winds, earthquakes, volcanic eruptions, and underwater landslides can shift significant amounts of ocean water, giving rise to tsunamis, which are enormous tidal waves, potentially reaching heights of upto 15 meters and causing huge destruction along coastal areas.

4. Explain the distribution of water in the world.

Ans. The three-fourth surface of the Earth is covered with the water.

The distribution of this water in percentage is given below

- 97.3% of total water is saline or salty in Oceans and seas.
- Only 3% of total water on the earth is freshwater. This freshwater can be found in ice-caps (2.0%), ground water (0.68%) fresh water lakes (0.009%) inland seas and salt lakes (0.009%), atmosphere (0.0019%) and rivers (0.0001%).

5. Differentiate between waves and tides **Competency Based**

Ans. Differences between waves and tides are

Waves	Tides
When the water on the surface of the ocean rises and falls alternately, they are called waves.	The rhythmic rise and fall of ocean water twice in a day is called a tide.
They are caused by wind blown.	They are caused by gravitational forces.
During a storm, the winds blowing at very high speed form huge waves. These may cause tremendous destruction.	It is high tide when water covers much of the shore by rising to its highest level. It is low tide when water falls to its lowest level and recedes from the shore.

6. Briefly explain, how spring and neap tides are formed.

Ans. Spring tides are formed during the full moon and new moon days when the sun, the moon and the Earth are in the same line and highest tides occur.

Neap tides are formed when the moon is in its first and last quarter, due to which the ocean waters are drawn in diagonally opposite directions by the gravitational pull of the sun and the moon and results in low tides.

7. Briefly state the use of high tides. **Diksha**

Ans. High tides are important for various reasons

- They raise the water level close to the shores. This helps the ships to arrive at the harbour more easily.
- The high tides also help in fishing. Many more fish come closer to the shore during the high tide. This enables fishermen to get a plentiful catch.
- The rise and fall of water due to tides is being used to generate electricity in some places.

8. Differentiate between warm ocean current and cold ocean current. **Competency Based**

Ans. Differences between warm ocean current and cold ocean current

Warm Ocean Current	Cold Ocean Current
It originates near the equator and move towards the poles.	It carries water from polar or higher latitudes to tropical or lower latitudes.
It brings warm temperature over land surface.	It brings cold temperature over land surface.
The Gulf Stream is a warm current.	The Labrador Ocean current is a cold current.

Long Answers Type Questions

1. How do we classify ocean movements? Explain.

Ans. The movements that occur in oceans can be broadly categorised as waves, tides and currents. These are given below

- **Waves** When the water on the surface of the ocean rises and falls alternately, they are called waves. During a storm, the winds blowing at very high speed form huge waves. These may cause tremendous destruction. An earthquake, a volcanic eruption or underwater landslides can shift large amounts of ocean water.
- **Tides** The rhythmic rise and fall of ocean water twice in a day is called a tide. It is high tide when water covers much of the shore by rising to its highest level. It is low tide when water falls to its lowest level and recedes from the shore.
- **Ocean Currents** These are streams of water flowing constantly on the ocean surface in definite directions which may be warm or cold. The warm ocean currents originate near the equator and move towards the poles. The cold currents carry water from polar or higher latitudes to tropical or lower latitudes.

2. Explain the occurrence of tsunami. Also given an example of tsunami that occured in history.

Ans. Tsunamis are massive tidal waves that result from natural events such as earthquakes, volcanic eruptions, or underwater landslides. These waves can be as high as 15 meters and travel at speeds exceeding 700 kilometers per hour. The term tsunami is of Japanese origin, meaning harbour waves, and these waves have a destructive impact, especially during storms or seismic activities.

One of the most devastating tsunamis in recent history occurred on 26th December, 2004, in the Indian Ocean. This was triggered by a massive undersea earthquake near Sumatra, with a magnitude of 9.0 on the Richter scale. The earthquake caused a significant shift in the sea floor, displacing it by about 10-20 meters and leading to a withdrawal of water mass from the coastlines in South and South-East Asia.

Some Indian Ocean islands, including the southernmost point of India, the Indira Point in the Andaman and Nicobar Islands, were entirely washed away.

3. Explain the different types of tides. Also explain about high tides.

Ans. Tides can be broadly categorised as follows

- **Spring Tides** During the full moon and new moon days when the sun, the moon and the Earth are in the same line, highest tides occur. These tides are called spring tides.

- **Neap Tides** When the moon is in its first and last quarter, the ocean waters are drawn in diagonally opposite directions by the gravitational pull of the sun, and the moon and results in low tides. These tides are called neap tides.

When the water of the Earth closer to the moon gets pulled under the influence of the moon's gravitational force and causes high tides are caused. High tides help in navigation. They raise the water level close to the shores which helps the ships to arrive at the harbour more easily. The high tides also help in fishing as more fish come closer to the shore during high tides.

4. Discuss the different types of ocean currents and how they originate. Also discuss their benefits. **Competency Based**

Ans. Ocean currents are continuous streams of water on the ocean surface with specific directions, categorised as either warm or cold currents.

Warm ocean currents typically originate near the equator and move towards the poles, while cold currents carry water from polar or higher latitudes to lower latitudes.

These currents play an important role in influencing local temperature conditions, as warm currents bring warmth to land surfaces. Regions where warm and cold currents converge offer some of the world's best fishing grounds. For example, seas around Japan and the Eastern coast of North America. However, these convergence areas also experience foggy weather, which poses challenges for navigation.

Case Based Question

1. Read the passage given below and answer the following questions.

Ocean currents are streams of water flowing constantly on the ocean surface in definite directions. The ocean currents may be warm or cold. Generally,

the warm ocean currents originate near the equator and move towards the poles. The cold currents carry water from polar or higher latitudes to tropical or lower latitudes. The Labrador Ocean current is cold current while the Gulf Stream is a warm current. The ocean current influence the temperature conditions of the area. Warm currents bring about warm temperature over land surface.

(i) How do ocean currents contribute to the temperature conditions of a region?

Ans. Ocean currents contribute to the temperature conditions by carrying warm or cold water to different latitudes.

Warm currents, originating near the equator, bring warm temperatures over land surfaces; while cold currents bring cold temperature.

(ii) Explain the significance of the Gulf Stream as a warm ocean current and is influence on the temperature conditions.

Ans. The Gulf Stream, as a warm ocean current originating near the equator, plays a significant role in increasing the temperatures over land surfaces. Its influences shows the relationship between ocean currents and local climate.

ASSESSMENT EXERCISE

Multiple Choice Questions (MCQs)

1. In which year did the tsunami hit the coastal areas of India?
   (a) 2005 (b) 2009
   (c) 2004 (d) 2008
2. Which of the following tide occurs during the full Moon?
   (a) Spring tides
   (b) Neap tides
   (c) High tides
   (d) None of the above
3. Which of the following area provide the best fishing ground?
   (a) Cold current
   (b) Warm current
   (c) Warm and cold current meets
   (d) None of the above

Subjective Questions (VSA, SA & LA)

1. Explain the distribution of waters on the Earth.
2. What are the different types of tides?
3. How does ocean current influences the temperature of the local area?
4. Explain water cycle in which water circulates between ocean, atmosphere and land.
5. How does wave formation occur in the ocean?
6. What do you mean by tsunami? Discuss its effect in India.
7. How is the movement of waves different from the tides? What causes them to occur?
8. Water is very important substance on the Earth. Suggest some major steps to conserve it.

Human Environment Interactions-The Tropical and the Subtropical Region

Our planet is a natural terrarium with varying characteristics including different climatic, longitudinal and latitudinal conditions. This leads to various uneven structures, for example, hot wet rainforests, dry deserts and frozen lands. In this chapter, we will learn about the life in **Amazon basin** and **Ganga-Brahmaputra Plains**.

6.1 Life in the Amazon Basin

The Amazon Basin lies in the tropical regions very close to the equator, between 10°N and 10°S. So, it is referred to as the **equatorial region**.

It is formed by joining of the **tributaries**[1] of the Amazon river which flows in the tropical region.

The Amazon river flows from the mountains to the West and reaches the Atlantic Ocean in the East.

The place where a river flows into another body of water is called the **river's mouth**.

The Amazon Basin is the **largest river basin**[2] in the world. It drains portions of Brazil, parts of Peru, Bolivia, Ecuador, Columbia and a small part of Venezuela.

• The Amazon Basin in South America

Discovery of Amazon River

The Amazon river was discovered by **Spanish explorers**. During the quest of discovery, they were attacked by a group of local tribes wearing headgears and grass skirts.

These people reminded them of the fierce tribes of women warriors who were known as the **Amazons** in ancient Roman Empire. Hence, the name was given Amazon.

Climate

The Amazon Basin stretches directly on the equator and is characterised by hot and wet climate throughout the year.

In Amazon Basin both day and nights are almost equally hot and humid and the skin feels sticky.

The region gets rain almost everyday. The day temperatures are high with very high humidity. At night, the temperature goes down but the humidity remains high.

Rainforests

The Amazon river basin is rich in the variety of life found here. Thick forests grow in the region of Amazon Basin as it gets heavy rainfall.

The forests are so thick that the dense 'roof' created by leaves and branches does not allow the sunlight to reach the ground.

The ground remains dark and damp. Only shade tolerant vegetation may grow in this region. For example, Orchids and **bromeliads** grow as plant parasites.

The rainforests have a diverse range of fauna, including birds like toucans, macaws and hummingbirds.

Various animals such as monkeys, sloths and ant-eating tapirs are found in the rainforests.

1 **Tributaries** These are small rivers that join the main river.

2 **River Basin** The main river along with all its tributaries that drain an area forms a river basin or the catchment area.

Various species of reptiles and snakes are also found in this region like crocodiles, pythons, anaconda and boa constrictor. Apart from these, many insect species and species of fish including flesh-eating Piranha fish is found in this region.

KNOWLEDGE PLUS Bromeliads are special plants that store water in their leaves. Animals like frogs use these pockets of water for laying their eggs.

People of the Rainforests

Hunting, fishing and farming are significant occupations for the people in the basin. Men are involved in hunting and fishing along the rivers, while women are responsible for taking care of the crops.

Due to uncertainty of hunting and fishing, women keep the families alive by feeding them the vegetables, they grow.

The people of the basin practice **slash and burn agriculture**, in which they grow most of their food in small areas after clearing some trees in the forest.

They mainly grow tapioca, pineapple and sweet potato as well as cash crops like coffee, maize and cocoa. The staple food is manioc which is also known as **cassava**, that grows under the ground, like potato. People also eat queen ants and egg sacs.

The rainforests provide a lot of wood for the houses. Hence, some families live in thatched houses shaped like beehives and other live in large apartment like houses called **Maloca** with a steeply slanting roof.

Slash and Burn Agriculture

Slash and burn is a way of cultivating land where farmers clear a piece of land by slashing or cutting down trees and bushes. These are then burnt, which releases the nutrients into the soil.

After this, crops are grown in this cleared field for a few years. After repeatedly using the patch of land, when the soil looses its nutrients, they leave this land and clear another plot of land to grow crops.

In the mean time, young trees grow in the old field that is abandoned. In this way, soil fertility is restored, and people can return to it and start cultivating it again.

Changing Life of the People

Life of the people of the Amazon Basin is slowly changing. In the older days, the central part of forest could be reached only by navigating rivers.

The construction of the **Trans Amazon Highway** in 1970 made all parts of the rainforest accessible. Aircrafts and helicopters are also used for reaching various places.

The indigenous population was forced to move out from the area and settle in new areas where they continued to practice their distinctive way of farming.

The developmental activities are leading to the gradual destruction of the biologically diverse rainforests. It is estimated that a large area of the rainforest has been disappearing annually in the Amazon Basin.

As a result of this destruction of forests, the topsoil is washed away by heavy rainfall and the dense forest turns into a barren landscape.

Try These

1. **The tributaries of which river form the Amazon Basin?**
2. **What are 'bromeliads'?**
3. **The term refers to the place where a river flows into another body of water. Identify the term.**
4. **Name some crops that are grown by the people of Amazon Basin.**

Life in the Ganga–Brahmaputra Basin

The **tributaries** of Ganga and Brahmaputra rivers together form the Ganga-Brahmaputra basin in the Indian **subcontinent**[3].

The basin lies in the sub-tropical region that is situated between 10°N to 30°N latitudes. It is drained by the tributaries of the Ganga river like the Ghaghra, the Son, the Chambal, the Gandak, the Kosi, and the tributaries of Brahmaputra river.

The plains of the Ganga and the Brahmaputra, the mountains and the foothills of the Himalayas and the Sundarbans delta are the main features of this basin.

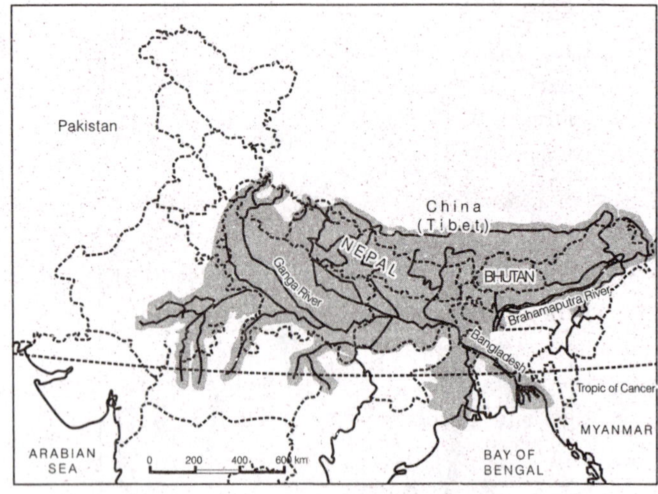

• Ganga-Brahmaputra Basin

3 **Subcontinent** A large landmass, such as India, that is part of a continent but is considered either geographically or politically as an independent entity.

Climate and Topography

The Ganga-Brahmaputra Basin is dominated by **monsoon climate**. The monsoon brings rains from mid-June to mid-September. The summers are hot and the winters are cool.

The basin area has varied topography. The environment plays a dominant role in the distribution of the population. The mountain areas with steep slopes have uninhabitable terrain. Therefore less number of people live in these areas. On the other hand, the plain areas provide the most suitable land for human habitation as the soil is fertile.

Agriculture in the Basin

Agriculture is the main occupation of the people in areas where flat land is available to grow crops. **The population density**[4] of the plains is very high.

The main crop is **paddy** which requires sufficient water to grow. Thus, it is grown in the areas where the amount of rainfall is high.

Wheat, maize, sorghum, gram and millets are the other crops that are grown in this basin. Cash crops like **sugarcane** and **jute** are also grown and banana plantations are seen in some areas of the plains.

In West Bengal and Assam tea is grown in plantations. Silk is produced through the cultivation of silk worms in parts of Bihar and Assam. In the mountains and hills, where the slopes are gentle, crops are grown through **terrace farming**[5].

Flora and Fauna of the Basin

The vegetation cover of the basin varies according to the type of landforms. In the Ganga and Brahmaputra plain, tropical deciduous trees grow, along with teak, sal and peepal whereas thick bamboo groves are common in the Brahmaputra plain. The delta area is covered with the mangrove forests.

In parts of **Uttarakhand**, **Sikkim** and **Arunachal Pradesh**, coniferous trees like pine, deodar and fir can be seen because the climate is cool and the slopes are steep.

A variety of animals are found in the basin in which elephants, tigers, deers and monkeys are common. The one-horned rhinoceros is found in the Brahmaputra plain. Bengal tiger and crocodiles are found in the delta area.

Aquatic life is found in the fresh river waters, the lakes and the Bay of Bengal sea. The most popular varieties of the fish are **rohu**, **catla** and **hilsa**. Fish and rice is the staple diet of the people living in the area.

Blind Dolphin

In the fresh waters of river Ganga and River Brahmaputra, a variety of dolphin locally called Susu (also called blind dolphin) is found. The presence of Susu is an indication of the health of the river.

Cities and Transport in the Basin

The Ganga-Brahmaputra plain has several big towns and cities like Allahabad, Kanpur, Varanasi, Lucknow, Patna and Kolkata with the population of more than ten lakhs.

The waste water from these towns and industries is discharged into the rivers that leads to the pollution of the rivers.

All the four ways of transport are well developed in the Ganga-Brahmaputra basin. In the plain areas, the roadways and railways transport the people from one place to another.

The waterways is an effective means of transport particularly along the rivers. **Kolkata** is an important port on the river Hooghly. The plain area has a large number of airports.

KNOWLEDGE PLUS The Prime Minister of India launched the **Swachh Bharat Mission** on 2nd October, 2014 to acceletrate the efforts for achieving universal sanitation coverage.

Namami Ganga Programme has been initiated to conserve the river Ganga.

Tourism in the Basin

Tourism is another important activity in the basin. Some of the tourist attractions are

- **Taj Mahal** on the banks of River Yamuna in Agra.
- Allahabad on the meeting of the Rivers Ganga and Yamuna.
- Buddhists stupas in Uttar Pradesh and Bihar, and Imambara in Lucknow.
- **Kaziranga** and **Manas wildlife sanctuaries** in Assam.
- Distinct tribal culture of Arunachal Pradesh.

Try These

1. **Name some tributaries of Ganga river.**
2. **Which type of farming is practiced by the people of Ganga-Brahmaputra Basin?**
3. **Mention the fish varieties popular in the Ganga-Brahmaputra Basin.**
4. **Name any one tourist place in the Ganga-Brahmaputra Basin.**

4 Population Density It refers to the number of persons that live in one square kilometer of an area.

5 Terrace Farming In this farming, terraces are built on steep slopes to create flat surfaces on which crops are grown. The slope is removed so that water does not run off rapidly.

HUMAN ENVIRONMENT INTERACTIONS-THE TROPICAL AND THE SUBTROPICAL REGION

Tropical Region
(e.g.– Amazon basin)

It lies between 10° N and 10°S latitude also known as equatorial region.

Sub-tropical Region
(e.g.-Ganga-Brahmaputra basin)

- It lies between 10° N to 30° N latitude.
- Rivers of this region include Ganga, Ghaghra, Son, Chambal, Gadak, Kosi and tributaries of Brahmaputra.

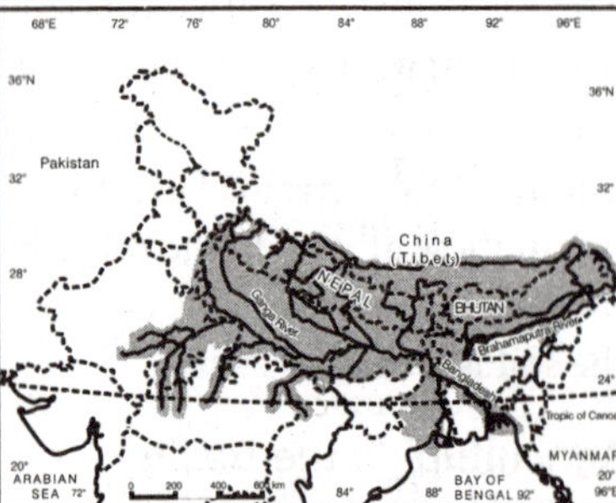

Climate

Climate

- In tropical region the climate remain Hot and wet throughout the year.
- Get rain almost everyday.
- Day temperature is high with humidity whereas in night temperature goes down.

Rainforests

- These are thick forests.
- Sunlight unable to reach the ground due to dense roof created by leaves and branches
- Flora–Orchids, bromeliads
- Fauna–Toucans, macaws and humming birds.

People of the Rainforest

- Main occupation-Hunting, fishing and farming
- Slash and burn agriculture is practiced.
- Fruits–Tapioca, pineapple and sweet potato
- Cash crops - Coffee, maize and cocoa
- Staple food – Manioc also known as cassava
- Houses are called Maloca

Climate and Topography

Moonsoon climate and has varied topography

Agriculture

- Crops–Paddy, wheat, maize, sorghum gram and millet
- Cash crops–Sugarcane, jute, banana, tea

Tourism

Taj Mahal, Buddhist stupas, Kaziranga and Manas wildlife sanctuaries

Cities and Transport

- **Cities**–Allahabad, Kanpur, Varanasi, Lucknow, Patna and Kolkata
- Railways, roadways, waterways and airways are well developed

Flora and Fauna

- Flora–Tropical deciduous trees, teak, sal and peepal, thick bamboo pine, deodar
- Fauna–Elephant, tigers, deers, monkeys, one-horned rhinoceros, Bengal tiger and crocodile

NCERT FOLDER

Covering Intext Questions and Exercises of NCERT

NCERT ON PAGE 41

Q.1 Some TV channels broadcast documentaries on the wildlife of the world. Try to watch some of the films and share your experience with the class.

Ans. Do it yourself.

NCERT ON PAGE 44

Q.2 River Brahmaputra is known by different names in different places. It is called Tsangpo in Tibet. Find the other names of the river.

Ans. The other names of Brahmaputra are Lohit, Jamuna (Bangladesh), Dihang or Siang (Arunachal Pradesh), Meghna etc.

Q.3 Collect some handicrafts made from jute, bamboo and silk. Display them in the class. Find out in which area they were made in?

Ans. Handicrafts from jute, bamboo and silk are made in Assam, West Bengal, Bihar and other North-Eastern states.

EXERCISES

Q.1 Answer the following questions.

(a) Name the continent in which the Amazon Basin is located.

Ans. The Amazon Basin is located in South America Continent.

(b) What are the crops grown by the people of the Amazon basin?

Ans. Crops grown by the people of Amazon basin are tapioca, pineapple, sweet potato, coffee, maize and cocoa.

(c) Name the birds that you are likely to find in the rainforests of the Amazon.

Ans. Birds that are likely to be found in the rainforests of the Amazon are toucans and hummingbirds.

(d) What are the major cities located on the river Ganga?

Ans. Major cities located on the river Ganga are Allahabad, Kanpur, Varanasi, Lucknow, Patna and Kolkata.

(e) Where is the one-horned rhinoceros found?

Ans. The one-horned rhinoceros is found in the Brahmaputra plain.

Q.2 Tick the correct answer.

(i) Toucans are a type of

(a) birds (b) animals (c) crops

(ii) Manioc is the staple food of

(a) Ganga basin (b) Africa (c) Amazon

(iii) Kolkata is located on the river

(a) Orange (b) Hooghly (c) Bhagirathi

(iv) Deodars and firs are a type of

(a) coniferous trees (b) deciduous trees
(c) shrubs

(v) Bengal tiger is found in

(a) mountains (b) delta area (c) Amazon

Ans. (i) (a) birds (ii) (c) Amazon
(iii) (b) Hooghly (iv) (a) coniferous trees
(v) (b) delta area

Q.3 Match the following.

	List I		List II
A.	Cotton textile	1.	Assam
B.	Maloca	2.	Terrace farming
C.	Piranha	3.	Sericulture
D.	Silk worm	4.	Slanting roof
E.	Kaziranga	5.	Ganga Plain
		6.	Varanasi
		7.	Fish

Ans. A. – 6 , B. – 4 , C – 7 , D – 3 , E – 1

Q.4 Give reasons.

(a) The rainforests are depleting.

Ans. The rainforests are depleting because of developmental activities which destroy the biological diversity of rainforests through deforestation and hunting.

(b) Paddy is grown in the Ganga-Brahmaputra plains.

Ans. The Ganga-Brahmaputra plain is best suited for paddy cultivation because it requires sufficient water and this region receive heavy rainfall which fulfil this condition.

REVIEW EXERCISE

Including Competency Based Questions

PART I

Multiple Choice Questions (MCQs)

1. Which river flows through the Amazon Basin and reaches the Atlantic Ocean?

(a) Nile (b) Ganges
(c) Amazon (d) Mississippi

2. After whom, the Amazon river named 'Amazon'?

(a) After a famous explorer
(b) After a Roman Emperor
(c) After the indigenous people who attacked Spanish explorers
(d) None of the above

3. What is the climate of the Amazon Basin?

(a) Cold and dry
(b) Hot and wet throughout the year
(c) Mild and rainy
(d) Extremely cold with heavy snowfall

4. Which plants are able to grow in the dark and damp conditions of the Amazon rainforest?

(a) Cacti (b) Sunflowers
(c) Orchids and bromeliads (d) Oak trees

5. What is the primary occupation of the people in the Amazon Basin?

(a) Hunting (b) Fishing
(c) Agriculture (d) All of these

6. What is the primary staple food of the people living in the Amazon Basin?

(a) Rice (b) Bread
(c) Manioc (cassava) (d) Corn

7. What is the farming method referred to as in the Amazon Basin, where land is cleared by cutting down trees and burning debris?

(a) Slash and Burn Agriculture (b) Conventional Farming
(c) Organic Farming (d) Aquaponics

8. Where is Ganga-Brahmaputra Basin situated? Diksha

(a) Sub-tropical region (b) Temperate region
(c) Polar region (d) Equatorial region

9. Which coniferous trees can be found in parts of Uttarakhand, Sikkim, and Arunachal Pradesh due to their cool climate and steep slopes?

(a) Pine, deodar, and fir (b) Oak, maple, and cedar
(c) Coconut, palm, and date (d) Bamboo, banyan, and teak

10. Which variety of dolphin, locally called Susu, is found in the fresh waters of the Ganga and Brahmaputra rivers?

(a) Killer whale
(b) Bottlenose dolphin
(c) Blind dolphin
(d) Gray dolphin

11. Which program was launched by the Prime Minister of India to accelerate efforts for universal sanitation coverage and focus on sanitation?

(a) Swachh Bharat Mission
(b) Namami Ganga Programme
(c) Clean Rivers Initiative
(d) Green India Campaign

12. Ankur from Indore , Madhya Pradesh decided to go to Allahabad (Prayagraj) for travelling and took blessing from sacred river Ganga. But he found the waste water from these towns and industries is discharged into the rivers that lead to the pollution of the rivers. What significant environmental concern is associated with the discharge of waste water from cities and industries into the rivers of the Ganga-Brahmaputra Basin? Competency Based

(a) Increase in aquatic biodiversity
(b) Improvement in water quality
(c) Decrease in pollution of the rivers
(d) Adverse effects on river ecosystems

13. 'Marking a shift in emphasis, the Union Government's flagship Namami Gange Programme, conceived to improve the sanitation levels in the Ganga river is now geared towards conservation, tourism and providing economic livelihoods.'

Source The Hindu

Should the implementation of such programme be considered in conservation and providing economic livelihoods? Competency Based

(a) Yes, such programme implementation helps in cleaning the river and aware about cleaniness of the river.
(b) Yes, such programme will benefit the government in portfolio making.
(c) No, such programme has negative impact on the river.
(d) No, there is no need of such programme as river is pure and clean.

14. Identify the correct option that describes about basin given below.

I. It lies between 10° N and 10° S.

II. It has high day temperature and high humidity.

III. Animals like monkeys, sloth and ant-eating tapirs are found here. **Competency Based**

Options

(a) Amazon Basin (b) Kaveri Basin
(c) Ganga Basin (d) Brahmaputra Basin

15. Choose the correct statement(s) from the following.

I. River Brahmaputra is also known as Jamuna.

II. Ganga is a tributary of Brahmaputra river.

III. Paddy cultivation does not require much water.

Codes

(a) I and II (b) Only I
(c) II and III (d) None of the above

16. Choose the incorrect statement(s) from the following.

I. The density of population of the plains is very low.

II. Kolkata is an important port on the river Hooghly.

III. Prime Minister of India launched the Swachh Bharat Mission on 2nd October, 2014.

Codes

(a) I and III (b) I, II and III
(c) Only I (d) Only III

Answers

1. (c) **2.** (c) **3.** (b) **4.** (c) **5.** (d)
6. (c) **7.** (a) **8.** (a) **9.** (a) **10.** (c)
11. (a) **12.** (d) **13.** (a) **14.** (a) **15.** (b)
16. (c)

Match the Following

1.

	List I		List II
A.	Amazon region	1.	River basin
B.	Orchids, bromeliads	2.	Special plants
C.	Manioc	3.	Staple food
D.	West Bengal and Assam	4.	Region near the equator

Codes

	A	B	C	D
(a)	1	2	3	4
(b)	1	3	2	4
(c)	4	2	3	1
(d)	2	3	1	4

2.

	List I	List II
A.	Ganga-Brahmaputra plain	1. Found in Amazon Basin
B.	Toucans	2. Located in Assam
C.	Bengal tiger	3. Region with monsoon climate
D.	Manas Wildlife Sanctuary	4. Found in the delta area

Codes

	A	B	C	D
(a)	3	1	4	2
(b)	4	1	2	3
(c)	2	3	1	4
(d)	3	4	1	2

Ans. 1. (c) 2. (a)

Assertion-Reason

1. Assertion (A) The Ganga-Brahmaputra Basin is dominated by a monsoon climate.

Reason (R) The monsoon brings rains from mid-June to mid-September in the region.

Codes

(a) Both A and R are true and R is the correct explanation of A
(b) Both A and R are true, but R is not the correct explanation of A
(c) A is true, but R is false
(d) A is false, but R is true

2. Assertion (A) Slash and burn agriculture is a common farming method in the Brahmaputra Basin.

Reason (R) This method involves clearing land by cutting down trees and burning debris to enrich the soil.

Codes

(a) Both A and R are true and R is the correct explanation of A
(b) Both A and R are true, but R is not the correct explanation of A
(c) A is true, but R is false
(d) A is false, but R is true

Ans. 1. (a) Both A and R are true and R is the correct explanation of A

2. (d) A is false, but R is true

Fill in the Blanks

1. The place where a river flows into another body of water is called the river's ....

2. The forests are in fact so thick that the dense .... created by leaves and branches does not allow the sunlight to reach the ground.

3. .... are special plants that store water in their leaves.

4. .... are built on steep slopes to create flat surfaces on which crops are grown.

5. To conserve the river Ganga, ... Programme has been initiated.

Ans. 1. mouth 2. roof
3. Bromeliads 4. Terraces
5. 'Namami' Ganga

True/False

1. The Amazon Basin lies between 20°N and 20°S latitudes.
2. The Amazon River flows from the East to the West.
3. The name 'Amazon' for the river and basin is derived from a group of fierce tribes of women warriors known in the ancient Roman Empire.
4. In the Amazon Basin, both day and night temperatures are almost equally hot and humid.
5. Terrace farming is a common practice in the mountainous and hilly areas of the Ganga-Brahmaputra Basin to maximise agricultural space.

Ans. 1. False 2. False 3. True 4. True 5. True

Picture Based Questions

1. **The image of one horned rhinoceros is shown below. In which region they are found mainly?**

(a) Brahmaputra plain (b) Ganga plain
(c) Amazon plain (d) Deccan plain

2. **There is an image shown of species found in Amazon rainforest. Identify the species.**

(a) Susu (b) Toucans
(c) Tiger (d) Crocodiles

Ans. 1. (a) Brahmaputra plain
2. (b) Toucans

Case Based Question

1. **Read the passage given below and answer the following questions.**

The plains of the Ganga and the Brahmaputra, the mountains and the foothills of the Himalayas and the Sundarbans delta are the main features of this basin. Ox-bow lakes dot the plain area. The area is dominated by monsoon climate. The monsoon brings rains from mid-June to mid-September. The summers are hot and the winters cool. The basin area has varied topography. The environment plays a dominant role in the distribution of the population. The mountain areas with steep slopes have inhospitable terrain. Therefore, less number of people live in the mountain area of the Ganga- Brahmaputra Basin. The plain area provides the most suitable land for human habitation. The soil is fertile. Agriculture is the main occupation of the people where flat land is available to grow crops. The density of population of the plains is very high.

(i) **What is the dominant climate pattern in the Ganga-Brahmaputra Basin?**
(a) Desert climate (b) Monsoon climate
(c) Arctic climate (d) Mediterranean climate

(ii) **Which season experiences hot and humid conditions in the Ganga-Brahmaputra Basin?**
(a) Spring (b) Summer
(c) Winter (d) Autumn

(iii) **Why do fewer people inhabit the mountain areas of the Ganga-Brahmaputra Basin?**
(a) Steep slopes make it difficult for agriculture
(b) Abundant fertile soil in the mountains
(c) Cooler climate in the mountains
(d) Presence of rich mineral resources

(iv) **What type of terrain is most suitable for human habitation and agriculture in the Ganga-Brahmaputra Basin?**
(a) Mountainous terrain
(b) Desert terrain
(c) Flat plain terrain
(d) Rainforest terrain

Ans. (i) (b) Monsoon climate
(ii) (b) Summer
(iii) (a) Steep slopes make it difficult for agriculture
(iv) (c) Flat plain terrain

PART II

Very Short Answer Type Questions

1. Where is the Amazon Basin located in terms of latitude?

Ans. The Amazon Basin is located near the equator, between 10°N and 10°S latitude.

2. How did the Amazon river get its name?

Ans. The Amazon river was named by Spanish explorers inspired by local tribes resembling the ancient Roman Amazons.

3. What prevents sunlight from reaching the ground in the Amazon rainforest?

Ans. The dense roof of leaves and branches in the Amazon rainforest prevents sunlight from reaching the ground.

4. Name some exotic birds found in the Amazon rainforest.

Ans. Exotic birds like toucans, macaws, and hummingbirds inhabit the Amazon rainforest.

5. What type of animals are found in the Amazon forests?

Ans. Animals found in the Amazon rainforests are monkeys, sloth and ant-eating tapirs.

6. What is the significance of bromeliads in the Amazon rainforest?

Ans. The significance of bromeliads in the Amazon rainforest is that they store water in their leaves, which is used by animals like frogs for laying their eggs.

7. What is the primary occupation of the people in the Amazon Basin?

Ans. The primary occupation of the people in the Amazon Basin is agriculture, particularly slash and burn agriculture.

8. What are some staple foods grown by the people in the Amazon Basin?

Ans. Staple foods grown by the people in the Amazon basin are tapioca, pineapple, sweet potato and manioc (cassava).

9. Who primarily engages in hunting and fishing in the Amazon Basin?

Ans. Men typically engage in hunting and fishing in the Amazon Basin.

10. Which two rivers form the Ganga-Brahmaputra Basin in the Indian sub-continent?

Ans. The Ganga and Brahmaputra rivers, along with their tributaries, form the Ganga-Brahmaputra Basin.

11. What is the main crop cultivated in the Ganga-Brahmaputra Basin?

Ans. Paddy (rice) is the main crop cultivated in the Ganga-Brahmaputra Basin.

12. Name a cash crop grown in the Ganga-Brahmaputra Basin.

Ans. Jute is a cash crop grown in the Ganga-Brahmaputra Basin.

13. How terraces are built?

Ans. Terraces are built on steep slopes to create flat surfaces on which crops are grown.

14. What is population density of West Bengal and Bihar?

Ans. The population density of West Bengal is 1029 and that of Bihar is 1102.

15. What is the primary means of transport in the Ganga-Brahmaputra Basin along the rivers?

Ans. Waterways serve is an effective means of transport in the Ganga-Brahmaputra Basin.

16. Which famous monument is located on the banks of the Yamuna river in Agra, within the Ganga-Brahmaputra Basin?

Ans. The Taj Mahal is located on the banks of the Yamuna river in Agra, within the Ganga- Brahmaputra Basin.

Short Answer Type Questions

1. Where is the Amazon Basin located. Discuss about its climate.

Ans. The Amazon Basin is located in tropical region which lies very close to the equator; between 10°N and 10°S.

The climate in the Amazon Basin is characterised by high temperatures and constant humidity. It experiences a tropical rainforest climate, with daily rainfall, hot daytime temperatures, and warm, sticky nights.

2. What special plants are found in the Amazon rainforest, and how they are used by animals?

Ans. In the Amazon rainforest, special plants like bromeliads are common. Bromeliads store water in their leaves, creating pockets of water.

These water-filled bromeliads are used by animals like frogs as breeding sites. Frogs lay their eggs in these pockets of water, which provide a safe and moist environment for their offspring to develop.

3. What is slash and burn agriculture, and how is it practiced in the Amazon Basin?

Ans. Slash and burn is a way of cultivating land where farmers clear a piece of land by slashing or cutting down trees and bushes. These are then burnt, which releases the nutrients into the soil.

After this, crops are grown in this cleared field for a few years. After repeatedly using the patch of land, when the soil looses its nutrients, they abandon or leave this land and clear another plot of land to grow crops.

In the mean time young trees grow in the old field that is abandoned. In this way, soil fertility is restored, and people can return to it and start cultivating it again.

4. What type of animals can be found in the Ganga-Brahmaputra Basin, and what role do they play in the region?

Ans. The Ganga-Brahmaputra Basin is home to a diverse range of wildlife, including elephants, tigers, deer, one-horned rhinoceros, Bengal tigers, crocodiles, etc. These animals play important roles in the region's ecosystem and contribute to its biodiversity. For example, the aquatic life, including various fish species like rohu, catla, and hilsa, is abundant in the rivers and lakes, providing a staple diet for the local population.

5. Write a short note on the activity of the people of the Ganga-Brahmaputra region.

Ans. The main activity of the people of the Ganga-Brahmaputra region is agriculture. The main crop is paddy. Wheat, maize, sorghum, gram and millets are the other crops that are grown. Cash crops like sugarcane and jute are also grown. Banana plantations are seen in some areas of the plain.

In West Bengal and Assam, tea is grown in plantations. Silk is produced through the cultivation of silkworms in parts of Bihar and Assam. In the mountains and hills, where the slopes are gentle, crops are grown on terraces.

6. How tourism flourished in the Ganga-Brahmaputra region?

Ans. Tourism flourished in the Ganga-Brahmaputra region due to a number of tourist attractions in this basis. These include

- Taj Mahal on the banks of River Yamuna in Agra
- Allahabad on the confluence of the Rivers Ganga and Yamuna
- Buddhists stupas in Uttar Pradesh and Bihar, and Imambara in Lucknow
- Kaziranga and Manas wildlife sanctuaries in Assam
- Distinct tribal culture of Arunachal Pradesh

7. Write the advantages of water transport. **Competency Based**

Ans. Water transport offers several advantages such as

- It is the most cost-effective means for transporting heavy and bulky goods. Its use dates back to ancient times, making it a well- established and reliable mode of transportation.
- It is fuel-efficient, as it requires less energy compared to other modes.
- It is environmentally friendly, producing fewer emissions and pollution, making it a sustainable choice for long-distance cargo and passenger transportation.

8. Differentiate between Amazon river basin and Ganga-Brahmaputra river basin. **Competency Based**

Ans. Differences between Amazon river basin and Ganga-Brahmaputra river basin are

Amazon River Basin	Ganga-Brahmaputra River Basin
It lies very close to the equator; between 10°N and 10°S. (Tropical region)	It lies in the sub-tropical region that is located between 10°N to 30°N latitudes.
The area is dominated by the tropical rainforests.	The area is dominated by monsoon climate and mangrove forests.

9. What was the main cause of pollution of river Ganga? **Diksha**

Ans. The main cause of pollution of river Ganga is the waste water from the towns and industries of Ganga-Brahmaputra plain which is discharged into the river. These towns include Allahabad, Kanpur, Varanasi, Lucknow, Patna and Kolkata with the population of more than ten lakhs.

Long Answer Type Questions

1. Amazon basin is extraordinarily rich in the variety of plants and animals. Explain.

Ans. Amazon basin is extraordinarily rich in the variety of plants and animals. Thick forests grow in the region of Amazon basin as it gets heavy rainfall. The forests are so thick that the dense 'roof' created by leaves and branches does not allow the sunlight to reach the ground.

The ground remains dark and damp. Only shade tolerant vegetation may grow in this region. For example, Orchids and bromeliads grow as plant parasites.

The rainforests have a diverse range of fauna, including birds like toucans, macaws and hummingbirds.

Various animals such as monkeys, sloths and ant-eating tapirs are found in the rainforests.

Various species of reptiles and snakes are also found in this region like crocodiles, pythons, anaconda and boa constrictor. Apart from these, many insect species and species of fish including flesh-eating Piranha fish is found in this region.

2. Discuss the flora and fauna of the Ganga-Brahmaputra Basin.

Ans. The flora of the Ganga-Brahmaputra Basin varies according to the type of landforms. In the Ganga and Brahmaputra plain, tropical deciduous trees grow, along with teak, sal and peepal whereas thick bamboo groves are common in the Brahmaputra plain. The delta area is covered with the mangrove forests.

In parts of Uttarakhand, Sikkim and Arunachal Pradesh, coniferous trees like pine, deodar and fir can be seen because the climate is cool and the slopes are steep.

A variety of animals is found in the basin in which elephants, tigers, deers and monkeys are common. The one-horned rhinoceros is found in the Brahmaputra plain. Bengal tiger and crocodiles are found in the delta area.

Aquatic life is found in the fresh river waters, the lakes and the Bay of Bengal sea. The most popular varieties of the fish are rohu, catla and hilsa.

3. What do you know about people living in Amazon Basin and how is their life changing? Diksha

Ans. The Amazon Basin is the world's largest rainforest people grow most of their food in small areas after clearing some trees in the forest. Men do hunting and fishing along the rivers and women take care of the crops.

They mainly grow tapioca, pineapple and sweet potato. Manioc, also known as cassava, is their staple food. They also eat queen ants and egg sacs.

Some families live in thatched houses shaped like beehives and others in large apartment–like houses called 'Maloca' with a steeply slanting roof.
Life of the people of Amazon basin is slowly changing. The heart of the forest could be reached only by navigating the river in older day. In 1970, the Trans Amazon highway made all parts of the forest accessible. Aircrafts and helicopters are also used for reaching various places.
The indigenous population was pushed out from the area and forced to settle in new areas. It is estimated that a large area of the rainforest has been disappearing annually in the Amazon Basin.

4. The Ganga-Brahmaputra Basin has several big towns and cities, and developed transport system. Explain. Competency Based

Ans. The Ganga-Brahmaputra plain has several big towns and cities like Allahabad, Kanpur, Varanasi, Lucknow, Patna and Kolkata with the population of more than ten lakhs.

The waste water from these towns and industries is discharged into the rivers that leads to the pollution of the rivers.

All the four ways of transport are well developed in the Ganga-Brahmaputra basin. In the plain areas, the roadways and railways transport the people from one place to another.

The waterways is an effective means of transport particularly along the rivers. Kolkata is an important port on the river Hooghly. The plain area has a large number of airports.

Case Based Question

1. Read the passage given below and answer the following questions.

People grow most of their food in small areas after clearing some trees in the forest. While men hunt and fish along the rivers, women take care of the crops. They mainly grow tapioca, pineapple and sweet potato. As hunting and fishing are uncertain it is the women who keep their families alive by feeding them the vegetables they grow. They practice "slash and burn agriculture". The staple food is manioc, also known as cassava that grows under the ground like the potato. They also eat queen ants and egg sacs. Cash crops like coffee, maize and cocoa are also grown. The rainforests provide a lot of wood for the houses. Some families live in thatched houses shaped like beehives. There are other large apartment-like houses called "Maloca" with a steeply slanting roof.

(i) How have people divided their jobs in the Amazon rainforest?

Ans. People have divided their jobs in the Amazon rainforest with men practising hunting and fishing along the rivers, and women taking care of the crops.

(ii) What plants are grown and consumed by people in the rainforest?

Ans. The plants grown and consumed by the people in the rainforest include tapioca, pineapple and sweet potato. The staple food is manioc, also known as cassava that grows under the ground like the potato. They also eat queen ants and egg sacs.

(iii) Write a short note on the houses of the people in the amazon rainforest.

Ans. The rainforests provide a lot of wood for the houses. Some families live in thatched houses shaped like beehives. There are other large apartment-like houses called "Maloca" with a steeply slanting roof.

(iv) What do you understand by the 'slash and burn agriculture'?

Ans. Slash and burn agriculture is a way of cultivating land where farmers clear a piece of land by slashing or cutting down trees and bushes. These are then burnt, which releases the nutrients into the soil.

Map Based Questions

1. Locate the tributaries of Ganga and Brahmaputra river on an outline map of India.

Ans.

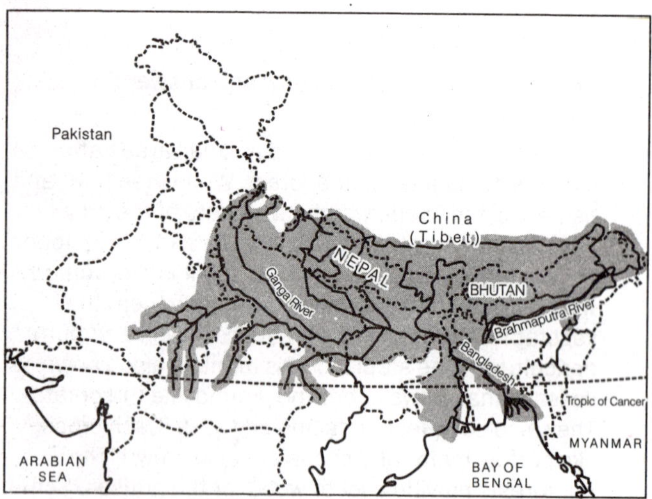

2. On the political map of South America, draw the equator. Mark the countries through which the equator passes.

Ans. The equator passes through Ecuador, Colombia, Peru and Brazil.

ASSESSMENT EXERCISE

Multiple Choice Questions (MCQs)

1. Who among of the following have discovered Amazon river?
   (a) Russian explorers (b) American explorers
   (c) Spanish explorers (d) Canadian explorers
2. Amazon river falls in which of the following oceans?
   (a) Atlantic ocean (b) Pacific ocean
   (c) Indian ocean (d) South China sea
3. Which of the following birds is found in rain forest?
   (a) Toucans (b) Hummingbirds
   (c) Plumage (d) All of these
4. Allahabad is situated on the bank of which river?
   (a) Ganga (b) Yamuna
   (c) Ganga and Yamuna (d) Chambal

Subjective Questions (VSA, SA & LA)

1. Which river is popular for having a variety of dolphins?
2. Name a place where a river flows into another body.
3. Write the name of birds which we commonly see in India.
4. Write the name of a flesh-eating fish.
5. What do you mean by tributaries?
6. Write a note on humidity and temperature of Amazon Basin.
7. Why does soil looses its fertility and how is it restored?
8. Write in detail about life in the Amazon Basin.
9. Write a brief account about the people of the rainforests and their different type of work.

CHAPTER 7

Life in the Deserts

In the world, there are some places where people have learned to cope with extremely harsh temperatures. Some of the places are hot as fire and some are cold as ice. These are the **desert areas** of the world. In this chapter, we will learn about the **Sahara Desert** and **Ladakh**.

7.1 Deserts

A desert is an arid region characterised by extremely high or low temperature and has scarce vegetation.

Deserts are characterised by low rainfall, scanty vegetation and extreme temperatures.

The people inhabit these lands wherever little water is available to practise agriculture.

The Hot Desert – Sahara

The Sahara desert covers a large part of North Africa. It is the **world's largest desert** with an area of around 8.54 million sq km.

The Sahara desert touches **eleven countries**. These are Algeria, Chad, Egypt, Libya, Mali, Mauritania, Morocco, Niger, Sudan, Tunisia and Western Sahara.

The Sahara desert is covered with vast stretches of sands, gravel plains and elevated plateaus with bare rocky surface which is more than 2500 m high at some places.

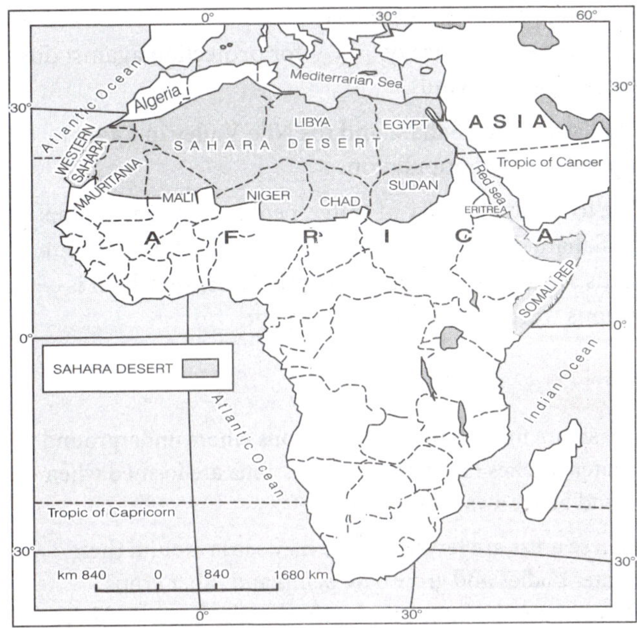

• Sahara in Africa

Climate

The climate of the Sahara desert is scorching hot (extreme heat) and parch dry (arid). It experiences a short rainy season, with clear and cloudless sky.

The moisture in the Sahara desert evaporates faster than its accumulation.

Days are very hot and the temperatures during the day may rise as high as 50°C. This heats up the sand and the bare rocks, which in turn radiates heat and makes everything around hot.

The nights may be freezing cold with temperatures nearing zero degrees.

Facts Related to Sahara Desert

Al Azizia in the Sahara desert, South of Tripoli, Libya recorded the **highest temperature** of 57.7°C in 1922.

Sahara once used to be a lush green plain. Cave paintings in Sahara desert show that there used to be rivers with crocodiles. Elephants, lions, giraffes, ostriches, sheep, cattle and goats. However, the change in climate has changed it to a very hot and dry region.

Flora and Fauna

Vegetation in the Sahara desert includes cactus, date palms and acacia. In some places there are oasis – green islands with date palms surrounding them.

Camels, hyenas, jackals, foxes, scorpions and many varieties of snakes and lizards are the prominent animal species living in the Sahara desert.

People

The Sahara desert despite its harsh climate has been inhabited by various groups of people, who practice different activities.

Bedouins and **Tuaregs** are nomadic tribes who live in Sahara desert and rear livestock such as goats, sheeps, camels and horses. These animals provide them with milk, hides (skin) from which they make leather for belts, slippers, water bottles, and their hairs are used for mats, carpets, clothes and blankets.

These tribes wear heavy **robes**[1] for protection against dust storms and hot winds.

The Oasis in the Sahara and the Nile Valley in Egypt supports settled population.

Due to the availability of water, people grow date palms in the Sahara desert. Crops such as rice, wheat, barley and beans are also grown here. **Egyptian cotton**, which is famous worldwide is grown in Egypt.

Oasis

Oasis are formed in the depressions where underground water reaches the surface. Depressions are formed when the wind blows away the sands.

These areas are fertile. People may settle around these water bodies and grow date palms and other crops. Sometimes the oasis may be abnormally large. **Tafilalet Oasis** in Morocco is a large oasis with an area of about 13,000 sq km.

Mineral Wealth and Cultural Landscape

The discovery of oil, a product in great demand throughout the world, in Algeria, Libya and Egypt is constantly transforming the Sahara desert.

The other important minerals found in the area include iron, phosphorus, manganese and uranium.

The cultural landscape of the Sahara is undergoing change. Office buildings with glass cased windows have been developed that are taller than mosques, and ancient camel paths have been replaced by super highways.

Trucks are replacing camels in the salt trade. Tuaregs are seen acting as guides to foreign tourists and nomadic herdsmen are moving to cities life for finding jobs in oil and gas operations.

The Cold Desert - Ladakh

Ladakh is a cold desert lying in the Great Himalayas, on the Eastern side of Jammu and Kashmir. Ladakh is made up of two words; **La** meaning **mountain pass** and **Dak** meaning **country**. It is also known as **Khapa-chan** which means snow land. It is surrounded by the Karakoram range in the North and the Zanskar mountains in the South.

Several rivers flow through Ladakh among which Indus is most important. The rivers form deep **valleys** and **gorges**.

Several **glaciers**[2] are found in Ladakh, for example the Gangri glacier.

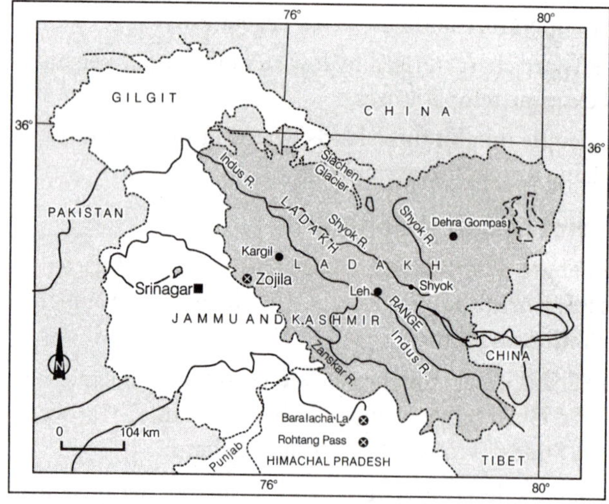

● Ladakh

Climate

The altitude in Ladakh varies from about 3000 m in Kargil to more than 8,000 m in the Karakoram.

Due to its high altitude, the climate is **extremely cold** and **dry**. The air of high altitude is so thin that the heat of the Sun can be felt intensely.

The day temperatures in summer are just above 0° and the night temperatures are below -30°C.

It is freezing cold in the winters when the temperatures may remain below-40°C for most of the time.

---

1 **Robes** Outerwear consisting of a long flowing garment used for official or ceremonial occasions.

2 **Glacier** It is slowly moving mass of ice.

As Ladakh lies in the rain shadow of the Himalayas, there is little rainfall, as low as 10 cm every year.

The area experiences freezing winds and burning hot sunlight. If we sit in the Sun with feet in the shade then we get suffer from both **sunstroke**[3] and **frostbite**[4] at the same time.

KNOWLEDGE PLUS Drass, one of the coldest inhabited places on Earth is located in Ladakh.

Flora and Fauna

There is sparse vegetation in Ladakh due to high aridity. This includes limited patches of grasses and shrubs available for animal grazing.

Groves of willows and poplars are seen in the valleys. The wood of the willow trees is used for making finest cricket bats.

Fruit trees such as apples, apricots and walnuts are grown in summers.

Several species of birds are seen in Ladakh such as robins, redstarts, Tibetan snowcock, raven and hoopoe. Some of these are migratory birds.

Common animals in Ladakh include wild goats, wild sheep, yaks, and special kinds of dogs. The animals are primarily reared for milk, meat and hides.

Yak's milk is used in cheese and butter production, while the hair of sheep and goat is used for making woolen products.

The **Chiru** or **Tibetan antelope**, is an endangered species hunted for its wool known as **shahtoosh**, which is light in weight and extremely warm.

People

The people in Ladakh are either Muslims or Buddhists. Several Buddhist monasteries are located in Ladakh with their traditional **gompas**[5]. Some famous monasteries in Ladakh include Hemis, Thiksey, Shey and Lamayuru.

During the summer season, people in Ladakh are engaged in the cultivation of crops such as barley, potatoes, peas, beans and turnips.

Women in Ladakh are very hard working. They work in the houses and fields, and also manage small businesses and shops.

Life of the people of Ladakh is undergoing change due to **modernisation**[6]. However, the people of Ladakh over the centuries have learned to live in balance and harmony with nature. Resources like water and fuel are used with care due to their scarcity and nothing is discarded or wasted.

Transport and Tourism

Leh, the capital of Ladakh, is well-connected by both road and air. The National Highway 1A connects Ladakh to the Kashmir Valley through the Zoji la Pass.

Tourism is a major industry, attracting visitors from India and abroad.

Important tourist activities include visiting gompas, treks to see the meadows and glaciers, and participating in local ceremonies and festivities.

KNOWLEDGE PLUS Manali-Leh highway crosses four passes, Rohtang la, Baralacha la, Lungalacha la and Tanglangla. This highway opens only between July and September when snow is cleared from the road.

3 **Sunstroke** It is an illness caused by spending too much time in strong heat and light from the sun.
4 **Frostbite** It is an injury caused by freezing of the skin.
5 **Gompas** It refers to a Tibetan monastery or temple.
6 **Modernisation** It is the process of updating something or making it work in a contemporary setting.

Mind Map

LIFE IN THE DESERTS

Desert
An arid region characterised by extremely high or low temperature and scare vegetation

Types of Deserts

Hot desert (Sahara)

Climate
- Extremely hot and dry
- Short rainy season
- Days are hot and temperature reach 50°C
- Nights are cold and temperature fall to 0° C

Flora and Fauna
- **Flora**–Cactus, date palm and acacia
- **Fauna**–Camels, hyenas, jackals, foxes, scorpions and varieties of snakes and lizards

People
- Bedouins and Tuaregs are nomadic tribes
- Crops–rice, wheat, barley and beans
- Heavy robes (Plothes) are worn by tribe for protection against dust storm and hot winds

Minerals
- Oil, iron, phosphorus, manganese and uranium

Cold desert (Ladakh)

Flora and Fauna
- Grass and shrubs willows trees
- Fruits–Apples, apricots and walnuts
- Birds–Robin, red starts Tibetan snowcock
- Animals–Goats, wild sheep and yaks

Climate
- Extremely cold and dry
- In summer day temperature is greater 0°c and in night, it is below −30°C
- In winter temperature remain below −40°C

People
- Agriculture is the main occupation
- Crops–Barley, potatoes, peas beans and turnips grown by people in summer
- People mainly belong to two religion groups i.e. Muslim and Buddhist

Transport and Tourism
- Well connected by road and airways
- NHAI connects Leh to Kashmir valleys through
- Famous monasteries–Hemis, Thiksey, Shey and Lamayuru

NCERT FOLDER

Covering Intext Questions and Exercises of NCERT

NCERT ON PAGE 51

Q.1 Scientists have actually found skeletons of fish in Sahara desert. What could have happened?

Ans. As scientists have found skeletons of fish in Sahara desert, it shows the presence of water bodies in that region. However, the change in climate has changed it to a very hot and dry region that makes species extinct.

EXERCISES

Q.1 Answer the following questions.

(a) What are the two types of deserts found in the world?

Ans. The two types of deserts found in the world are

- Hot desert
- Cold desert

(b) In which continent is the Sahara desert located ?

Ans. The Sahara desert is located in African continent.

(c) What are the climatic conditions of the Ladakh desert?

Ans. The climatic conditions of the Ladakh desert are extremely cold and dry. The air of high altitude is so thin that the heat of the Sun can be felt intensely.

(d) What mainly attracts tourists to Ladakh?

Ans. Tourists are mainly attracted to Ladakh to visit gompas, going on treks to see the meadows and glaciers, and participating in local ceremonies and festivities.

(e) What type of clothes the people of the Sahara desert wear?

Ans. The people of the Sahara desert wear heavy robes for protection against dust storms and hot winds.

(f) Name the trees that grow in Ladakh.

Ans. The trees that grow in Ladakh are willows, poplars, apples, apricots and walnuts

Q.2 Tick the correct answer.

1. Sahara is located in which part of Africa?

(a) Northern (b) Eastern (c) Western

2. Sahara is what type of desert?

(a) Cold (b) Hot (c) Mild

3. The Ladakh desert is mainly inhabited by

(a) Christians and Muslims
(b) Buddhists and Muslims
(c) Christians and Buddhists

4. Deserts are characterised by

(a) scanty vegetation
(b) heavy precipitation
(c) Iow evaporation

5. Hemis in the Ladakh is a famous

(a) temple (b) church
(c) monastery

6. Egypt is famous for growing

(a) wheat (b) cotton (c) maize

Ans. 1. (a), 2. (b), 3. (b), 4. (a), 5. (c), 6. (b)

Q.3 Match the following.

List I	List II
A. Oasis	1. Libya
B. Bedouins	2. Monastery
C. Oil	3. glacier
D. Gangri	4. depressions with water
E. Lamayuru	5. cold desert
	6. Sahara

Ans. A — 4, B — 6, C — 1, D — 3, E — 2

Q.4 Give reasons.

(a) There is scanty vegetation in the deserts.

Ans. There is scanty vegetation in the deserts because in the deserts there is little rainfall and the temperature is extremely high so, evaporation takes place at a faster rate.

(b) People of the Sahara desert wear heavy robes.

Ans. People of the Sahara desert wear heavy robes to protect themselves from dust storms and hot winds.

REVIEW EXERCISE

Including Competency Based Questions

PART I

Multiple Choice Questions (MCQs)

1. What is the Sahara desert primarily characterised by?

(a) Dense vegetation
(b) Low temperatures
(c) High rainfall
(d) Extreme heat and arid conditions

2. How many countries does the Sahara desert touch?

(a) 5 (b) 8 (c) 11 (d) 15

3. Which desert is known for its extremely high daytime temperatures, reaching up to 50 °C?

(a) Sahara (b) Gobi
(c) Atacama (d) Arabian

4. What causes the formation of oasis in the Sahara desert?

(a) Strong winds
(b) Sand dunes
(c) Underground water reaching the surface
(d) Frequent rainfall

5. Which of the following animals is commonly found in the Sahara desert?

(a) Polar bears (b) Penguins
(c) Camels (d) Kangaroos

6. What is the traditional occupation of the Bedouins and Tuaregs in the Sahara desert?

(a) Fishing (b) Agriculture
(c) Nomadic herding (d) Mining

7. What important mineral resource has been discovered in the Sahara desert?

(a) Gold (b) Silver
(c) Oil (d) Diamonds

8. Which desert is described as a cold desert in the chapter?

(a) Sahara (b) Gobi (c) Atacama (d) Ladakh

9. What is the main river that flows through Ladakh?

(a) Nile (b) Amazon
(c) Indus (d) Yangtze

10. How does the climate of Ladakh affect its agriculture? Competency Based

(a) It allows for year-round crop cultivation.
(b) It leads to abundant rainfall for crop growth.
(c) It limits crop cultivation to the summer season.
(d) It supports the growth of tropical crops.

11. Akshay, who belongs to Maharashtra, recently went to Ladakh in winters. He soon fell sick. Which of the following is a characteristic of Ladakh's climate? Competency Based

(a) Extremely high annual rainfall
(b) Mild temperatures throughout the year
(c) Scorching hot summers with temperatures exceeding 50°C
(d) Harsh cold winters with temperatures dropping well below freezing

12. What significant transportation route links Leh, the capital of Ladakh, to the Kashmir Valley?

(a) Sea route (b) Underground tunnels
(c) Mountain passes (d) National Highway 1A

13. What is a notable characteristic of Ladakhi people's lifestyle as mentioned in the information?

(a) Excessive use of resources
(b) Balance and harmony with nature
(c) Rapid industrialisation
(d) Disregard for water conservation

14. Identify the correct option that describe about the region given below.

(i) There is little rainfall as low as an in this region.
(ii) The willow trees are found in this region.
(iii) The Chiru, an endangered species is also found in this region.

Options

(a) Ladakh (b) Shimla
(c) Sahara (d) Jammu

15. Identify the correct option that describes the region given below. Competency Based

(i) It is lying in the Great Himalayas.
(ii) Indus being the most important river in this region.
(iii) In this region, the air at this altitude is so thin that the heat of the Sun can be felt intensely.

Options

(a) Jammu and Kashmir (b) Ladakh
(c) Sahara desert (d) Tibet

16. Choose the correct statement(s) from the following.

I. Tafilalet Oasis is situated in Morocco with an area of about 13, 000 sq km.
II. The altitude in Ladakh varies from 100 m to 1000 m.

III. Thiksey Monastery is situated in Ladakh.

Codes

(a) Only I (b) I and II
(c) I and III (d) Only III

17. Choose the incorrect statement(s) from the following.

I. Birds like robins, red starts are found in Sahara desert.

II. There is heavy rainfall in Ladakh region due to Himalayas.

III. Indus is an important river of Ladakh region.

Codes

(a) Only I (b) I and II (c) Only II (d) II and III

Answers

1. (d)	**2.** (c)	**3.** (a)	**4.** (c)	**5.** (c)
6. (c)	**7.** (c)	**8.** (d)	**9.** (c)	**10.** (c)
11. (d)	**12.** (d)	**13.** (b)	**14.** (a)	**15.** (b)
16. (c)	**17.** (b)			

Match the Following

1.

List I	List II
A. Sahara	1. Libya
B. Ladakh	2. India
C. Tuaregs	3. Nomadic tribe
D. Monastery	4. Thiksey

Codes

	A	B	C	D		A	B	C	D
(a)	1	2	3	4	(b)	3	1	4	2
(c)	2	1	3	4	(d)	2	3	1	4

2.

List I	List II
A. Gompas	1. Date palms
B. Chiru	2. Tibet
C. Oasis	3. Endangered species
D. Karakoram	4. Buddhist monasteries

Codes

	A	B	C	D		A	B	C	D
(a)	4	1	3	2	(b)	1	2	3	4
(c)	4	3	1	2	(d)	1	3	2	4

Ans. 1. (a) 2. (c)

Assertion-Reason

1. Assertion (A) The Sahara Desert was once a lush green plain with rivers and abundant wildlife.

Reason (R) Climate change transformed the Sahara into a hot and dry region, leading to the disappearance of rivers and wildlife.

Codes

(a) Both A and R are true and R is the correct explanation of A
(b) Both A and R are true, but R is not the correct explanation of A
(c) A is true, but R is false
(d) A is false, but R is true

2. Assertion (A) Tourism is a major industry in Ladakh, attracting visitors from India and abroad.

Reason (R) Ladakh's modernisation is causing significant harm to the local environment and traditional way of life.

Codes

(a) Both A and R are true and R is the correct explanation of A
(b) Both A and R are true, but R is not the correct explanation of A
(c) A is true, but R is false
(d) A is false, but R is true

Ans. 1. (a) Both A and R are true and R is the correct explanation of A

2. (b) Both A and R are true, but R is not the correct explanation of A

Fill in the Blanks

1. The climate of the Sahara desert is scorching hot and ....

2. .... in the Sahara and the Nile Valley in Egypt supports settled population.

3. .... are replacing camels in the salt trade.

4. Ladakh is a cold desert lying in the ...., on the Eastern side of Jammu and Kashmir.

5. The National Highway .... connects Leh to Kashmir Valley through the Zoji la Pass.

Ans. 1. parch dry. 2. The Oasis
3. Trucks 4. Great Himalayas
5. 1A

True/False

1. The Sahara desert is the world's largest desert.

2. The Sahara desert touches nine countries.

3. The Sahara desert once used to be a lush green plain with crocodiles and various animals.

4. In Ladakh, the day temperatures in summer are usually well above 30°C.

5. Tourism is not a major industry in Ladakh.

Ans. 1. True 2. False 3. True
4. False 5. False

Picture Based Questions

1. **There is a oasis shown in the figure. Which trees are mainly found in oasis?**

(a) Willows (b) Poplars
(c) Mangrove (d) Date palm

2. **Thiksey Monastery is shown in the image. To which religion it belongs?**

(a) Hindu (b) Sikhs
(c) Jain (d) Buddhists

Ans. 1. (d) Date palm 2. (d) Buddhists

Case Based Question

1. **Read the passage given below and answer the following questions.**

Vegetation in the Sahara desert includes cactus, date palms and acacia. In some places there are oasis - green islands with date palms surrounding them. Camels, hyenas, jackals, foxes, scorpions, many varieties of snakes and lizards are the prominent animal species living there. The Sahara desert despite its harsh climate has been inhabited by various groups of people, who pursue different activities.

Among them are the Bedouins and Tuaregs. These groups are nomadic tribes rearing livestock such as goats, sheep, camels and horses. These animals provide them with milk, hides from which they make leather for belts, slippers, water bottles; hair is used for mats, carpets, clothes and blankets. They wear heavy robes as protection against dust storms and hot winds.

(i) **Which types of vegetation are mentioned in the Sahara desert?**
(a) Oak trees
(b) Cactus, date palms and acacia
(c) Pine trees
(d) Maple trees

(ii) **What are the green islands with date palms in the Sahara called?**
(a) Jungles (b) Meadows
(c) Oasis (d) Orchards

(iii) **Which animals are prominent in the Sahara desert?**
(a) Polar bears and penguins
(b) Tigers and elephants
(c) Camels, hyenas and jackals
(d) Kangaroos and koalas

(iv) **What products do the hides of the livestock provide for the Bedouins and Tuaregs?**
(a) Chocolate bars
(b) Leather for belts, slippers and water bottles
(c) Silk scarves
(d) Diamond jewellery

Ans. (i) (b) Cactus, date palms and acacia
(ii) (c) Oasis
(iii) (c) Camels, hyenas, and jackals
(iv) (b) Leather for belts, slippers and water bottles

PART II

Very Short Answers Type Questions

1. **What is the Sahara desert known for?**

Ans. The Sahara desert is known for its extreme heat and arid conditions.

2. **Name the countries that Sahara desert touch.**

Ans. The Sahara desert touches eleven countries. These are Algeria, Chad, Egypt, Libya, Mali, Mauritania, Morocco, Niger, Sudan, Tunisia and Western Sahara.

3. **What is the main source of water in Sahara's oasis?**

Ans. The main source of water in Sahara's oasis is the underground water that reaches the surface due to wind erosion.

4. **What is the highest recorded temperature in the Sahara desert?**

Ans. The highest recorded temperature in the Sahara was 57.7°C in Al Azizia, Libya, in 1922.

5. What is the significance of date palms in Sahara oasis regions?

Ans. The significance of date palms in Sahara oasis is that they provide a crucial source of food.

6. Which minerals are found in the Sahara desert, besides oil?

Ans. Minerals such as iron, phosphorus, manganese, and uranium are found in the Sahara desert.

7. How has modernisation impacted the traditional lifestyle in the Sahara desert? **Competency Based**

Ans. Modernisation has led to changes in the traditional lifestyle in the Sahara desert by introducing some changes like the use of trucks in the salt trade and the shift of some nomadic herdsmen to city jobs in oil and gas operations.

8. What does 'Ladakh' mean, and where is it located?

Ans. Ladakh is made up of two words; 'La' meaning 'mountain pass' and 'Dak' meaning 'country'.

Ladakh is a cold desert lying in the Great Himalayas, on the Eastern side of Jammu and Kashmir.

9. Which mountain ranges enclose Ladakh?

Ans. Ladakh is enclosed by the Karakoram range in the North and the Zanskar mountains in the South.

10. What is the highest temperature typically recorded in Ladakh during the summer?

Ans. The highest temperature typically recorded in Ladakh during the summer is just above zero degrees Celsius.

11. What types of vegetation are found in Ladakh's valleys?

Ans. The type of vegetation found in Ladakh valleys includes groves of willow and poplar trees, along with fruit trees like apples, apricots and walnuts.

12. What are some common bird species found in Ladakh?

Ans. Common species of birds found in Ladakh include robins, redstarts, Tibetan snowcock, raven and hoopoe. Some of these are migratory birds.

13. Which animals are primarily reared by the people of Ladakh?

Ans. People in Ladakh primarily rear yaks, special breeds of dogs, and other livestock for milk, meat and hides.

14. How do Ladakhi people use the wool of the Tibetan antelope?

Ans. The wool of the Tibetan antelope, known as shahtoosh, is used for making fine and warm woolen products.

15. What is the significance of willow trees in Ladakh?

Ans. The significance of willow trees in Ladakh is that they are used to make cricket bats, known for their fine quality.

16. What are 'gompas' in Ladakh's cultural landscape?

Ans. 'Gompas' are Buddhist monasteries that are prominent in Ladakh's cultural landscape.

17. What are the main crops cultivated in Ladakh during the summer season?

Ans. During the summer season, people in Ladakh cultivate crops like barley, potatoes, peas, beans and turnips.

18. How are the resources of water and fuel managed in Ladakh?

Ans. Ladakhi people use water and fuel resources with great care, avoiding waste and unnecessary disposal due to resource scarcity.

19. What is the primary mode of transportation to Leh, the capital of Ladakh?

Ans. The primary mode of transportation to Leh is air and road. National Highway 1A links it to the Kashmir valley via the Zoji la Pass.

20. What is the primary industry that attracts visitors to Ladakh?

Ans. The primary industry that attracts visitors of Ladakh is tourism.

Short Answer Type Questions

1. What are the key features of the Sahara desert's climate, and how do they impact the region?

Ans. The Sahara desert's climate is characterised by extreme heat, aridity and limited precipitation.

These conditions result in rapid moisture evaporation, daytime temperatures reaching as high as 50°C and night time temperatures dropping significantly. The lack of cloud cover and clear skies intensify these conditions. These harsh climate factors make agriculture difficult and force people to adapt to arid conditions.

2. How has the Sahara desert's climate changed over time, and what evidence supports this change?

Ans. The Sahara desert has become a hot and dry region due to climatic change.

This transformation is supported by both historical records and geological research. Historical evidence, such as cave paintings showing rivers with crocodiles, elephants, lions, and giraffes, suggests that the Sahara was once a lush green plain.

3. Briefly write about the distribution of flora and fauna in Sahara. **Diksha**

Ans. The distribution of flora and fauna in Sahara is very unique due to it's very hot and dry weather. Cactus, date palms and acacia are popular vegetation in Sahara desert. There are oasis with date palms surrounding them in some places.

Camels, hyenas, jackals, foxes, scorpions many varieties of snakes and lizards are the prominent animal species of Sahara. The plants and animals are mostly found near the area of water spots in the desert, where it is a little easier to survive.

4. How do oasis regions form in the Sahara desert, and what role do they play for the local population?

Ans. Oasis regions in the Sahara desert form when the wind erodes the sand, allowing underground water to reach the surface.

These fertile areas support settled populations and agriculture, mainly date palms. Crops like rice, wheat, barley, beans and the famous Egyptian cotton are also grown in oasis regions, providing important resources for the local population.

5. What impact has the discovery of oil and other minerals had on the Sahara desert's landscape and people?

Ans. The discovery of oil in countries like Algeria, Libya, and Egypt has impacted the Sahara desert, leading to modernisation with gleaming glass-cased office buildings and superhighways.

Additionally, other minerals like iron, phosphorus, manganese, and uranium have contributed to economic development and changes in the region. Nomadic herdsmen have found jobs in oil and gas operations, and trucks are replacing camels in the salt trade.

6. What is the role of willow and poplar trees in Ladakh's vegetation, and how do they impact the environment?

Ans. In Ladakh's valleys, groves of willow and poplar trees are essential for providing shade and contributing to the limited vegetation in the region. These trees also add to the local biodiversity and offer habitat for various bird species. Additionally, willow trees serve as a valuable resource for wood, particularly in the making of cricket bats.

7. What is the significance of the 'gompas' in Ladakh, and how do they influence the local culture?

Ans. Gompas are Buddhist monasteries in Ladakh that play a significant role in the region's cultural and religious life. They are centers for Buddhist worship, study, and community gatherings.

These monasteries contribute to the unique cultural landscape of Ladakh and are sites of pilgrimage and festivals that brings a sense of community and spirituality among the people.

8. How do Ladakhi people cope with the extreme cold and arid climate of the region?

Ans. Ladakhi people cope with the extreme cold and arid climate of the region by engaging in summer crop cultivation, including barley, potatoes, peas, beans, and turnips.

During the harsh winters, they focus on festivities and ceremonies to stay engaged and maintain their sense of community and culture.

9. How do the Ladakhi people value and manage their limited resources like water and fuel?

Ans. Ladakhi people have developed a lifestyle that values the responsible use of resources like water and fuel due to their scarcity.

They manage water and fuel with great care to avoid waste and unnecessary disposal, reflecting their commitment to sustainable living in a challenging environment.

Long Answer Type Questions

1. Write a note on the hot desert-Sahara.

Ans. The Sahara desert is the world's largest hot desert. It covers an area of around 8.54 million square km. The Sahara desert touches eleven countries. These are Algeria, Chad, Egypt, Libya, Mali, Mauritania, Marocco, Niger, Sudan, Tunisia and Western Sahara. Besides the vast stretches of sands that Sahara desert is also covered with, there are also gravel plains and elevated plateaus with bare rocky surface. These rocky surfaces are more than 2500m high at some places.

Sahara desert is very dry and scorching hot. It has a short rainy season. The temperature in the Sahara during day rise as high as 50°C and during winter it goes low of below 0°C.

Sahara desert is home to a variety of plants and animals. Cactus, date palms and acacia are popular vegetation of it. Camels, hyenas, jackals, foxes, scorpions, many varieties of snakes and lizards are found here. Bedouins and Tuaregs, nomadic tribes of Sahara desert, inhabited here and they rear livestock such as goats, sheep, camels and horses. The Oasis in the Sahara and the Nile Valley in Egypt supports settled population. Date palms are grown in these regions.

2. Discuss the major occupations of the people of the cold desert-Ladakh.

Ans. Major occupation of the people of Ladakh is agriculture. The people of Ladakh grow crops such as barley, wheat, buckwheat, peas, rapeseed and beans. The Indus river is the main source of irrigation for agriculture in Ladakh.

The people of Ladakh also rear sheep, goats, yaks and other animals for their milk, meat, wool and fur. The Chiru or the Tibetan antelope is an endangered species. It is hunted for its wool known as shahtoosh, which is light in weight and extremely warm.

The people of Ladakh also manage small business and shops. Ladakh is also famous tourist destination because of its beautiful mountains, lake and Buddhist monastries.

People visit gompas, go on treks to see meadows and glaciers, and attend ceremonies and festivities. Some famous monasteries are Hemis, Thiksey, Shiy and Lamayuru. Many people of Ladakh work in the tourism industry as hotel staff, tour guides and drivers.

3. Write a short note on the flora and fauna found in the Ladakh desert.

Ans. Ladakh desert is a high altitude desert in the Great Himalayas, on the Eastern side of Jammu and Kashmir. It is home to a variety of flora and fauna, which is adapted to cold weather. The vegetation is sparse due to high aridity. There are scanty patches of grasses and shrubs for animals to graze. Groves of willows and poplars are seen in the valleys. Fruit trees such as apples, apricots and walnuts bloom during the summers.

Several species of birds such as robins, redstarts, Tibetan snowcock, raven and hoopoe are common in this region. Some of these are migratory birds. Wild goats, wild sheep, yak and special kinds of dogs are found in Ladakh. The animals are reared to provide milk, meat and hides. Yak's milk is used to make cheese and butter. The hair of the sheep and goat is used to make woollens.

4. Explain the climatic condition of Ladakh. **Diksha**

Ans. Ladakh is situated in the Northern most part of India. Its high-altitude location in the Himalayas and Karakoram ranges contributes to the unique weather conditions. It experiences extremely cold and dry winters. It is often below freezing point.

The altitude in Ladakh varies from about 3000 m in Kargil to more than 8000 m in the Karakoram. The air at this altitude is so thin that the heat of the Sun can be felt intensely. In summers, the day temperatures are just above 0° and the night temperatures well below-30°C. In winters, it is freezing cold when the temperatures may remain below -40°C for most of the time.

There is little rainfall as it lies in the rain shadow of the Himalayas. Rainfall is as low as 10 cm every year. Ladakh enjoys abundant sunshine throughout the year due to its high elevation and clear skies.

5. Differentiate between the Sahara desert and Ladakh desert. **Competency Based**

Ans. The differences between the Sahara and Ladakh deserts are

Sahara desert	Ladakh desert
It is the world's largest hot desert with an area of around 8.54 million sq km.	Ladakh is a cold desert lying in the Great Himalayas.
The climate of the Sahara desert is scorching hot and parch dry. It has a short rainy season.	Due to its high altitude, the climate is extremely cold and dry.
Camels, hyenas, jackals, foxes, scorpions, many varieties of snakes and lizards are the prominent animal species found here.	The animals found in Ladakh are wild goats, wild sheep, yak and special kinds of dogs.
Vegetation in the Sahara desert includes cactus, date palms and acacia.	Due to high aridity, the vegetation is sparse in Ladakh. There are scanty patches of grasses and shrubs for animals to graze. Groves of willows and poplars are seen in the valleys.

Case Based Question

1. Read the passage and answer the following questions.

Ladakh is a cold desert lying in the Great Himalayas, on the eastern side of Jammu and Kashmir. The Karakoram Range in the north and the Zanskar mountains in the south enclose it. Several rivers flow through Ladakh, Indus being the most important among them. The rivers form deep valleys and gorges. Several glaciers are found in Ladakh, for example the Gangri glacier.

The altitude in Ladakh varies from about 3000m in Kargil to more than 8,000m in the Karakoram. Due to its high altitude, the climate is extremely cold and dry. The air at this altitude is so thin that the heat of the sun can be felt intensely. The day temperatures in summer are just above zero degree and the night temperatures well below –30 °C.

(i) Why does Ladakh experience extremely cold and dry conditions, with temperatures dropping well below -30 °C in the winters and little rainfall, despite its high altitude in the Himalayas?

Ans. Ladakh experience extremely cold and dry conditions due its location in the rain shadow of the Himalayas. The mountain range blocks the moist air from reaching the region, resulting in limited rainfall, as low as 10 cm annually. This lack of moisture, along with high altitudes, leads to freezing winds, burning sunlight, and exceptionally low temperatures in both summer and winter.

(ii) How does a person suffers from both sunstroke and frost bite at the same time in Ladakh?

Ans. A person may suffer from both sunstroke and frost bite at the same time in Ladakh due to its location as the area experiences freezing winds and burning hot sunlight.

Map Based Questions

1. On the outline map of Africa, mark the Sahara desert and any four countries around it.

Ans.

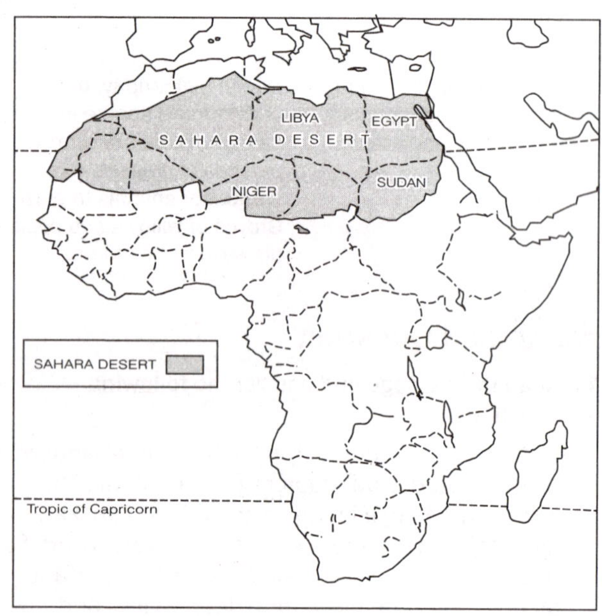

2. On the outline map of India, mark the Karakoram range, Zanskar range, Ladakh and Zoji la Pass.

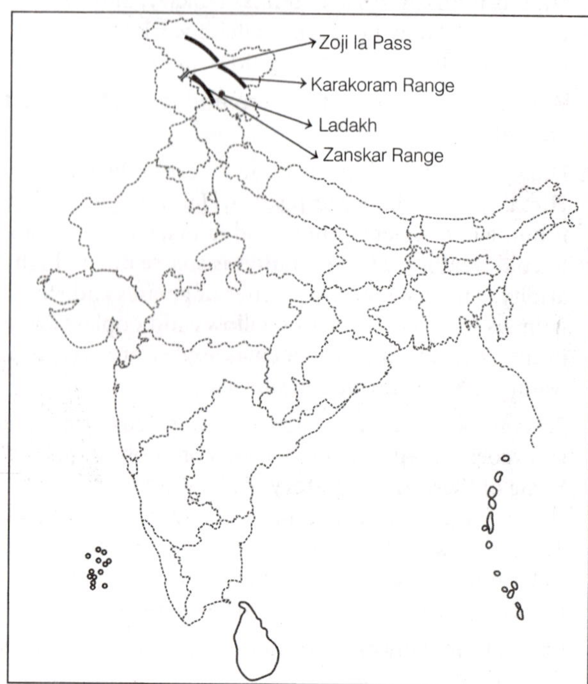

ASSESSMENT EXERCISE

Multiple Choice Questions (MCQs)

1. Identify the largest desert of the world among the following.
   (a) Gobi desert (b) Atacama desert
   (c) Sahara desert (d) None of these
2. Which of the following is not a characteristic features of desert?
   (a) Low rainfall
   (b) Scanty vegetation
   (c) Extreme temperature
   (d) Great diversity
3. Which of the following is a condition of desert region?
   (a) Moisture evaporates faster than it accumulates
   (b) Moisture accumulates faster than it evaporates
   (c) Moisture evaporates and accumulates at the same rate
   (d) None of the above
4. Name the Northern most pass of India.
   (a) Bara Lacha (b) Rohtang Pass
   (c) Sipkila Pass (d) Zoji la Pass

Subjective Questions (VSA, SA & LA)

1. What are the other important minerals found in Sahara desert other than oil resources?
2. Name the mountain ranges which encloses Ladakh region from North.
3. Write the use of hair of sheep and goat.
4. Write the names of Buddhists monasteries located in the Ladakh region.
5. What are oasis and how are they formed?
6. How does discovery of oil constantly transforming the Sahara desert?
7. What are the different activities involved with the people of Ladakh region?
8. Explain about the effects of extreme high and low temperature in desert region.
9. Write a short note on the nomadic tribes of Sahara desert.

On Equality

CHAPTER 1

India is a democratic country in which the principle of equality of all the persons is recognised. Equality is a key feature of democracy and influences all aspects of its functioning.

In this chapter, we will learn what is equality, why is it important and how it is a global phenomena and a feature of many democratic countries.

1.1 Equality in Indian Democracy

Equality[1] in Indian **democracy**[2] is ensured by recognising each and every individual in the country as equal, no matter to which caste, religion, tribe, educational and economic background the individual belongs.

Earlier, no law existed to protect people from discrimination and ill-treatment. Now, there are several laws that work to see that people are treated with **dignity**[3] and as equals.

The **Constitution**[4] of India recognises every person as equal. This recognition of equality includes some of the following provisions in the **Constitution**

- Every person is equal before the law.
- No person can be discriminated on basis of their religion, race, caste, place of birth, etc.
- Every person has access to all public places including playgrounds, hotels, shops, etc.
- Untouchability in any form is abolished.

Article 15 of the Indian Constitution

Article 15 prohibits of discrimination on grounds of **religion**, **race**, **caste**, **sex** or **place of birth**. The provisions under this article are

- The State shall not discriminate against any citizen on grounds only of religion, race, caste, sex, place of birth or any of them.
- On grounds only of religion, race, caste, sex, place of birth or any of them, no citizen shall be subject to any disability, liability, restriction or condition with regard to
  (a) access to shops, public restaurants, hotels and places of public entertainment.
  (b) use of wells, tanks, bathing ghats, roads and places of public resort which are maintained wholly or partly through State funds, or dedicated to the use of the general public.

Government Initiatives for Equality

Government has made efforts to implement equality through laws and also by implementing programmes and schemes to help disadvantaged communities.

For example, a **Mid-day meal scheme** was introduced in government elementary schools in order to provide children with cooked lunch.

1 **Equality** It is the quality or state of being equal i.e. having the same rights, social status, etc.
2 **Democracy** It is a system of government in which eligible citizens may participate.
3 **Dignity** It refers to thinking of oneself and other persons as worthy of respect.
4 **Constitution** This document lays forth the fundamental rules and laws that the citizens and government of the country must follow.

In 2001, in India, **Tamil Nadu** was the **first state** to introduce this scheme. This resulted in an increase in enrollment and regularity of student's attendance in schools.

This programme has also helped reduce caste prejudices because children of all castes in the school eat this meal together. **Dalit**[5] women have been employed to cook the meal.

Inspite of government programmes and schemes, incidents of people being treated unequally can still be observed. This is because attitudes of people change very slowly.

Equality can only be established when people begin to believe that no one is inferior, and that every person deserves to be treated with dignity.

Establishing equality in a democratic society is a continuous struggle in which individuals and communities both need to contribute.

1.2 Issues of Equality in Other Democracies

There are many democratic countries around the world which are struggling with the issue of equality. For example, inequality faced by African-Americans in the United States of America. The **Civil Rights Movement**[6] took place in the late 1950s for equal rights for African-Americans.

The **Civil Rights Act,** 1964 prohibited discrimination on the basis of race, religion and national origin. However, a majority of African-Americans still continue to be among the poorest in the country.

1.3 Challenge of Democracy

No country can be described as fully democratic. Individuals and communities are always trying to expand the idea of democracy and demanding a greater recognition of equality on existing as well as new issues. The struggle for the recognition of every individual as equal and their dignity is to be maintained.

5 **Dalit** It means 'broken' and is used to address so-called lower castes.

6 **Civil Rights Movement** A movement that began in USA in 1950s in which African-American people demanded equal rights and an end to racial discrimination.

ON EQUALITY

Equality in Indian Democracy

- The Constitution of India recognises every person as equal.
- Provisions for equality in the Constitution
  - Every person is equal before law.
  - No person can be discriminated on the basis of their religion, caste, etc.
  - Every person has access to all public places.
  - Untouchability in any form is abolished.

Issues of Equality in other Democracies

- The Civil Rights Movement took place in the late 1950s for equal rights for African-Americans.
- The Civil Rights Act, 1964 prohibited discrimination on the basis of race, religion and national origin.

Challenges of Democracy

- No country can be described as fully democratic.
- Recognition of every individual as equal and their dignity is to be maintained.

Article 15

Prohibits discrimination on grounds of religion, race, caste, sex or any of them.

Government Initiatives for Equality

- Implementing equality through laws and programmes and schemes to help disadvantaged communities, e.g. Mid-day Meal Scheme.
- Tamil Nadu was the first state to introduce Mid-day Meal Scheme.

NCERT FOLDER

Covering Intext Questions and Exercises of NCERT

NCERT ON PAGE 4

Q.1 Can you think of an incident in your life in which your dignity was violated? How did this make you feel?

Ans. Yes, my dignity was violated while I was in Vth class. My English teacher treated me unfairly in comparison to my classmate. The teacher gave my friend more marks than me for the same answer. Due to which I felt disgusted.

NCERT ON PAGE 6

Q.2 What is the Mid-day meal programme? Can you list three benefits of the programme? How do you think this programme might help promote greater equality?

Ans. The Mid-day meal programme is an initiative taken by the government in order to provide children of elementary schools with cooked lunch all over the country.

Three benefits of the programme are

(i) It helped in reducing the hunger of poor students who cannot concentrate on their studies because of empty stomachs.

(ii) The programme also helped in improving the attendance of the students.

(iii) This programme has also helped reduce caste discrimination because children of all castes in the school eat this meal together.

This programme helped in promoting equality as it will help in reducing caste prejudices as both lower and upper caste children will sit together to eat their meals. In some places, dalit women have been employed to cook the meals.

Q.3 Find out about one government scheme in your area. What does this scheme do? Whom is this scheme set-up to benefit?

Ans. In my area, a government scheme known as Pradhan Mantri Jan Dhan Yojna (PMJDY) was launched.

This scheme is set-up to benefit the weaker sections and low-income groups by ensuring access to various financial services such as basic savings bank accounts, loans, remittances, insurance and pension etc.

EXERCISES

Q.1 In a democracy, why is Universal Adult Franchise Important?

Ans. The Universal Adult Franchise is important in a democracy because it serves as the basis for all elections that are held to choose the government at all levels.

Universal Adult Franchise means that all the adults who are 18 years of age and above, have the right to vote, irrespective of their religion, caste, colour, race, economic and educational conditions. In a democracy, the people rule the country and make all decisions. This is only possible if each and every individual is free to choose the type of government they want.

Q.2 Re-read the box on Article 15 and state two ways in which this Article addresses inequality?

Ans. Article 15 addresses discrimination based on religion, race, caste, gender, place of birth, and so on. It addresses inequality and discrimination by

- allowing access to shops, public places, hotels, restaurants and places of public entertainment.
- allowing the general public to use the wells, tanks, bathing ghats and roads which are maintained fully or partly by state funds.

Q.3 What do you understand by the term "all persons are equal before the law"? Why do you think it is important in democracy?

Ans. "All persons are equal before the law" means that all citizens, regardless of their class or economic background, are equal and there are same laws for every one. No one should be discriminated against under the law on the basis of race, religion, caste, or gender. Each and every person, that is, from the President of the country to the domestic workers should be treated equally and have to follow the same laws.

In a democracy, equality is important because it suggests no one should be treated unfairly due to their caste, colour, religion, gender, or any other factor. Equality also reflects the real character of democracy. It ensures that everyone has equal opportunities and live in dignity.

Q.4 According to the Rights of Persons with Disabilities Act, 2016, persons with disabilities have equal rights, and that the government should make possible their full participation in society. The government has to provide free education and integrate children with disabilities into mainstream schools. This law also states that all public places including buildings, schools, etc., should be accessible and provided with ramps.

Look at the photograph and think about the boy who is being carried down the stairs. Do you think the above law is being implemented in his case? What needs to be done to make the building more accessible for him? How would his being carried down the stairs affect his dignity as well as his safety?

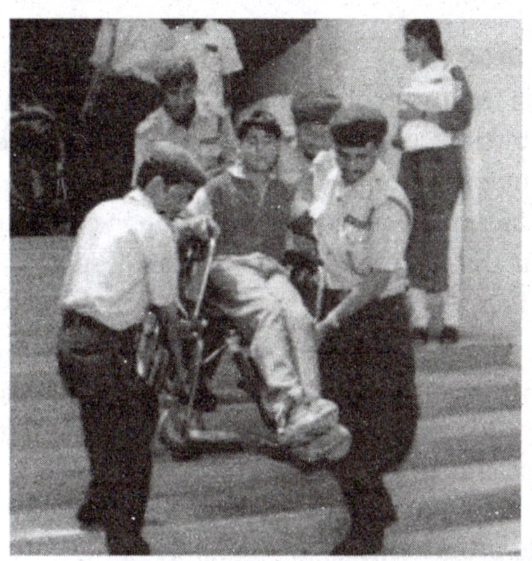

Ans. The boy in the photograph clearly has a disability. The Disabilities Act, 1995 is not being implemented in this case.

The building is not accessible for him and in order to make it possible ramps should be constructed.

The boy's dignity is affected as he's being carried down by others, which may make him feel dependent on others. It also affects his safety as he may anytime fall from the chair due to negligence and incapacity.

REVIEW EXERCISE

Including Competency Based Questions

PART I

Multiple Choice Questions (MCQs)

1. The Indian Constitution recognises
(a) all people are equal
(b) all people are not equal
(c) all people are economically sound
(d) None of the above

2. Where has the Mid-day meal scheme been started?
(a) In government offices (b) In private schools
(c) In income tax department (d) In government schools

3. When was the Mid-day meal scheme introduced for the first time?
(a) 2001 (b) 2002
(c) 2000 (d) 2005

4. Mid-day meal was firstly introduced in
(a) Kerala (b) Rajasthan
(c) Tamil Nadu (d) West Bengal

5. When persons are treated unequally their
(a) status is violated (b) freedom is violated
(c) dignity is violated (d) pride is violated

6. African-Americans are discriminated against in
(a) Africa (b) South America
(c) USA (d) South Africa

7. Who started the Civil rights movement ?
(a) Rose Mary (b) Anug San
(c) Nelson Mandela (d) Rosa Parks

8. The Civil Rights Act was passed in
(a) 1955 (b) 1964 (c) 1946 (d) 1965

9. Universal Adult Franchise states that every adult has
(a) no vote (b) one vote
(c) multiple vote (d) All of these

10. Which Article of the Indian Constitution defines equality?
(a) Article 10 (b) Article 12 (c) Article 15 (d) Article 21

11. In 1893, New Zealand became the first country to provide women the Right to Vote. Rwanda established a 30% quota for women in elected offices in 2003, and it now boasts the largest proportion of women in any parliament in the world, at 61.3%.

Source The Print

What is the main objective of all the above actions taken by different countries? Competency Based

(a) To increase women's participation in politics
(b) To increase women's participation in economy
(c) To increase women's participation in sports
(d) To increase women's participation in Academics

12. Identify the correct option from the following information. Competency Based

(i) This programme has helped reduce caste prejudices.
(ii) Tamil Nadu was the first state in India to introduce this programme.
(iii) This programme helps encourage students to come to school by providing food.

Codes

(a) Sarva Siksha Abhiyan (b) Mid-day meal
(c) Right to Education (d) Bal Bandhu Scheme

13. Choose the correct statements from the following.

I. The Indian Constitution recognises every person as equal.
II. Rosa Parks was a journalist from Chennai.
III. Untouchability has been abolished.

Codes

(a) I and II (b) I and III
(c) II and III (d) All of these

14. Choose the incorrect statements from the following.

I. Universal Adult Franchise means Right to Equality.
II. Right to Vote is granted to the citizens of India who are above 10 years of age.
III. The Civil Right Movement was started in the 1950s in Africa.

Codes

(a) I, II and III (b) I and II
(c) Only III (d) None of these

Answers

1. (a) **2.** (d) **3.** (a) **4.** (c) **5.** (c)
6. (c) **7.** (d) **8.** (b) **9.** (b) **10.** (c)
11. (a) **12.** (b) **13.** (b) **14.** (a)

Match the Following

1.

List I	List II
A. Rosa Parks	1. Dalit leader
B. B R Ambedkar	2. Fought against racial discrimination in South Africa
C. Universal Adult Franchise	3. African-American
D. Mahatma Gandhi	4. Right to Vote

Codes

	A	B	C	D
(a)	3	1	4	2
(b)	2	4	3	1
(c)	1	3	4	2
(d)	4	1	3	2

Ans. (a)

Assertion-Reason

1. Assertion (A) Supreme Court asked all state governments to begin Mid-day-meal scheme in their schools within six months.

Reason (R) Tamil Nadu was the first state in India to introduce Mid-day-meal scheme.

Codes

(a) Both A and R are true and R is the correct explanation of A.
(b) Both A and R true, but R is not the correct explanation of A
(c) A is true, but R is false
(d) A is false, but R is true

2. Assertion (A) Government programmes play an Important role in increasIng equality of opportunity.

Reason (R) Civil Right Movement was started in India to prohibit discrimination.

Codes

(a) Both A and R are true and R is the correct explanation of A
(b) Both A and R true, but R is not the correct explanation of A
(c) A is true, but R is false
(d) A is false, but R is true

Ans. 1. (b) Both A and R true, but R is not the correct explanation of A
2. (c) A is true, but R is false

Fill in the Blanks

1. .... is a key feature of democracy. Diksha
2. The idea of .... is based on the idea of equality. Diksha
3. The Mid-day-meal programme has helped increase the .... and .... of poor children in school.
4. In the United States of America, the .... trace their ancestry back to the slaves who were transported from Africa.
5. The issue of .... continues to be the key issue around which communities struggle.
6. The act of considering oneself and others to be deserving of respect is referred to as ....

Ans. 1. Equality 2. Universal Adult Franchise
3. enrollment, attendance 4. African-Americans
5. equality 6. dignity

True/False

1. The Mid-day meal programme has helped to reduce caste prejudices.
2. Rosa Parks was an African-American woman.
3. According to BR Ambedkar, self-respect is the most vital factor in life.
4. One of the most common forms of inequality in India is the caste system.
5. Establishing equality in a democratic society is a continuous struggle.

Ans. 1. True 2. True 3. True
4. True 5. True

Picture Based Question

1. **The image given below is of Dr B R Ambedkar. What is Dr B R Ambedkar best known for?**

(a) Leading India's struggle for Independence
(b) Firiting National Anthem
(c) Famous Bureaucrat
(d) Advocating for the Rights of the Dalits

Ans. 1. (d) Advocating for the Rights of the Dalits

Case Based Question

1. **Read the passage given below and answer the following questions**

The two ways in which the government has tried to implement the equality that is guaranteed in the Constitution is first through laws and second through government programmes or schemes to help disadvantaged communities. There are several laws in India that protect every person's right to be treated equally. In addition to laws, the government has also set up several schemes to improve the lives of communities and individuals who have been treated unequally for several centuries. These schemes are to ensure greater opportunity for people who have not had this in the past.

(i) On what basis government is trying to implement equality?
(a) Religion
(b) Caste
(c) Gender
(d) All of the above

(ii) What is the main focus of the government scheme?
(a) Economic growth
(b) Education reforms
(c) Improving the lives of disadvantage communities
(d) Environment sustainability

(iii) Which of the following has been abolished to bring equality in society?
(a) Religious practices
(b) Traditional methods
(c) Untouchability
(d) Public gathering

(iv) According to the Constitution, what does it mean for every person to be "Equal before the law"?
(a) They have the same income
(b) They have the same rights
(c) They must obey the same laws
(d) They can discriminate based on their preferences

Ans. (i) (d) All of the above
(ii) (c) Improving the lives of disadvantage communities
(iii) (c) Untouchability
(iv) (b) They have the same rights

PART II

Very Short Answer Type Questions

1. **What type of government does India have?**

Ans. India have a democratic government where people elect their representatives.

2. **Who has been employed to cook the meal under the Mid-day meal scheme?**

Ans. Dalit women have been employed to cook the meal under the Mid-day meal scheme.

3. **What do you understand about the Universal Adult Franchise?**

Ans. Universal Adult Franchise states that every adult, irrespective of their religion, caste, education, colour, race, economic conditions is free to vote.

4. What does the term Dalit refer to?

Ans. The term Dalits means 'broken' and is used to address the so-called lower castes.

5. What do you understand by 'dignity'? Diksha

Ans. Dignity is the quality of being worthy of honour or respect.

6. What do you understand about the Constitution?

Ans. The Constitution is a body of fundamental principles or established rules according to which a state is governed.

7. How did BR Ambedkar view self-respect?

Ans. BR Ambedkar was a Dalit leader. He viewed self-respect as the most vital factor in life without which man is nothing.

8. Who is allowed to vote in India? Competency Based

Ans. In India, all adults i.e. persons who are 18 years or above are allowed to vote irrespective of their religion, gender, caste.

9. What is the aim of the Civil Rights Act of 1964?

Ans. The Civil Rights Act of 1964 prohibited discrimination on the basis of race, religion or national origin.

10. Can a state discriminate against any citizen on the ground of caste and religion?

Ans. No, a state cannot discriminate against any citizen on the ground of caste and religion.

11. What are common forms of inequality that exist in India? Diksha

Ans. Inequality on the basis of caste, religion, disability, gender, and financial status exist in India.

Short Answer Type Questions

1. Describe the basis on which people are treated unequally. How equality can be established?

Ans. The people are treated unequally on the basis of caste, religion, tribe, educational and economic background.

Equality can only be established when people begin to believe that no one is inferior, and that every person deserves to be treated with dignity.

2. Write a short note on equality in Indian democracy. Diksha

Ans. Equality in Indian democracy is ensured by recognising each and every individual in the country as equal, no matter to which caste, religion, tribe, educational and economic background the individual belongs.

In Indian Democracy, citizens elect their representatives through voting. The Constitution of India states that no one can be prohibited equality before the law or equal protection under the law by the government.

3. What are the two ways in which the government has tried to implement the equality that is guaranteed in the Constitution?

Ans. The two ways in which the government has tried to implement the equality that is guaranteed in the Constitution are

(i) Firstly, through the laws.

(ii) Secondly, through government programmes or schemes to help disadvantaged communities.

4. When persons are discriminated, their dignity is violated. How the Indian Constitution respects the dignity of all persons? Competency Based

Ans. When persons are discriminated against, they feel embarrassed and humiliated, which hurts their dignity.

The Indian Constitution respects the dignity of all the people as they have the right to be treated equally with respect and to be valued for who they are.

5. Describe the challenges of democratic nation. Competency Based

Ans. The challenges of democratic nation are

- One of the most serious challenges to democracy is the presence of corrupt and dishonest political leaders.
- Democracy include inequalities, and misuse of power.
- The socio-economic differences among the population is another significant challenge in democracy.

6. What is the significance of Universal Adult Franchise in a democracy?

Ans. The Universal Adult Franchise is an important aspect of democratic societies as it offers all adult citizens the right to Vote despite their economic or social status.

It promises that all adult citizens in the country have the right to vote without considering caste, colour, creed, or religion.

7. What is the basic requirement for reducing/eliminating inequality in Indian society? Diksha

Ans. The basic requirement for reducing/eliminating inequality in Indian society is to empower women and create opportunities for youth and disadvantaged communities.

Equality can only be established when people begin to believe that no one is inferior, and that every person deserves to be treated with dignity.

8. Briefly explain about the struggle for equality led by the African-Americans. Diksha

Ans. The fight for equal rights was brought to the forefront of America's attention during the African American Civil Rights Movement of the 1950s. African Americans are an ethnic group of Americans who have ancestry from some of Africa's racial groups.

The Civil rights movement was founded in order to end legal racial discrimination against African-Americans.

Long Answer Type Questions

1. What do you know about the Civil rights movement? Describe the incident that happened with Rosa Parks. What does the Civil Rights Act prohibited? Competency Based

Ans. The Civil rights movement is a movement started in the USA in the late 1950s to push for equal rights for African- Americans.

Rosa Parks was an African-American woman who refused to give up her seat in a bus to a white man. Her refusal started a huge protest against the unequal ways in which African- Americans were treated and this came to be known as the Civil rights movement.

The Civil rights act 1964, prohibited discrimination on the basis of race, religion or national origin. It also stated that all schools would be open to African-Americans and they would no longer have to attend separate schools.

2. Establishing equality in a democratic society is a continuous struggle. Comment. Competency Based

Ans. Establishing equality in a democratic society is a continuous struggle because attitudes of people in the society change very slowly. Even though people are aware that discrimination is against the law they continue to treat people unequally on the basis of their caste, religion, disability, economic status and gender. Change in attitude is a slow process and hence, establishing equality in a democratic society is a continuous struggle.

Equality can only be established when people begin to believe that no one is inferior, and that every person deserves to be treated with dignity.

Establishing equality in a democratic society is a continuous struggle in which individuals and communities both need to contribute.

3. What provisions are there in the Indian Constitution to recognise equality?

Ans. The Constitution of India recognises every person as equal. This recognition of equality includes some of the following provisions in the Constitution

- Every person is equal before the law.
- No person can be discriminated on basis of their religion, race, caste, place of birth, etc.
- Every person has access to all public places including (playgrounds, hotels, shops, etc.)
- Untouchability in any form is abolished.

Picture Based Question

1. Look at the picture given below of Mid-day meal provided in school and answer the following questions.

(i) How do the students get advantaged by the Mid-day meal?

Ans. The students in schools get advantaged through the healthy Mid-day meal as it reduces classroom hunger.

(ii) What are the places where the government serves the Mid-day meal to students?

Ans. The places where the government serves the Mid-day meal to students are government schools, government-aided local body, innovative education centres, Madarsas and Maqtabs supported by Sarva Shiksha Abhiyan, and National Child Labour Project schools run by the Ministry of Labour.

Case Based Question

1. Read the passage given below and answer the following questions.

In the United States of America, the African-Americans whose ancestors were the slaves who were brought over from Africa, continue to describe their lives today as largely unequal. This, despite the fact that there was a movement in the late 1950s to push for equal rights for African- Americans. Prior to this,

African-Americans were treated extremely unequally in the United States and denied equality through-law. For example, when traveling by bus, they either had to sit at the back of the bus or get up from their seat whenever a white person wished to sit. Rosa Parks (1913-2005) was an African-American woman.

Tired from a long day at work she refused to give up her seat on a bus to a white man on 1st December, 1955. Her refusal that day started a huge agitation against the unequal ways in which African-Americans were treated and which came to be known as the Civil Rights Movement. The Civil Rights Act of 1964 prohibited discrimination on the basis of race, religion or national origin. It also stated that all schools would be open to African-American children and that they would no longer have to attend separate schools specially set up for them.

However, despite this, a majority of African-Americans continue to be among the poorest in the country. Most African-American children can only afford to attend government schools that have fewer facilities and poorly qualified teachers as compared to white students who either go to private schools or live in areas where the government schools are as highly rated as private schools.

(i) Who was Rosa Parks? How she initiated the Civil Rights Movement?

Ans. Rosa Parks (1913-2005) was an African-American woman. Tired from a long day at work she refused to give up her seat on a bus to a white man on 1st December, 1955. Her refusal started a huge protest against the unequal ways in which African-Americans were treated and which came to be known as the Civil Rights Movement.

(ii) What was the condition of the African-Americans before the movement in the late 1950's?

Ans. Before the movement in the late 1950's, African-Americans were treated extremely unquality in the United States and were denied equality through law.

(iii) What was the Civil Rights Act of 1964?

Ans. The Civil Rights Act of 1964 prohibited discrimination on the basis of race, religion or national origin. It also stated that all schools would be open to African-American children and that they would no longer have to attend separate schools specially set up for them.

ASSESSMENT EXERCISE

Multiple Choice Questions (MCQs)

1. Which of the following is the most essential aspect of all democracies?
(a) Universal Adult Franchise
(b) Freedom of Association
(c) Right to free education
(d) Total ban on child labour

2. .... is an important aspect of democracy and influences all spheres of its functioning.
(a) Liberty (b) Justice
(c) Equality (d) Secularism

3. One of the most common forms of inequality in India is
(a) single citizenship
(b) reservation
(c) caste system
(d) None of the above

Subjective Questions (VSA, SA & LA)

1. What does it mean to be recognised as equal?

2. Name some schemes that improved the lives of unequally treated persons.

3. How Mid-day meal scheme has helped to reduce cast prejudice?

4. Why the issue of caste continues to be in the mind of highly educated urban Indians?

5. Write briefly about the practice of unequal treatment to the African-Americans in USA.

6. Write some challenges of democracy. Write about the provisions of Constitution for equality.

7. What were the views of BR Ambedkar about self-respect?

Role of the Government in Health

CHAPTER 2

In a democracy, people expect the government to work for their well-being. This could be done by providing education, health, employment, housing facilities, etc by the government. In this chapter, we will learn about healthcare in India, facilities provided through private and public healthcare services and equality in healthcare in India.

2.1 Health

Health means our capability to remain free of illness and injuries. Health is not just about diseases; there are other factors also that affect our health. Some of them are

- Clean drinking water
- Pollution free environment
- Adequate food to eat
- Proper living conditions
- Life without mental strain or stress

Healthcare in India

Healthcare in India consists of a large number of doctors, clinics and hospitals. India has significant experience and knowledge in running a **public healthcare system**[1]. Some of the significant features of healthcare in India are as follows

- India has the **largest number of medical colleges** in the world and is one of the largest producers of doctors.
- India is a large exporter of medicines and the third-largest producer of medicines in the world.
- India receives a large number of **medical tourists**[2] from various countries. They travel to India to receive medical care at some of the top facilities in the world.

In order to prevent and treat illnesses appropriate healthcare facilities are required, such as

- Health centres and hospitals
- Laboratories for testing
- Ambulance services
- Blood banks
- Health workers, nurses and qualified doctors
- Health professionals to advise, diagnose and treat
- Medicines and equipments

2.2 Public and Private Healthcare Services

Healthcare services can be categorised into two parts

- **Public**[3] health services
- **Private**[4] health facilities

Public Health Services

Public health services comprise a network of health centres and hospitals run by the government.

These are available both in rural and urban areas.

- At the rural or village level, health centres include a nurse and a village health worker who are trained and work under the supervision of doctors at **Primary Health Centre (PHCs)**[5].
- At the urban or district level, the District Hospital supervises the health centres. Large cities have many governments as well as specialised government hospitals.
- Public healthcare services are known as 'Public' because resources required to run these services are obtained

1 **Public Healthcare System** It is a system of hospitals and health centres run by the government.

2 **Medical Tourists** These refer to foreigners who come to a country specifically for medical treatment at hospitals that offer world class facilities at a lower cost than what they would have to pay in their own countries.

3 **Public** It is an activity or service that is meant for all people in the country and is mainly organised by the government. This includes schools, hospitals, telephone services, etc.

4 **Private** It is an activity or service that is organised by an individual or company for their own gain.

5 **Primary Health Centre (PHCs)** They are also known as Public Health Centres. They are state owned rural healthcare facilities in India.

- Public healthcare services are known as 'Public' because resources required to run these services are obtained from the general public in the form of taxes. So, these facilities are meant for everyone.
- They provide quality services either free of cost or at low cost.
- They prevent the spread of diseases such as TB, malaria, jaundice, cholera, etc.

Public health services can be made effective only when there is a **participation of people**. Indian Constitution states that it is the primary responsibility of the government to ensure the welfare of the people and to provide health care to all. The government must protect the **Right to Life** of every person.

Private Health Facilities

Private health facilities are those which are privately owned and not owned or controlled by the government.

A large number of private health facilities exist in India both in rural and urban areas. There are **Registered Medical Practitioners** (RMPs) in rural areas, and large number of doctors are available in urban areas, some of which provide specialised services.

Urban areas also have hospitals and nursing homes that are privately owned. There are many laboratories that provide special facilities such as X-ray, ultrasound, etc and medical shops from where we can buy medicines.

Patients have to pay a lot of money for private health facilities in comparison to public healthcare services.

2.3 Healthcare and Equality : Availability of Adequate Healthcare in India

In India, only **private services**[6] are increasing. Private services are mainly concentrated in urban areas and they are run for profit. The cost of these services is high and medicines are expensive.

Many people in India cannot afford private services or have to borrow money during illness. It is only 20% of the population who can afford medicines and treatment for illnesses. Apart from lack of money, there are some other reasons preventing people from getting proper medical treatment. For example,

- Women's health concerns are considered to be less important than men's health.
- Many tribal areas have few health centres, and they do not run properly. These areas also does not have private health services.

Initiatives to be Taken

Apart from healthcare services, health is also dependent upon the basic amenities and the social conditions of the people. Hence, it is important to work on both to improve the health situation of the people.

Some examples which provide ways to improve the health condition are discussed below

The Kerala Experience

In Kerala, efforts have been made to provide adequate healthcare to its people. In 1996, State Government gave its 40% budget to the Panchayats in order to provide better facilities and check the existing ones.

Water, food, women's development and education were provided. Working of schools and anganwadis was ensured. However, despite these efforts some problems like shortage of medicines, lakh of hospital bed and doctor, were needed to be addressed.

The Costa Rican Approach

Costa Rica is considered as one of the healthiest countries in Central America. The Costa Rican Government spend its money for health, education and other basic needs of the people, instead of spending money on building an army.

People were provided with safe drinking water, sanitation, nutrition and housing facilities. Health education was considered significant as knowledge about health was important at all levels.

The Costa Rican Government believes that a country can develop only when its people are healthy. Thus, it pays a lot of attention to the health of its people.

6 **Private Service** It is an activity or service which is owned and controlled by private owners.

ROLE OF THE GOVERNMENT IN HEALTH

Health

- Capability to remain free of illness and injuries.
- Some factors that affect health
  - Clean drinking water
  - Pollution free environment
  - Adequate food to eat
  - Proper living conditions
  - Life without mental stress

Healthcare in India

- India has largest number of medical college and the largest exporter of medicines.
- India receives large number of medical tourist from various countries.
- Some healthcare facilities that are required
  - Health centres and hospitals
  - Laboratories for testing
  - Ambulance services
  - Health workers, nurses and qualified doctors
  - Medicines and equipments

Healthcare and Equality

- Only private healthcare services are increasing in urban areas.
- Medicines are expensive.
- Only 20% of the population can afford medicines and treatment for illnesses.
- Services are not meant for poor people of the society.
- Women health is concerned less importance than man.

Initiative to be Taken

- Government to provide quality health care service to all.
- Provide fresh drinking water, sanitation, nutrition to all.
- Examples of ways to improve health conditions
  - Kerala spend 40% of it budget on health sector.
  - Costa Rice became one of the healthiest country of Central America by providing proper health service.

Healthcare Services

Public

- Network of health centres and hospitals run by the government.
- Facilities are meant for everyone.
- At rural level, health centres include a nurse and a village health worker, both trained under doctors at **Primary Health Centres (PHCs).**
- At urban level, health centres are supervised by District Hospital.

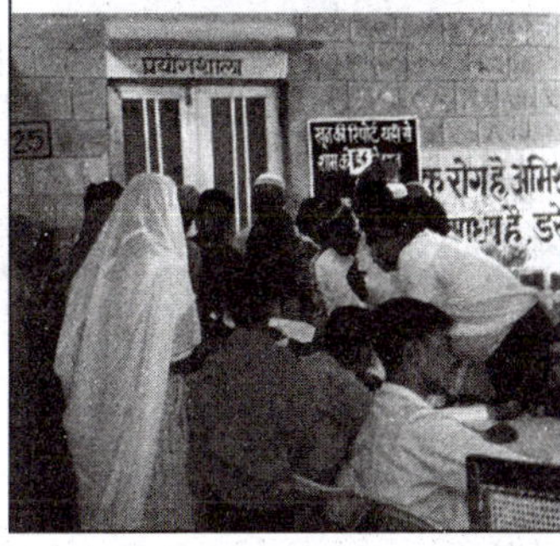

Private

- Privately owned and not controlled by government.
- Facilities meant only for those who can afford.
- There are **Registered Medical Practitioners (RMPs)** in rural areas.
- There are large number of doctors in urban areas.

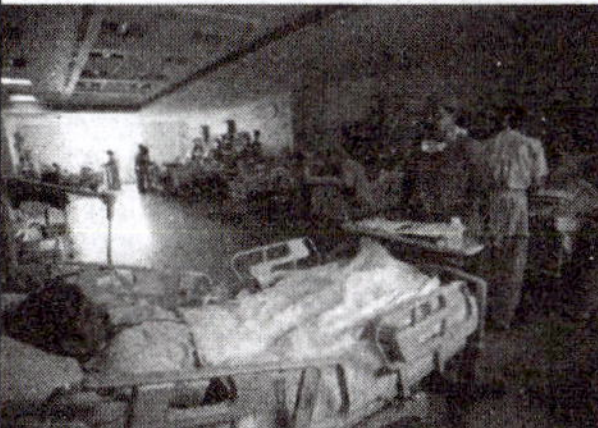

NCERT FOLDER

Covering Intext Questions and Exercises of NCERT

NCERT ON PAGE 13

Q.1 Would you associate all or some of these pictures with health? In what ways? Discuss in groups?

Ans. Yes, we associate all of these pictures with health because the conditions shown in these pictures directly or indirectly affects the health of a person.

Q.2 Pick out two situations from the collage that are not related to illness and write two sentences on how they are related to health.

Ans. Two situations from the collage that are not related to illness are

(i) A woman carrying two earthen pots on her head and going to fetch water.

(ii) Two garbage containers are shown kept in front of the houses in a slum.

In the first situation, the woman might have collected water from open tanks or wells which is not clean and creates health problems.

In the second situation, the containers might contain all types of wastes. The house flies sitting on these wastes carry pathogenic germs to our eatables, which can lead to illness.

NCERT ON PAGE 14

Q.3 Can you provide a title to these columns?

Column I	Column II
India has the largest number of medical colleges in the world and is among the largest producers of doctors. Approximately, 15000 new doctors qualify every year.	Most doctors settle in urban areas. People in rural areas have to travel long distances to reach a doctor. The number of doctors with respect to the population is much less in rural areas.
Healthcare facilities have grown substantially over the years. In 1950, there were only 2717 hospitals in India. In 1991, there were 11174 hospitals. In 2000, the number grew to 18218.	About 5 lakh people die from tuberculosis every year. This number is almost unchanged since Independence! Almost 2 million cases of malaria are reported every year and this number isn't decreasing.
India gets a large number of medical tourists from many countries. They come for treatment in some of the hospitals in India that compare with the best in the world.	We are not able to provide clean drinking water to all. 21% of all communicable diseases are water borne. e.g. diarrhoea, worms, hepatitis, etc.
India is the fourth largest producer of medicines in the world and is also a large exporter of medicines.	Half of all children in India do not get adequate food to eat and are undernourished.

Ans. **Column I** – India's flourishing medical landscape

Column II – Challenges and drawbacks in India's Healthcare system

Q.4 In India, it is often said that we are unable to provide health services for all because the government does not have enough money and facilities. After reading the above left hand column, do you think this is true? Discuss.

Ans. After reading the above column, I don't think it is true.

The reasons for the same are

- India has the largest number of medical colleges in the world.
- Number of hospitals is increasing constantly.
- Foreigners come to India for treatment.
- India ranks fourth in production of medicines.

NCERT ON PAGE 18

Q.5 Why did Ranjan have to spend so much money? Give reasons.

Ans. Ranjan had to spend so much money because he took his treatment from private hospital and they charge lots of unnecessary money from the patients.

Q.6 What problems did Aman face in the public hospital? How do you think the hospital can work in a better manner? Discuss.

Ans. Aman was suffering from a viral fever hence his parents took him to the public hospital. He faced a lot of problems while he was there in hospital.

Some of them are

- He had to wait in a long queue at the Out Patient Department (OPD) counter, leaning on his father all the time.
- They again had to stand in a long queue for blood tests.
- Government hospitals are not well organised and managed.

Proper actions should be taken in order to avoid adverse situations. More hospitals and trained person should be provided with better facilities to work in. Proper appointment system should be adopted and the patient should be told about the timings. There should not be frequent changes of doctors.

Q.7 Where do you go when you are ill? Are there any problems that you face? Write a paragraph based on your experience.

Ans. I prefer to go to a private health centre whenever I am not well. Private centres are hygienic, clean and properly administered. There is no rush in private hospitals and therefore, treatment is done quickly.

Q.8 What problems do we face in private hospitals? Discuss.

Ans. In private hospitals, we have to face problems such as

- Non-availability of expert doctors
- Expensive treatment
- Extra tests prescribed by doctors
- Extra medicines, which can be avoided still prescribed by doctors.

NCERT ON PAGE 19

Q.9 In what ways is the public health system meant for everyone?

Ans. Public health system is meant for everyone as there are a number of hospitals, healthcare centres, dispensaries available for general public. They treat people free of cost or at low cost.

Q.10 List some Public Health Centres (PHCs) or hospitals near your place. From your experience (or by visiting any one of them), find out the facilities provided and people who run the centre.

Ans. Public health centres which are situated near my area are RML Hospital and Saroj Hospital.

These centres are run by people appointed through government. RML lacks in the cleanliness aspect, while Saroj is quite near, well equipped and advanced.

NCERT ON PAGE 20

Q. 11 Private health facilities can mean many things. Explain with the help of some examples from your area.

Ans. Private health facilities can mean many things as. There are countless doctors and private clinics run for profit motive in the urban areas. They provide specialised services. There are many laboratories that do tests and offer facilities like X-ray, ultrasound, etc.

Today all these services are run by big companies which in turn also run many businesses related to these private centres such as medical shops, etc.

Q. 12 How can healthcare be made more affordable?

Ans. Healthcare can be made more affordable in the following ways

- Discounts on healthcare should be given.
- Government should focus on improving the basic amenities and social conditions of the people because health is dependent on both these aspects.
- People should be encouraged to opt for health insurance.

EXERCISES

Q.1 In this chapter you have read that health is a wider concept than illness. Look at this quote from the Constitution and explain the terms 'Living standard' and 'Public health' in your own words.

Ans. **Living standard** It means level of wealth, comfort, material goods and necessities available to the people.

If the basic amenities are barely satisfied, then it is of low level and if people are living in hygienic conditions with all comforts, then level of living is high.

Public health It refers to all organised measures that are provided by government to prevent diseases and promote health among the population as a whole. Government provides quality healthcare services either free or at low cost.

Q.2 What are the different ways through which the government can take steps to provide healthcare for all? Discuss.

Ans. The different ways through which the government can provide healthcare for all are

- Setting up new primary health centres, hospitals and family welfare centres.
- Preventing spread of diseases such as TB, jaundice, malaria, etc.
- Spreading health related knowledge among general public.
- Organising free camps and diagnostic centres.

Q.3 **What differences do you find between private and public health services in your area?**

Facility	Cost of services	Availability of services
Private		
Public		

Ans.

Facility	Cost of services	Availability of services
Private	Very expensive	Quality services but available to only the economically well-off.
Public	Free or low cost	Easily available, ordinary services, not maintained

Q.4 **"Improvement in water and sanitation can control many diseases." Explain with the help of examples.**

Ans. Improvement in water and sanitation can control many diseases since both water and sanitation are parts of basic amenities. If water and sanitation are of poor quality, this will lead to poor health.

Diseases like malaria, diarrhoea, jaundice are water borne diseases caused due to contaminated water and diseases like plague, fever, etc are caused due to unhygienic sanitary conditions.

Thus, improvement in water and sanitation will surely control many diseases, thereby increasing standard of living and good health.

REVIEW EXERCISE

Including Competency Based Questions

Part I

Multiple Choice Questions (MCQs)

1. Good health depends on
(a) clean drinking water (b) pollution free environment
(c) adequate food to eat (d) All of these

2. To prevent and treat illness, we need
(a) health centres (b) ambulance services
(c) laboratories for testing (d) All of these

3. It is the primary duty of the government to ensure the welfare of the
(a) VIPs (b) rich persons
(c) poor persons (d) all its citizens

4. What is the main motive of private health services?
(a) Profit earning (b) Social service
(c) Both (a) and (b) (d) None of these

5. According to one study, how much per cent of the people who are admitted to a hospital have to borrow and sell their possession to pay expenses?
(a) 20% (b) 40%
(c) 30% (d) 10%

6. Aman, a student of class VII, went to government hospital to treat his fever and cold. What are the situations he may face at hospital? Competency Based
(a) A long queues (b) Good doctors
(c) Costs very low (d) All of these

7. With Covid having exposed India's public health system, particularly at the primary healthcare level, there is unanimity that the country's health sector needs extensive infrastructure support.

Source Mint Competency Based

Should government focus on primary healthcare level to maintain strong healthcare system?
(a) Yes, primary healthcare level is used by rich people therefore it is necessary.
(b) Yes, primary healthcare level should be focused as it provide healthcare facilities to all citizens at affordable cost.
(c) No, primary healthcare level is not useful to maintain strong healthcare system.
(d) No, primary healthcare level is only burden, it should be avoided.

8. Identify the correct option that describes the statements given below. Competency Based

I. It is considered to be one of the healthiest countries in Central America.
II. It decided not to have an army.
III. It provided safe drinking water, sanitation, nutrition, etc to every citizens.

Options
(a) San Francisco (b) Costa Rica
(c) Panama (d) El Salvador

9. Choose the correct statement(s) from the following.

I. Health is only about disease.

II. 21 per cent of all communicable diseases are air born.

III. India is the fourth largest producer of medicines in the world.

Codes

(a) Only I (b) Only II (c) I and II (d) Only III

10. Choose the incorrect statement(s) from the following.

I. Half the population of children in India don't get adequate food to eat and are therefore undernourished.

II. Patients usually have to wait in long queues in government hospitals.

III. 80 per cent of the population can afford all the medicines that they require during an illness.

Codes

(a) Only I (b) Only II (c) I and II (d) Only III

Answers

1. (d)	2. (d)	3. (d)	4. (a)	5. (b)
6. (d)	7. (b)	8. (b)	9. (d)	10. (d)

Match the Following

1.

	List I		List II
A.	Costa Rica	1.	Free of cost
B.	Private Service	2.	Profit motive
C.	Public Service	3.	Rural areas
D.	RMPs	4.	Healthiest country

Codes

	A	B	C	D		A	B	C	D
(a)	3	2	1	4	(b)	1	2	3	4
(c)	4	3	1	2	(d)	4	2	1	3

Ans. (d)

Assertion-Reason

1. Assertion (A) Health is not only about disease.

Reason (R) It isn't healthy to be dull, inactive, anxious or scared for long stretches of time.

Codes

(a) Both A and R are true and R is the correct explanation of A

(b) Both A and R are true, but R is not the correct explanation of A

(c) A is true, but R is false

(d) A is false, but R is true

2. Assertion (A) India gets a large number of medical tourists from many countries.

Reason (R) Private health facilities provide services at cheaper prices in compaion to public health facilities.

Codes

(a) Both A and R are true and R is the correct explanation of A

(b) Both A and R are true, but R is not the correct explanation of A

(c) A is true, but R is false

(d) A is false, but R is true

Ans. 1. (a) Both A and R are true and R is the correct explanation of A

2. (c) A is true, but R is false

Fill in the Blanks

1. PHC stands for ....
2. 40% of the Kerala's budget is given to ....
3. .... service is organised by individual or company for their own profit.
4. System of hospitals and health centres run by government is called as ....
5. India is the .... largest producer of medicines in the world and is also a large .... of medicines.

Ans. 1. Primary Health Centre 2. Panchayats
3. Private 4. public healthcare system
5. second, exporter

True/False

1. OPD stands for Old Patient Department.
2. Communicable diseases can also spread from animal to human beings.
3. Kerala Government gave its 60% budget to Panchayats.
4. India is the largest producer of medicine in the world.
5. In rural areas, a jeep is often used to serve as a mobile clinic for patients.

Ans. 1. False 2. True 3. False
4. False 5. True

Picture Based Question

1. The image shown below is one of the sustainable development goals. How many goals are adopted at United Nations?

(a) 5 (b) 9 (c) 11 (d) 17

Ans. 1. (d) 17

Case Based Question

1. Read the following passage and answer the questions.

In order to prevent and treat illnesses we need appropriate healthcare facilities such as health centres, hospitals, laboratories for testing, ambulance services, blood banks, etc., that can provide the required care and services that patients need. In order to run such facilities we need health workers, nurses, qualified doctors and other health professionals who can advice, diagonse and treat illnesses. We also need the medicines and equipment that are necessary for treating patients. These facilities are required to take care of us.

(i) Which factor is not considered as symptom of healthy person?

(a) Adequate sleep (b) Healthy food
(c) Stressful (d) Pollution free environment

(ii) Which country has largest number of medical college in the world?

(a) USA (b) Canada
(c) China (d) India

(iii) Which facilities are run by government?

(a) District Hospital
(b) Apollo Hospital
(c) Medanta
(d) MAX Hospital

(iv) Which term is used to describe professionals who can advise, diagnose and treat illnesses?

(a) Fitness trainers (b) Nutritionists
(c) Medical experts (d) Health enthusiast

Ans. (i) (c) Stressful
(ii) (d) India
(iii) (a) District Hospital
(iv) (c) Medical experts

Part II

Very Short Answer Type Questions

1. Define medical tourists.

Ans. Medical tourists are the people who travel to India especially for medical treatment because hospitals here in India offer them world-class facilities at lower costs.

2. What do you understand by communicable diseases?

Ans. Communicable diseases are those which spread from one person to another or from animal to a person through air, food and water.

3. Define health.

Ans. Health can be defined as our capacity to remain free of illness and injuries.

4. What are the expectations of people from government in a democratic country?

Ans. In a democratic country, people expect that government should work for their well-being and welfare.

5. What are the two types of healthcare services discussed in this chapter?

Ans. The two types of healthcare services are

(i) Public health services
(ii) Private health facilities

6. What does constitution say with respect to welfare of people?

Ans. According to our Constitution, it is the primary duty of the government to ensure the welfare of the people and provide healthcare services to all.

7. What do you understand by public healthcare system?

Ans. Public healthcare system is a system of hospitals and health centres run by government.

8. Why do poor people fall ill more often?

Ans. Poor people fall ill more often because they are deprived of basic amenities of life and hence they are more prone to diseases.

9. Which kind of services are easily available in rural areas?

Ans. Public healthcare services are easily available in rural areas.

10. Where are RMPs mostly found?

Ans. RMPs stands for Registered Medical Practitioners and they are mostly found in rural areas.

Short Answer Type Questions

1. What factors other than diseases affect our health?

Ans. The other factors apart from diseases that affect our health are

- Clean drinking water
- Pollution free environment
- Adequate food to eat
- Proper living conditions
- Life without mental strain or stress

2. Discuss positive aspects of healthcare in India.

Ans. Positive aspects of healthcare in India are

- India has the largest number of medical colleges and produces the largest number of doctors.
- Number of hospitals have been increasing continuously over the years.

- A number of medical tourists visit India for their treatment.
- India is the fourth largest producer of medicines in the world.

3. Discuss negative aspects of healthcare in India.

Ans. The negative aspects of healthcare in India are

- There is scarcity of doctors in rural areas as most doctors settle in urban areas.
- Many people die from tuberculosis every year and the number isn't decreasing.
- Clean drinking water is not available which causes water borne diseases.
- Lack of adequate food causes malnourishment in children.

4. Is adequate health services available to all? Discuss.

***Or* "Adequate healthcare services are not available to all citizens in India". Briefly explain.** Competency Based

Ans. No, adequate health services are not available to all. This is because private services are increasing but public services are not. Thus, private services are available at very high cost to the people living in urban areas only.

Poor people hardly afford these services. They have to borrow money or sell their possessions to pay for their treatment.

5. What can be done to improve health situation in our country?

Ans. To improve the health situation in our country several steps can be taken as follows

- At first, a healthcare system should be established that is available and accessible to all citizens.
- Public health awareness programmes should be started to raise awareness and educate people about healthy lifestyle.
- Healthcare facilities in rural areas are much important as most of population of our country lives in villages.

6. To prevent and treat ill health, what facilities are required?

Ans. To prevent and treat ill health, facilities given below are required

- Health centres and hospitals
- Laboratories for testing
- Ambulance services
- Health workers, nurses and qualified doctors
- Health professionals to advise, diagnose and treat patients
- Medicines and equipment

7. Why are public healthcare services known as 'public'? What are their functions?

Ans. Public healthcare services are known as 'public' because resources required to run these centres are obtained from the general public in a way of taxes. So, these facilities are meant for everyone.

They provide quality services either free of cost or at very low cost. Their function is to prevent spread of diseases such as TB, malaria, jaundice, etc.

8. What are Private Health Services?

Ans. Private Health Services are those which are privately owned and controlled. There are large number of private health facilities in our country because many doctors run their own private clinics.

There are RMPs in rural areas and specialised doctors in urban areas. A number of privately owned hospitals, nursing homes, laboratories, medical shops are also there in urban areas. In private services, people have to pay a lot of money for their treatment.

9. Health and education are fundamental pillars of society. These are basic civil rights as well. A year before our Independence, the Bhore Committee presented a report that became the template on which independent India built her healthcare infrastructure, from Primary Health Centres (PHCs), Secondary Health Centres (SHCs) to District hospitals. Competency Based

Source Forbes India

(i) Why are health and education called fundamental pillars of society?

Ans. Health and education are called fundamental pillars of society as health provides a quality life and education enables individuals with knowledge and skills need to contribute in society's progress.

(ii) Who runs primary health centres, secondary health centres and district hospitals and why?

Ans. Government runs primary health centres, secondary health centres and district hospitals to provide affordable and accessible facilities to all citizen.

Long Answer Type Questions

1. Discuss the changes made by Kerala Government in the state in 1996.

Ans. Kerala Government has made efforts to provide adequate healthcare to its people. In 1996, the State Government gave its 40% budget to the Panchayats in order to provide better facilities and check the existing ones.

Problems such as water supply schemes, specific problems of village were taken up. Proper planning was done for betterment of people.

Water, food, women's, development and education were provided health centres were improved.

Working of schools and anganwadis was ensured. All other problems were checked though some problems are there which have to be addressed.

Some problems like shortage of doctors, medicines and beds etc are still there, but the situation has improved in terms of health of people.

2. Explain the Costa Rican approach.

Or **What is Costa Rican approach in health? Explain.** **Diksha**

Ans. Costa Rica is considered one of the healthiest countries in South America. The main reason for this is found in Costa Rican Constitution. The government here took an approach of not having an army and instead allotting its money for health, education and other basic amenities.

People were provided with safe drinking water, sanitation, nutrition and housing facilities. Health education was considered significant as knowledge about health was important at all levels. According to Costa Rican Government, a country can develop only when its people are healthy. Thus, they paid significant attention to the health of the people.

3. "The government can take steps to reduce healthcare costs in India." What are your suggestions for that? **Competency Based**

Ans. It is important to reduce healthcare costs in India and make it affordable and accessible for all citizens. Some suggestions to consider for this are

- Implementation of a complete universal healthcare system that provides basic healthcare services at very low cost or free.
- There should be implementation of strict price controls on essential medicines and medical equipment to prevent price rise by hospitals and medical companies.
- Health insurance policies should be promoted and regulated to make them affordable.
- There should be remote healthcare consultations to save time and money.
- Generic medicines should be encouraged over the branded ones, which are more affordable and equally effective.
- There should be investment in research and development for medical purposes and provide incentives for that to develop affordable drugs and equipments.
- There should be an increase in number of hospitals and medical colleges so that shortage of doctors could be reduced.

Picture Based Question

1. Look at the picture and identify what kind of hospital is shown in it. State some features of such hospitals.

Ans. The picture shown above is of a government hospital. Following are the features of government hospital

- Resources needed to run these services are obtained from the money that the public pays to the government as taxes.
- It provides quality health care services either free or at a low cost, so that even the poor can seek treatment.
- It takes action to prevent the spread of diseases such as TB, malaria, chikungunya, cholera, etc.

Case Based Question

1. Read the passage given below and answer the following questions.

"Government uses tax money for providing many public services for the benefit of all citizens. Some services such as defence, police, judicial system, highways, etc benefit all citizens. Otherwise, the citizens cannot organise these services for themselves.Taxes fund developmental programmes and services such as education, health care, employment, social welfare, vocational training, etc required for needy citizens. Tax money is utilised for relief and rehabilitation in case of natural disasters such as floods, earthquakes, tsunami, etc. Space, nuclear, and missile programmes are also funded from the revenues collected as taxes."

(i) Why do you think it is necessary for citizens to pay taxes?

Ans. It is necessary for citizens to pay taxes because it helps the government to provide important services like defence, police, education and healthcare. Taxes also support programmes for those in need and help the country respond to natural disasters. It is a way for everyone to contribute to the nation's well-being.

(ii) Why is it important for the government to organise services like defence, police and highways?

Ans. It is important for the government to organise services like defence, police and highways because citizens cannot organise these services for themselves, so the government takes the responsibility with the help of tax money to ensure the well-being of all citizens.

(iii) Name some specific programmes funded by taxes that are meant for needy citizens.

Ans. Taxes help to fund programmes like education, health care, employment opportunities and social welfare.

ASSESSMENT EXERCISE

Multiple Choice Questions (MCQs)

1. In a democracy which of the following could not be provision for welfare of people?
(a) Employment (b) Health
(c) Education (d) Profit earning

2. Which of the following factor affect our health?
(a) Healthy environment (b) Clean drinking water
(c) Safe food (d) All of these

3. Which of the following states provided 40% of the entire state budget to Panchayats?
(a) Tamil Nadu (b) Kerala
(c) Uttar Pradesh (d) Punjab

Subjective Questions (VSA, SA & LA)

1. Do you think that a dull, inactive, anxious person is healthy?

2. What are the requirements for appropriate healthcare facilities?

3. Name some diseases which are prevented by public healthcare.

4. Why are governments health services called as 'Public health service'?

5. Why are public services not increasing in parallel with private services?

6. How is health dependent on basic amenities and social conditions?

7. Differentiate the health services of urban and rural areas.

8. Costa Rica's decision not to have an army has placed it as one of the healthiest countries in South America. Explain.

How the State Government Works

The word 'government' refers to government departments and various ministers who head them.The government works at three levels – local, state and national. **Members of Legislative Assembly** (MLAs) are important in the functioning of the government at state level.

3.1 Member of Legislative Assembly (MLA)

Every state in India has a Legislative Assembly and each state is divided into several constituencies. The people elect one member as their representative from each **constituency**[1] by voting. This elected member becomes an MLA.

MLAs may belong to different parties. They are elected by the people, thus they are said to represent people.

A political party whose MLAs have won more than half the number of constituencies in a state can be said to be in a **majority**. The political party that has the majority is called the **ruling party** and all other members are called the **opposition**.

In a democracy, MLAs have the main authority. These members can ask questions, debate over an important issues decide where money should be spent, etc.

MLAs are together responsible for the work of the government. There are some MLA's who have a **dual responsibilities**- as an MLA and as a minister.

All the MLAs who gather together (assemble) in the Legislative Assembly are called the **Legislature**[2].

Chief Minister and Other Ministers

After the elections MLA's from the ruling party elect their leader who becomes the Chief Minister. He is also called as the **Head of the Executive**[3]. The Chief Minister selects other MLAs as ministers.

It is the Governor of the state who appoints the Chief Minister and other ministers. The Governor is called the **Head of the State** appointed by the Central Government. He/She is appointed to ensure that the State Government works within the rules and regulations of the Constitution.

Chief Minister along with other ministers are responsible for running various government departments and ministries. They have separate offices.

3.2 Debate in the Legislative Assembly

Legislative Assembly is the place where all the MLA's from the ruling party and the opposition party meet and discuss various important things.

A debate is generally held in Legislative Assembly to discuss current problems. MLAs take part in the debate by asking questions, expressing their opinions or giving suggestions to the government.

After all the discussion, the concerned minister replies and assures the assembly that adequate steps are being taken.

1 **Constituency** It is a particular area from which all the voters living there choose their representatives.
2 **Legislature** It is the organ of the state which is responsible for making laws.
3 **Executive** It is the organ of the government which is responsible for executing the laws. It comprises of Chief Minister and other ministers.

Chief Minister along with other ministers have to take all the decisions. However, these decisions have to be approved by the Members of Legislative Assembly.

3.3 Working of The Government

The Legislative Assembly is not the only place where opinions are expressed about the work of the government and action is demanded. There are several newspapers, organisations and TV channels which regularly talk about the government.

The government works in the following ways after the debate in the Legislative Assembly

- According to the discussions in the Legislative Assembly, the Chief Minister and the ministers have to take action on the particular issue discussed in the Legislative Assembly.
- They do this through various government departments like Public Works Department, Agriculture Department, Health Department, Education Department, etc.
- A press conference[4] is generally held by a particular minister who explains the steps taken by the government. Media persons then report these discussions in several newspapers.
- New laws can also be implemented by the State Government on certain issues in the Legislative Assembly of the respective state.

In a democracy, there are various ways through which people express their views and also take action. It is the people who have the main authority, because they are the ones who elect their representatives. They have the power to organise meetings, to voice their opinions and protest against the government.

4 Press Conference It is a gathering of journalists who have been invited to hear and ask questions on a particular issue and then are expected to report on this to the larger public.

HOW THE STATE GOVERNMENT WORKS

Legislative Assembly

The place where MLAs gather to express opinion related to work of government.

Debates in the Legislative Assembly

- Generally, current problems are discussed in the debate.
- MLAs take part in debate by asking questions, expressing opinions or giving suggestions.
- After discussion, concerned minister assures the assembly that adequate steps are being taken.
- CM with other ministers has to take all the decisions, but they have to be approved by MLAs.

Members of Legislative Assembly (MLA)

- Elected by people.
- They have main authority.
- Have dual responsibilities.
- All the MLAs who gather together in the Legislative Assembly are called the Legislature.
- Ruling Party–The political party that has majority.
- Opposition–Members other than majority.

Chief Minister and other Ministers

- Chief Minister (CM) is Head of the Executive.
- CM is appointed by the Governor who is Head of the State.
- CM selects other MLAs minister.
- CM along with other ministers is responsible for running various government departments and ministries.

Working of the Government

- The issues discussed in Legislative solved by State Government through Public.
- Works Department, Agriculture Department, Health Department, etc.
  - There are various ways through which people express their views in a democracy.
  - They have the power to organise meetings, voice their opinions and protest against the government.

NCERT FOLDER

Covering Intext Questions and Exercises of NCERT

NCERT ON PAGE 25

Q.1 What is happening in Patalpuram?

Ans. Patalpuram is experiencing the problem of shortage of water which has resulted in outbreak of diarrhoea in the city.

Q.2 Why is this problem serious?

Ans. The problem is serious because according to TV news, ten people have died from diarrhoea. It was necessary to take immediate action to bring the situation under control.

Q.3 What action do you think can be taken in the above situation and who do you think should take this action? Discuss.

Ans. In the above situation, Health Minister should take the required action like improving health services and clean drinking water should be supplied to people, etc.

NCERT ON PAGE 26

Q.4 Discuss the following terms with your teacher

(a) Public meeting (b) States in India
(c) Constituency (d) Majority
(e) Ruling party (f) Opposition

Ans. (a) **Public meeting** It is the meeting of general public which focusses on current issues faced by the people.

(b) **States in India** Our country has been divided into several units with properly defined boundaries. These units with specified boundaries are defined as states.

(c) **Constituency** Constituency is an area from which people living there elect one representative, who then becomes a Member of Legislative Assembly (MLA).

(d) **Majority** It is the political party whose MLAs have won more than half the number of constituencies in a state.

(e) **Ruling Party** It is a political party which has attained majority.

(f) **Opposition** Opposition are the elected members in the state Legislature Assembly who have not attained majority.

Q.5 Can you explain the following terms majority, ruling party, opposition with reference to your state?

Ans. In any state i.e. Rajasthan, Bharatiya Janata Party is the majority and ruling party and the opposition party is Indian National Congress.

A political party whose MLAs have won more than half the number of constituencies in a state is a **majority party**. The political party that has the majority is called the **ruling party** and all other members are called the **opposition**.

NCERT ON PAGE 27

Q.6 Construct a table, similar to the one given for Himachal Pradesh, for your state.

Ans. Do it yourself.

Q.7 At times, the ruling party may not be single party but a group of parties working together. This is called a coalition. Discuss with your teacher.

Ans. A coalition is a pact or treaty among different parties in which they cooperate and join together to get majority and form the government. In a parliamentary system, Coalition Government is made up of coalition of parties.

When no one party is able to get the majority, then many parties come together to form the government.

NCERT ON PAGE 30

Q.8 What were the main arguments put forward by different MLAs who thought that the government was not taking the situation in a serious manner?

Ans. The main arguments put forward by different MLAs who thought that the government was not taking the situation in a serious manner, were

- As per MLA 1, the government had not been able to check a simple problem like diarrhoea in his constituency and there had been 15 deaths due to this.
- Similarly, MLA 2 and 5 argued that the government hospitals were in a very bad situation in the district and no medical staff was being appointed.
- MLA 3 claimed that there was serious shortage of water in his constituency.

Q.9 If you were the Health Minister, how would you respond to the discussion given in your NCERT textbook on page 34 and 35.

Ans. If I were the Health Minister, I would have taken a note of all the problems being faced by the people in constituencies.

Further, I would have convinced the fellow MLAs that the Health Ministry is taking proper action in this regard by launching initiatives and doing everything it can to resolve problems.

Q.10 Do you think the debate given on page 34 and 35 of your NCERT textbook would have been useful in some ways? How? Discuss.

Ans. Yes, the given debate would have been very useful. Firstly, the concerned ministers would come to know what problems are being faced by public that need to be resolved. Secondly, the respective MLAs would come to know what steps the government is taking to resolve the issues in their constituency.

Q.11 In the working of the government, explain the difference between being an MLA and an MLA who is also a minister.

Ans. If an MLA is selected by the Chief Minister to handle a particular ministry, then he will be a minister and also an MLA. In this case, on one side he has to take care of the problems being faced in his constituency and bring it to the notice of the minister concerned.

On the other side, he has to respond to other MLAs also in regard to the working of his ministry.

NCERT ON PAGE 33

Q.12 Find out with the help of your teacher, the work done by the government departments mentioned in your NCERT textbook on page 39 and fill in the table.

Name of Department	Examples of their work
School Education	
Public Works Department	
Agriculture	

Ans.

Name of Department	Examples of their work
School Education	Construction of new schools. Appointing adequate number of teachers. Providing good infrastructure facilities in schools.
Public Works Department	Provision of clean drinking water and electricity. Construction of roads. Construction of government buildings and staff quarters.
Agriculture	Provision of good quality seeds and fertilisers. Provision of adequate irrigation facilities. Providing loans and subsidies to farmers.

NCERT ON PAGE 34

Q.13 Do a similar wallpaper project about any issue connected with the working of your State Government like an education programme, any law and order, issue, mid-day meal scheme, etc.

Ans. Do it yourself.

EXERCISES

Q.1 Use the terms 'constituency' and 'represent' to explain who an MLA is and how is the person elected?

Ans. Member of the Legislative Assembly is elected by the people and hence, this way they 'represent' people.

A person is elected as an MLA in the following manner

- Each state is divided into different areas or constituencies.
- Elections are organised in each constituency.
- People from each constituency vote for their representatives. The person attaining maximum votes is then elected as an MLA.

Q.2 How did some MLAs become ministers?

Ans. The Chief Minister after his/her election by the MLAs selects other people as ministers among the MLAs. After the elections, the Governor of the state appoints the Chief Minister and other ministers. In this way, some MLAs become ministers.

Q.3 Why should decisions taken by the Chief Minister and other ministers be debated in the Legislative Assembly?

Ans. The decisions taken by Chief Minister and other ministers should be debated in the Legislative Assembly because of the following reasons

- In this debate, MLAs can communicate their views and can ask queries related to the issues. They can give some suggestions as to what steps the government can take.
- The Chief Minister and other ministers can reply to the queries and assure people about their decisions.

Q.4 What was the problem in Patalpuram? What discussion/action was taken by the following? Fill in the table.

Public Meeting
Legislative Assembly
Press Conference
Chief Minister

Ans. Patalpuram was experiencing the problem of shortage of water which resulted in diarrhoea in the city.

Public Meeting	In public meeting, people protested against the problem of diarrhoea and water crisis faced by them.
Legislative Assembly	The issue was debated in the assembly and the required measures to be taken were decided.
Press Conference	Journalists asked questions on a particular issue and the Health Minister explained the actions taken by government.
Chief Minister	He visited Patalpuram and announced compensation for the families of victims.

Q.5 What is the difference between the work that MLAs do in the assembly and the work done by government departments?

Ans. Differences between the work that MLAs do in the assembly and the work done by the government departments is that an **MLA** works for the well-being of people. He raises relevant issues in the Legislative Assembly and demands solution to the problems. On the other hand, the **government departments** implement decisions taken in the Legislative Assembly.

REVIEW EXERCISE

Including Competency Based Questions

Part I

Multiple Choice Questions (MCQs)

1. MLA stands for
(a) Member of Long Assembly
(b) Member of Legislative Assembly
(c) Member of Law Assembly
(d) None of the above

2. Political party that has attained majority is known as
(a) Opposition party (b) Ruling party
(c) Coalition party (d) Majority party

3. What is the head of the State known as?
(a) MLA (b) Chief Minister
(c) Governor (d) Minister

4. Who appoints the Chief Minister?
(a) MLA (b) Governor
(c) Prime Minister (d) None of these

5. To attain majority, political party is required to win
(a) less than half the number of constituencies.
(b) more than half the number of constituencies.
(c) hundred per cent constituencies.
(d) None of the above

6. Laws for the entire country are made by
(a) Legislative Assembly (b) Parliament
(c) Governor (d) Chief Minister

7. Rita, a class 7th student was discussing with her friend Ritika about working of different government departments. Who is responsible for working of schools and colleges? **Competency Based**
(a) Home Minister
(b) Prime Minister
(c) Chief Minister
(d) Education Minister

8. Identify the correct option that describes the state given below. **Competency Based**
I. It has 68 constituencies.
II. It's capital is Shimla.
III. Punjab and Uttarakhand are South of this state.
Options
(a) Jammu and Kashmir
(b) Haryana
(c) Himachal Pradesh
(d) Uttar Pradesh

9. **Identify from the following statements, who is being talked about?**
   I. He is the Head of the State.
   II. He is in charge of appointing the head of executive and other ministers selected by Chief Minister.
   III. He is appointed by the President.

   Options
   (a) Governor (b) Minister of Parliament
   (c) MLA (d) Chief Minister

10. **Choose the correct statement(s) from the following.**
   I. Members of the Legislative Assembly are elected by the people.
   II. The political party that has the majority is called the opposition.
   III. MLAs does not become ministers.

   Codes
   (a) Only I (b) Only II
   (c) I and II (d) I and III

Answers

1. (b)	2. (b)	3. (c)	4. (b)	5. (b)
6. (b)	7. (d)	8. (c)	9. (a)	10. (a)

Match the Following

1.

List I	List II
A. Party in minority	1. Ruling party
B. Party in majority	2. Opposition party
C. Legislative Assembly	3. Vidhan Sabha

Codes

	A	B	C		A	B	C
(a)	2	1	3	(b)	3	1	2
(c)	3	2	1	(d)	1	2	3

2.

List I	List II
A. Governor	1. Members of Legislative Assembly
B. Chief Minister	2. Head of government
C. MLA	3. Real authority
D. People	4. Head of State

Codes

	A	B	C	D		A	B	C	D
(a)	1	2	3	4	(b)	4	2	1	3
(c)	3	1	2	4	(d)	4	3	2	1

Ans. 1. (a) 2. (b)

Assertion-Reason

1. **Assertion** (A) The Governor of the state appoints the Chief Minister and other ministers after the elections.

   Reason (R) The Chief Minister and other ministers are elected by the MLAs belonging to the ruling party.

   Codes
   (a) Both A and R are true and R is the correct explanation of A
   (b) Both A and R are true, but R is not the correct explanation of A
   (c) A is true, but R is false
   (d) A is false, but R is true

2. **Assertion** (A) The Indian National Congress was the major opposition party because it has the largest number of MLAs after the BJP.

   Reason (R) The BJP won the majority of seats in the 2017 Assembly Elections.

   Codes
   (a) Both A and R are true and R is the correct explanation of A
   (b) Both A and R are true, but R is not the correct explanation of A
   (c) A is true, but R is false
   (d) A is false, but R is true

Ans. 1. (a) Both A and R are true and R is the correct explanation of A
2. (b) Both A and R are true, but R is not the correct explanation of A

Fill in the Blanks

1. .... is the other name for Legislative Assembly.
2. A state is divided into different areas known as ....
3. MLAs belonging to the .... elect their leader as Chief Minister.
4. Some MLAs have dual responsibility one as an MLA and other as the ....

Ans. 1. Vidhan Sabha 2. constituencies
3. ruling party 4. minister

True/False

1. There are only two levels of government.
2. Himachal Pradesh is divided into 70 constituencies.
3. MLAs together are responsible for the working of government.
4. Chief Minister is the head of the Government.

Ans. 1. False 2. False 3. True 4. True

Picture Based Questions

1. **The figure shown below is an image of type of activity in the classroom to do research on particular topic. What is the name of activity?**

(a) Drawing Project (b) Class Project
(c) PPT Project (d) Wallpaper Project

2. **The image shown below is the map of Himachal Pradesh. Which of the following state is not the neighbouring state of Himachal Pradesh?**

(a) Punjab
(b) Rajasthan
(c) Uttarakhand
(d) Jammu and Kashmir

Ans. 1. (d) Wallpaper Project
2. (b) Rajasthan

Case Based Question

1. **Read the passage given below and answer the following questions.**

Every state in India has a Legislative Assembly. Each state is divided into different areas or constituencies. The state of Himachal Pradesh is divided into 68 assembly constituencies. From each constituency, the people elect one representative who then becomes a Member of the Legislative Assembly (MLA). You would have noticed that people stand for elections in the name of different parties.

These MLAs, therefore, belong to different political parties. A political party whose MLAs have won more than half the number of constituencies in a state can be said to be in a majority. The political party that has the majority is called the ruling party and all other members are called the opposition. For example, the Legislative Assembly of the state of Himachal Pradesh has 68 MLA constituencies.

(i) How are Members of the Legislature Assembly (MLA) elected in India?
(a) Elected by Governor
(b) Chosen by the president
(c) Directly elected by the people
(d) Selected by political parties

(ii) What is the role of opposition in a Legislative Assembly?
(a) To make laws
(b) To appoint the Chief Minister
(c) To challenge and scrutinise the ruling party
(d) To approve budget

(iii) How is the ruling party different from the opposition in a Legislature Assembly?
(a) By the number of MLAs elected
(b) By constituencies members
(c) By alphabetical order
(d) By party names

(iv) What happens if a political party's MLA win more than half the constituencies in a state?
(a) They form a coalition.
(b) They become opposition.
(c) They dissolve Legislative Assembly.
(d) They are in the majority and become the ruling party.

Ans. (i) (c) directly elected by the people
(ii) (c) To challenge and scrutinise the ruling party
(iii) (a) By the number of MLAs elected
(iv) (d) They are in the majority and become the ruling party.

Part II

Very Short Answer Type Questions

1. What are the three levels of government in India?

Ans. The three levels of government in India are

(i) National level

(ii) State level

(iii) Local level

2. By whom are the MLAs elected?

Ans. Members of the Legislative assembly are elected by the people.

3. How is the Governor of a state appointed?

Ans. Governor of a state is appointed by the Central Government.

4. State the meaning of Legislative Assembly.

Ans. Legislative Assembly is a place where all MLAs from ruling as well as opposition party meet to debate and discuss various issues.

5. What do you mean by government?

Ans. The word 'government' refers to government departments and various ministers who had them.

6. Define constituency.

Ans. Constituency is a particular area from which all the voters living there choose their representatives.

7. What is the objective of organising public meetings?

Ans. The objective of organising public meetings is to protest and demand for the rights of the people.

Short Answer Type Questions

1. Who is an MLA? Is it important to be a part of any political party to become an MLA?

Ans. MLA is a Member of Legislative Assembly and is elected by people representing a particular constituency.

It is not important for a person to be a part of any political party to become an MLA. The person can contest elections as an independent candidate also.

2. How do opposition parties affect the working of ruling party?

Ans. Opposition parties affect the working of the ruling party as they play a significant role in the working of government by keeping an eye on the actions of the ruling government.

They ask questions and queries and give suggestions for the working of the government.

3. Differentiate between ruling party and opposition. Competency Based

Ans. The differences between ruling party and opposition are

Ruling Party	Opposition Party
The ruling party hold the offices in government and implements policies.	The opposition's role is to criticise, provide alternatives and check the government's power.
Ruling party members hold key government positions	Opposition members are not a part of the government's executive.
The ruling party usually has more access to resources and government machinery.	The opposition depends on its parliamentary or legislative role.

4. How do you think press conference plays an important role in democracy?

Ans. Press conference plays an important role in democracy because in a press conference, large number of people from different newspapers, media, gather and ask questions to ministers and report them in various newspapers and TV channels. This way, the general public comes to know about the working of government.

5. The Chief Minister and other ministers have to take decisions and run the government. We usually hear about them or see them in the news channels or in the papers. Competency Based

(i) What is a Legislative Assembly?

Ans. A Legislative Assembly is a place where all the MLAs, whether from the ruling party or from the opposition, meet to discuss various things.

(ii) What are the functions of Chief Minister and other ministers?

Ans. Chief Minister lead the state government and formulate policies. Other ministers manage specific portfolios and help in different departments like education, health or irrigation.

6. In the 2017 elections held in Himachal Pradesh, BJP had majority with 44 MLA's and it became the ruling party. All other MLA's became the opposition. INC was the major opposition party.

(i) How is the ruling party decided? Mention the criteria.

Ans. The party which has maximum number of its MLA's elected to the state legislature is called a ruling party. Rest other parties are the opposition.

(ii) Who decides the chief minister?

Ans. The chief minister is decided by the elected members of the ruling party.

7. Neha, Rohan and a few other students from their school travelled to the Legislative Assembly. They were excited. After all the security checks, they were seated inside a hall, upstairs. Competency Based

(a) What is a legislature?

Ans. Legislature refers to a group of people who have the power to make and change laws. All the MLAs who gather together (assemble) in the legislative assembly are called the Legislature.

(b) Write a short note on debates in the state Legislative Assembly.

Ans. Debates and discussions are held in the legislative assembly to talk about current problems.

MLAs take part in the debate by asking questions, expressing their opinions or giving suggestions to the government. The concerned minister replies and assures the assembly that adequate steps are being taken.

Long Answer Type Questions

1. Discuss the procedure for government formation in a state.

Ans. The following procedure is followed to form a government in a state

- General elections are contested to elect representatives from various constituencies.
- A political party obtaining more than half of the total seats is said to be in majority and this party forms the government.
- MLAs belonging to ruling party elect their leader who then becomes Chief Minister.
- The Chief Minister then selects other people as ministers.
- Finally, the Governor appoints the chief Minister and other ministers.

2. Explain with the example of Himachal Pradesh, the working of a State Legislative Assembly.

Ans. Himachal Pradesh is divided into 68 assembly constituencies. From each constituency, people elect one representative who then becomes a member of Legislative Assembly. From 68 constituencies, a party needs more than 34 MLAs in order to gain majority.

In 2017, Bharatiya Janta Party (BJP) had majority with 44 MLAs and it became the ruling party. All other MLAs became the opposition. The Indian National Congress (INC) was the major opposition party as it had the second largest number of MLAs.

After the elections, the MLAs belonging to the ruling party elected their leader who became the Chief Minister. The Chief Minister selects other people as ministers. Governor of the state appoints the Chief Minister and the other ministers. .

3. What did the Chief Minister and the Health Minister do in the next week of the assembly session?

Ans. In the week after the assembly session, the Chief Minister and the Health Minister visited Patalpuram district.

They did the following in the district

- They visited the families who had lost their relatives.
- They visited people in hospitals.
- The government announced compensation for the families.
- The Chief Minister said, a high-level enquiry committee will be asked to look into the needs of the district to provide sanitation facilities.
- The Chief Minister said he would request the minister of public works to take care of the needs of proper water supply in the region.

4. Briefly explain the working of government in detail.

Ans. The government works in the following ways after the debate in the Legislative Assembly

- According to the discussions in the Legislative Assembly, the Chief Minister and the ministers have to take action on the particular issue discussed in the Legislative Assembly. They do so through various government departments like Public Works Department, Agriculture Department, Health Department Education Department etc.
- A press conference is generally held by a particular minister who explains the steps taken by the government. Media persons then report these discussions in several newspapers.
- New laws can also be implemented by the State Government on certain issues in the Legislative Assembly of the respective state. Laws for the entire country are made in the Parliament.

Picture Based Question

1. Observe the following picture and answer the questions that follow.

(i) What do you infer from the above picture?

Ans. From the above picture, it is inferred that people have gathered to raise their opinion for some issue and protest the government.

(ii) In which type of government, such action is allowed?

Ans. This type of public action is allowed in democratic government.

Case Based Question

1. Read the following passage and answer the question.

Government Smells the Garbage : Chief Minister Promises Funds for Work

During the last few weeks, there have been many deaths in some districts of our state. There has been a strong reaction that the government has not taken this seriously.

The Health Minister explained today at a press conference that his government has asked all the collectors and the chief medical officers to take urgent measures. The most important problem is that of drinking water. The minister said that they intend to supply drinking water to every village through tanker trucks.

The Chief Minister has promised funds for this work. They also plan to start a campaign to inform people about the steps that can be taken to prevent diarrhoea. When a reporter asked him as to what steps are being taken to see that garbage that has been lying around for months is quickly collected, the Chief Minister said that he would look into this.

(i) Write two measures that the government undertook for controlling diarrhoea.

Ans. The two measures taken by the government are

(a) The Chief Minister promised to set aside funds to supply clean drinking water to every village through tanker trucks.

(b) The Health Ministry planned to start a campaign to inform people about steps that can be taken to prevent diarrhoea.

(ii) What is the purpose of a press conference? How does the press conference help you get information on what the government is doing?

Ans. The press conference is generally organised by ministers to answer the questions on their working and to provide clarifications on some issues.

Large number of TV and newspaper reporters are present in a press conference who ask questions to ministers. These discussions are then reported in newspapers or the press conferences are shown on TV through which we get to know about what the government is doing.

ASSESSMENT EXERCISE

Multiple Choice Questions (MCQs)

1. Government works at which of the following level?
(a) State
(b) Local
(c) National
(d) All of the above

2. Chief Minister have to take action through various departments like
(a) Agriculture department
(b) Health department
(c) Space department
(d) Both (a) and (b)

3. Which one of the following is a most powerful organ in a democracy?
(a) Chief Minister (b) Governor
(c) People (d) Minister

Subjective Questions (VSA, SA & LA)

1. How do people demand action from government in a democracy?

2. Who are responsible for making laws on certain issues?

3. Why did Chief Minister and the minister for health visit Patalpuram district?

4. What do you understand by Legislative Assembly?

5. How can you say that MLAs are representative of people?

6. Mention the role played by press conference in a democracy.

7. Write in detail about the decisions that have been taken by Chief Minister.

8. Discuss about the role of members of Legislative Assembly.

Growing up as Boys and Girls

Being a girl or a boy is an important part of one's **identity**[1]. It is the society that teaches us about the kind of behaviour that is acceptable in society for boys and girls.

Different societies assign different roles to men and women. The role and work of women is valued less in comparison to men. This led to inequalities between men and women in the area of work.

4.1 Ways of Growing Up

There are many different ways of growing up. The distinction between boys and girls start at a very young age.

Both girls and boys are given different toys to play with and this is a way of telling children that they have different roles in the society.

The society we live in does not value the work of men and women equally. There is a difference in their status. There are also differences in the way of dressing, way of talking and the games that are played by girls and boys.

The different ways for growing up are discussed below through the following examples

Growing up in Samoa in the 1920s

The Samoan islands are a large group of small islands in the Southern part of the Pacific Ocean. According to research reports on Samoan society of 1920s, children grew in the following ways

- The children in Samoa islands did not go to school. They learnt to take care of children and do household work from other older children and adults.
- When children began to walk, they were looked after by their older brothers and sisters who were often as young as 5 years old.
- At the age of 9, boys started learning outdoor jobs like **fishing** and **planting coconuts**. Girls still continued to look after small children.
- Girls were given more freedom in their teenage years. After the age of 14, they also started going on fishing trips, working in plantations and learning to weave baskets.
- Cooking was done in special cooking houses, where boys were supposed to do most of the work while girls helped them in preparations.

Growing up in Madhya Pradesh in the 1960s

According to an account of experiences of people from a small town in Madhya Pradesh in the 1960s, children grew up in the following ways

- After 6th class, boys and girls went to separate schools which were designed very differently. Girl's school had a central courtyard while boy's school had no such courtyard.
- Girls used the streets to get straight to home whereas boys used them to play, stand idle and try out tricks with their bicycles.
- Girls always went in groups because they were afraid of being teased or attacked.

4.2 Valuing Housework

In most societies, the work that men and women do, is not valued equally. Many women work in offices and many women only do housework.

In some cases, the women work both inside and outside the home, which is often reffered to as **double burden** of women's work.

1 **Identity** It is a sense of self-awareness of who or what a person is. Typically, a person can have several identities. For example, a person can be a girl, a sister and a musician.

It is the main responsibility of a women for doing housework and performing **care-giving tasks**[2] like looking after the family, especially children, elderly and sick members. However, the work of the women within the home is not recognised as work.

Housework also involves many different tasks, some of which require a lot of physical work. For example, in both rural and urban areas, women and girls have to fetch water. In rural areas, women have to carry heavy loads of firewood.

Washing clothes, cleaning, sweeping and cooking requires bending, lifting, carrying and standing for long hours. Housework and care-giving tasks are time-consuming. Women have much less time for leisure as compared to men, but still their work is undervalued.

4.3 Lives of Domestic Workers

In many towns and cities, domestic workers are employed to do a lot of work like sweeping, cleaning, washing clothes and dishes, cooking and taking care of young children or elderly.

Most of these domestic workers are women. Sometimes, young boys or girls are employed to do this work.

Wages[3] of domestic workers are very low as domestic work does not have much value. They start their work as early as five in the morning and end as late as twelve at night. They are not given respect by their employers despite their hardwork.

4.4 Women's Work and Equality

The low value that is given for women's household and care-giving work is a part of a larger system of inequality between men and women present in society. This inequality cannot be dealt by an individual or family alone but also by the government.

Equality is an important principle of our Constitution according to which, being male or female should not become the reason for discrimination. However, inequality still exists between the two sexes.

The government understands the reasons for inequality and is taking positive steps for the same.

For example,

- The government has set up **Anganwadis** or **childcare centers** in several villages.
- It has passed a law making it mandatory for the organisation that have more than 30 women workers to provide **creche facilities**[4].
- Creche facilities help women to take up employment outside the home. These also make it possible for more girls to attend schools.

2 **Care-giving Tasks** These refer to a range of tasks related to looking after and nurturing. Besides physical tasks, they also involve a strong emotional aspect.

3 **Wages** It is the salary paid for the work done.

4 **Creche Facilities** It is a facility which enables parents to leave their children while th[illegible] at work.

GROWING UP AS BOYS AND GIRLS

Valuing Housework

- Women work both inside and outside the home, referred to as double burden of women's work.
- The work of the women within the home is not recognised as work.
- The main responsibility of women is doing housework and performing care-giving tasks.
- Housework involves different tasks, some of which require a lot of physical work.

Ways of Growing UP

- The distinctions between boys and girls start at a very young age.
- Society does not value the work of men and women equally.

Lives of Domestic Workers

- Domestic workers are employed in many towns and cities to do a lot of work like sweeping, cooking, cleaning, washing clothes, etc.
- Most of them are women, young boys or girls.
- Wages are very low.
- Workers were not given respect by their employees.

Women's Work and Equality

- The low value given to women's work is a part of a larger system of inequality.
- This inequality to be dealt both by individual and the government.
- The government has set up Anganwadis or Childcare centres in villages.
- It is mandatory for the organisation to have more than 30 women workers.

NCERT FOLDER

Covering Intext Questions and Exercises of NCERT

NCERT ON PAGE 39

Q.1 In what ways do the experiences of Samoan children and teenagers differ from your own experiences of growing up? Is there anything in this experience that you wish was part of your growing up?

Ans. In the Samoan society, children and teenagers did not go to school. They looked after the younger siblings at home. However, we as children and teenagers go to school regularly and had no such responsibility to look after the younger siblings.

No, there is nothing in this experience that I wish was a part of my growing up.

NCERT ON PAGE 40

Q.2 Make a drawing of a street or a park in your neighbourhood. Show the different kinds of activities young boys and girls may be engaged in. You could do this individually or in groups.

Ans. Do it yourself.

Q.3 Are there as many girls as boys in your drawing? Most probably you would have drawn fewer girls. Can you think of reasons why there are fewer women and girls in your neighbourhood streets, parks and markets in the late evenings or at night?

Ans. No, there are less girls in my drawing.

There are fewer women and girls in our neighbourhood streets, parks and markets, during late evenings or at night, because they have a fear of being teased or attacked.

Q.4 Are girls and boys doing different activities? Can you think of reasons why this might be so? What would happen if you replaced the girls with the boys and vice-versa?

Ans. Yes, the girls and boys are doing different activities because the nature has made them different. There are some specific works which have to be done differently by girls and boys.

The landscape would change completely, when girls are replaced with boys.

NCERT ON PAGE 43

Q.5 Were Harmeet and Shonali correct in saying that Harmeet's mother did not work?

Ans. No, Harmeet and Shonali were not correct in saying that their mother did not work because their mother used to stay at home and do all the household work for which she was not paid. They developed false notion that she did not work.

Q.6 What do you think would happen if your mother or those involved in doing the work at home went on a strike for a day?

Ans. If my mother or those involved in doing the work at home went on a strike for a day, the house will be all spoiled, because it is the mother who manages all the work in the house.

Q.7 Why do you think that men and boys generally do not do housework? Do you think they should?

Ans. Men and boys generally do not do the housework because they believe that household work is the responsibility of women and they are not taught to do such work from the beginning.

Yes, from my point of view, they should participate in the household work as housework is a joint responsibility of all the members who live in the house. If women can work both outside and inside the home, then men should also work in the house.

Q.8 Study the table and answer the questions that follow.

State	Haryana	Tamil Nadu
Women paid (work hours per week)	23	19
Women unpaid (housework hours per week)	30	35
Women (Total)	?	?
Men paid (work hours per week)	38	40
Men unpaid (housework hours per week)	2	4
Men (Total)	?	?

(a) What are the total number of work hours spent by women in Haryana and Tamil Nadu each week?

(b) How does this compare with the total number of work hours spent by men?

Ans. (a) Total number of work hours spent by women in Haryana is 53 and in Tamil Nadu is 54 in a week.

(b) Total number of work hours spent by men in Haryana is 40 and Tamil Nadu is 44 in a week. Women contribute more than 33% of their work hours in household work and men contribute just 5% of their total work hours in household work.

EXERCISES

Q.1 Are the statements given below true or false. Support your answer with the use of an example.

(a) All societies do not think similarly about the roles that boys and girls play.

(b) Our society does not make distinctions between boys and girls when they are growing up.

(c) Women who stay at home do not work.

(d) The work that women do is less valued than that of men.

Ans. (a) **True** There are a lot of societies that think differently about the role of girls and boys in society. The work that they do is not valued equally society expects that housework should be done by women, on the other hand, men should be involved in office work.

(b) **False** The distinctions between boys and girls begin from a very young age. For example, they are given different toys to play with. While boys are given cars to play with, girls are given dolls.

(c) **False** Women do more work than men and as such they do not get leisure time. The responsibility of housework i.e. cooking washing dishes, looking after children, etc is upon women. Women are involved in the houshold work from working to the might.

(d) **True** While men are paid for the work they do in offices, women who work from morning to night in house are not paid.

Q.2 Housework is invisible and unpaid work. Housework is physically demanding. Housework is time consuming. Write in your own words what is meant by the terms 'invisible', 'physically demanding' and 'time consuming'? Give one example of each based on the household tasks undertaken by women in your home.

Ans. 'Invisible' means the work can be seen only when it is not done. For examples, the care of the house and keeping a watch on the activities of domestic help are invisible.

'Physically demanding' means we have to do hard manual labour to complete a task. For examples, washing of clothes is physically demanding.

'Time consuming' means the work which needs considerable time to be completed. For examples, cooking food and cleaning the house is time consuming.

Q.3 Make a list of toys and games that boys typically play and another for girls. If there is a difference between the two lists, can you think of some reasons why this is so? Does this have any relationship to the roles children have to play as adults?

Ans. List of toys and games that boys and girls play are

Boys Cars, Guns, Football, Cricket, Kabaddi, Hockey.

Girls Dolls, Kitchen set, Badminton, Ludo, Cooking items.

Yes, there is a difference between the two sets of toys and games as there is a difference between boys and girls in respect of strength, stamina, etc.

The games they play are a way of telling that they have specific roles to play in their future as men and women.

Q.4 If you have someone working as a domestic help in your house or locality, talk to her and find out a little bit more about her life—Who are her family members? Where is her home? How many hours does she work? How much does she get paid? Write a small story based on these details.

Ans. Yes, I know one domestic helper who works in my neighbourhood.

Her name is Chameli. She is married and has two children and lives with her husband in a nearby slum area.

She is employed as a full-day worker. She has to work for almost 14 hours i.e. 7 in the morning to 9 in the night.

She receives ₹2000 for a month, which is very less according to the work she performs and the time she gives for her job.

REVIEW EXERCISE

Including Competency Based Questions

Part I

Multiple Choice Questions (MCQs)

1. In society, men and women do not have the same

(a) status (b) height
(c) weight (d) None of these

2. Girls in Samoan Islands were given freedom after the age of

(a) nine (b) five (c) twelve (d) fourteen

3. Which of the following is an important activity of Samoan Islands?

(a) Farming (b) Cooking
(c) Fishing (d) Plantation

4. In Madhya Pradesh, boys and girls went to separate school from class

(a) VII (b) VI
(c) V (d) VIII

5. The government has set up Angawadi centres in several in villages. These are Competency Based

(a) Yoga centres (b) Entertainment centres
(c) childcare centres (d) Education centres

6. The government has passed laws that makes it mandatory for organisation on that have more than 30 women employees to provide creches facilities.

How the provision of creches helps women? Competency Based

(a) Encourages women to start working from home.
(b) Encourages women to work outside the home.
(c) Both (a) and (b)
(d) None of the above

7. A coach for a youth sports team encourages both girls and boys to participate in all sports and provides equal opportunities for training and playing time. What is the objective of coach? Competency Based

(a) To discourage girls from participating in sports.
(b) To focus mainly on boys sports skills.
(c) To promote gender equality.
(d) To limit participation based on gender.

8. Identify from the following statements the term referred to here.

I. It is generally observed that women typically labour both inside (housework) and outside.
II. It is used to describe women's situation.
III. A huge number of women face this situation.

Options

(a) Double burden (b) Double work
(c) Double labour (d) Double situation

9. Choose the correct statement(s) from the following.

I. The roles women play and the work they do are usually valued less than the roles men play and the work they do.
II. Boys are given cars to play while girls are given dolls.
III. Girls always went in groups in Samoa, perhaps because they also carried fears of being teased.

Codes

(a) I and II (b) I and III
(c) Only III (d) I, II and III

10. Choose the incorrect statement(s) from the following.

I. Society devalues the household work.
II. In both rural and urban areas, women and girls have to fetch water.
III. Equality is not an important principle of our Constitution.

Codes

(a) Only I (b) I and II
(c) Only III (d) I, II and III

Answers

1. (a) **2.** (d) **3.** (c) **4.** (b) **5.** (c)
6. (b) **7.** (c) **8.** (a) **9.** (d) **10.** (c)

Match the Following

1.

	List I		List II
A.	Children did not go to school	1.	Women
B.	Schools were designed differently	2.	Madhya Pradesh
C.	Housework and care-giving tasks	3.	Samoan islands

Codes

	A	B	C		A	B	C
(a)	3	1	2	(b)	1	2	3
(c)	2	3	1	(d)	3	2	1

2.

	List I		List II
A.	Housework hours for men in Tamil Nadu	1.	23 hours
B.	Paid work hours for women in Haryana	2.	19 hours
C.	Physical work	3.	Housework
D.	Paid work hours for women in Tamil Nadu	4.	4 hours

Codes

	A	B	C	D		A	B	C	D
(a)	4	1	3	2	(b)	3	4	1	2
(c)	2	3	1	4	(d)	1	2	3	4

Ans. 1. (d) 2. (a)

Assertion-Reason

1. **Assertion** (A) Societies make clear distinctions between boys and girls from a very young age.

   Reason (R) Boys are given cars to play and girls dolls.

   Codes

   (a) Both A and R are true and R is the correct explanation of A

   (b) Both A and R are true, but R is not the correct explanation of A

   (c) A is true, but R is false

   (d) A is false, but R is true

2. **Assertion** (A) Being a boy or a girl is an important part of one's identity.

   Reason (R) In rural areas, women carry heavy loads of firewoods.

   Codes

   (a) Both A and R are true and R is the correct explanation of A

   (b) Both A and R are true, but R is not the correct explanation of A

   (c) A is true, but R is false

   (d) A is false, but R is true

Ans. 1. (a) Both A and R are true and R is the correct explanation of A

2. (b) Both A and R are true, but R is not the correct explanation of A

Fill in the Blanks

1. Housework is .... and ....
2. Care-giving tasks are associated with ....
3. .... mother went on strike for a day.
4. .... is the significant principle of Indian Constitution.

Ans. 1. physically demanding, time consuming

2. women

3. Harmeet's

4. Equality

True/False

1. Our society sees men and women equally.
2. Domestic workers have very low salary.
3. Women spend most of their time watching television.
4. Women suffer from double burden.

Ans. 1. False 2. True 3. False 4. True

Picture Based Questions

1. **The image shown below is of a Samoan child. What is the major activity of Samoan Islands?**

(a) Cutting trees (b) Agriculture

(c) Cooking (d) Fishing

2. **The image below shows girls going to school together in group. Why do you think they are travelling in a groups?**

(a) Don't know the route (b) Afraid of dogs

(c) Parents say it (d) Fear of being teased

Ans. 1. (d) Fishing

2. (d) Fear of being teased

Case Based Question

1. Read the passage given below and answer the following questions.

As we have seen the low value attached to women's household and care-giving work is not an individual or family matter. It is part of a larger system of inequality between men and women. It, therefore, has to be dealt with through actions not just at the level of the individual or the family but also by the government. As we now know, equality is an important principle of our Constitution.

The Constitution says that being male or female should not become a reason for discrimination. In reality, inequality between the sexes exists. The government is, therefore, committed to understanding the reasons for this and taking positive steps to remedy the situation. For example, it recognises that burden of child-care and housework falls on women and girls.

(i) Who bears the burden of the child-care and household?

(a) Men and women equally
(b) Mainly men
(c) Mainly women and girls
(d) Government

(ii) What does the government commit to do regarding gender inequality?

(a) Ignore it
(b) Promote it
(c) Acknowledge it but no action
(d) Understand it and take positive action.

(iii) Which is not a example of gender inequality?

(a) Gender pay gap
(b) Recruitment in armed forces.
(c) Limited access to education
(d) Unequal division of household labour.

(iv) What does the text say regarding the equality between women and men?

(a) Equality doesn't exist.
(b) equality is a significant challenge.
(c) Equality is a minor issue.
(d) Equality varies by region.

Ans. (i) (c) Mainly women and girls
(ii) (d) Understand it and take positive action.
(iii) (b) Recruitment in arm forces.
(iv) (a) Equality doesn't exist.

Part II

Very Short Answer Type Questions

1. What does society teach us?

Ans. The society teaches us about the kind of behaviour that is acceptable in society for boys and girls.

2. What can you say about the value of work of men and women?

Ans. The work of men and women is not equally valued in our societies.

3. Where is Samoa?

Ans. Samoa islands are part of a large group of small islands in the Southern part of Pacific Ocean.

4. List the primary activities in Samoa that boys start performing at the age of nine.

Ans. The primary activities that boys start performing in Samoa at the age of nine includes fishing and planting coconut.

5. Why did the girls' schools in Madhya Pradesh have a courtyard ?

Ans. Girls' schools had a central courtyard so that they could play with proper security and safety.

6. Why were girls so purposeful while walking on the streets ?

Ans. The girls were purposeful while walking on the streets as their main aim was to reach home safely.

7. How do societies look at girls and boys? Competency Based

Ans. The societies discriminate between girls and boys from a very young age.

8. List some tasks related to housework.

Ans. Housework involves sweeping, cleaning, washing clothes and dishes, cooking, etc.

9. Why are the wages of domestic workers so low?

Ans. Wages of domestic workers are low because their work is not valued in society.

10. What is the name given to the child-care centres in several villages?

Ans. The name given to child-care centres in villages is Anganwadis.

11. Define care-giving.

Ans. Care-giving means looking after and nurturing the family with great sincerity.

12. What do you mean by double burden?

Ans. Double burden refers to the situation where women work both outside and inside the home.

Short Answer Type Questions

1. Describe the childhood of Samoan islands children.

Ans. According to research reports on Samoan society of 1920s, children grew in the following ways

- The children in Samoa islands did not go to school. They learnt to take care of children and do household work from other older children and adults.
- When children began to walk, they were looked after by their older brothers and sisters who were often as young as 5 years old.
- At the age of 9, boys started learning outdoor jobs like fishing and planting coconuts. Girls still continued to look after small children.

2. Discuss the growing up of boys and girls in Madhya Pradesh.

Ans. According to an account of experiences of people from a small town in Madhya Pradesh in the 1960s, children grew up in the following ways

- After 6th class, boys and girls went to separate schools which were designed very differently. Girl's school had a central courtyard while boy's school had no such courtyard.
- Girls used the streets to get straight to home whereas boys used them to play, stand idle and try out tricks with their bicycles.
- Girls always went in groups because they were afraid of being teased or attacked.

3. Why do society devalue the women's work at home? Diksha

Ans. Society devalues the women's work at home because inequality exists between the genders in the society.

It is usually assumed that household work care-giving tasks are something that comes naturally to women. Works of household like dish washing, cooking, cleaning house maintenance are also assumed easy work and less valued.

4. In a locality in Agra, streets full of girls and boys playing games, talking, and riding bicycles can be seen in the evening. However, as soon as it gets dark, less number of girls are seen as they head back home. Competency Based

(i) Why are girls often seen in groups?

Ans. Girls often travel in groups because they feared of being attacked or teased. It is for their safety that they head back home early and in groups.

(ii) Are ways of growing up the same in every society?

Ans. No, ways of growing up differs in each society. The discrimination starts at a very young age which can be seen in the toys given to them.

5. How does our Constitution protect people from discrimination? Competency Based

Ans. Constitution protect people from discrimination as equality is a significant principle of our Constitution. The Indian Constitution says that being male or female should not become reason for discrimination. It is the duty of the government to understand the reason for the inequality that exists and take positive steps. For the same, government has set-up anganwadis in several villages. The government has passed laws that make compulsory for organisations which have more than 30 women employees to provide creche facilities.

6. Payal is a housewife who takes care of all the family needs and caregiving tasks like looking after the sick members of the family and taking care of children. She wakes up at 6 in the morning and gets free by 10 at night. Yet, her family never recognised her work. Competency Based

(i) Who has the main responsibility for housework across the world?

Ans. Across the world, women are responsible for household work and care-giving tasks such as looking after family.

(ii) Why does society not consider housework as real work?

Ans. The work that women do within the home is not recognised as work because it is assumed that this is something that comes naturally to women. It, therefore, does not have to be paid for. Society devalues this work and such work remains invisible.

Long Answer Type Questions

1. "We also realise that societies make clear distinction between boys and girls". Explain.

Ans. It is true that societies make clear distinctions between boys and girls. The way societies make distinctions can be seen from the examples of growing up of children of Samoan islands and Madhya Pradesh as follows

- The children in Samoa islands did not go to school. They learnt to take care of children and do household work from other older children and adults. When children began to walk, they were looked after by their older brothers and sisters who were often as young as 5 years old.

- In Madhya Pradesh, after 6th class, boys and girls went to separate schools which were designed very differently. Girl's school had a central courtyard while boy's school had no such courtyard. Girls used the streets to get straight to home whereas boys used them to play, stand idle and try out tricks with their bicycles.

2. Take reference of Melani, a household worker to explain about working condition of household worker.

Ans. The working condition of household worker or domestic worker is not good. Wages of domestic workers are very low as domestic work does not have much value. They start their work as early as five in the morning and end as late as twelve at night. They are not given respect by their employers despite their hardwork.

Housework also involves many different tasks some of which require a lot of physical work. For example, in both rural and urban areas, women and girls have to fetch water. In rural areas, women have to carry heavy loads of firewood.

Washing clothes, cleaning, sweeping and cooking requires bending, lifting, carrying and standing for long hours. Housework and care-giving tasks are time-consuming.

3. Write a note on the main features of the Samoan society.

Ans. The main features of the Samoan society are as follows

- Children did not go to school they learnt household work and things like how to take case of other children and adults.
- As soon as the babies learnt to walk, their parents other adults did not look after them.
- Both boys and girls as young as 5 years old looked after their siblings.
- When boys turned 9 years old, they joined the older boys in fishing and other outdoor activities like planting coconuts.
- Till they reached teenage, girls had to continue looking after children or do errands for adults. They got much more freedom once they entered teenage after the age of around 14 years. They went out for fishing, worked in the plantations learnt how to weave baskets, etc.
- Cooking was done in special cooking houses where boys did most of the work and girls helped with preparations.

Picture Based Questions

1. Answer the question based on picture.

What do you think this poster is trying to say?

Ans. This poster is all about the rights of women. The picture above is trying to highlight the importance of women in life.

The lines written on the picture states that now, no more ignorance of women is possible and they should be given their place of dignity.

2. Write an interesting slogan for the poster given below.

Ans. Slogan for the poster could be 'The Power of Women'.

Case Based Question

1. Read the passage and answer the following questions.

The boys' school had no such courtyard and our playground was just a big space attached to the school. Every evening, once school was over, the boys watched as hundreds of school girls crowded the narrow streets.

As these girls walked on the streets, they looked so purposeful.

This was unlike the boys who used the streets as a place to stand around idle, to play, to try out tricks with their bicycles. For the girls, the street was simply a place to get straight home.

The girls always went in groups, perhaps because they also carried fears of being teased or attacked.

(i) "The boys school had no such courtyard". Which courtyard is being talked about ?

Ans. Here, the courtyard is the playground or a big space attached to the school where boys and girls used to play. The boys' school and the girls' school were designed differently as boys school had no courtyard as the girls school had.

(ii) For what purpose did the boys use the street?

Ans. The boys used the streets as a place to stand around idling, to play, to try out tricks with their bicycles, etc. While for girls, the street was simply a place to get back straight to home.

ASSESSMENT EXERCISE

Multiple Choice Questions (MCQs)

1. Boys and girls learn about behaviour from ....

(a) schools (b) society

(c) parents (d) All of these

2. At Samoan islands what was the work of nine years old boys?

(a) Looked after the younger siblings

(b) Learning outdoor jobs

(c) Cooking

(d) Both (b) and (c)

3. In most societies, the works done by men and women are valued as

(a) equally (b) women does not work

(c) not equally (d) None of these

Subjective Questions (VSA, SA & LA)

1. What did Harmeet's family think about Jaspreet's work?

2. Which type of work is assumed to be something that comes naturally to women?

3. What is the duration of work for a domestic worker?

4. Which have more leisure time men or women (as domestic worker)?

5. Write about the constructional features of girls school.

6. How can you say that the role of streets are different for boys and girls?

7. What are the similarities in the domestic works of rural and urban women?

8. How can you say that girls childhoods were different from boys in Madhya Pradesh in the 1960s?

9. Write in detail about the difficulties faced by Harmeet and his father when his mother was on strike.

Women Change the World

CHAPTER 5

Women have faced a lot of inequalities since earlier times and they are still struggling and making efforts to overcome this challenge through various movements.

Women work both inside and outside the home but there are some occupations which are considered more suitable for men than women. One way in which new opportunities can be created for women is getting education.

5.1 Fewer Opportunities and Rigid Expectations

Many people believe in **stereotypes**[1] which give rise to inequality in the society.

Many people think that certain jobs should only be done by men and some only by women. For example, it is believed by many people that women make better nurses because they are more patient and gentle.

They also believe that girls and women are not capable of dealing with technical things.

Thus, they are not supported like boys to become doctors and engineers.

In most families, girls are encouraged to get married, once they finish their schooling.

In our society children are pressurised in the form of demands from adults and unfair teasing by friends. For example, boys are pressurised to think about getting a job with a good salary or to behave like other boys.

5.2 Learning for Change

Going to school is an important part of life today. However, in the past, only a few people had skills to read and write. Most of the children learnt the work that was done by their family members or elders.

Girls during this time were not allowed to learn, to read and write. Even in families where skills like pottery, weaving and craft were taught, women's role was regarded only as supportive.

In the 19th century, new ideas about learning and education emerged. Schools started becoming common and children from all communities started going to schools. However, there was still opposition for providing education to girls.

KNOWLEDGE PLUS The book titled **Amar Jiban** is the first known autobiography written by an Indian woman, **Rashsundari Devi.**

5.3 Schooling and Education Today

Today, both girls and boys attend school in large numbers but there are still differences between the education of boys and girls.

India conduct **census** in every 10 years. It counts the entire population of the country and gathers information about the people living in India like their age, schooling, occupation, the number of literate people, the ratio of men and women, etc.

In 1961 census, the percentage of literate people in India was 40% and 15% for men and women, respectively.

1 **Stereotype** It refers to the practice of unfair belief that all people belonging to a particular group are bound to have certain fixed characteristics.

According to 2011 census, the percentage of literate people is 82% and 65% for men and women, respectively.

This shows that number of literate people among both men and women has increased but gap among men and women literacy still exists.

Schooling and Social Groups

It has been observed that girls belonging to **Dalits** (SC) and **Adivasi** (ST) communities leave school early. Muslim girls, in comparison to these communities, leave school even without completing primary school.

There are several reasons due to which these communities leave school. Some of these are

- There are no proper schools and teachers on regular basis especially in rural and poor areas.
- Schools are far from people's homes. There are no facilities for transportation like buses, vans, etc.
- Many families are poor and unable to bear the cost of educating their children.
- Many children also leave school because they are discriminated against by their teacher and classmates.

5.4 Women's Movement

Women's movement refers to the struggle of women both individually and collectively to bring about changes in spheres like legal reforms, violence and health.

Individual women and women's organisations from different parts of the country are part of the movement.

Different strategies have been used to spread awareness, fight **discrimination**[2] and seek justice which include

- **Campaigning** Campaigns are a significant part of women's movement in order to fight discrimination and violence. Several laws have been passed as a result of campaigning. For example,
  - Supreme court framed guidelines in 1997 to protect women from **sexual harassment**[3] at workplace and in educational institutions.
  - Dowry laws were changed to punish families who seek dowry which led to dowry deaths.
  - A law regarding **domestic violence** was passed in 2006, to protect women against physical and mental violence within homes.
- **Raising Awareness** Women's movement raises public awareness on women's right issues through street plays, songs and public meetings.
- **Protesting** It is a way of raising voice against **Violations**[4] in the form of public rallies and demonstrations.
- **Showing Solidarity** The women's movement is about showing **solidarity**[5] with other women and causes.

KNOWLEDGE PLUS International Women Day is celebrated on 8th March.

2 **Discrimination** It means to treat people unequally or with disrespect.
3 **Sexual harassment** It refers to physical or verbal behaviour that is sexual in nature.
4 **Violation** It is the act of doing something which is not allowed by a law or rule.
5 **Solidarity** It is a feeling of unity between people who have the same interests and goals.

WOMEN CHANGE THE WORLD

Fewer Opportunities and Rigid Expectations

- Many people believe in stereotypes.
- Women were given fewer opportunities.
- Girls are encouraged in most families to get married after their schooling.
- Children are pressurised in the form of demands from adults and unfair teasing by friends.

Learning for Change

- Going to school is an important part of life.
- Opposition for providing education to girls.
- In the 19th century, children from all communities started going to school.
- **Amar Jiban** is the first known autobiography written by an Indian woman, **Rassundari Devi**.

Schooling and Education Today

- Both girls and boys attend school in large numbers today, but there is difference in education of boys and girls.
- According to 1961 Census, there were 40% literate men and 15% literate women in India.
- According to 2011 Census, there were 82% literate men and 65% literate women in India.
- The number of literate people among both men and women has increased but the gap among their literacy still exists.

Schooling and Social Groups

- Girls belonging to Dalits (SC) and Adivasi (ST) communities leave school early. Muslim girls leave school even without completing primary school.
- Some reasons for leaving school
  - No proper schools and teachers on regular basis
  - Schools are far from people's homes
  - Many families are poor and unable to bear cost of education
  - Many children are discriminated in school, so they leave school

Women's Movement

- Women's movement refers to the struggle of women to bring about changes in spheres like legal reforms, violence and health.
- Strategies to spread awareness, fight discrimination and seek justice include
  - Campaigning
  - Raising Awareness
  - Protesting
  - Showing solidarity
- Some laws passed for women welfare
  - Guidelines framed by Supreme Court in 1997 to protect women from sexual harassment
  - Dowry laws were changed to punish families seeking dowry
  - Law regarding domestic violence passed in 2006

NCERT FOLDER

Covering Intext Questions and Exercises of NCERT

NCERT ON PAGE 49

Q.1 See what images your class drew by filling in the table below. Add up the number of male and female images separately for each occupation.

Category	Male image	Female image
Teacher		
Farmer		
Factory worker		
Nurse		
Scientist		
Pilot		

(i) Are there more images of men than women?

(ii) In what kinds of jobs were there more images of men than women?

(iii) Have all the nurses been drawn as females? Why?

(iv) Are there fewer images of female farmers? If so, why?

Ans.

Category	Male image	Female image
Teacher	10	40
Farmer	25	01
Factory worker	20	03
Nurse	0	35
Scientist	30	03
Pilot	10	01

(i) Yes, there are more images of men than women.

(ii) In the following jobs, there were more images of men women

- Manual works
- Military and Defence
- Office jobs
- Industries and Factories
- Farmers
- Factory Workers
- Scientists
- Pilots

(iii) Mostly nurses have been drawn as females because male nurses are very few. Females are generous, kind, compassionate, considerate and enduring. Hence, they are preferred as nurses and not males.

(iv) Yes, there are fewer images of female farmers because the work of a farmer is very hard. Women cannot do such physical work though there are a few females who are engaged in farming.

NCERT ON PAGE 50

Q.2 How does your class exercise compare with Rosie Ma'am's class exercise?

Rosie Ma'am's class has 30 children. She did the same exercise in her class and here is the result. (See Figure in NCERT Textbook on page 56)

Category	Male image	Female image
Teacher	5	25
Farmer	30	0
Factory worker	25	5
Nurse	0	30
Scientist	25	5
Pilot	27	3

Ans. Our class exercise is comparable to that of Rosie Ma'am's class exercise in the following ways

- Females are more in teaching profession than males.
- Not a single woman is engaged as farmer in Rosie's exercise but in our exercise a few women are engaged as farmers.
- Very few women work in factories.
- No man works as a nurse in both the exercises.
- The number of women is far less as scientists. Likewise very few females are pilots.

NCERT ON PAGE 56

Q.3 Study the given table and answer the following questions:

This table shows the percentage of girls and boys leaving schools

Level	All			SC			ST		
	Boys	Girls	Total	Boys	Girls	Total	Boys	Girls	Total
Primary (Classes 1-5)	4.36	3.88	4.13	4.71	4.20	4.46	7.02	6.84	6.93
Elementary (Classes 6-8)	3.49	4.60	4.03	5.00	6.03	5.51	8.48	8.71	8.59
Secondary (Classes 9-10)	17.21	16.88	17.06	19.64	19.05	19.36	24.94	24.40	24.68

Source : Select Education Survey, GIO 2003-2004

(a) What percentage of children leave school at the elementary level?

(b) At which level of education do you see the highest percentage of children leaving?

(c) Why do you think that the percentage of Adivasi girls and boys leaving school is higher than that of any other group?

Ans. (a) 52% of children leave school at the elementary level.

(b) The highest percentage of children leave school at the secondary level.

(c) The percentage of Adivasi girls and boys leaving school is higher than that of other group because of the following reasons

- Lack of proper schools and teachers.
- Remoteness of schools from homes.
- Lack of proper transportation.

NCERT ON PAGE 57

Q.4. From the table given below convert the figures of primary class children who leave school into a bar diagram.

Level	All			SC			ST		
	Boys	Girls	Total	Boys	Girls	Total	Boys	Girls	Total
Primary (Classes 1-5)	4.36	3.88	4.13	4.71	4.20	4.46	7.02	6.84	6.93
Elementary (Classes 6-8)	3.49	4.60	4.03	5.00	6.03	5.51	8.48	8.71	8.59
Secondary (Classes 9-10)	17.21	16.88	17.06	19.64	19.05	19.36	24.94	24.40	24.68

Ans.

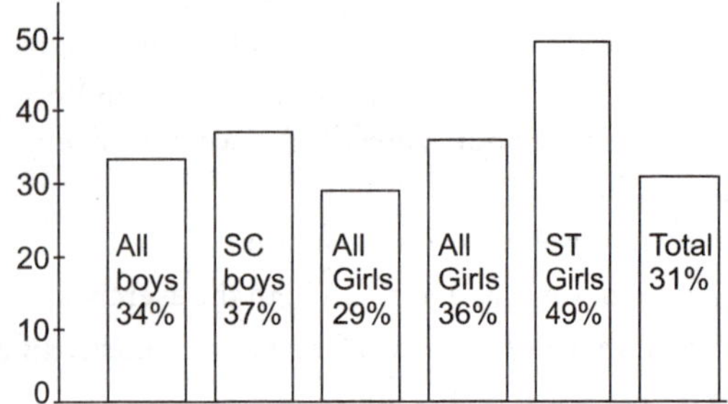

EXERCISES

Q.1 How do you think stereotypes, about what women can or cannot do, affect women's right to equality?

Ans. Stereotypes, about what women can or cannot do, affect women's right to equality in the following ways

- They are considered inferior to men, and do not get the same support that boys get.
- They are not sent to educational institutions, they are not paid equally to men for the same work, and are married early instead of higher education.

Q.2 List one reason why learning the alphabet was so important to women like Rashsundari Devi, Ramabai and Rokeya?

Ans. Learning the alphabet was important to Rashsundari Devi, Ramabai and Rokeya because by learning they could share their thoughts and views with the society through stories, writings and autobiography.

Q.3 "Poor girls drop out of school because they are not interested in getting an education." Explain why this statement is not true.

Ans. The statement "Poor girls drop out of school because they are not interested in getting an education" is not true and the reasons are

- There are no proper schools and teachers in rural and poor areas.
- Schools are far from people's residences and there is lack of transportation facilities.
- Some families can't bear the cost of education.

Q.4. Can you describe two methods of struggle that the women's movement used to raise issues? If you had to organise a struggle against stereotypes, about what women can or cannot do, what method would you employ from the ones that you have read about? Why would you choose this particular method?

Ans. Two methods of struggle that the women's movement used to raise issues are described below

- **Campaigning** Campaigns are a significant part of women's movement in order to fight against discrimination and violence. Campaigning has led to many positive results such as passage of several laws.
- **Protesting** It helps in raising voices against violations in the form of public rallies and demonstrations which draw attention to injustices.

If I had to organise a struggle against stereotypes, I would engage people in raising awareness. In every country women face inequality of one or the other kind, which is often overlooked, and for this to change, we need more people raising awareness.

I would choose this method because awareness is the first step in bringing about a positive change.

REVIEW EXERCISE

Including Competency Based Questions

PART I

Multiple Choice Questions (MCQs)

1. Ramabai was given the title of
(a) Captain (b) Pandita
(c) Master (d) None of these

2. Rashsundari Devi was born at which place?
(a) Maharashtra
(b) Kerala
(c) Tamil Nadu
(d) West Bengal

3. Amar Jiban was written by
(a) Rokeya Sakhawat Hossain
(b) Ramabai
(c) Rashsundari Devi
(d) Satyarani

4. Which among the following languages, did Rokeya Sakhawat Hossain knew how to read and write?
(a) Hindi (b) English (c) Urdu (d) Bangla

5. What is the official name for Scheduled Tribe ?
(a) Adivasi (b) Dalits
(c) Muslim Minorities (d) Both (a) and (b)

6. Passage of law on domestic violence in 2006 was the result of
(a) raising awareness (b) protesting
(c) campaigning (d) showing solidarity

7. The Supreme Court of India issued guidelines in 1997 to safeguard women from ....
(a) dowry death (b) domestic violence
(c) sexual harassment (d) mental violence

8. "In India, cultural and religious restrictions often come in the way of women realising their full potential. Education is a tool for self-awareness that helps them to stand up for themselves, have a better awareness of their rights and to change subjugation and patriarchy". **Competency Based**

Source Times of India

Which of the following is a cultural or religious restriction that can come in the way of women realising their full potential in India?
(a) Lack of access to education (b) Child marriage
(c) Gender discrimination (d) All of these

9. Identify the correct option from the information given below.

I. It involves counting the total population and measuring the sex ratio, number of literates, etc.
II. It is done after every 10 years.

Codes
(a) Census (b) Examination (c) Study (d) Survey

10. Identify the correct option from the information given below.

I. She was given the title 'Pandita' as she could read and write Sanskrit.
II. She set up a mission in Khedgaon in 1898.
III. She encouraged to women to learn skills like carpentry, sewing, printing press, etc that are not usually taught to women. **Competency Based**

Codes
(a) Sarala Bai (b) Kasturba Gandhi
(c) Savitri Bai Phule (d) Ramabai

11 Choose the correct statement(s) from the following.

I. 83.6% of working women in India are engaged in textile industry.
II. It is believed that science requires a technical mind and girls and woman are not capable of it.

Codes
(a) Only I (b) Only II
(c) Both I and II (d) None of these

12. Choose the incorrect statement(s) from the following.

I. Due to stereotypes, many girls do not get the same support that boys get to study.
II. Boys are not pressurised to think about getting a job that will pay a good salary.
III. In 16th century, many ideas about education and learning emerged. **Competency Based**

Codes
(a) Only I (b) Only II (c) Only III (d) I and III

Answers

1. (b)	2. (d)	3. (c)	4. (c)	5. (a)
6. (c)	7. (c)	8. (d)	9. (a)	10. (d)
11. (b)	12. (b)			

Match the Following

1.

	List I		List II
A.	Women's movement	1.	Worked for widows and poor women
B.	Ramabai	2.	15% girls and women were literate
C.	Rokeya Sakhawat Hossain	3.	Sultana's Dream
D.	1961 Census	4.	54% girls and women were literate
E.	2011 Census	5.	Protesting

Codes

	A	B	C	D	E		A	B	C	D	E
(a)	5	1	3	2	4	(b)	1	2	3	4	5
(c)	4	3	2	1	5	(d)	1	2	3	5	4

Assertion-Reason

1. Assertion (A) Rokeya Sakhawat knew how to read and write Urdu but was stopped from learning Bangla and English.

Reason (R) English was seen as a language that would expose girls to new ideas.

Codes

(a) Both A and R are true and R is the correct explanation of A
(b) Both A and R are true, but R is not the correct explanation of A
(c) A is true, but R is false
(d) A is false, but R is true

2. Assertion (A) Ramabai wrote her biography Amar Jiban in Bangla.

Reason (R) Lady land is a place where women had the freedom to study, work and create inventions.

Codes

(a) Both A and R are true and R is the correct explanation of A
(b) Both A and R are true, but R is not the correct explanation of A
(c) A is true, but R is false
(d) A is false, but R is true

Ans. 1. (a) Both A and R are true and R is the correct explanation of A
2. (d) A is false, but R is true

Fill in the Blanks

1. .... means forcefully breaking the rules and laws.

2. Messages through songs, street plays and public meetings are spread while ....

3. After learning the alphabets, Rashsundari Devi read ....

4. Public rally is an example of ....

Ans. 1. Violation
2. raising awareness
3. Chaitanya Bhagabat
4. protesting

True/False

1. Boys are pressurised to think about getting married after they complete their schooling.

2. Rokeya Sakhawat Hossain started a school for both boys and girls.

3. Women's movement is also supported by men.

4. Girls from SC's and ST's are less likely to leave school than Muslim girls.

Ans. 1. False 2. False
3. True 4. True

Picture Based Questions

1. The image shown below is of printing press mostly managed by women. Who taught printing to women?

(a) Rashsundari Devi (b) Rokeya Hossain
(c) Ramabai (d) Sarojini Naidu

2. The image shown is the logo of initiative started by Government, named 'Beti Bachao Beti Padhao'. When was the initiative launched?

(a) 2014 (b) 2015
(c) 2016 (d) 2017

Ans. 1. (c) Ramabai 2. (b) 2015

Case Based Question

1. Read the passage given below and answer the following questions.

Going to school is an extremely important part of your life. As more and more children enter school every year, we begin to think that it is normal for all children to go to school. Today, it is difficult for us to imagine that school and learning could be seen as "out of bounds" or not appropriate for some children. But in the past, the skill of reading and writing was known to only a few. Most children learnt the work their families or elders did. For girls, the situation was worse. In communities that taught sons to read and write, daughters were not allowed to learn the alphabet. Even in families where skills like pottery, weaving and craft were taught, the contribution of daughters and women was only seen as supportive. For example, in the pottery trade, women collected the mud and prepared the Earth for the pots. But since they did not operate the wheel, they were not seen as potters.

(i) Which of the following SDG Goal is for quality education?

(a) Goal 1 (b) Goal 2
(c) Goal 3 (d) Goal 4

(ii) In which of the following century new ideas about education and learning are emerged?

(a) Eighteenth century (b) Nineteenth century
(c) Twentieth century (d) Twenty-first century.

(iii) Which one of the following work is not considered for women?

(a) Cooking (b) Teaching
(c) Engineering (d) Nursing

(iv) Who wrote the first known autobiography of an Indian woman?

(a) Rashsundari Devi (b) Laxmi Devi
(c) Sumitra Devi (d) Sarala Devi

Ans. (i) (d) Goal 4
(ii) (b) Nineteenth century
(iii) (c) Engineering
(iv) (a) Rashsundari Devi

PART II

Very Short Answer Type Questions

1. Why according to stereotypes, girls can't study science?

Ans. According to stereotypes, girls can't study science because it requires a technical mind and girls and women are not capable of dealing with technical things.

2. Why don't girls get the same support as boys? Competency Based

Ans. Many girls do not get the same support as boys because of the stereotypes which prevents girls and boys to be looked at as unique individuals and not according to their gender.

3. What is the role played by women in pottery trade?

Ans. Women play the role of collecting mud and preparing Earth for the pots.

4. Who was Rashsundari Devi?

Ans. Rashsundari Devi, born in West Bengal, was a housewife from a rich landlord's family. She wrote Amar Jiban.

5. How did Rokeya Sakhawat Hossain contributed in education of girls?

Ans. Rokeya Sakhawat Hossain contributed in education of girls by starting a school for girls in Kolkata.

6. Define solidarity.

Ans. Solidarity is a feeling of unity between people who have the same interests and goals.

7. How much percentage of women are engaged in agricultural work in India?

Ans. 83.6% of women are engaged in agricultural work in India.

8. Why is women's work at home not recognised as work?

Ans. Women's work at home is not recognised as work because it does not bring any money or income.

9. How is International Women's Day celebrated?

Ans. On International Women's Day, women all over the world come together to celebrate and renew their struggles.

10. Who was the first woman engine driver for Northern Railways?

Ans. Laxmi Lakra, a woman from a poor tribal family in Jharkhand, was the first woman engine driver for Northern Railways.

Short Answer Type Questions

1. "We live in a society in which all children face pressures from the world around them." Discuss.

Ans. We live in a society in which children face pressures from the world around them in the form of demands from adults. Sometimes they are teased by their friends.

For example, boys are pressurised to get a job that will pay good salary and sometimes when they do not behave properly they are being teased and bullied. Boys from an early age are encouraged not to cry in front of others.

2. What are the rigid expectations from men and women in our society? Competency Based

Ans. The rigid expectations from men and women in our society involves stereotypes, such as women can work better work as nurses and men as army officers.

It is thought that women are more patient and gentle, hence they can be better nurses and as science requires a technical mind, women are not capable of dealing with technical things. Due this kind of thinking, girls do not get the same support as boys. Also girls are encouraged to get married after they complete their schooling.

3. "In the 19th century, many new ideas about education and learning emerged." How? Competency Based

Ans. In the 19th century, many new ideas about education and learning emerged. Schools became more common and communities that had never learnt reading and writing, started sending their children to schools. Despite so much of opposition, many women and men made efforts to open schools for girls. Women struggled to learn to read and write.

4. Rokeya Sakhawat Hossain was stopped from learning English and Bangla. Why? How did she manage to learn these languages?

Ans. Rokeya Sakhawat Hossain was stopped from learning English and Bangla because in those days English was seen as a language that would expose girls to new ideas. People thought these ideas were not correct for them.

She managed to learn these languages with the support of her elder brother and sister.

5. What do you know about census? Give an account of 1961 and 2011 census?

Ans. Census is the process of counting the number of people in a country and collecting information about them such as their age, schooling, job, etc.

This information is also used to calculate the number of literate people, ratio of men and women, etc.

The 1961 Census recorded that 40% of males and 15% of females are literate whereas the 2011 figures recorded that 82% of males and 65% of females are literate.

6. Write about various social groups and their schooling.

Ans. There are several social groups such as Scheduled Castes (SCs) (official term for Dalits), Schedule Tribes (STs) 'official term for Adivasis', Muslim Communities, etc.

It has been observed that girls belonging to SC and ST communities are less likely to remain in school and girls from Muslim community drop out without even completing their primary school. Girls from SC and ST communities remain in school for around four years where as Muslim girls spend just three years.

7. "Girls from poor families drop out of schools more in number". Why is it so? Diksha

Ans. Girls from poor families who drop out of schools are more in number due to various reasons such as there are no schools nearby and there is no transportation facilities to reach school as it costs much more.

Poor families are not able to afford the fees and expenses to continue the study. Some kind of discrimination also exists as boys are given more preference in comparison to girls.

8. What do yo mean by women's movement? Discuss.

Ans. Women's movement refers to struggle by women to bring changes in spheres like education, legal reforms, violence, health, etc.

There are spheres where situation of women has improved but a lot has to be done in order to change and improve the situation. Women individually and collectively come together to bring these changes. Various women organisations also contribute to overcome the negative situations.

9. Sunita Devi, is a dedicated advocate for women's rights, who found herself sitting outside the state legislature building with a bundle of legal documents. She had been leading a constant legal fight to seek justice for her sister, who had fallen victim to domestic violence and dowry harassment. Sunita's efforts were part of a broader movement to address gender based violence and change societal attitudes. Competency Based

(i) What are dowry deaths?

Ans. Dowry deaths are when a newly married woman is harmed or killed by her in-laws or husband because they are not satisfied with the dowry given by her family at the time of marriage.

(ii) Briefly explain two ways in which women can raise their voice against issues like dowry death?

Ans. Women can raise their voice against issues like dowry deaths in several ways. Two among them are

(i) **Raising awareness** The message against such evil practices like dowry can be spread through street plays, songs and public meetings.

(ii) **Campaigning** It is an important part of the women's movement which is used to fight discrimination and violence against them. Women work in an organised and collective manner to achieve their certain goals.

10. 'Women are the backbone of our society. They are the ones who raise child, who make communities stronger and vibrant. They are fighting for equality, justice and peace. They are making the world a better place'. **Competency Based**

(i) In what ways are women changing the world for the better?

Ans. Women are changing the world for better by leading businesses, making scientific discoveries, making government and policies, and by advocating for social justice.

(ii) What are some examples of women who had made a positive impact on the world?

Ans. Ramabai, Rokeya Sakhawat Hossain and Rashsundari Devi are some examples of women who had made a positive impact on the world.

Long Answer Type Questions

1. Many in the community believed that women were only suited for roles of teaching and homemaking. They were discouraged from pursuing careers in fields like engineering or construction.

However, Priya Sharma defied these expectations. Belonging to a conservative town in Rajasthan, she pursued a degree in civil engineering and went on to become a successful construction project manager, breaking all gender stereotypes in her community.

(i) What is a stereotype? **Competency Based**

Ans. Stereotypes are certain irrational beliefs that people belonging to particular groups based on religion, wealth, language are bound to have certain fixed characteristics or can only do a certain type of work.

For example, it is seen that girls including Priya were discouraged from entering into fields like civil engineering because society thought they did not have a scientific mind. It's important to make sure that women are treated equally and have the same opportunities as men without any discrimination.

(ii) How is women's role within the family linked to their work outside the home?

Ans. Women's role within the family is linked to their work outside the home as women are considered to be fragile, weak, and gentle at heart, who are fit for the care-giving tasks at home. Likewise, they are considered suitable for the jobs which involve gentleness and patience, for example, nurses.

Society doesn't consider girls to be capable of dealing with technical things. Assuming that a person's job be based on the basis of their given nature and gender is a misconception that leads to discrimination.

Individuals should be free to pursue any career they choose, regardless of their gender.

2. An editor is writing an article about the life of Rashsundari Devi. Elaborate the life experience of Rashsundari and discuss how she learnt to write.

Or **Discuss about the experience of Rashsundari Devi.**

Ans. Rashsundari Devi was born in West Bengal. When she was 60, she wrote her autobiography *Amar Jiban* in Bangla. She was a housewife from a rich landlord's family and at that time it was considered bad luck for husbands if women learnt to read and write. Even then, she was determined to read and write.

According to her autobiography, she used to work whole day and without taking any rest she learned to read. Though various negative thoughts crossed her mind, still she was keen on studying. She secretly stole a page from her husband's 'Chaitanya Bhagabat and a page from her eldest son's copy.

She matched the letters of manuscript with her son's copy page and tried to learn. With great care and pains, she learnt how to read. Her writing gave the world an opportunity to know about women's lives in those days and her everyday experiences in detail.

3. Write down any three methods of struggle adopted by women's movements.

Ans. Three methods of struggle adopted by women's movements are

(i) **Campaigning** Campaigns are a significant part of women's movement to fight discrimination and violence. Several laws have been passed as a result of campaigning

- A law regarding domestic violence was passed in 2006 so that women can be legally protected against physical and mental violence within their homes.
- The Supreme Court formed guidelines in 1997 to protect women from sexual harassment at workplace and in educational institutions.
- Case regarding dowry deaths was being raised by women's groups in 1980s which made it a public issue in newspapers and society. Dowry laws were also changed to punish families who ask for dowry.

(ii) **Raising Awareness** It means to raise public awareness about women's right issues through street plays, songs and public meetings. They are significant part of women's movement.

(iii) **Protesting** Protesting and raising voice against violations in the form of public rallies and demonstrations help in drawing attention to injustices.

Picture Based Questions

1. Answer the following questions based on picture given below.

(i) Identify the person in above picture.

(ii) Which title was she given and why?

(iii) What was the purpose of mission set up by her?

Ans. (i) The person in the above picture is Ramabai with her daughter.

(ii) Ramabai was given the title of 'Pandita' because she was able to read and write Sanskrit.

(iii) She set-up a mission in Khedgaon near Pune in 1898, where widows and poor women were motivated to become literate and independent.

2. Answer the following questions based on picture given below.

(i) Who is the person in the above picture?

(ii) Where is she sitting and why?

Ans. (i) The person in the picture is Satyarani, an active member of the women's movement.

(ii) She is sitting on the steps of Supreme Court to seek justice for her daughter who was murdered for dowry.

3. Read the story and answer the questions given below.

(i) If you were Xavier, what subject would you choose and why?

(ii) In your experience, what are some other pressures that boys experience?

Ans. (i) If I was Xavier, I would have chosen History as my subject as I love to study History and it is an interesting subject which helps to know about the past.

(ii) Some other pressures that boys have to experience are

- Think about getting a job that pays good salary.
- They are forced to make their careers in technical fields.

Case Based Question

1. Read the passage and answer the questions given below

Rokeya Sakhawat Hossain knew how to read and write Urdu, she was stopped from learning Bangla and English. In those days, English was seen as a language that would expose girls to new ideas, which people thought were not correct for them. Rokeya learnt to read and write Bangla and English with the support of her elder brother and an elder sister. She went on to become a writer.

She wrote a remarkable story titled Sultana's Dream in 1905 to practice her English skills when she was merely 25 years old. This story imagined a woman called Sultana who reaches a place called Ladyland.

Ladyland is a place where women had the freedom to study, work and create inventions like controlling rain from the clouds and flying air cars.

(i) Who was Rokeya Sakhawat Hossain?

(ii) Which story did she write?

(iii) What are the values of Rokeya's character highlighted in the passage?

Ans. (i) Rokeya Sakhawat Hossain, was born in a rich family and owned a lot of land.

(ii) She wrote a remarkable story titled 'Sultana's Dream.'

(iii) Values highlighted through Rokeya's character are independence, creativity, and eagerness to learn.

ASSESSMENT EXERCISE

Multiple Choice Questions (MCQs)

1. In stereotype families, the girl are encouraged to become

(a) doctors (b) engineers

(c) housewife (d) Both (a) and (b)

2. In Pottery trade, why women were not seen as potters?

(a) They did not operate the wheel

(b) They did not do anything

(c) They are helpers

(d) None of the above

3. Rashsundari Devi was born in which state?

(a) Mumbai (b) West Bengal

(c) Pune (d) Hyderabad

Subjective Questions (VSA, SA & LA)

1. How do women represent their thinking about inequalities?

2. What was the dream of Rokeya Sakhawat Hossain?

3. How women have earned the right to study?

4. Write about struggle faced by Laxmi Lakra to become an engine driver.

5. Why Xavier forced to take Maths or Science irrespective of his interest in History?

6. Write a short note on struggles faced by Rashsundari Devi to learn reading manuscript.

7. Write in detail about the reasons why children drop out of school in rural and poor areas.

8. How did women's group ensure justice for dowry victims in 1980s?

9. Discuss the changes that have been brought by women struggles.

Understanding Media

CHAPTER 6

Media is the plural form of the term 'medium' which describes the various ways through which we communicate in society. It refers to all means of communication which include TV, radio and newspapers. As they reach millions of people across the world, they are called **mass media**.

6.1 Media and Technology

The **technology**[1] that mass media uses keeps on changing. Newspapers, television and radio can reach millions of people because they use certain technologies.

Media has been categorised into two categories as follows

(i) Print Electronic Media (TV and radio)

(ii) Print Media (newspapers and magazines)

Their names are related to the technologies they use.

Changing technology helps the media to reach more people.

For example, technology improved the quality of image and sound that we see and hear on television.

Television has brought the world closer to the people, as it enables the people to view news and entertainment channels from other parts of the world.

For example, technology invited to quality of second and image that he see learn of television

KNOWLEDGE PLUS 'Televisor' was an early form of television invented by **John L Baird.**

6.2 Media and Money

The different technologies used in mass media are expensive. For example, a TV studio has lights, cameras, sound recorders, transmission satellites, etc which are very costly.

It requires money to pay the newsreaders as well as other people who help in **broadcasting**[2]. As the technology used in mass media keeps changing, a lot of money is required for getting the latest technology. Thus, most television channels and newspapers are part of big business houses.

One way in which mass media earns money is from **advertisements** that are repeatedly shown to make people buy different products.

6.3 Media and Democracy

In a democracy, media plays a very important role in providing news and discussing events taking place in the country and the world. The people learn about the working of government through this information.

The people can also take action on the basis of this information by organising public protest, campaign, asking the government to rethink its programme, etc.

Balanced Report and Independent Media

It is important for the media to provide information which is balanced. A **balanced report** is one which discusses all points of view of a particular story and then leaves it to the readers to make up their minds.

Information provided by the media should be reliable and not biased. A balanced report requires media to be independent.

1 **Technology** It is the use of science in industry, to invent useful things to solve problems.

2 **Broadcast** It means to make things public by means of radio or television.

An **independent media** means that its coverage of news is not under the control and influence of any one.

It is important in a democracy that media should be independent. However, it is not independent because government controls media through censorship.

When the government prevents either a news item, or scenes from a movies or lyrics of a song from being shared with the larger public, it is called **censorship**. An example of government censoring the media is in period of Emergency between 1975-1977.

Media is no longer considered independent because of its close links to business. The continuous need of money for media and its links to advertising means that it becomes difficult for media to report against people who give them advertisements.

KNOWLEDGE PLUS Social advertisements refer to advertisements made by the Government or private agencies that have a larger message for society.

Setting Agendas

Media plays an important role in deciding what stories to focus on and what is newsworthy. As media plays an important role in our lives and in shaping our thoughts, it is commonly said that the media 'sets the **agenda**[3]'.

Media should focus on issues that are significant in our lives and not on those which make money for it.

Local Media

It refers to the media that covers small issues involving ordinary people and their daily lives. It **publishes**[4] news of local importance.

The usage of community radios to tell farmers about the prices of crops and the documentary films showing real life conditions of poor communities, are some examples of local media.

Another example of local media is a newspaper called **Khabar Lahriya** which is run by eight Dalit women of Chitrakoot district in Uttar Pradesh. It reports on Dalit issues and cases of violence against women.

3 **Agenda** It refers to a plan or list of matters to be acted upon for the welfare of the society.

4 **Publish** When news reports, article interviews are printed in newspapers ,magazines and books for a large number of citizens to reason, it is known as published.

UNDERSTANDING MEDIA

Media and Technology

- Changing technology helps the media to reach more people.
- Improves the quality of sounds and images.

Media and Money

- Media needs a lot of money to keep up with new technology.
- Mass media earns money from advertisements.
- TV channels and newspapers are part of big business houses.

Print Electronic Media
(TV and Radio)

Print Media
(Newspapers and Magazines)

Media and Democracy

- In democracy, media plays a very important role in providing news.
- People come to know about the government works.

Setting Agendas

- Media decides what is considered newsworthy by choosing which stories to focus on.
- Media sets the agenda by shaping our thoughts.

Balanced Report and Independent Media

- Media should provide balanced information.
- A balance report discusses all point of view of a particular story.
- Media should be independent in its coverage of news.
- Government controls media through censorship, e.g. government censored media during Emergency between 1975 and 1977.

NCERT FOLDER

Covering Intext Questions and Exercises of NCERT

NCERT ON PAGE 65

Q.1 Look at the collage and list six various kinds of media that you see.

Ans. The various kinds of media in the collage are

- Radio
- Television
- DVD
- Transistor
- Computer
- Internet

Q.2 Ask older members of your family about what they used to listen to on the radio when there was no TV around. Find out from them when the first TV came to your area. When was cable TV introduced?

Ans. Older members of my family used to listen Vividh Bharati on the radio. The first TV came in 1984 in our area. Cable TV was introduced in 1990 in our area.

Q.3 How many people in your neighbourhood use the internet?

Ans. Most of the people in my neighbourhood use internet.

Q.4 List three things that you know about some other part of the world from watching television.

Ans. The things I know about some other part of the world from watching television are

- Tsunami in Indonesia
- Rita and Caterina in USA
- Blast in Samjhauta Express

NCERT ON PAGE 66

Q.5 Can you list three different products that are advertised during your favourite TV programme?

Ans. Three products advertised during my favourite TV programme are

- Chocolates
- Electronics
- Clothing

Q.6 Take a newspaper and count the number of advertisements in it. Some people say that newspapers have too many advertisements. Do you think this is true and why?

Ans. Yes, it is true that newspaper have too many advertisements.

These advertisements are necessary as they reduce the cost of newspaper and make it affordable for the people.

Q.7 ***News of India Report***

Crackdown on Polluting Factories

Protestors Block Roads and Disrupt Traffic

Violent protests by owners and workers brought the city to a standstill today. People getting to work could not do so on time because of huge traffic jams. The owners and workers are protesting the government's decision to close down polluting factory units.

Although, the government did take this decision rather hastily,the protestors have known for quite some time that their units are not legal. Moreover, the levels of pollution in the city will be greatly reduced by this closure. Mr Jain a well known figure in the city said, "With our city gradually becoming India's new business hub, it is important that it be a clean and green city. Polluting factories should be moved. The factory owners and workers should accept the relocation being offered by the government instead of protesting".

India Daily Report

Closure of factories causes unrest

The closure of one lakh factories in the city's residential areas is likely to become a serious issue. On Monday, thousands of factory owners and workers took to the streets to strongly protest this closure. They said that their livelihoods would be lost. They say that the fault lies with the municipal corporation because it continued to issue licenses for new factories to be set up in residential areas.

They also say that there were no adequate relocation efforts. The owners and workers plan a one-day city bandh to protest against this closure. Mr Sharma, one of the factory owners said, "The government says that it has done a lot to relocate us.

But the areas they have sent us to have no facilities and have not been developed for the last-five years."

Questions

(i) Are the above stories in the two newspapers similar? And if not, why not? What in your view, are the similarities and the differences?

(ii) If you read the story in the News of India, what would you think about the issue?

Ans. (i) No, the above two stories are not similar. Although both are related to the closure of factories but information provided in each of them differs.

Difference between the two is that according to the report in News of India, closure of factories will lead to clean and green city, whereas report in India daily states that closure of factories will result in loss of livelihoods.

Similarity in both of them is that both the reports deal with the protests by owners and workers of the factories and government is assuring the protestors to relocate the factories somewhere else.

(ii) After reading the story in the News of India report, it can be said that workers and owners should accept the proposal for relocation of factories, instead of protesting.

This is because the city is emerging as a new business hub, and it is necessary to keep it green, clean and free from pollution.

NCERT ON PAGE 69

Q.8 Do you think it is important to know both sides of story? Why?

Ans. Yes, it is important to know both sides of story in order to develop correct views about that information and give opinions.

Q.9 Pretend that you are a journalist for a newspaper and write a balanced story from the two news reports.

Ans. Balanced story

- The government order closure of polluting factories in the city. The pollution had already reached dangerous levels.
- Factory owners and workers protested violently against the closure. The city life came to a standstill.
- For clean and green city, closure of factories was essential.
- The government should have relocated the factories at suitable locations with proper time frame.

NCERT ON PAGE 71

Q.10 What is the consequence of the media 'setting the agenda' by reporting on the Fashion Week rather than the slum demolitions?

Ans. By 'setting the agenda' on the Fashion Week rather than the slum demolitions, media houses will earn huge amount of money.

Q.11 Can you think of an issue that does not seem important to you because it is never featured in the media?

Ans. Issue which is important but never featured in media is the poor sanitary conditions of the people living below the poverty line.

EXERCISES

Q.1 In what ways does the media play an important role in a democracy?

Ans. In a democratic country, media plays a significant role in following ways

- Media makes the citizens aware of the recent issues.
- It is through media only that people come to know about the working of the government.
- Media propagates the policies and programmes of the government.
- People forms opinion based on the information provided by media.

Q.2 Can you give this diagram a title? What do you understand about the link between media and big business from this diagram?

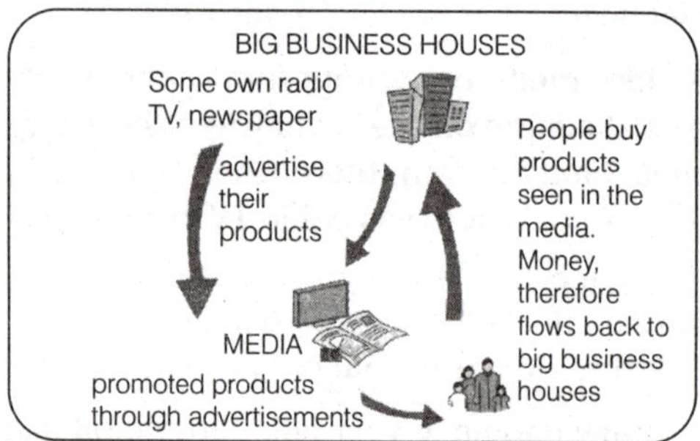

Ans. The appropriate title should be 'Big Business Houses and Media'

The link between media and big business houses is that maximum number of media houses are owned by big business houses. They advertise their products through these media houses and media houses earn heavy amount in return. People get attracted towards these products and buy them. It is a mutually beneficial relationship between the media and business houses.

Q.3 You have read about the ways in which the media 'sets the agenda'.What kind of effect does this have in a democracy? Provide two examples to support your point of view.

Ans. Media 'setting the agenda' has following effects in democracy

- It is through the media that people come to know about working of the government.
- People form opinion based on the agenda set by the media.

- Sometimes government prevents the media from publishing particular things and is known as censorship.
- Media is also under the influence of big business houses. They make media work for their own interests and hence balanced report is not prepared.

Some examples of these effects are

- Clean drinking water is a major issue but media is never seen discussing this issue.
- News of fashion week formed the headlines of front page which largely benefitted the media houses.

REVIEW EXERCISE

Including Competency Based Questions

Part I

Multiple Choice Questions (MCQs)

1. The word media includes

(a) radio (b) TV
(c) newspapers (d) All of these

2. Which among the following is/are included in electronic media? Diksha

(a) Newspapers (b) Magazines
(c) Radio (d) All of the above

3. Which among the following does print media include?

(a) Magazines (b) TV
(c) Radio (d) None of these

4. What is the name for an early television?

(a) Teleview (b) TV
(c) Televisor (d) Telecom

5. Which among the following was invented by John L Baird ? Competency Based

(a) Radio (b) Electronic typewriter
(c) Televisor (d) Cameras

6. Which has brought the world closer to us? Diksha

(a) Television (b) Taperecorder
(c) Typewriter (d) None of these

7. TV studio in which newsreader sits consists of

(a) lights (b) cameras
(c) transmission satellites (d) All of these

8. Which is the main source of income of media? Diksha

(a) Advertisements (b) Articles
(c) General news (d) None of these

9. Government control over the media through which process?

(a) censorship (b) Emergency
(c) Independence (d) None of these

10. Government censored the media during emergency period between Diksha

(a) 1972-1974 (b) 1975-1978
(c) 1975-1977 (d) None of these

11. What does local media include among the following?

(a) Community radios
(b) Documentary films
(c) Newspapers
(d) All of the above

12. What is Khabar Lahariya?

(a) Local Magazines
(b) Local Newspaper
(c) story book
(d) None of the above

13. Shiva, a student of class VII, got to know about the policy on education which he did not find good for students. What are the ways in which he can show concern to the government? Competency Based

(a) Public Protest
(b) Starting a signature campaign
(c) Writing letters to education minister
(d) All of the above

14. Identify the correct option that represent the following information. Competency Based

I. It covers small issues which the media will not be interested to cover.
II. It is also made in documentary films by cheap cameras.
III. It is generally represented in regional language.

Options

(a) Mass media (b) Social media
(c) Print media (d) Local media

15. **Choose the correct statement from the following**

I. Newspapers, television and radio can reach millions of people because they use certain technologies.

II. Media is the singular form of the word 'medium'.

III. Changing technology restrains media to reach more people.

Codes

(a) Only I (b) Only II

(c) I and II (d) Only III

Answers

1. (d)	**2.** (c)	**3.** (a)	**4.** (c)	**5.** (c)
6. (a)	**7.** (d)	**8.** (a)	**9.** (a)	**10.** (c)
11. (d)	**12.** (b)	**13.** (d)	**14.** (d)	**15.** (a)

Match the Following

1.

	List I		List II
A.	Media role	1.	Censorship
B.	Local Media	2.	John L Baird
C.	Television	3.	Setting Agendas
D.	Government restriction on Media	4.	Khabar Lahariya
E.	Printing	5.	Gutenberg

Codes

	A	B	C	D	E		A	B	C	D	E
(a)	3	4	2	1	5	(b)	2	1	5	4	3
(c)	5	4	2	3	1	(d)	4	1	5	3	2

Ans. (a)

Assertion-Reason

1. **Assertion** (A) Newspapers and magazines are often referred to as print media.

Reason (R) The technology that mass media uses is static and unchanging.

Codes

(a) Both A and R are true and R is the correct explanation of A

(b) Both A and R are true, but R is not the correct explanation of A

(c) A is true, but R is false

(d) A is false, but R is true

2. **Assertion** (A) Changing technology in the media industry primarily aims to reduce the reach of mass media.

Reason (R) Modernising technology helps media reach more people and improve the quality of content.

Codes

(a) Both A and R are true and R is the correct explanation of A

(b) Both A and R are true, but R is not the correct explanation of A

(c) A is true, but R is false

(d) A is false, but R is true

Ans. 1. (c) A is true, but R is false

2. (d) A is false, but R is true

Fill in the Blanks

1. ...... is the earliest form of mass media.
2. .... media is important in a democracy.
3. Technologies used in mass media are very ....
4. With .... typewriters, journalism underwent a change in the .... **Diksha**
5. Mass media earns money through .... **Diksha**

Ans. 1. Print media 2. Independent

3. expensive 4. electronic, 1940s

5. advertisements

True/False

1. Changing technology improves the quality of sound and the images. **Diksha**
2. Asking the government to rethink its programme is one of the ways people react.
3. The media decides what to focus on and in this way, 'it sets the agenda'. **Diksha**
4. The first printed book 'The Bible' was published by Gutenberg.
5. Balanced report discusses only one point of view or one side of story.

Ans. 1. True 2. True 3. True 4. True 5. False

Picture Based Questions

1. **The image shown below is an artist's impression of invention of the printing press. What was the name of inventor?**

(a) Johannes Gutenberg (b) Leonard da Vinci

(c) Else Wyrich (d) Nikola Tesla

2. **What is the primary purpose of the media shown in the image?**

(a) Business promotion
(b) Social media sharing
(c) Entertainment
(d) Information and news circulation

Ans. 1. (a) Johannes Gutenberg
2. (d) Information and news circulation

Case Based Question

1. **Read the passage given below and answer the following questions.**

While the government does continue to censor films, it does not really censor the media's coverage of news. Despite the absence of censorship by the government, most newspapers nowadays still fail to provide a balanced story. The reasons for this are complicated. Persons who research the media have said that this happens because business houses control the media. At times, it is in the interest of these businesses to focus on only one side of the story. Media's continual need for money and its links to advertising means that it becomes difficult for media to be reporting against people who give them advertisements. Media is, thus, no longer considered independent because of its close links to business.

(i) **What is the term used when government restrict a new item or movie scenes from being shared?**
(a) Publish (b) Editing
(c) Posting (d) Censorship

(ii) **What is the main challenge of ensuring balanced and objective reporting in the media today?**
(a) The media's close relationship with business
(b) Government interference
(c) Media's focus on sensationalism and distortion
(d) All of the above

(iii) **According to the passage, is media considered independent?**
(a) No
(b) Yes
(c) Only partially
(d) It depends on the government

(iv) **Which of the following is the best way to stay informed about current events?**
(a) Read only from one source
(b) Read from various source
(c) Watch cable network
(d) None of the above

Ans. (i) (d) Censorship
(ii) (d) All of the above
(iii) (a) No
(iv) (b) None of the above

Part II

Very Short Answer Type Questions

1. **What do you mean by the term media.** Diksha

Ans. Media is a term used to define all forms of communication like radio, TV, newspapers, internet, etc.

2. **Give one merit of changing technology with respect to media.**

Ans. Merit of changing technology to media is that it helps media to reach more people.

3. **Give one merit of television.**

Ans. One merit of television is that it has made us to think of ourselves as members of a larger global world.

4. **Define mass media.** Diksha

Ans. Mass media is a form of media that reaches millions of people or the masses across the country and the world through TV, radio and newspapers.

5. **Why do same advertisements are shown repeatedly on TV?**

Ans. Some advertisements are repeatedly shown on TV in the hope that people will go out and buy the product that is advertised.

6. **How do people come to know about working of government?**

Ans. People come to know about the working of government through the information provided by media.

7. **Define balanced report.**

Ans. Balanced report is one which deals with all point of views of the story and the story/ information should not be biased.

8. **What do you understand by independent media?** Diksha

Ans. Independent media is one which is not under the influence and control of anyone.

9. Mention any two ways how people show their dissatisfaction with the government decisions. Diksha

Ans. Two ways people show their dissatisfaction with the government decisions are by

(i) Organising public protest

(ii) Starting a signature campaign

10. Define signature campaign.

Ans. Signature campaign is a letter or a petition signed by large number of people to demonstrate support for a cause or an action.

11. On what factor does the cost to advertise on a news channel depend? Competency Based

Ans. The cost to advertise on a news channel depends on the popularity of the channel. It varies from ₹ 1000 to ₹ 1,00,000 per 10 sec.

Short Answer Type Questions

1. "Everything ranging from the stall at the local fair to the programme that you see on TV can be called media." Discuss. Competency Based

Ans. Everything ranging from the stall at local fair to the programme that we see on TV can be called media. Media is a word frequently used to collectively refer television, radio, newspapers, internet and various other forms of communication. Media is something that affects our daily lives. It is a plural form of the term 'medium' and includes all things through which we communicate in society.

2. How does television affect our lives? Diksha

Ans. Television affects our lives so much that we cannot think of our lives without it. It has brought the world closer to us.

Television helps us to view news and entertainment channels from other parts of the world. For example, we can see images of a storm that has hit the coast of Florida, United States by sitting in India.

3. The media serves a fundamental purpose by supplying the information essential for informed discussions. A wall functioning democracy relies on citizens making knowledgeable decisions and this lies on the type of information they access.

(i) What is the role of media in democracy?

Ans. Role of democracy in media is to provide information that is reliable and unbiased. It helps the citizens to know about the working of the government.

Media propagates (spreads) the policies and programs of the government and criticizes unpopular policies.

(ii) What do you mean by balanced report by media? Diksha

Ans. A balanced report is one that discusses all points of views of a particular story and then leaves it to the readers to make up their minds.

4. Explain about the importance for media to be balanced.

Ans. It is important for the media to provide information which is balanced. A balanced report is one which discusses all points of view of a particular story and then leaves it to the readers to make up their minds.

Information provided by the media should be reliable and not biased. A balanced report requires media to be independent. An independent media means that its coverage of news is not under the control and influence of any one.

5. 'The reality is that media is far from independent' Comment. Competency Based

Ans. The media is far from independent because it is always under the government control.

Government controls the media by censoring the information to prevent news items, scenes from movies, lyrics of song, etc from being shared with the larger public. Sometimes, it is the interest of big business houses which controls the media's coverage.

6. Write a brief note on 'local media'. Diksha

Ans. Local media is news and information about local area which raises issue that involves ordinary people and their daily lives. It is usually started in local groups. Several people use community radio to tell farmers about the prices of different crops. Others make documentary films with fairly cheap and easily available video cameras on the real-life conditions faced by different poor communities.

For example Khabar Lahariya, a local Bundeli language newspaper, is run by eight Dalit women in Uttar Pradesh. It reports and publishes on Dalit issues and cares of violence againt women and political corruption.

7. What is social advertising? Why do you think social advertising is important?

Ans. When advertising is done with a view to educate the public about a certain issue or publicise a government scheme. Social advertising is essential because it raises awareness about important issues and inspires people to make a positive difference. It can address a wide range of causes like environmental protection, kindness, health awareness and more.

Long Answer Type Questions

1. Discuss the role of technology in media.

Ans. Technology is the use of science in industry to invent useful things or to solve problems. Cable television and extensive use of the internet is a recent phenomenon. Technology used by media is dynamic. Newspaper, magazines etc are called print media and they use various technologies to present the material in an attractive way. TV and radio are called electronic media which have brought the world closer to us.

The dynamic nature of technology helps media to spread its effect to more people with better quality of sound and images. Technology also contributes in changing the way people think.

2. An article is published about the role of huge money in changing the media. Why does the media require huge amount of money? Explain how mass media earn money. **Competency Based**

Ans. Media require huge amount of money because the various technologies that are used in mass media are very costly. If we take an example of TV studio, we see, it has lights, cameras, sound recorders, transmission satellites, etc which are too expensive. Besides a number of other people are also paid who helps in broadcasting.

A lot of money is spent in using changing technologies and hence a big amount of money is required for the same. This makes television channels and newspapers part of big business houses.

Mass media earns money by advertising various items like cars, phones, electronics, etc. Advertisements are repeated during a telecast of movies, serials and matches. Media receives huge amounts of money from business houses as they give media the major part of advertisements.

3. Why do you think that existence of local media is important? Explain with example, the ways through which people at local level get informed.

Ans. The existence of local media is important as other big media houses are not interested in covering 'small' issues that involve ordinary people and their daily lives. This forced several groups to come together and start their own media.

There are various ways through which people at local level get informed. One of them is community radio which keeps farmers up to date.

Making documentary films is another cheap way to inform citizens about real-life conditions. Another example is publishing local newspapers in local language, so that each corner of the country can be informed.

An example of local media is khabar Lahariya, a local Bundeli Language newspaper which is run by 8 Dalit women in Uttar Pradesh. It reports and publishes on Dalit issues and cases of violence against women and political corruption.

4. Last month, the media covered all the news related to celebrity gossip, but they seemed to ignore the pressing issue of pollution in our city.
Pollution created a lot of problems for the people of the city, yet the media failed to cover it. **Competency Based**

(i) Why is it important for the media to balance entertainment and news about critical issues?

Ans. It is essential for the media to strike a balance between entertainment news and critical issues. While entertainment news can be fun and enjoyable, it's equally important to inform the public about crucial matters like pollution, health and safety. Media is a powerful tool to educate people and create awareness. Neglecting important issues can lead to ignorance and hinder necessary actions. By providing a mix of both types of news, the media can ensure that people are well-informed and can make informed decisions about their lives, communities and the world.

(ii) What is the role of media in our lives?

Ans. The media plays a very important role in our lives in the following ways

- It helps us stay informed about what's happening in the world, in our country, and in our local communities.
- The media also acts as a watchdog, keeping an eye on the government and other powerful people to make sure that they are doing their jobs properly and not being corrupt.

5. What do you mean by an independent media? Why is it important for the media to be independent?

Ans. Independent media is the media that is not controlled by any government, corporation or any other business group which has self interest. It is free to report on the news without any influence or fear.

Independent media is important because

- It helps to hold the government accountable, inform the public, and also provide platform to raise their voice.
- An independent media can help to promote transparency and accountability in the government and the private sector.
- It provides accurate and unbaised information about important issues to the public.

Picture Based Question

1. Study the two pictures and answer the following questions.

Picture 1

Picture 2

(a) What is the first picture about? What was its effect?

(b) Identify the person in the second picture.

(c) What was his invention?

Ans. (a) The first picture is of electronic typewriter. It brought changes in journalism drastically in the 1940s.

(b) John L Baird is sitting in the second picture.

(c) John L Baird invented the 'televisor', an early television.

Case Based Question

1. Read the passage given below and answer the following questions.

In many of our homes. TV is on for a very long time. In many ways a lot of our impressions about the world around us are formed by what we see on TV it is like a window on the world. TV has different types of programmes, soap operas like Saas Bhi Kabhi Bahu Thi, game shows, like Kaun Banega Crorepati, reality TV shows like Big Boss, news, sports and cartoons. Before, in between and after each programme are advertisements. Since, TV time costs so much money, only those programmes that can attract the maximum number of viewers are shown.

We need to think about what TV does to us, how it shapes our views of the world, our beliefs, attitudes and values. We need to realise that it gives us a partial view of the world. While we enjoy our favourite programmes, we should always be aware of the large exciting world beyond our TV screens. There is so much happening out there that TV ignores. A world beyond film stars, celebrities and rich lifestyles, a world that all of us need to reach out to and respond to in various ways. We need to be active viewers, who question whatever we see and hear, while we may enjoy it too!

(a) What does TV do to us?

(b) Do television programmes show us all the happenings around the world?

Ans. (a) Television plays a significant role in lives of people. We form a lot of impressions about the world around us by watching TV. It influences our thinking and helps us to develop various view points.

(b) No, there is so much happening around the world that TV ignores. There is a world beyond film stars, celebrities, etc which we need to see and respond to.

ASSESSMENT EXERCISE

Multiple Choice Questions (MCQs)

1. Journalism underwent a sea-change in the 1940s because of

(a) internet (b) television

(c) radio (d) electronic typewriters

2. When there is no control and influence on the coverage of news in media it is called as

(a) Dependent media

(b) Independent media

(c) Free media

(d) All of these

3. Which one of the fortnightly was run by eight dalit women in Chitrakoot (Uttar Pradesh)?

(a) Khabary (b) Bharat news

(c) Khabar Lahariya (d) All of these

Subjective Questions (VSA, SA & LA)

1. What do you mean by Public protest?

2. Write one instance when media failed to focus on issue that is significant in our lives.

3. Differentiate between electronic media and print media.

4. Write positive as well as negative aspect of censorship.

5. How does media influences our thoughts, feelings and actions?

6. Explain media's close relationship with businessman. How does it affect a balanced report?

7. How mass media earn financial support? Write about the cause of repeated advertisement.

8. Write a short note on satellites and how is it useful for mass media.

CHAPTER 7

Markets Around Us

A place where we visit to purchase things such as clothes, vegetables, stationery, etc is referred to as a **market**. There are various types of markets, which include shops, hawker's stall in our neighbourhood, a weekly market, a large shopping complex and mall.

7.1 Weekly Market

A weekly market is held on a specific day of the week. Weekly markets have the following features

- **No Permanent Shops** Weekly markets do not have permanent shops. Traders establish their shops for a single day and then close them up in the evening. They establish their shops somewhere else the next day.
- **Cheap Rate** Things of daily requirements are available in these markets. Many things available in weekly markets are at cheaper rates.

  This is because the owners themselves manage the shop with the help of their family members. They don't have their shops in permanent buildings thus they do not have to pay rent, electricity and fees to the government, and hire workers and pay wages to them.
- **Competition** These markets have a large number of shops selling the same goods, thus there is a competition among them.
- **All Things Available at One Place** One of the advantages of weekly markets is that most of the things that people need are available at one place. People do not have to go to different areas to buy different things.
- **Choice and Variety** People in the market have a choice and a variety of goods, as there are many shops selling same as well as different goods.

7.2 Shops in the Neighbourhood

There are many shops in our neighbourhood from where we buy the daily goods. Many of these are permanent shops, while others are roadside stalls such as that of the vegetable **hawker**[1], the fruit vendor, the mechanic, etc.

Shops in the neighbourhood are useful in many ways such as

- They are near our home and we can go there any time we want.
- These shops also provide goods on credit as the buyer and seller usually know each other.

7.3 Shopping Complexes and Malls

Markets in the urban areas that have many shops are called shopping complexes.

Malls are large multi-storeyed air conditioned buildings in urban areas with shops on different floors.

In these urban markets, both **branded** and **non-branded** goods are available. Branded goods are more expensive and better in quality than non-branded goods.

The branded goods are sold by companies through shops and special showrooms in large urban markets. Only a few people can afford branded goods.

1 **Hawker** A hawker is a vendor who sells inexpensive items and do not have permanent shops.

7.4 Chain of Markets

Goods are produced in factories, on farms or in homes. However, we do not directly purchase goods from factory or farm and the producers do not sell their goods to us in small quantities.

There are people who act as link between **producers** and the final **consumers** who are known as the **traders**. The **wholesale[2] trader** buy large quantities of goods and then sell them to other traders.

In the markets, buying and selling takes place between traders. There are wholesale markets in every city where goods are bought for the first time and then supplied to other traders.

The roadside hawker buys items from the wholesale trader in the town, who in turn have bought these from other big wholesaler trader in the city.

The wholesale trader in the city bought these goods in large quantity from the factory and stored them in a godown.

The trader who finally sells the goods to the consumer is called the **retailer[3]**. This could be a trader in a weekly market, a hawker in the neighbourhood or a shop in a shopping complex. In this way, a **chain of markets[4]** is established.

7.5 Markets Everywhere

Markets exists everywhere and all the markets in a specific locality work in a particular manner and time.

However, it is not necessary for a person to go to the market to buy goods. Orders can be placed on phone or through the **internet**, for variety of things and they are delivered at home. Thus, buying and selling can be done through various ways and not necessarily through shops in market places.

7.6 Markets and Equality

The shop owners in weekly markets and in a shopping complex are different from each other. One is a small trader with little money to run the shop while other spends a lot of money to establish the shop.

They also earn unequal amounts. The weekly market traders earn little profit as compared to the profit of a regular shop owner in a shopping complex.

Similarly the people who buy goods are different from one another. There are many people who cannot afford even the cheapest of goods whereas some people buy goods from malls. Thus, a person to be a buyer or seller in different markets depend upon the money he/she have.

When things are sold, it encourages production and new opportunities are created for people.

2 Wholesale This refers to buying and selling in large quantities. Most products, including vegetables, fruits and flowers have special wholesale markets.
3 Retailer It is the middlemen between wholesaler and the consumer. Retailer directly deals with consumer.
4 Chain of Markets This refers to a series of markets that are connected links in a chain because products pass from one market to another.

MARKETS AROUND US

Weekly Market

- Held on a specific day of the week.
- Features
  - No permanent shops
  - Things available at cheaper rates
  - Competition is there in the market
  - All things are available at one place
  - Offer a large choice and variety of goods

Shops in the Neighbourhood

- Accessible very easily.
- Trustworthy and reliable.
- Examples–Vegetable hawker, the fruit vendor, the mechanic, etc.
- Useful for the following
  - Nearby our homes
  - Provide goods on credit

Chain of Markets

- Goods travel from factories to wholesale traders, then to various markets and finally to retailers who sell to consumers.
- The trader who finally sells the goods to the consumer is called a retailer.

Markets Everywhere

- All the markets work in a specific locality work in a particular manner and time.
- Buying and selling can be done through various ways, e.g. through phone or internet.

Markets and Equality

- Shop owners in weekly markets and shopping complexes are different from each other in the following ways
  - Shop owner in a weekly market is a trader with little money while owner in a shopping complex spends a lot of money to setup a shop.
  - A trader in a weekly market earns little profit than a trader in shopping complex.

Shopping Complexes and Malls

- Shopping Complexes are the markets in the urban areas having many shops.
- Malls are large multi-storeyed air conditioned buildings in urban areas with shops on different floors.
- Both branded and non-branded goods are available.

NCERT FOLDER

Covering Intext Questions and Exercises of NCERT

NCERT ON PAGE 78

Q.1 Why do people go to a weekly market? Give three reasons.

Ans. People go to a weekly market because

- Things are available at cheaper rates.
- Almost all things are available at one place.
- People have a choice while shopping in weekly markets.

Q.2 Who are the sellers in a weekly market ? Why don't we find big business persons in these markets?

Ans. The sellers in a weekly market are the small traders, who establish their shops for a single day and store things at home.

Big business persons are not seen in these markets because they run their business from their permanent establishments.

Q.3 Why are things cheap in the weekly market?

Ans. Things are cheap in the weekly market because the shops established here are not permanent.
The owners themselves manage the shop with the help of their family members. They don't have their shops in permanent buildings thus, they don't have to pay rent, electricity and fees to the government, and hire workers and pay them wages.

Q.4 Explain with an example how people bargain in the market. Can you think of a situation where the bargain would be unfair?

Ans. People bargain in the market because the sellers charge very high prices of the products. Buyers want the products at low prices and they try to bargain and bring down the prices. This way the price of good is bargained and the rate is fixed on mutually agreed price.

Bargain would be unfair for the products where the seller has not charged high prices.

Q.5 What are different kinds of shops that you find in your neighbourhood? What do you purchase from them?

Ans. The different kinds of shops in my neighbourhood are departmental stores, dairy, stationery, chemist, bakery, etc.

We buy goods like milk, butter, ghee, groceries, pen, pencils, medicines, biscuits, cakes, etc from them.

Q.6 Why are goods sold in permanent shops costlier than those sold in the weekly markets or by roadside hawkers?

Ans. Goods sold in permanent shops are costlier than those sold in the weekly markets or by roadside hawkers because owners of permanent shops have to bear a lot of expenditure such as rent, electricity, fees to government and wages to their workers.

Roadside hawkers or traders in weekly markets do not have to bear such expenses and hence their goods are cheaper.

NCERT ON PAGE 81

Q.7 Why do people not bargain in shops located in malls whereas they bargain in weekly markets?

Ans. People do not bargain in shops located in malls because they usually sell branded items with price tags on them. Branded items are traded at fixed prices.

It is easy to bargain in weekly markets because prices are not fixed as goods are not branded.

Q.8 How do you think your neighbourhood shop gets its goods? Find out and explain with some examples.

Ans. Our neighbourhood shops get their goods from wholesalers.

For example, nearby departmental store is a retailer who purchases its stock in bulk from the wholesaler.

Q.9 Why is a wholesale trader necessary ?

Ans. Wholesale trader is necessary as he/she acts as a link between retailer and producer. It is wholesale trader who collects goods from producers and supply them to the retailers for final sale.

EXERCISES

Q.1 In what ways is a hawker different from a shop owner?

Ans. Differences between a hawker and shopkeeper are

Hawker	Shopkeeper
Hawker is a trader who sells his goods and products by shouting, roaming from one place to another.	Shopkeeper is a trader who owns a shop in market and where both shopkeeper and buyer know each other.
Hawkers don't have permanent shops and buyer and seller are not known to each other, thereby goods are purchased in cash.	Shopkeeper sells goods on credit also.
Hawker generally sell non-branded items.	Shopkeeper sells branded as well as non-branded items.

Q.2 **Compare and contrast a weekly market and a shopping complex on the following.**

Market	Kind of goods sold	Prices of goods	Sellers	Buyers
Weekly market				
Shopping complex				

Ans.

Market	Kind of goods sold	Prices of goods	Sellers	Buyers
Weekly market	Daily use products, not packaged, not branded	Cheap	Small traders hawkers	Low income group people
Shopping complex	Branded products, packaged, all need products	Expensive	Big shop owners	Upper-middle class and high-class people

Q.3 **Explain how a chain of markets is formed. What purpose does it serve?**

Ans. The chain of markets is established after various steps. First of all, goods are produced in factories, on farms or in homes.

The wholesale trader buy large quantities of goods and then sell them to other traders.

In the markets, buying and selling takes place between traders. The trader who finally sells the goods to the consumer is called the retailer. This could be a trader in a weekly market, a hawker in the neighbourhood or a shop in a shopping complex.

The roadside hawker buys items from the wholesale trader in the town, who in turn have bought these from other big wholesaler trader in the city. The wholesale trader in the city would have bought these goods in a large quantity from the factory and stored them in a godown. In this way, a chain of markets is established.

The chain of markets serve following purposes

- Consumers get their goods in small quantities.
- Producers can sell their goods in bulk easily.
- Consumer get their goods nearby their homes.

Q.4 **'All persons have equal rights to visit any shop in a marketplace'. Do you think this is true of shops with expensive products? Explain with examples.**

Ans. Yes, every person had an equal right to visit any shop in a marketplace, even those selling expensive items.

For example, Sujata and Kavita had every right to enter the shop selling readymade branded clothes in 'Anzal Mall'. The security guard looked at them as if he wanted to stop them from entering the shop because they appeared poor. Even if they could not afford to buy any cloth from that shop, they had the right to visit it.

Q.5 **'Buying and selling can take place without going to a marketplace'. Explain this statement with the help of examples.**

Ans. 'Buying and selling can take place without going to a marketplace' as it is not always compulsory for one to go to the marketplace to purchase goods. This is an era of internet. We can place orders of a variety of things through internet or phone. The goods are delivered at our home.

For example, in clinics and nursing homes, there are sales representatives waiting for doctors. These persons are also involved in selling of goods.

REVIEW EXERCISE

Including Competency Based Questions

Part I

Multiple Choice Questions (MCQs)

1. **People go to weekly markets to buy**

(a) branded clothes (b) cars
(c) goods of everyday requirements (d) All of these

2. **What is the market called which is held on a specific day of a week?**

(a) Daily market (b) Vendor market
(c) Weekly market (d) None of these

3. **Shopkeepers in a weekly market are**

(a) large traders (b) wholesalers
(c) big businessmen (d) small traders

4. **Which among the following is not available in weekly markets?**

(a) Branded clothes (b) Vegetables
(c) Daily requirement items (d) None of these

5. **Market that caters to the immediate needs of the people in an area is called** Diksha

(a) super market (b) neighbourhood market
(c) shopping mall (d) weekly market

6. **In many urban areas, large multi-storeyed air-conditioned building with shops on different floors is known as**

(a) shops (b) complexes (c) market place (d) malls

7. **Branded goods are sold in**

(a) malls (b) roadside shops
(c) weekly markets (d) All of these

8. **Why less number of people can purchase branded products?** **Diksha**

(a) These products are sold by street vendors.
(b) These products are very costly.
(c) These products one sold in showrooms.
(d) These products are promoted by celebrities.

9. **Chain of markets involves** **Competency Based**

(a) Producer → Wholesaler → Retailer → Consumer
(b) Producer → Retailer → Wholesaler → Consumer
(c) Wholesaler → Retailer → Consumer
(d) Producer → Consumer

10. **What refers to buying and selling in large quantities?**

(a) Mall (b) Weekly market
(c) Wholesale (d) Complex

11. **Shopkeepers procure their goods from**

(a) factories (b) farms (c) wholesaler (d) All of these

12. **Identify the correct option which describes the type of market given below.** **Competency Based**

I. They establish their shops next day somewhere else.
II. These market face competition as there are many shops of same kind.
III. They do not have permanent buildings where they pay rent.

Codes

(a) Neighbourhood market (b) Weekly market
(c) Malls (d) Online market

13. **Choose the correct statement(s) from the following.**

I. Many things in weekly markets are at higher rates.
II. In urban markets, both branded and non-branded goods are a!vailable. **Competency Based**
III. Wholesale trader buys goods in large quantities.

Codes

(a) I and II (b) II and III
(c) I, II and III (d) None of these

14. **Choose the incorrect statement(s) from the following.** **Competency Based**

I. The trader who finally sells goods to the consumer is the retailer.
II. Wholesale markets are the place where goods reached first and then supplied to other traders.
III. There are some markets that we may not be aware of.

Codes

(a) I, II and III (b) Only III
(c) I and III (d) None of these

Answers

1. (c)	**2.** (c)	**3.** (d)	**4.** (a)	**5.** (b)
6. (d)	**7.** (a)	**8.** (b)	**9.** (a)	**10.** (c)
11. (d)	**12.** (b)	**13.** (b)	**14.** (d)	

Match the Following

1.

List I	List II
A. Weekly Markets	1. Buyer and seller know each other.
B. Neighbourhood shops	2. Provide goods at cheaper prices.
C. Shopping complexes and malls	3. Branded and non-branded goods are available.
D. Traders	4. People between producers and consumers.

Codes

	A	B	C	D		A	B	C	D
(a)	2	1	3	4	(b)	1	2	3	4
(c)	1	4	3	2	(d)	2	3	4	1

Ans. (a)

Assertion-Reason

1. **Assertion** (A) Weekly markets are held on a specific day of the week.

Reason (R) Weekly markets do not have permanent shops and traders set up shops for the day.

Codes

(a) Both A and R are true and R is the correct explanation of A
(b) Both A and R are true, but R is not the correct explanation of A
(c) A is true, but R is false
(d) A is false, but R is true

2. **Assertion** (A) The final consumer is the one who buys goods in large quantities from wholesalers.

Reason (R) Retailers play a minimal role in the distribution of goods.

Codes

(a) Both A and R are true and R is the correct explanation of A
(b) Both A and R are true, but R is not the correct explanation of A
(c) A is true, but R is false
(d) A is false, but R is true

Ans. 1. (a) Both A and R are true and R is the correct explanation of A

2. (d) A is false, but R is true

Fill in the Blanks

1. .... means buying and selling in large quantities.
2. .... is used for making online purchases.
3. The people in between the producer and the final consumer are the ....
4. Sameer is a .... trader in weekly market. **Competency Based**
5. ....products are usually sold in the shopping malls. **Diksha**
6. A wholesale trader sells the goods to a ....

Ans. 1. Wholesale 2. Internet
3. traders 4. small
5. Branded 6. retailer

True/False

1. Wholesaler sells the goods finally to the consumers.
2. The weekly market trader earns little profit compared to a regular shop owner in shopping complex.
3. Shopping malls and complexes are found mostly in urban areas.
4. Weekly markets sell both branded and non-branded goods.
5. Weekly markets do not have permanent shops.

Ans. 1. False 2. True 3. True
4. False 5. True

Picture Based Question

1. **The image shown below is of shop in neighbourhood. Which of the following is not the feature of neighbourhood shop?**

(a) Buyers and seller know each other
(b) Shop is near home
(c) Buyer can pay later
(d) Shop open weekly on particular day

Ans. (d) Shop open weekly on particular day

Case Based Question

1. **Read the passage given below and answer the question that follows.**

The people in between the producer and the final consumer are the traders. The wholesale trader first buys goods in large quantities. For example, the vegetable wholesale trader will not buy a few kilos of vegetables, but will buy in large lots of 25 to 100 kilos. These will then be sold to other traders. In these markets, buying and selling takes place between traders. It is through these links of traders that goods reach far away places. The trader who finally sells this to the consumer, is the retailer. This could be a trader in a weekly market, a hawker in the neighbourhood or a shop in a shopping complex.

(i) What is stored in a godown?
(a) Small quantities of goods
(b) Goods for selling there
(c) Consumer goods to stock
(d) Vegetables

(ii) Where do city wholesale traders typically purchase goods from?
(a) From retailer
(b) From consumer
(c) From smaller traders
(d) From factory

(iii) Who is the final link in the chain of markets before goods reach the consumer?
(a) Producers
(b) Wholesale traders
(c) Retailers
(d) Hawkers

(iv) Which term is used to purchase goods through internet?
(a) Online shopping (b) Mall shopping
(c) Retailing (d) Trading

Ans. (i) (c) Consumer goods to stock
(ii) (d) From factory
(iii) (c) Retailers
(iv) (a) Online shopping

Part II

Very Short Answer Type Questions

1. What do you mean by market?

Ans. Market is a place where buying and selling occurs.

2. What all things do we buy from markets?

Ans. We buy many things such as vegetables, groceries, medicines, clothes stationery, eatables, etc from the markets.

3. What kind of shops do the weekly market traders have?

Ans. Weekly market traders have temporary shops which they set up for the day and then close in the evening.

4. There is a competition among the shops in the weekly market. Why? Competency Based

Ans. There is a competition among the shops in the weekly market because there are many shops selling same products at cheap prices.

5. Why do people go to the weekly markets? Diksha

Ans. People go to the weekly markets for their everyday requirements.

6. What kind of shops we find in our neighbourhood?

Ans. We find many shops in our neighbourhood, some are permanent shops while others are roadside stalls.

7. What kind of markets are there in urban area ?

Ans. Urban areas have markets with many shops, mainly known as shopping complexes.

8. What kind of goods do you get in the urban markets?

Ans. Both branded and non–branded goods are available in the urban markets.

9. Why are branded goods expensive?

Ans. Branded goods are expensive because they are advertised and claims better quality.

10. Where are goods produced?

Ans. Goods are produced in factories, on farms and in homes.

11. Give reason why we do not buy goods directly from producers. Competency Based

Ans. We don't buy goods directly from producers because they are not interested in selling goods in small quantities.

12. Who buys goods from producers ?

Ans. Wholesale traders buy goods from producers.

13. Who acts as link between wholesalers and consumers?

Ans. Retailer acts as a link between wholesalers and consumers.

14. How can buyers be different people?

Ans. The buyers can be different from each other as there are many buyers who cannot afford even the cheapest goods while other buyers frequently visit malls and buy different items.

Short Answer Type Questions

1. What are the advantages of weekly market? Diksha

Ans. Advantages of weekly market are

- Most things we need are available at one place.
- People prefer going to a market where they have choice and a variety of goods so they go to weekly markets.
- Many things in weekly market are available at cheaper rates.
- If some trader were to charge a high price, people would move to another shop where the same thing may be available more cheaply or where the buyer can bargain and bring price down.

2. How are shops in neighbourhood useful? Diksha

Ans. Shops in neighbourhood are useful in many ways

- They are near our home and we can go there on any day of the week.
- Buyer and seller know each other and thus they also provide goods on credit. This means that you can pay for the purchases later.

3. Maya, a regular customer in the neighbourhood market, goes to her local grocery store to buy essential items. Due to unforeseen circumstances, Maya realises that she doesn't have enough cash with her. The kind shopkeeper, Mr. Sharma, knows Maya well and understands her situation. Instead of turning her away, he allows Maya to take the groceries she needs and promises to pay the amount later when she has the money. Competency Based

(i) What is pay on credit?

Ans. Pay on credit is when a customer obtains goods or services with the promise to pay for them later. In a neighbourhood market, if someone like Maya , faces a temporary shortage of cash, the shopkeeper may allow them to take essential items, trusting them to settle the payment at a later date.

(ii) How might this practice of pay on credit impact the relationship between the shopkeeper and the customer in the long run?

Ans. The practice of pay on credit can positively impact the relationship between the shopkeeper and the customer in the long run. It builds trust and a sense of understanding. The shopkeeper's flexibility to allow the customer to pay later increase loyalty, creating a lasting bond. Over time, this relationship can strengthen, as the customer values the shopkeeper's support and continues to choose the neighbourhood market for their needs.

4. 'Shop-owners in a weekly market and those in a shopping complex are different people'. Discuss. Competency Based

Ans. Shop-owners in a weekly market and those in a shopping complex are different people in the following ways

Shop-owners in Weekly Market	Shop-owners in Shopping Complex
They are small traders with little money to run the shop.	They spend a lot of money to establish the shop.
The weekly market traders earn little profit.	The profit of a regular shop owner in a shopping complex is more than the shop owner in weekly market.

5. From where do you think shop-owners procure their goods? Explain.

Ans. Shop-owners procure their goods through traders. Goods are produced in farms, factories and at homes. But goods are not bought directly from the producers i.e. from factory or farm. There are people between producers and customers who help in procuring goods. These people in between are known as traders.

6. Discuss the role of wholesaler and retailer.

Ans. Wholesalers and retailers are the people between producers and consumers.

Wholesaler is the first who buys goods in large quantities and then sells them to the retailers. Retailer is the trader who finally sells them to the consumers.
This connection of traders helps goods to reach far away places. Thus, wholesaler is in direct contact with producer while retailer is in direct contact with consumers.

7. What do you know about the online marketing? Diksha

Ans. Online markets are those markets through which buyer can buy or shop anything without going to market.

Buyers can buy almost everything through internet these days by sitting at home. It is not needed for the buyers to go to shop through malls, shop or retail store.

There are many online websites and application which can be used to buy goods. Goods purchased are delivered at home in available time. Money can also be paid through online transition. It makes shopping easy and convenient for people.

Long Answer Type Questions

1. Discuss in detail about kinds of markets in urban areas.

Ans. Urban areas have markets with many shops mainly known as shopping complexes. Also there are large member of multi-storeyed air-conditioned buildings with shops on different floors, referred to as malls.

Both branded and non-branded goods are available in these markets. Branded goods are expensive and promoted by advertising claiming better quality. The producers of these brands sell them with the help of shops and special showrooms in large urban markets. Only few people can afford these branded goods.

2. An economic advisor to a business man is making report on market chain to understand business in better way. Discuss the key point that should be mentioned to under the chain of market. Competency Based

Ans. The term chain of markets refers to the inter connected network of various levels through which goods and services pass from their initial production, to their consumers.

Goods are produced in factories, on farms or in homes. There are people who act as link between producers and the final consumers when are known as the traders. The wholesale trader buy large quantities of goods and then sell them to other traders.

In the markets, buying and selling takes place between traders. The trader who finally sells the goods to the consumer is called the retailer. This could be a trader in a weekly market, a hawker in the neighbourhood or a shop in a shopping complex.

The roadside hawker buys items from the wholesale trader in the town, who in turn have bought these from other big wholesaler trader in the city. The wholesale trader in the city would have bought these goods in a large quantity from the factory and stored them in a godown. In this way, a chain of markets is established.

3. Sunita is a wholesale rice distributor in her town. Her business day begins early at the local grain market. Around 4 am, trucks loaded with bags of rice from various rice mills start arriving. The market comes alive with the hustle and bustle of buyers and sellers. Sunita takes part in the bidding process, deciding on the rice varieties and quantities she wants to purchase. After winning the bids, she stores the rice in her warehouse within the market.

Around 7 am, local grocery stores and restaurant owners come to the market to purchase rice for their businesses. They need to make their purchases early so that they can open their shops and restaurants by 9 am.

Why is a wholesale trader necessary?

Or **How does a wholesale trader contribute to the overall economy of a region?**

Ans. A wholesale trader is necessary for several reasons as follows

- They help bridge the gap between manufacturers or producers and retailers. Manufacturers often produce goods in large quantities, while retailers sell them in smaller portions. Wholesale traders buy products in bulk from manufacturers and then distribute them to retailers in smaller quantities. This simplifies the supply chain, making it easier for retailers to access a wide variety of goods.

- Wholesale traders help maintain prices. By buying in bulk, they can negotiate better prices with manufacturers, which can lead to cost savings for retailers and ultimately, consumers.

Overall, wholesale traders play a crucial role in ensuring the efficient and cost effective distribution of goods, supporting the economy by connecting producers and retailers while helping to maintain stable prices.

4. Markets exist everywhere. Explain.

Ans. Markets exists everywhere, i.e. in every locality and work with proper procedure and time. Although, it is not compulsory for one to go to the market to buy goods. Orders can be placed on phone or through internet for variety of things and goods are delivered at our door steps.

For instance, there are sales representatives waiting for doctors in clinics and nursing homes, they are the people involved in the selling of goods. Hence, buying and selling can be done through various ways and not necessarily through shops in market places.

There are some markets that we don't recognise because there are goods which are traded but we don't use them directly. It means we don't normally see buying and selling but only the final product like the car in showroom.

Picture Based Question

1. On the basis of given picture, answer the questions that follows

(i) Who is the person in the above picture?

Ans. The person in the above picture is Aftab.

(ii) What kind of trader is he?

Ans. Aftab is one of the wholesale trader of vegetables. He has a shop in the market where he stores the vegetables that he has bought and sells to hawkers and shopkeepers.

Case Based Questions

1. Read the passage given below and answer the question that follows.

Sujata and Kavita were sent to buy groceries from their neighbourhood shop. This was the shop they usually went to. It was crowded today. The shop owner managed the shop herself with two helpers. When they managed to get into the shop, Sujata dictated a list to her. She in turn began asking her helpers to weigh and pack the items. Meanwhile Kavita looked around...

On the top left shelf there were different brands of detergent cakes. Another shelf had toothpastes, talcum powder, shampoo, hair oil. The different brands and different colours looked so attractive.
On the floor lay a few sacks.

It took almost 20 minutes to weigh and pack all the groceries. Then Sujata showed her "notebook." The woman noted the amount of
₹ 1550 in the notebook and gave it back. She also noted the amount in her big register.

Then Sujata took the heavy bags out of the shop. Her family will pay for the purchases in the first week of next month.

(i) Why did Sujata carry a notebook?

Ans. Sujata carried a notebook, so that amount of credit can be noted down in it.

(ii) Do you think this system is useful ? Can there be problems?

Ans. Yes, according to me this system is useful. People with low income can utilise this system.

The system of credit is totally dependent on trust between buyer and seller. If honesty is there, there can be no problems.

2. Read the passage given below and answer the question that follows.

Anzal Mall is a five-floor shopping complex. Kavita and Sujata were enjoying going up and down in the lift. It seemed as if it was made of glass and they were able to see outside as they went up. It was fascinating to see so many different kinds of shops such as the ice-cream, burger, pizza and other food shops; shops full of home appliances; footwear and leather items as well as bookshops.

While wandering about on the third floor they entered a shop that was selling branded ready-made clothes.

The security guard looked at them as if he wanted to stop them but he did not say anything. They looked at some dresses and then looked at the price tag.

None of them was less than ₹ 2000, almost five times the weekly market price! Sujata whispered to Kavita, "I'll take you to another shop which has good quality ready-made clothes at more reasonable prices".

(i) Why do you think guard wanted to stop Kavita and Sujata from entering the shop?

Ans. The guard wanted to stop Kavita and Sujata from entering the shop because he might have thought that they belong to poor family and cannot afford the items kept in shop.

(ii) What would you say if someone stops you from entering a shop in a market?

Ans. If anyone tries to stop me from entering a shop, I would speak up for my right and will stop that person from violating my dignity.

ASSESSMENT EXERCISE

Multiple Choice Questions (MCQs)

1. Which of the following is the characteristic of weekly market?

(a) Held on specific day
(b) Have permanent shops
(c) Used for everyday requirement
(d) Both (a) and (c)

2. Which of the following markets have maximum competition among traders?

(a) Neighbourhood
(b) Weekly market
(c) Malls
(d) None of the above

3. Which are the shops that provide goods on credit?

(a) Weekly market
(b) Malls
(c) Neighbourhood market
(d) All of the above

Subjective Questions (VSA, SA & LA)

1. What are people in between the producer and the final consumer called?

2. What do you mean by chain of markets?

3. Branded goods are sold in which type of market?

4. Name the market which do not have permanent shops.

5. How can you say that competition among shopkeepers in weekly market is in favour of consumer?

6. Write about the goods that are bought and sold by less aware markets.

7. Why many things are available at cheaper rate in weekly markets?

8. Write a short note on shopping complexes.

9. What are the processes involved in between production and consumption of goods?

10. Differentiate between shop owners of malls and weekly market.

CHAPTER 8

A Shirt in the Market

The making of a shirt, involves a large process starting from the production of cotton to the sale of the shirt. A chain of markets links the producer of cotton to the buyer of the shirt in the supermarket. This chain involves continuous buying and selling at every step.

8.1 Cotton Farmer in Kurnool

Cultivation[1] of cotton is expensive and difficult. In Kurnool (Andhra Pradesh), small farmers like Swapna grow cotton on their small piece of land.

After harvesting of cotton, farmers collect the cotton bolls. This harvest is taken to the local traders instead of selling it at Kurnool cotton market.

This is because farmers borrowed money at a **high interest rate** from the local trader, to buy seeds, fertilisers and pesticides for cultivation of cotton.

Even though the market price is high, the trader buys the harvest at a low price from the farmer.

8.2 The Cloth Market at Erode

The bi-weekly market of Erode in Tamil Nadu is one of the biggest cloth markets in the world. Cloth made by the weavers in the villages around Erode is sold in this market.

There are offices of cloth merchants around the market who buy this cloth. Many **South Indian traders** of other states also come to purchase the cloth in this market.

The cloth merchants purchase yarn and supply it to the weavers to make cloth according to their need. After the cloth has been produced by the weavers, the merchants supply the cloth on order to garment manufacturers and exporters around the country.

Putting Out System

It is a system where the merchants distribute work among the weavers according to the orders they have received.

The weavers get the yarn from the merchant and supply him the cloth.

This system is prevalent in the weaving industry in most regions of India.

This benefits the weavers in two ways as followos

- They do not have to spend money on the purchase of yarn.
- They do not have to care about the selling of finished cloth.

However, there are also some disadvantages as follows

- Weavers have to depend on merchants for raw materials and markets, which make merchants very powerful.
- Weavers are paid very less for making the cloth.

8.3 The Garment Exporting Factory Near Delhi

The Erode merchant supplied the cloth to a garment exporting factory near Delhi, to make shirts. The shirts will then be exported to the foreign buyers which include businessmen from US and Europe.

1 **Cultivation** It is the process of preparing and using soil for growing plants.

These businessmen run a chain of large stores on their own terms. They demand low prices from the supplier, high standards of quality and timely delivery. They do not accept any **defects** or **delay** in delivery.

This pressure from the buyers results in**cost**[2] cutting by garment factories who get the maximum work done by the workers at the lowest possible wages. In this way, they can maximise their profits and supply garments to foreign buyers at a cheap price.

Weaver's Cooperative

It is way to reduce the dependence of weaver on the merchant and to earn a higher income for the weavers. In a cooperative, people with common interests come together and work for their mutual benefit.

In a weaver's cooperative, the weavers form a group and take up certain activities collectively. They acquire yarn from the yarn dealer and distribute it among the weavers.

The cooperative also does the marketing. So, the role of the merchant is reduced, and weavers get a fair price on the cloth. Sometimes, the government helps the cooperatives by buying cloth from them at a reasonable price.

8.4 Gainers in the Market

In the market, some people made profits and some people did not gain as much from the buying and selling. They earned little despite their hard work.

Market and Equality

Everyone does not gain equally in the market. There are some people who make more profits than others.

The foreign businesspersons make huge profits in the market, while the garment**exporter**[3] make only moderate profits.

The earnings of the workers at the garment export factory are very low that they can only fulfil their day-to-day needs. The small cotton farmers and weavers do not get the fair price in the market for what they produced.

The merchant or traders earn more in comparison to the weavers, however it is less than the exporter.

It is usually the rich and the powerful people that get the maximum earnings from the market. These people have money and owns large shops, large land holdings, etc.

The poor have to depend on the rich and powerful for various things which include loans, raw materials and marketing of their goods and employment.

The poor are exploited in the market due to this dependence. There are some ways to overcome this exploitation such as formation of producers **cooperatives**[4] and ensuring that laws are followed strictly.

---

2 **Cost** It is the actual amount of expenditure incurred on a product.

3 **Exporter** It refers to a person who sells goods abroad.

4 **Cooperatives** It is an organisation that is owned and operated by the people who work there or people who use its services.

A SHIRT IN THE MARKET

Cotton Cultivation

- Expensive and difficult work.
- Farmers collect the cotton boils after harvest, and sell it to the local traders instead of cotton market.
- The trader buys the harvest at a low price than the market price.

Market and Equality

- Everyone does not gain equally in the market.
- The rich and powerful get the maximum profit.
- Poor depend on the rich for many things.
- Some ways to overcome exploitation of poor in the market
  - Formation of producers cooperatives
  - Ensuring that laws are followed strictly

Exports of Garments

- Demand low prices from the supplier, high standards of quality and timely delivery.
- Do not accept any defects or delay in delivery.

Weaver's Cooperative

- Weaver's form a group and take up certain activities collectively.
- Cooperative also does the marketing, so the role of merchant is reduced, and weavers get a fair price on the cloth.
- Sometimes, government helps the cooperative by buying cloth from them at reasonable price.

Putting Out System

- Weavers get the yarn from the merchant and supply him cloth.
- Advantages of the system
  - Weavers do not have to spend money on purchase of yarn.
  - They do not have to care about the selling of finished cloth.
- Disadvantages of the system
  - Weavers have to depend on merchants for raw materials and markets.
  - They are paid very less for making cloth.

NCERT FOLDER

Covering Intext Questions and Exercises of NCERT

NCERT ON PAGE 87

Q.1 Did Swapna get a fair price on the cotton?

Ans. No, Swapna did not get a fair price on the cotton.

Q.2 Why did the trader pay Swapna a low price?

Ans. The trader paid Swapna a low price because she was poor and financially dependent on the trader. She also could not sell her harvest in the market because she had promised to sell cotton to the trader trader in return of the loan taken by her.

Q.3 Where do you think large farmers would sell their cotton? How is their situation different from Swapna?

Ans. Large farmers would sell their cotton in the markets at higher rates. Their situation is different from Swapna as

- She is a small farmer.
- She has taken loan from the trader.
- She has promised to sell cotton to the trader.

NCERT ON PAGE 89

Q.4 What are the following people doing at the Erode cloth market

(a) Merchants (b) Weavers

(c) Exporters

Ans. (a) **Merchants** are selling/supplying the woven cloth in order to garment manufacturers and exporters around the country.

(b) **Weavers** are bringing cloth to the market which they have made on order from the merchant.

(c) **Exporters** are arranging cloth for exports.

Q.5 In what ways are weavers dependent on cloth merchants?

Ans. Weavers are dependent on cloth merchants for

- Raw materials
- Marketing their cloth

NCERT ON PAGE 90

Q.6 If the weavers were to buy yarn on their own and sell cloth, they would probably earn three times more. Do you think this is possible? How? Discuss.

Ans. If weavers were to buy yarn on their own and sell cloth, they would for sure earn more because in this case they would purchase yarn at lowest rates and would sell cloth at the highest possible rate. The middlemen i.e. trader will get removed from chain and hence, it will be the weaver who would earn all the profit.

Q.7 Do you find similar *'putting-out'* arrangements in making papads, masalas, beedis? Find out about this in your area and discuss in class.

Ans. Do it yourself.

Q.8 You might have heard of cooperatives in your area. It could be in milk, provisions, paddy, etc. Find out for whose benefit they were set up?

Ans. Cooperatives have been set up to help producers in the following ways

- To provide financial assistance at low interest rate.
- To purchase products from producers on reasonable prices.
- To save them from middlemen and traders.
- To increase bargaining power of the producers.

NCERT ON PAGE 91

Q.9 What are the demands foreign buyers make on the garment exporters? Why do the garment exporters agree to these demands?

Ans. The demands foreign buyers make on the garment exporters are

- Lowest prices for the garments.
- High standards for quality of production.
- Timely delivery with no defects.

The exporters agree to these demands because selling products to these powerful buyers will help them in earning profits.

Q.10 How do garment exporters meet the conditions set by the foreign buyers?

Ans. The garment exporters try to meet the conditions set by foreign buyers by cutting the costs. They get the maximum work done from the workers at lowest wages. This helps them in maximising profits.

NCERT ON PAGE 92

Q.11 Why do you think more women are employed in the Impex garment factory? Discuss.

Ans. More women are employed in the Impex garment factory because women are hard working and they work at cheaper rate. They are mostly employed as helpers for thread cutting, buttoning and ironing. These jobs have the lowest wages.

Q.12 Write a letter to the minister asking for what you think would be proper payments to the workers.

Ans. Do it yourself

NCERT ON PAGE 111

Q.13 Compare the earnings per shirt of the worker in the garment factory, the garment exporter and the businessperson in the market abroad. What do you find?

Ans. The earnings per shirt of different persons in the garment factory are

- Worker gets ₹ 15 per shirt.
- Garment exporter gets ₹ 100 per shirt.
- Foreign businessperson gets ₹ 600 per shirt.

The worker who contributes maximum earns very less whereas exporter and businesspersons earns a good amount.

Q.14 What are the reasons that the businessperson is able to make a huge profit in the market?

Ans. The businesspersons is able to make huge profit in the market due to the following reasons

- The businesspersons advertise their shirts in very attractive manner, which increases its sales.
- The businesspersons sell the garments to consumers who belong to high income group.
- The businessperson knows the ways to get the work done by workers at lowest price.

Q.15 You have read the chapter on advertising. Why does the businessperson spend ₹ 300 per shirt on advertising? Discuss.

Ans. The businessperson spends ₹ 300 per shirt on advertising because

- Advertising helps in building brands.
- Advertisements influences the lives of people and convince them to buy the product.
- It presents the shirt in such a way that people want to buy them instantly.

Q.16 Fill in the box.

People who gained in the market
1. ______
2. ______
3. ______
People who didn't gain as much in the market
1. ______
2. ______
3. ______

Ans. People who gained

- Foreign businesspersons
- Garment exporter
- Merchant

People who didn't gain as much in the market

- Weavers
- Farmers
- Workers

EXERCISES

Q.1 What made Swapna sell the cotton to the trader instead of selling at the Kurnool cotton market?

Ans. Swapna had to sell the cotton to the trader instead of selling at the Kurnool cotton market as she had borrowed money from a local trader at the beginning of the crop season. The local trader lent Swapna the required money but on a condition that she would sell all her cotton to him.

Q.2 Describe the conditions of employment as well as the wages of workers in the garment exporting factory. Do you think the workers get a fair deal?

Ans. The conditions of employment and wages of workers in the garment exporting factory are

- The workers have to work atleast 10-12 hours in a day.
- Their job is not permanent i.e. workers are hired on temporary basis.
- Their wages are fixed according to their skills.

According to me, workers are not getting a fair deal.

Q.3 **Think of something common that we use. It could be sugar, tea, milk, pen, paper, pencil, etc. Discuss through what chain of markets this reaches you. Can you think of the people that help in the production or trade?**

Ans. One common thing that we use is Sugar.

Chain of markets through which it reaches us include

People that help in the production or trade of sugar are as follows

- Farmers
- Workers
- Retailer
- Millowner
- Wholesaler
- Consumer

Q.4 **Arrange the statements given alongside in the correct order and then fill in the numbers in the cotton bolls accordingly. The first two have already been done for you.**

(i) Swapna sells the cotton to the trader.

(ii) Customers buy these shirts in a supermarket.

(iii) Trader sells cotton to the ginning mill.

(iv) Garment exporters buy the cloth from merchants for making shirts.

(v) Yarn dealers or merchants give the yarn to the weavers.

(vi) The exporter sells shirts to the businessperson from the USA.

(vii) Spinning mill buys the cotton and sells yarn to the yarn dealers.

(viii) Weavers return with the cloth.

(ix) Ginning mill cleans the cotton and makes it into bales.

Ans.

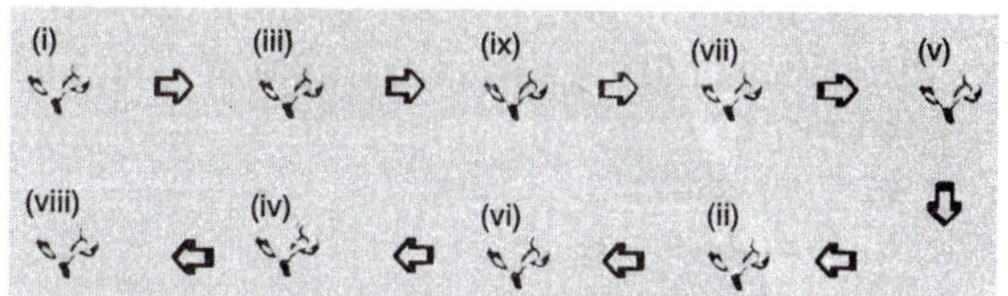

REVIEW EXERCISE

Including Competency Based Questions

Part I

Multiple Choice Questions (MCQs)

1. **Swapna is a small farmer in Kurnool and grows ....**

(a) wheat (b) rice
(c) cotton (d) maize

2. **Which is one of the largest cloth market in the world?**

(a) Delhi (b) Kolkata
(c) Tamil Nadu (d) Agra

3. **Who among the following is part of putting out system?**

(a) Farmer (b) Weavers
(c) Consumer (d) Foreign buyers

4. **Foreign buyers involve businesspersons from**

(a) US and Europe (b) US and South Africa
(c) Europe and Australia (d) China and Japan

5. **The series of markets that are connected in the form of a chain and pass goods from one market to others are** **Diksha**

(a) weekly markets (b) shopping malls
(c) online market (d) chain of market

6. **In what work are the women at the Impex garment factory involved in**

(a) Buttoning (b) Thread cutting
(c) Ironing (d) All of these

7. **What is the price of the shirt in United States at which it is sold ?**

(a) $ 26 (b) $ 24
(c) $ 28 (d) $ 22

8. The Erode merchants send the cloth to the garments export centre in Delhi. The garments factory makes shirts to be sold to the chain of business from the US and the Europe.

Identify the person who sends the manufactured garments to other countries of the world.

Options

(a) Manufacturer (b) Importer
(c) Exporter (d) Worker

9. The weavers live in villages around and take the yarn supplied by these traders to their homes where the looms are located in sheds adjacent to their houses. The weavers and their families spend long hours working on these looms. A variety of sarees, towels, shirting, ladies dress material and bedsheets are produced in these looms. They then bring back the finished cloth to the traders. Here, they can be seen getting ready to go to the merchant in the town.

The trader keeps an account of the yarn given and pays them money for weaving this into cloth.

The above passage is an example of what among the following?

(a) Cooperatives
(b) Manufacturing
(c) Putting out system
(d) Marketing

10. Choose the correct statement(s) from the following.

I. Small farmers generally take the harvest of cotton to the local trader and sell it to them.

II. The arrangement between the merchant and the weavers is an example of putting-out system.

Codes

(a) Only I (b) Only II
(c) Both I and II (d) None of these

11. Choose the incorrect statement(s) from the following.

I. The government does not help the cooperatives of weavers.

II. The Erode merchant supplies the cotton cloth produced by the weavers to a garment exporting factory near Delhi.

Codes

(a) Only I (b) Only II
(c) Both I and II (d) None of these

Answers

1. (c)	2. (c)	3. (b)	4. (a)	5. (d)
6. (d)	7. (a)	8. (c)	9. (c)	10. (c)
11. (a)				

Match the Following

1.

List I	List II
A. Tamil Nadu Government	1. Arrangement between the merchant and the weaver
B. Putting-out-system	2. Total cost of shirt in United States
C. Advertising, storage and purchase forms	3. Free school uniform programme
D. Erode's cloth market	4. Bi-weekly

Codes

	A	B	C	D		A	B	C	D
(a)	3	1	2	4	(b)	4	3	1	2
(c)	4	1	3	2	(d)	4	1	2	3

Ans. (a)

Assertion-Reason

1. **Assertion** (A) The exporter tries his best to meet the conditions set by the powerful buyers.

Reason (R) The exporter wants to maintain a good business relationship with the foreign businessperson.

Codes

(a) Both A and R are true and R is the correct explanation of A
(b) Both A and R are true, but R is not the correct explanation of A
(c) A is true, but R is false
(d) A is false, but R is true

2. **Assertion** (A) Garment exporting factories try to increase the cost by maximising worker productivity.

Reason (R) Businesspersons from the US and Europe run a chain of stores and set high standards for quality.

Codes

(a) Both A and R are true and R is the correct explanation of A
(b) Both A and R are true, but R is not the correct explanation of A
(c) A is true, but R is false
(d) A is false, but R is true

Ans. 1. (a) Both A and R are true and R is the correct explanation of A
2. (d) A is false, but R is true

Fill in the Blanks

1. Cultivation of ...... requires high levels of inputs.
2. Weavers are dependent on merchants for ...... and .... .

3. Merchant supplies cotton cloth to a ...... factory.
4. .... and the ...... gets the maximum earnings from the market.
5. Chain of markets link the producer to the ....

Ans. 1. cotton 2. raw materials and market
3. garment exporting 4. Rich, powerful
5. consumer

True/False

1. Buying and selling takes place only at last stage in the chain.
2. Erode's bi-weekly market is one of the largest cotton markets in the world.
3. A chain of markets links the producer of cotton to the buyer at the supermarket.
4. It is the foreign businesspersons who earns maximum profit in the market.

Ans. 1. False 2. True 3. True 4. True

Picture Based Question

1. The image given below is of a cloth shop in Erode which is one of the largest cloth markets in the world. Where is Erode situated?

(a) Rajasthan (b) Andhra Pradesh
(c) Telangana (d) Tamil Nadu

Ans. (d) Tamil Nadu

Case Based Question

1. Read the passage given below and answer the following questions.

We have seen that the weavers are paid little by the merchant under the putting out system. Weaver's cooperatives are one way to reduce the dependence on the merchant and to earn a higher income for the weavers. In a cooperative, people with common interests come together and work for their mutual benefit. In a weaver' cooperative, the weavers from a group and take up certain activities collectively. They procure yarn from the yarn dealer and distribute it among the wavers. The cooperative also does the marketing. So, the role of the merchant is reduced, and weavers get a fair price on the cloth.

(i) What is the main goal of weaver's cooperation?
(a) Increase income (b) Reduce dependence
(c) Yarn Procurement (d) Marketing

(ii) How does the merchant's role change in weaver's cooperatives?
(a) Reduced (b) Increased
(c) Unchanged (d) Eliminate

(iii) What state government runs the Free School Uniform Program?
(a) Karnataka (b) Tamil Nadu
(c) Kerala (d) Maharashtra

(iv) Which of the following SDG Goal is about decent work and economic growth?
(a) Goal 6 (b) Goal 7 (c) Goal 8 (d) Goal 9

Ans. (i) (b) Reduce dependence (ii) (a) Reduced
(iii) (b) Tamil Nadu (iv) (c) Goal 8

Part II

Very Short Answer Type Questions

1. Who is Swapna?

Ans. Swapna is a small cotton farmer in Kurnool, Andhra Pradesh.

2. Where does Swapna sell cotton?

Ans. Swapna sells cotton to the local trader, instead of selling cotton at the Kurnool cotton market.

3. How much is the earning of Swapna from cotton cultivation?

Ans. Swapna's earning from cotton cultivation is barely more than what she might have earned as a wage labourer.

4. "The small farmers need to borrow money to meet these expenses". Which expenses is being talked about. Discuss. Competency Based

Ans. The small farmers, like Swapna need to borrow money to meet the expenses for the cultivation of crop (cotton). The cultivation of cotton demands high level of inputs like fertilisers and pesticides for which huge amount of money is required.

5. What reason did trader gave for low price of cotton?

Ans. The reason trader gave for low price of cotton was that cotton was selling cheap and there was a lot of cotton in the market.

6. On what basis does the merchant distribute the work?

Ans. The merchant distributes the work based on the orders he has received for cloth.

7. For what purpose does the garment exporting factory will use the cloth?

Ans. The garment exporting factory will use the cloth for making the shirts.

Short Answer Type Questions

1. "Though Swapna knows that cotton will sell for atleast ₹ 1800 per quintal, she doesn't argue further". Discuss.

Ans. Swapna sold cotton at a price of ₹ 1500 per quintal and didn't argue for a higher price as the trader was a powerful man in the village and the farmers were dependent on him for loans and for money required for meeting their needs like illness, school fees, etc.

During no work period of the year, the farmers have to borrow money for their survival.

2. Discuss about the one of the largest cloth markets in the world discussed in the chapter.

Ans. Erode's bi-weekly cloth market situated in Tamil Nadu is one of the largest cloth markets in the world.

Large variety of cloth is available in this market. Cloth made by weavers of villages are also brought here for sale. Merchants and traders from many South Indian towns come to this market to buy cloth.

On market days, weavers bring cloth that has been made on order from the merchant. These merchants supply cloth on order to garment manufacturers and exporters around the country. They purchase the yarn and give instructions to the weavers about the kind of cloth to be made.

3. The merchant distributes work among the weavers based on the orders he has received for cloth. The weavers get the yarn from the merchant and supply him the cloth. Competency Based

(i) What is the advantage of weavers from merchant distributer?

Ans. The advantages of weavers from merchant distributer are

- They do not have to spend money on the purchase of yarn.
- They do not have to care about the selling of finished cloth.

(ii) What is the disadvantage of weavers from merchant distributer?

Ans. The disadvantages of weavers from merchant distributer are

- Weavers have to depend on merchants for raw materials and markets, which make merchants very powerful.
- Weavers are paid very less for making the cloth.

4. Why do the garment exporters meet the conditions set by the foreign buyers? How do they meet the conditions set by foreign buyers?

Ans. Indian garment exporters meet the conditions set by foreign buyers because it helps them in the form of increased business and income. Ensuring quality standards and timely deliveries builds trust, leading to repeat orders.

This supports their livelihoods, increases economic growth, and helps maintain a positive global reputation for Indian garment exports, ensuring long-term success for both parties.

The garment exporters meet the conditions set by foreign buyers by cutting the cost of producing. They get the maximum work out of the workers at the lowest possible wages.

5. Who are the gainers in the market? Does everyone gain equally in the market? Explain.

Ans The gainers in the market include the foreign business person garment exporter and merchant.

No, everyone does not gain equally in the market. There are some people who make more profits than others. The foreign businesspersons make huge profits in the market. Compared to this, the garment exporter make only moderate profits.

The earnings of the workers at the garment export factory are very low that they can only cover their day-to-day needs.

The small cotton farmers and weavers do not get the fair price in the market for what they produced. The merchant or traders earn more in comparison to the weavers, however it is less than the exporter.

Long Answer Type Questions

1. Suresh is planning to engage in the cloth exporting business. He asked his cloth merchant friend to tell him about the business of cloth. Write in detail what point his friend should mention to understand the cloth exporting business. Competency Based

Ans. The cloth exporting buisness involves a process in which the merchant supplied the cloth to a garment exporting factory, which is used to make shirts and other garments. The garments will then be exported to the foreign buyers which include businessmen from US and Europe.

These businessmen run a chain of large stores on their own terms. They demand low prices from the supplier, high standards of quality and timely delivery. They do not accept any defects or delay in delivery.

This pressure from the buyers results in cost cutting by garment factories who get the maximum work done by the workers at the lowest possible wages this way, they can maximise their profits and supply garments to foreign buyers at a cheap price.

2. To increase the sale of hand-woven textiles, the government operates stores under the brand "Gujarat Handloom Emporium." These stores serve as a platform for handloom weaver's cooperatives to showcase and sell their products. The government's involvement ensures fair trade practices and provides a direct link between consumers and producers.

(i) What are weaver's cooperatives of producers? Explain.

Ans. Weaver's cooperatives are a way to reduce the dependence of weaver on the merchant and to earn a higher income for the weavers. In a cooperative, people with common interests come together and work for their mutual benefit.

In a weaver's cooperative, the weavers form a group and take up certain activities collectively. They acquire yarn from the yarn dealer and distribute it among the weavers.

The cooperative also does the marketing. So, the role of the merchant is reduced, and weavers get a fair price on the cloth.

(ii) How are weavers dependent on merchants?

Ans. Weavers are dependent on merchants in the following ways

- Cloth merchants act as intermediaries, connecting the weaver's products to a wider market. Weavers often lack direct access to consumers, and merchants bridge this gap, helping them sell their textiles.
- Cloth merchants also provide financial support by purchasing the fabrics in bulk, guaranteeing a steady income for the weavers.

3. 'The poor depend on rich and powerful for loans. Because of this dependence, the poor are exploited.' Explain how. Also discuss the ways to overcome this exploitation. Competency Based

Ans. The poor depend on rich and powerful for loans. Because of this dependence, the poor are exploited.

It is usually the rich and the powerful people that get the maximum earnings from the market. These people have money and own large shops large land holdings, etc.

The poor have to depend on the rich and powerful for various things which include loans, raw materials and marketing of their goods. and employment. The poor are exploited in the market due to this dependence.

There are some aways to overcome this exploitation such as formation of producers cooperatives and ensuring that laws are followed strictly.

Picture Based Questions

1. Observe the picture given below and answer the questions that follow.

Picture 1

Picture 2

Picture 3

(i) What do you understand by looking at picture 1?

(ii) What do you know about powerlooms?

(iii) What are the traders doing in the 3rd picture?

Ans. (i) This is a merchant's shop in the bazaar. Over the years, these traders have developed extensive contacts with garment firms around the country from whom they get orders. These traders purchase the yarn (thread) from others.

(ii) Powerloom is a type of mechanised loom that is run by electricity instead of hand.

Most weaving units have about 2-8 powerlooms on which the yarn is woven into cloth. A variety of sarees, towels, shirting, ladies dress material and bedsheets are produced in these looms.

(iii) Here, traders here can be seen getting ready to go to the merchant in the town. The trader keeps an account of the yarn given and pays them money for weaving this into cloth.

2. The shirt given below shows the profit made by the businessperson and the various costs that he had to pay. Find out from the diagram below, what the cost price includes.

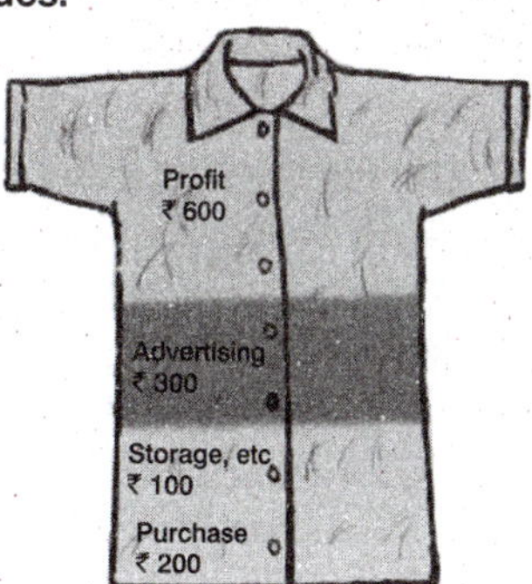

Ans. The cost price of the shirt includes

Advertising + Storage + Purchase

$= ₹\ 300 + ₹\ 100 + ₹\ 200 = ₹\ 600$

Case Based Question

1. Read the passage given below and answer the following questions.

The weavers get the yarn from the merchant and supply him the cloth. For the weavers, this arrangement seemingly has two advantages. The weavers do not have to spend their money on purchase of yarn. Also, the problem of selling the finished cloth is taken care of. Weavers know from the outset what cloth they should make and how much of it is to be woven. However, this dependence on the merchants both for raw materials and markets means that the merchants have a lot of power. They give orders for what is to be made and they pay a very low price for making the cloth. The weavers have no way of knowing who they are making the cloth for or at what price it will be sold. At the cloth market, the merchants sell the cloth to the garment factories. In this way, the market works more in favour of the merchants.

(i) How do merchants have a lot of power?

Ans. Merchants have a lot of power as the weavers are dependent on them both for raw materials and markets.

(ii) How do merchants exploit the weavers?

Ans. Merchants exploit the weavers by giving orders for what is to be made and they pay a very low price for making the cloth.

(iii) What are the advantages for the weavers in the arrangement explained above?

Ans. The advantages for the weavers are that they do not have to spend their money on purchase of yarn. Also, the problem of selling the finished cloth is solved.

ASSESSMENT EXERCISE

Multiple Choice Questions (MCQs)

1. Which high levels of inputs are required in cultivation of cotton?

(a) Water (b) Fertilisers
(c) Pesticides (d) Both (b) and (c)

2. One of the which is largest markets in the world situated in Tamil Nadu?

(a) Kurnool cotton (b) Erode's bi-weekly
(c) Local bazaar (d) Both (a) and (b)

3. Government exporting factories get the maximum work out of the workers at

(a) maximum wages (b) lowest possible wage
(c) free of cost (d) None of these

Subjective Questions (VSA, SA & LA)

1. Why small farmers need to borrow money for cotton cultivation?
2. Who distribute works among the weavers?
3. Give an example of putting-out-system.
4. Why Swapna take the harvest to the local trader?
5. Write about advantages of weavers in the arrangement with merchant.
6. Why weavers earned little despite their hard work?
7. How can you say that merchants have a lot of power?
8. Discuss about shirts in the United States.
9. Write in detail about difficulties faced by small farmers.
10. Write a short note on market and equality.

SAMPLE QUESTION PAPERS

Sample Question Paper 1 (Solved)

Social Science

Time : 3 hrs M.M. : 80

General Instructions

1 All questions are compulsory.

2 Marks for each question are indicated against the question.

Multiple Choice Questions (MCQs)

1. In which century did the geographer Al-Idrisi create the map showing the Indian sub-continent from land to sea? (1)

(a) 10th century (b) 11th century
(c) 12th century (d) 13th century

2. During which historical period was the wall relief of Vishnu as Narasimha created? (1)

(a) Gupta period (b) Maurya period
(c) Rashtrakuta period (d) Chola period

3. Match the following. (1)

	List I		List II
A.	Qutbuddin Aibak	1.	1266-1287
B.	Shamsuddin Iltutmish	2.	1210-1236
C.	Raziyya	3.	1236-1240
D.	Ghiyasuddin Balban	4.	1206-1210

Codes

	A	B	C	D		A	B	C	D
(a)	4	2	3	1	(b)	1	3	2	4
(c)	3	2	1	4	(d)	2	4	1	3

4. Consider the following statements and identify in whose reign these conditions existed. (1)

(i) Revenue collected from jagir was often less than the salary of the mansabdar.

(ii) Peasantry was suffering tremendously.

(iii) The number of mansabdars had increased to 79.

Options

(a) Akbar (b) Aurangzeb (c) Shah Jahan (d) Jahangir

5. What does population density measure? (1)

(a) The size of a population in a given area
(b) The number of animals in a specific habitat
(c) The number of persons per square kilometer
(d) The total area covered by a population

6. Which of the following best defines the term 'biotic'? (1)

(a) Inanimate objects
(b) Non-living matter
(c) The world of living organisms
(d) Geological formations

7. What is the thinnest layer among the Earth's layers? (1)

(a) Mantle (b) Outer core (c) Inner core (d) Crust

8. Which device records seismic waves caused by earthquakes? (1)

(a) Telescope (b) Microscope
(c) Seismograph (d) Spectrometer

9. A recent report from the Yale Program on Climate Change Communication and C Voter International reveals that a large majority of the Indian public, specifically 82%, are either alarmed or concerned about global warming.

Should reports on global warming be taken into account by the government? (1)

(a) Yes, global warming is happening, government should make plans to tackle it.
(b) Yes, global warming is going to happen in future, government should make policy for it.
(c) No, global warming is only politically motivated issue.
(d) No, there is no impact of global warming, it is hypothetical concept.

10. What is the approximate salinity level of the dead sea in grams per liter of water? (1)

(a) 150 grams (b) 250 grams
(c) 340 grams (d) 500 grams

11. Which of the following statements accurately defines the principle of equality as recognised in the Indian Constitution? (1)

Statement I "Equality under the Indian Constitution means the absence of any form of inequality, ensuring identical treatment for all individuals regardless of their background."

Statement II "The recognition of equality in the Indian Constitution ensures that every person is treated as identical, disregarding any differences in caste, religion or economic status."

Codes

(a) Statement I is true, but Statement II is false
(b) Statement I is false, but Statement II is true
(c) Both statements I and II are correct
(d) Both statements I and II are incorrect

12. Under whose supervision do the nurses and village health workers operate at the village-level health centers? **(1)**

(a) Specialists from urban hospitals
(b) Community leaders in the village
(c) Doctors at the Primary Health Centre (PHC)
(d) Non-Governmental Organisation (NGO) representatives

13. Assertion (A) The establishment of anganwadis and mandatory creche facilities by the government has positively impacted female employment and girls' education.

Reason (R) The provision of crèches in organisations and child-care centers in villages has enabled women to pursue employment opportunities and increased school attendance for girls. **(1)**

Codes

(a) Both A and R are true and R is the correct explanation of A
(b) Both A and R are true, but R is not the correct explanation of A
(c) A is true, but R is false
(d) A is false, but R is true

14. What does censorship refer to in the context of media? **(1)**

(a) The promotion of news items and movies to the public
(b) The act of preventing for sharing the certain news items, movie scenes, or song lyrics with the larger public
(c) The encouragement of open discussions on controversial topics
(d) The regulation of media for profit maximisation

Fill in the Blanks

1. Shankara, one of the most influential philosophers of India, was born in .... in the 8th century. **(1)**

2. The place where a river flows into another body of water is called the .... **(1)**

3. .... is the first known autobiography written by an Indian woman. **(1)**

True or False

1. The term kathak is derived from katha, a word used in Sanskrit and other languages for story. **(1)**

2. The climate of the Sahara desert is scorching wet and parch dry. **(1)**

3. The arrangement between the merchant and the weavers is an example of putting-out system. **(1)**

Very Short Answer Type Questions

1. Why did Alauddin Khalji and Muhammad Tughlaq face administrative challenges in Delhi? **(2)**

2. Every morning Ravi waits for the arrival of trucks filled with vegetables from the farm. The shopkeepers rush towards him to stock up the fresh products for their own businesses. What is the role of Ravi as described here? **(2)**

3. What is the uppermost layer of the Earth's surface called? **(2)**

Or

What process leads to the formation of sedimentary rocks?

4. What impact does changing technology have on the ways media reaches people and influences their perceptions? **(2)**

5. What succession tradition did the Mughals follow? **(2)**

Or

What does the term 'mansabdar' signify in the Mughal context?

Short Answer Type Questions

1. Explain the challenges historians face with ancient manuscripts. **(3)**

2. Write about the cultural influence and contributions of the Cheras in Kerala. **(3)**

Or

Describe how food habits in Bengal were influenced by local resources and cultural norms.

3. Why is it important for citizens to pay taxes to the government? **(3)**

4. Abhishek, who belongs to Karnataka, recently went to Ladakh in winter and after he returned home he told his friend about the scenic beauty of Ladakh and its climate.

   Describe the geographical features and climate of Ladakh. **(3)**

5. How does the environment influence agriculture in the Ganga-Brahmaputra basin? **(3)**

6. Explain the concept of equality in the Indian Constitution. **(3)**

   Or

   Discuss the protections provided by Article 15 of the Indian Constitution.

Long Answer Type Questions

1. Trace the historical evolution of Kathak and its significance in Indian dance forms. **(5)**

   Or

   Kavita watched a Bengali film with one of her friends and she got interested in the language. So, she went to her Bengali friend's house and asked her grandmother about the evolution of Bengali language and its influence through history.

   How would Kavita's grandmother explain here about the Bengali language?

2. Describe India's healthcare infrastructure and its global significance. **(5)**

   Or

   Why is the public health service considered essential according to the Constitution?

3. Explain the various ways in which a river shapes the landscape. **(5)**

   Or

   Explain the movement of lithospheric plates and their impact on the Earth's surface.

Case Based Questions

1. **Read the given passage and answer the questions that follow. (4)**

   Delhi first became the capital of a kingdom under the Tomara Rajputs, who were defeated in the middle of the 12th century by the Chauhans (also referred to as Chahamanas) of Ajmer. It was under the Tomaras and Chauhans that Delhi became an important commercial centre. Many rich Jaina merchants lived in the city and constructed several temples. Coins minted here, called dehliwal, had a wide circulation. The transformation of Delhi into a capital that controlled vast areas of the sub-continent started with the foundation of the Delhi Sultanate in the beginning of the 13th century. The Delhi Sultans built many cities in the area that we now know as Delhi.

   (i) Who were the early rulers of Delhi before the foundation of the Delhi Sultanate? (1)

   (ii) What made Delhi an important commercial center during the Tomara and Chauhan rule? (2)

   (iii) When did the transformation of Delhi into a vast capital territory begin? (1)

2. **Read the given passage and answer the questions that follow. (4)**

   Carbon dioxide released in the atmosphere creates a green house effect by trapping the heat radiated from the Earth. It is therefore called a greenhouse gas and without it the Earth would have been too cold to live in. However, when its level in the atmosphere increases due to factory smoke or car fumes, the heat retained increases the temperature of the Earth. This is called global warming. This rise in temperature causes the snow in coldest parts of the world to melt. As a result, the sea level rises, causing floods in the coastal areas. There may be drastic changes in the climate of a place leading to extinction of some plants and animals in the long run.

   (i) What is the role of carbon dioxide in the atmosphere? (1)

   (ii) What happens when the level of carbon dioxide in the atmosphere increases due to human activities? (1)

   (iii) How does global warming contribute to changes in the Earth's climate? (2)

3. **Read the given passage and answer the questions that follow. (4)**

   The government can also decide to make new laws for the state regarding sanitation and health facilities. For example, it may make it compulsory for municipal corporations to ensure that there are adequate toilets in every urban area. It may also ensure that a health worker is appointed in every village. This act of making laws on certain issues is done in the Legislative Assembly of each state. The various government departments then implement these laws. Laws for the entire country are made in the Parliament. In a democracy, it is the people who elect their representatives as Members of the Legislative Assembly (MLAs) and, thus, it is the people who have the main authority. The ruling party members then form the government and some members are appointed ministers.

(i) Where are state laws regarding sanitation and health facilities made? (1)

(ii) Who has the primary authority in a democracy according to the given information? (1)

(iii) What role do ruling party members play in a democracy? (2)

Map Based Question

1. (a) On the political map of India, locate the following. (3)

(i) The place captured by Ibrahim Lodhi – Panipat

(ii) The place of Rajput ruler of Amber – Jaipur

(iii) The place in Gujarat where earthquake hit in 2001 – Bhuj

(b) On the given political outline map of India, identify the following. (2)

(i) A mountain range

(ii) The region ruled by Sisodia Rajput

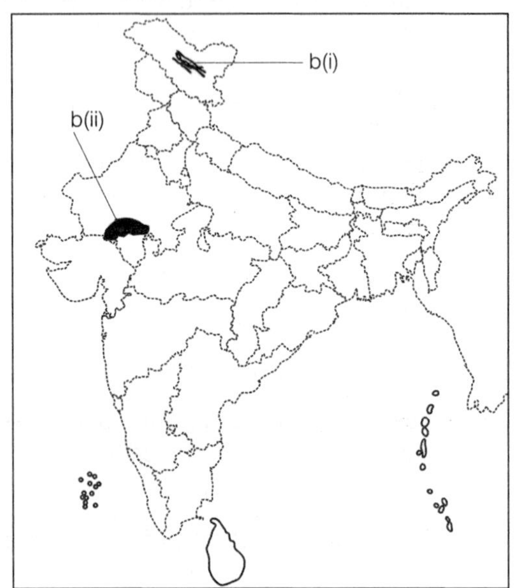

Answers

Multiple Choice Questions

1. (b)	**2.** (c)	**3.** (a)	**4.** (b)	**5.** (c)
6. (c)	**7.** (d)	**8.** (c)	**9.** (a)	**10.** (c)
11. (d)	**12.** (c)	**13.** (a)	**14.** (b)	

Fill in the Blanks

1. Kerala **2.** river's mouth **3.** Amar Jiban

True or False

1. True **2.** False **3.** True

Very Short Answer Type Questions

1. Alauddin Khalji and Muhammad Tughlaq had a hard time to face administrative challenges in Delhi because they had to deal with frequent attacks from the Mongols. To protect against these attacks, they had to maintain a big army, which was tough to handle.

2. Ravi here is described as a wholesale trader who purchases vegetables in bulk from farms and then sells these goods to shopkeepers of city markets, thereby facilitating the distribution of goods from farms to consumers.

3. The uppermost layer of the Earth's surface is called the crust, and it is the thinnest layer among all the layers.

Or The sedimentary rocks are formed when tiny particles called sediments, made from broken down rocks, are carried by wind or water, then compressed and hardened over time.

4. Changing technology significantly broadens media outreach, enhancing audio-visual quality and altering perspectives on life. Advanced tools enable instant access to diverse content, shaping opinions through personalised information, potentially impacting perspectives and beliefs significantly.

5. Mughals divided their inheritance among all sons, unlike giving everything to the eldest son. They followed succession inheritance, sharing the estate among multiple sons instead of just one.

Or A 'mansabdar' in the Mughal system was someone with a specific rank and salary decided by a number called zat. This number determined their military duties and position.

Short Answer Type Questions

1. Historians face several challenges when studying ancient manuscripts, which are handwritten documents from the past. Some of the main challenges are
   - Preservation of manuscripts are often centuries old and can be incredibly delicate. The ink may have faded, the paper may have decay, or the document may have been damaged over time. These issues can make it challenging to decode the text accurately.
   - Interpretation can contain different languages, scripts, styles, and genres of writing. They can also reflect the biases, perspectives, and agendas of the scribes who copied them. These factors can make it difficult to understand the meaning and context of the manuscripts.
   - Fragmentation of manuscripts are often incomplete or broken into pieces due to accidents, fires, wars, or vandalism. They may also be separated from their original contexts or bindings due to transfers or migrations. These situations can make it hard to reconstruct the whole manuscript and its original appearance.
2. The cultural influence and contributions of the Cheras in Kerala were as follows
   - The Chera kingdom, formed in the 9th century in present-day Kerala, played a significant role in promoting Malayalam language and script.
   - They notably used Malayalam in official inscriptions, among the earliest instances in the sub-continent.
   - While emphasising regional language, the Cheras also valued Sanskritic traditions. They incorporated Sanskrit stories into Kerala's temple theatre.
   - The earliest Malayalam literary works, dating back to the 12th century, were influenced by Sanskrit.

Or The food habits in Bengal primarily revolve around locally available resources, prominently rice and fish due to the region's riverine nature. Even among financially challenged Bengalis, rice and fish remain staple foods. While Brahmanas traditionally avoided non-vegetarian food, the popularity of fish in Bengal's diet led to the relaxation of this prohibition.

The Brihaddharma Purana from the 13th century, originating in Bengal, specifically permitted Bengal Brahmanas to consume certain fish varieties, showcasing the influence of local culture on dietary practices.

3. It is important for citizens to pay taxes to the government because taxes are the main source of revenue for the government and it uses tax money to provide various public goods and services that benefit the society. Some of the reasons why paying taxes is important are
   - Taxes are required to fund development programme and services, such as health care, education and social welfare.
   - Taxes contribute to the welfare schemes that help different sectors of the society, such as employment programs, subsidy on home loans, concession on cooking gas, pension schemes, etc. These schemes improve the quality of life and reduce poverty and inequality among the citizens.
   - Tax money is utilised for relief and rehabilitation in case of natural disasters.
4. The geographical features and climate of Ladakh are as follows
   - Ladakh is situated in the Great Himalayas within Jammu and Kashmir. It is enclosed by mountain ranges, specifically the Karakoram Range to the North and the Zanskar mountains to the South.
   - Ladakh's altitude varies from 3,000 m to over 8,000 m.
   - The area experiences extremely cold and dry weather due to its high altitude. The thin air at this altitude intensifies the Sun's heat.
   - During summers, daytime temperatures just rise above zero, while nights temperature below –30°C and in winter temperature remain below –40°C for most of the time..
5. The environment in the Ganga-Brahmaputra basin significantly influences agriculture in the following ways
   - The main river Ganga and Brahmaputra drain the area to make soil fertile.
   - The fertile soil is suitable for agriculture, resulting in a high population.
   - Agriculture is the main occupation in the plain areas where crops like paddy, wheat, maize, sorghum, gram and millets are grown.
   - Cash crops such as sugarcane and jute are also cultivated in the plain areas.
   - Banana plantations are found in some regions, while tea is grown in plantations in West Bengal and Assam.
6. The concept of equality in the Indian Constitution means that all citizens are equal before the law and have equal rights and opportunities in matters of public life. The Constitution also prohibits discrimination on the

basis of religion, race, caste, sex, place of birth, or any other grounds. The Constitution also abolishes untouchability and titles that confer social privileges.

The concept of equality is derived from the Preamble of the Constitution, which states that India is a sovereign, socialist, secular, democratic republic that secures justice, liberty, equality and fraternity to all its citizens. It is also reflected in various fundamental rights and directive principles of state policy that aim to promote social justice and welfare for all sections of society.

Or The protections provided by Article 15 of the Indian Constitution are as follows

- Article 15 of the Indian Constitution prohibits discrimination solely based on religion, race, caste, sex, or place of birth.
- It ensures that the state cannot discriminate against any citizen on these grounds. Moreover, citizens are safeguarded from facing any form of disability, restriction, or condition in accessing public places like shops, restaurants, or entertainment venues.
- Additionally, they cannot be deprived of using facilities like wells, roads, or bathing ghats maintained or dedicated to the public due to these factors, ensuring equal treatment and access for all.

Long Answer Type Questions

1. The historical evolution of Kathak and its significance in Indian dance forms are as follows

Historical Evolution

- Kathak, initially associated with North Indian temples, originated from the Kathaks, who were storytellers integrating gestures and songs.
- Its evolution occurred during the 15th and 16th centuries, influenced by the bhakti movement, portraying Radha-Krishna tales in folk plays such as rasa lila.
- Mughal patronage refined Kathak in court performances, leading to distinct gharanas in Jaipur and Lucknow.
- By the 19th century, Kathak expanded to regions like Punjab, Haryana, Jammu and Kashmir, Bihar, and Madhya Pradesh.

Significance

- The dance form emphasised intricate footwork, elaborate costumes, and storytelling.
- Despite British disapproval, Kathak persisted through courtesan performances.
- It gained recognition as one of India's classical dance forms post-independence, signifying its enduring cultural significance.

Or The evolution of Bengali language and its influence through history was as follows

- The Bengali language, also called Bangla, is an Indo- European language that evolved from the Indo- Aryan languages, such as Magadhi, Prakrit and Pali.
- In the mid-first millennium BCE, Sanskrit texts suggest that the people of Bengal did not originally speak Sanskritic languages.
- From the fourth-third centuries BCE, commercial ties between Bengal and Magadha (South Bihar) grew, potentially increasing the influence of Sanskrit.
- In the seventh century, the Chinese traveler Xuan Zang noted the prevalence of languages related to Sanskrit in Bengal, indicating a significant linguistic influence from Sanskrit.
- By the eighth century, Bengal became the center of a regional kingdom under the Palas, fostering the development of a regional language.
- By the fifteenth century, the Bengali group of dialects was united by a common literary language based on the spoken language of the Western part of the region, leading to the emergence of modern Bengali.
- Modern Bengali incorporated a wide range of non-Sanskrit words from various sources, including tribal languages, Persian and European languages, enriching its vocabulary.

2. India's healthcare infrastructure and its global significance are as follows

Healthcare in India

- India hosts the largest number of medical colleges globally, producing over 30,000 new doctors each year, showcasing its significant contribution to the healthcare workforce.
- Renowned hospitals in India attract numerous medical tourists seeking high-quality treatment, reflecting the country's advancement in providing world-class healthcare services.
- As the third-largest producer of medicines globally, India exports pharmaceuticals extensively, contributing significantly to the global healthcare market.

Global Significance

- India's renowned hospitals attract numerous medical tourists worldwide, underscoring its global reputation for offering superior healthcare services.
- Being a significant exporter of medicines, India's pharmaceutical industry plays a crucial role in meeting global healthcare demands.
- India's step in medical sciences, including the development of advanced technologies and treatment procedures, signify its global contribution to the healthcare domain.

Or The Constitution considers the public health service essential as it upholds citizens' right to life and welfare. According to the Constitution, the government is mandated to ensure healthcare accessibility for all. This service is sustained by funds derived from taxpayers and aims to deliver accessible healthcare to everyone. Its primary goal is safeguarding the right to life by providing timely medical interventions.

The public health service also includes measures such as improving water and sanitation, organising free camps for check-ups, spreading health awareness, and providing emergency services. The Constitution also supports a view that the right to health is an aspect of our fundamental rights. Therefore, the public health service is essential for fulfilling our basic needs and protecting our well-being.

3. Ways in which a river shapes the landscape are as follows

- **Erosion and Waterfalls** Rivers erode the landscape through the force of running water, particularly over hard rocks or steep valleys, forming waterfalls.
- **Meanders** In plains, rivers create large bends known as meanders, formed due to continuous erosion and deposition along their sides.
- **Ox-bow Lakes** Ongoing erosion causes the ends of meander loops to come closer until they eventually cut off, forming ox-bow lakes.
- **Floodplain Formation** River flooding results in the deposition of sediments along the banks, creating fertile floodplains. Raised banks formed during flooding are termed levees.
- **Distributaries and Delta Formation** As rivers approach the sea, reduced speed leads to the creation of distributaries—multiple streams branching out. These distributaries deposit their load, forming individual mouths. The accumulation of sediments from these mouths contributes to the formation of a delta.

Or The movement of lithospheric plates is the theory that explains how the Earth's outer layer, called the lithosphere, is divided into several rigid and irregular-shaped plates that carry continents and ocean floors. These plates move very slowly because of the movement of the molten magma inside the earth, which acts as a lubricant.

The movement of these plates causes impacts on the surface of the Earth, such as

- **Volcanic activity** When two plates collide or diverge, they create zones of subduction or rifts, where magma rises to the surface and forms volcanoes.
- **Earthquakes** When two plates slide past each other or move away from each other, they create friction and stress along their boundaries. This can result in sudden movements of large masses of rock, called faults, which cause earthquakes.
- **Mountain-building** When two plates converge or diverge, they push up or pull down on each other, creating highlands or lowlands.

Case Based Questions

1. (i) The Tomara Rajputs early ruled Delhi until their defeat by the Chauhans (Chahamanas) of Ajmer in the 12th century.

(ii) During the Tomara and Chauhan rule, Delhi became significant due to rich Jaina merchants residing there who constructed temples, and the wide circulation of dehliwal coins.

(iii) The transformation commenced at the start of the 13th century with the establishment of the Delhi Sultanate, which led to the construction of multiple cities in the area now known as Delhi.

2. (i) Carbon dioxide acts as a greenhouse gas, trapping heat radiated from the Earth, creating a livable temperature; without it, the Earth would be too cold.

(ii) Increased carbon dioxide causes global warming, raising Earth's temperature. This melting results in rising sea levels and coastal floods, altering climate and potentially causing plant and animal extinctions.

(iii) Global warming from increased carbon dioxide levels leads to temperature rise, causing snowmelt, rising sea levels, coastal floods, and eventual climate changes, potentially resulting in plant and animal extinctions.

3. (i) State laws on sanitation and health facilities are made in the Legislative Assembly of each state.
(ii) In a democracy, the people hold the primary authority as they elect their representatives (MLAs) who make laws in the Legislative Assembly.
(iii) Members of the ruling party who are elected by the people, constitute the government at the state level. They are responsible for appointing ministers and overseeing the implementation of laws passed in the Legislative Assembly.

Map Based Question

1.

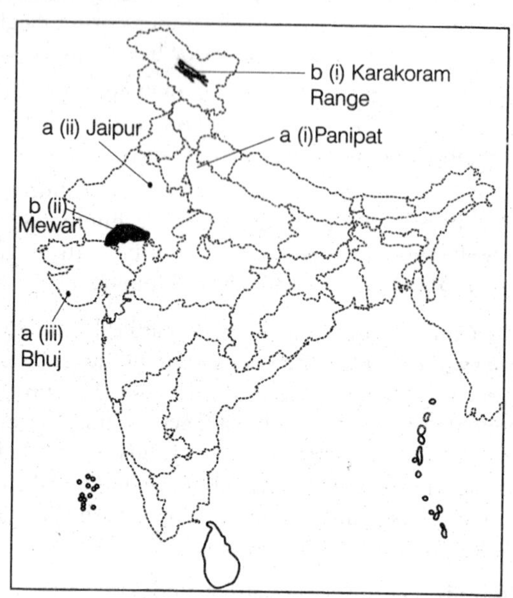

Sample Question Paper 2 (Unsolved)

Social Science

Time : 3 hrs M.M. : 80

General Instructions

1 All questions are compulsory.

2 Marks for each question are indicated against the question.

Multiple Choice Questions (MCQs)

1. Which of the following best defines an archive? (1)

(a) A place for storing personal belongings
(b) A facility for keeping historical monuments
(c) A location to maintain old official records and manuscripts
(d) A space exclusively for scientific experiments

2. What was Mahmud of Ghazni's primary motive behind his raids in the Indian sub-continent? (1)

(a) Economic prosperity
(b) Political dominance
(c) Religious motivation
(d) Cultural exploration

3. "In India, cultural and religious restrictions often come in the way of women realising their full potential. Education is a tool for self-awareness that helps them to stand up for themselves, have a better awareness of their rights and to change subjugation and patriarchy."

Source Times of India

Which of the following is a cultural or religious restriction that can come in the way of women realising their full potential in India? (1)

(a) Lack of access to education
(b) Child marriage
(c) Gender discrimination
(d) All of the above

4. Who utilised the Banjaras to transport grain to city markets? (1)

(a) Emperor Akbar
(b) Sultan Alauddin Khalji
(c) Emperor Jahangir
(d) Sultan Muhammad bin Tughlaq

5. Match the following .

List I	List II
A. Abul Fazl	1. Revenue system based on crop data
B. Todar Mal	2. Conducted a revenue survey
C. Zabt	3. Akbar Nama
D. Zamindars	4. Term for intermediaries in Mughal administration

Codes

	A	B	C	D
(a)	3	2	1	4
(b)	4	3	2	1
(c)	3	2	4	1
(d)	2	3	4	1

6. Which term refers to the domain encompassing various water sources and different water bodies like rivers, lakes, seas and oceans? (1)

(a) Atmosphere
(b) Lithosphere
(c) Biosphere
(d) Hydrosphere

7. Which minerals primarily constitute the continental mass? (1)

(a) Gold and Silver
(b) Silica and Alumina
(c) Iron and Copper
(d) Diamond and Quartz

8. Which waterfall is recognised as the highest waterfall in the world? (1)

(a) Niagara falls
(b) Victoria falls
(c) Angel falls
(d) Iguazu falls

9. Consider the statements given below about the impact of human activities on carbon dioxide levels in the atmosphere. Choose the correct statements. **(1)**

I. Green plants use carbon dioxide for photosynthesis.
II. Animals release carbon dioxide into the atmosphere.
III. Burning fuels like coal and oil contributes billions of tons of carbon dioxide annually.
IV. The Earth's weather and climate are affected by the increased volume of carbon dioxide.

Codes
(a) Both I and II
(b) Both II and III
(c) Both III and IV
(d) Both I and IV

10. On which date is World Water Day celebrated? **(1)**
(a) 22nd April (b) 22nd March
(c) 22nd May (d) 22nd February

11. What was one significant change brought about by the Civil Rights Act of 1964 regarding African-American children? **(1)**
(a) Establishment of separate schools for African-American children
(b) Integration of schools, allowing African-American children to attend any school
(c) Mandating higher fees for African-American children's education
(d) Enforcing racial segregation in educational institutions

12. Assertion (A) In a democracy, the people hold the secondary authority as they elect their representatives.

Reason (R) The ruling party members in the Legislative Assembly are responsible for forming the government and appointing ministers who oversee different government departments. **(1)**

Codes
(a) Both A and R are true and R is the correct explanation of A
(b) Both A and R are true, but R is not the correct explanation of A
(c) A is true, but the R is false
(d) A is false, but the R is true

13. Identify the text from its features given below. **(1)**

I. It was circulated orally and cannot be precisely dated.
II. It was popular where the influence of Brahmanas was weak.
III. It included stories concerning the Worship of Dharma Thakur, fairy tales, folk tales and ballads.

Codes
(a) Malayalam text Lilatilakam
(b) Bengali text dependent on Sanskrit
(c) Bengali text independent of Sanskrit
(d) Sanskrit text Brihaddharma Purana

14. What does the Constitution emphasise regarding discrimination based on gender? **(1)**
(a) The Constitution promotes discrimination based on gender.
(b) The Constitution prohibits discrimination based on gender.
(c) The Constitution allows discrimination based on gender in certain situations.
(d) The Constitution ignores the issue of gender discrimination.

Fill in the Blanks

1. The mother of Jahangir was a .... princess, daughter of the Rajput ruler of Amber. **(1)**

2. .... is the most plentiful gas in the air. **(1)**

3. .... is the first known autobiography written by an Indian woman. **(1)**

True or False

1. The forces which act in the interior of the Earth are called as Exogenic forces. **(1)**

2. In 1236, Sultan Iltutmish's daughter, Raziya, became Sultan. **(1)**

3. A political party whose MLAs have won more than half the number of constituencies in a state can be said to be in a minority. **(1)**

Very Short Answer Type Questions

1. Ram and Ravi were talking in the class about a person who came to their village to know about the culture and lifestyle of the village.
   The head of the village called that person, a foreigner. Ram asked his teacher, what is the meaning of foreigner. How will teacher explain this to Ram? **(2)**

2. Define the term 'medical tourists'. **(2)**

Or What directive does the Medical Council of India's Code of Medical Ethics emphasise regarding drug prescription by physicians?

3. How does an increase in atmospheric carbon dioxide lead to global warming? **(2)**

Or Define atmosphere.

4. What are the four domains of the natural environment? **(2)**

5. What were the primary forms of tax mentioned in the inscriptions of the Cholas in Tamil Nadu? **(2)**

Short Answer Type Questions

1. Who were Raziya, Rudrama Devi and Didda? How did their approaches to rulership differ during their reigns? **(3)**

2. What did 'mansabdar' mean during the Mughal period? How was someone's position as a mansabdar decided? **(3)**

3. Explain the purpose and workings of a weaver's cooperative, emphasising its impact on the relationship between weavers and merchants. **(3)**

Or How does the described market scenario showcase income disparities among different groups?

4. What factors contribute to the affordability of goods in weekly markets? **(3)**

5. What are sedimentary rocks? How are they created? **(3)**

Or Arpita was playing in the ground with her friends. One of her friend pick up a rock and said, in school her teacher told them rocks are made up of minerals and minerals are very helpful to us. Arpita become interested to know about mineral and asked her sister, what are minerals? How are they useful for mankind?

6. What is 'slash and burn agriculture'? How is it practiced in the Amazon Basin? **(3)**

Or Write about the different flora and fauna found in Ganga Brahmaputra basin.

Long Answer Type Questions

1. What were the significant expansions and achievements during the reign of Rajaraja I and Rajendra I in the Chola dynasty? **(5)**

Or How was the administration structured during the Chola period, particularly regarding villages and larger units? Who held significant control over these units?

2. Sita was watching news on the TV and got to know a women's movement is going on in the middle Eastern countries. She got interested about the topic and asked her mother what is the need of women's movement? What are the changes occurring in our country through this movement? **(5)**

Or Explain in brief the role of the Legislative Assembly in a state democracy.

3. Discuss the different types of ocean currents and their causes. **(5)**

Or

Do you think the statement "Our planet is similar to a terrarium" is accurate? Explain your answer by discussing the water cycle in an easy and understandable way.

Case Based Questions

1. **Read the given passage and answer the questions that follow.** **(4)**

   Tribal people were found in almost every region of the sub-continent. The area and influence of a tribe varied at different points of time. Some powerful tribes controlled large territories. In Punjab, the Khokhar tribe was very influential during the 13th and 14th centuries. Later, the Gakkhars became more important. Their chief, Kamal Khan Gakkhar, was made a noble (mansabdar) by Emperor Akbar. In Multan and Sind, the Langahs and Arghuns dominated extensive regions before they were subdued by the Mughals. The Balochis were another large and powerful tribe in the North-West. They were divided into many smaller clans under different chiefs.

(i) **How did tribes in the Indian sub-continent differ from the caste-based societies in terms of social organisation and livelihood? (1)**

(ii) **Who were the prominent tribes dominating Multan and Sind before the Mughal rule? (2)**

(iii) **Under whose reign did Mughal forces capture many Chero fortresses and subjugate the tribe? (1)**

2. Read the given passage and answer the questions that follow. (4)

Life of the people of the Amazon basin is slowly changing. In the older days, the heart of the forest, could be reached only by navigating the river. In 1970, the Trans Amazon highway made all parts of the rainforest accessible. Aircrafts and helicopters are also used for reaching various places. The indigenous population was pushed out from the area and forced to settle in new areas where they continued to practice their distinctive way of farming. The developmental activities are leading to the gradual destruction of the biologically diverse rainforests. It is estimated that a large area of the rainforest has been disappearing annually in the Amazon basin.

(i) **What major development opened up the Amazon rainforest to easier access? (1)**

(ii) **How were the indigenous populations affected by the developmental activities in the Amazon basin? (2)**

(iii) **What is happening to the Amazon rainforest due to ongoing developmental activities? (1)**

3. Read the given passage and answer the questions that follow. (4)

Going to school is an extremely important part of your life. As more and more children enter school every year, we begin to think that it is normal for all children to go to school. Today, it is difficult for us to imagine that school and learning could be seen as "out of bounds" or not appropriate for some children. But in the past, the skill of reading and writing was known to only a few. Most children learnt the work their families or elders did. For girls, the situation was worse. In communities that taught sons to read and write, daughters were not allowed to learn the alphabet. Even in families where skills like pottery, weaving and craft were taught, the contribution of daughters and women was only seen as supportive.

(i) **How was education perceived for many children in the past? (1)**

(ii) **What was the situation for girls regarding education in communities where sons were taught to read and write? (1)**

(iii) **How was the contribution of daughters and women viewed in families where craft and skills were taught? (2)**

Map Based Question

1. (a) **On the political map of India, locate the following.**

(i) Capital of Sawai Raja Singh - Jaipur **(3)**

(ii) Locate Chittorgarh Fort

(iii) Pass that crosses Manali - Leh Highway

(b) **On the given political outline map of India, identify the following. (2)**

(i) The place also known as Khapa-Chan

(ii) The place where Chatrapati Shivaji Maharaj born

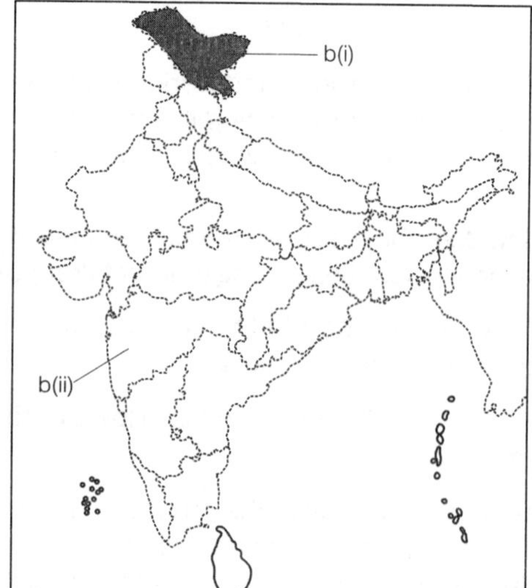

Answers

Multiple Choice Questions

1. (c)	2. (c)	3. (d)	4. (b)
5. (a)	6. (d)	7. (b)	8. (c)
9. (c)	10. (b)	11. (b)	12. (d)
13. (c)	14. (b)		

Fill in the Blanks

1. Kachhwaha
2. Nitrogen
3. Amar Jiban

True or False

1. False
2. True
3. False

Map Based Question

1.

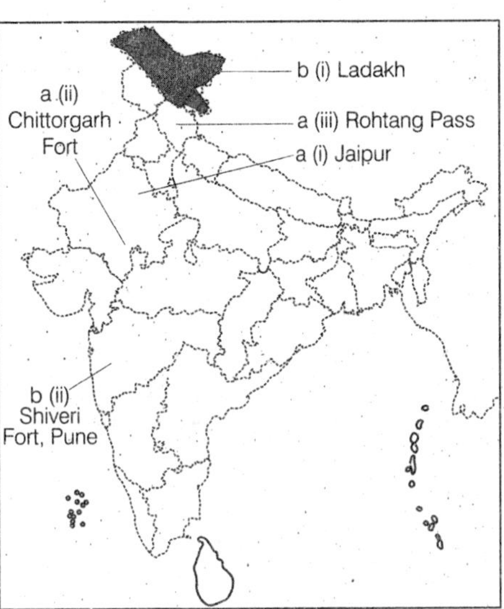

Sample Question Paper 3 (Unsolved)
Social Science

Time : 3 hrs	M.M. : 80

General Instructions
1 All questions are compulsory.
2 Marks for each question are indicated against the question.

Multiple Choice Questions (MCQs)

1. Which religious movements emerged between the 7th and 9th centuries, led by saints devoted to Shiva and Vishnu respectively? (1)
(a) Bhakti and Sufi movements
(b) Nayanars and Alvars movements
(c) Vedic and Upanishadic movements
(d) Jain and Buddhist movements

2. What was the original profession of the Kathaks in North India? (1)
(a) Temple priests (b) Sculptors
(c) Story-tellers in temples (d) Musicians

3. Who was responsible for the construction of five astronomical observatories, commonly known as Jantar Mantar? (1)
(a) Akbar the Great
(b) Raja Ram Mohan Roy
(c) Sawai Jai Singh
(d) Maharana Pratap

4. According to Minhaj-i-Siraj in the 13th century, what did the term "Hindustan" refer to? (1)
(a) Only the region of Bengal
(b) Areas between the rivers Ganga and Yamuna
(c) Entire South Asian continent
(d) Regions near the Arabian Sea

5. Match the defeated kings or rulers mentioned in the Sanskrit prashasti with the regions or kingdoms they belonged to. (1)

List I	List II
A. King of Vanga	1. Part of Bengal
B. King of Anarta	2. Part of Maharashtra
C. King of Malwa	3. Part of Madhya Pradesh
D. King of Vatsa	4. Part of North India

Codes

	A	B	C	D
(a)	1	2	3	4
(b)	4	3	2	1
(c)	3	2	1	4
(d)	2	3	4	1

6. Who decides which stories are important enough to be covered in the media? (1)
(a) Government officials
(b) Celebrities
(c) Journalists and media professionals
(d) Religious leaders

7. How do traders operate in a weekly market? (1)
(a) They have permanent shops.
(b) They trade every day of the week.
(c) They set up shops for the day and close them in the evening.
(d) They sell their goods online.

8. Which Indian city hosts one of the world's largest cloth markets known for its variety of fabrics? (1)
(a) Chennai
(b) Erode
(c) Madurai
(d) Coimbatore

9. Which of the following statements are true regarding the government's efforts to implement equality in India? (1)
Statement I Laws are one way through which the government ensures equality by protecting every person's right to fair treatment.
Statement II Government schemes aim to improve the lives of disadvantaged communities and individuals to provide greater opportunities for those historically treated unequally.

Codes

(a) Only Statement I is true
(b) Only Statement II is true
(c) Both Statement I and Statement II are true
(d) Neither Statement I nor Statement II is true

10. **Assertion** (A) India has the largest number of medical colleges globally and produces a significant number of doctors annually.
Reason (R) Despite this, the majority of doctors prefer to settle in rural areas, leading to a shortage of medical professionals in urban regions. **(1)**

Codes

(a) Both A and R are true and R is the correct explanation of A
(b) Both A and R are true, but R is not the correct explanation of A
(c) A is true, but R is false
(d) A is false, but R is true

11. Where is the deepest mine in the world located? **(1)**

(a) United States
(b) South Africa
(c) Australia
(d) Russia

12. Which area is formed by the combination of a main river and all its tributaries? **(1)**

(a) Floodplain
(b) River delta
(c) River basin or catchment area
(d) Estuary

13. How did the extreme temperature recorded in Al Azizia in 1922 influence subsequent scientific research and understanding of climatic phenomena? **(1)**

(a) It led to the relocation of indigenous communities to cooler regions.
(b) It prompted international collaborations to study desert ecosystems.
(c) It sparked investigations into the impact of climate change on desert regions.
(d) It served as a benchmark for assessing temperature measurement techniques and data acuracy.

14. What role does the atmosphere play in relation to protecting the Earth? **(1)**

(a) It generates heat to counter the Sun's rays
(b) It blocks the Sun's rays completely
(c) It traps harmful rays and heat from the Sun
(d) It reflects harmful rays back into space

15. Identify the term from the following statements. **(1)**

I. It is generally observed that women typically labour both inside (housework) and outside.
II. It is used to describe women's situation.
III. A huge number of women face this situation.

Options

(a) Double burden
(b) Double work
(c) Double labour
(d) Double situation

Fill in the Blanks

1. Vijayalaya, who belonged to the ancient chiefly family of the Cholas from ...., captured the delta from the Muttaraiyar in the middle of the 9th century. **(1)**

2. The crust forms only .... per cent of the volume of the Earth, 84 per cent consists of the mantle. **(1)**

3. The public health service is a chain of health centres and hospitals run by the .... **(1)**

True or False

1. A clan is a group of families or households claiming descent from a common ancestor. **(1)**

2. The Sun's heat causes evaporation of air into vapour. **(1)**

3. The women's movement led the Supreme Court to formulate guidelines in 1997 to protect women against sexual harassment at the workplace and within educational institutions. **(1)**

Very Short Answer Type Questions

1. At what age did Babur ascend to the throne of Ferghana, and what circumstance led to his accession? **(2)**

2. What is the composition of the Earth's crust ? **(2)**

3. What determines the path for MLAs to become ministers or Chief Ministers in a State Government? **(2)**

Or

What is the primary purpose of a press conference?

4. Earth's salinity i.e. the salt concentration in its water bodies, primarily oceans and seas, varies due to factors like evaporation, precipitation and freshwater input. **(2)**
   (i) What proportion of Earth's water exists in saline form and is primarily found in oceans and seas?
   (ii) How does Earth's salinity impact climate patterns?
5. How did the Khaljis and Tughlaqs utilise individuals of humble origin in their administrations? **(2)**

Short Answer Type Questions

1. Who were the Nayanars and Alvars ? What was their role in the emergence of a new religious movement in South India? **(3)**
2. What defines tribal societies? How do they differ from caste-based societies? **(3)**

   Or

   Who were the Banjaras? How did they contribute to trade during the Mughal era?
3. The media serves a fundamental purpose by supplying the information essential for informed discussions. A functioning democracy relies on citizens making knowledgeable decisions, and this lies on the type of information they access. **(3)**
   (i) What do you mean by a balanced report by the media?
   (ii) What is the significance of the media in democracy?
4. How are Members of the Legislative Assembly (MLAs) elected? **(3)**
5. Explain briefly the formation of spring and neap tides. **(3)**

Or Explain water cycle with a neat and labelled diagram.

6. Describe the factors that contributed to the flourishing of tourism in the Ganga-Brahmaputra region. **(3)**

Long Answer Type Questions

1. What were the expansions and political involvements of key Rajput rulers? **(5)**

Or Describe the Marathas' military strategies and their territorial expansions from 1720 to 1761, notably impacting the Mughal Empire.

2. Last month, the media covered all the news related to celebrity gossip, but they seemed to ignore the pressing issue of pollution in our city. Pollution created a lot of problems for the people of the city, yet the media failed to cover it. **(5)**
   (i) Why is it important for the media to balance entertainment and news about critical issues?
   (ii) What is the role of the media in our lives?
3. Explain the structure of atmosphere in brief. **(5)**

Or Explain the term 'Air pressure' and its significance in brief.

Case Based Questions

1. **Read the given passage and answer the questions that follow. (4)**

   Peasant and zamindari rebellions in many parts of Northern and Western India added to these problems. These revolts were sometimes caused by the pressures of mounting taxes. At other times, they were attempts by powerful chieftains to consolidate their own positions. Mughal authority had been challenged by rebellious groups in the past as well. But these groups were now able to seize the economic resources of the region to consolidate their positions. The Mughal emperors after Aurangzeb were unable to arrest the gradual shifting of political and economic authority into the hands of provincial governors, local chieftains and other groups.

   (i) What were some reasons behind peasant and zamindari rebellions in Northern and Western India? (2)

   (ii) How did Mughal authority weaken after Aurangzeb's reign? (1)

   (iii) What contributed to the gradual transfer of political and economic power away from Mughal emperors in India? (1)

2. **Read the given passage and answer the questions that follow.** **(4)**

The rhythmic rise and fall of ocean water twice in a day is called a tide. It is high tide when water covers much of the shore by rising to its highest level. It is low tide when water falls to its lowest level and recedes from the shore.The strong gravitational pull exerted by the Sun and the Moon on the Earth's surface causes the tides. The water of the Earth closer to the Moon gets pulled under the influence of the Moon's gravitational force and causes high tide. During the full Moon and new Moon days, the Sun, the Moon and the Earth are in the same line and the tides are highest.

(i) **Explain the concept of high tide and low tide with respect to the ocean's water level.** **(1)**

(ii) **How do tidal patterns vary in different geographical locations around the world?** **(1)**

(iii) **How do tidal patterns differ depending on the Moon's phases and its relative position to the Earth and the Sun?** **(2)**

3. **Read the given passage and answer the questions that follow.**

A weekly market is so called because it is held on a specific day of the week. Weekly markets do not have permanent shops. Traders set up shops for the day and then close them up in the evening. Then they may set up at a different place the next day. There are thousands of such markets in India. People come here for their everyday requirements. Many things in weekly markets are available at cheaper rates. This is because when shops are in permanent buildings, they incur a lot of expenditure – they have to pay rent, electricity, fees to the government. They also have to pay wages to their workers. In weekly markets, these shop owners store the things they sell at home. Most of them are helped by their family members and, hence, do not need to hire workers. Weekly markets also have a large number of shops selling the same goods which means there is competition among them.

(i) **Why are goods often available at cheaper rates in weekly markets compared to permanent shops?** **(1)**

(ii) **How do weekly markets differ from shops in permanent buildings?** **(1)**

(iii) **What are the advantages of traders in weekly markets over those in permanent shops?** **(1)**

Map Based Question

1. (a) **On the political map of India, locate the following.** **(3)**

(i) The city formed by Akbar – Fatehpur Sikri

(ii) The palace of Raja Ajit Singh – Jodhpur

(iii) Capital of Jammu and Kashmir – Srinagar

(b) **On the given political outline map of India, identify the following.** **(2)**

(i) An important river of Ladakh

(ii) Place where Golden Temple is situated

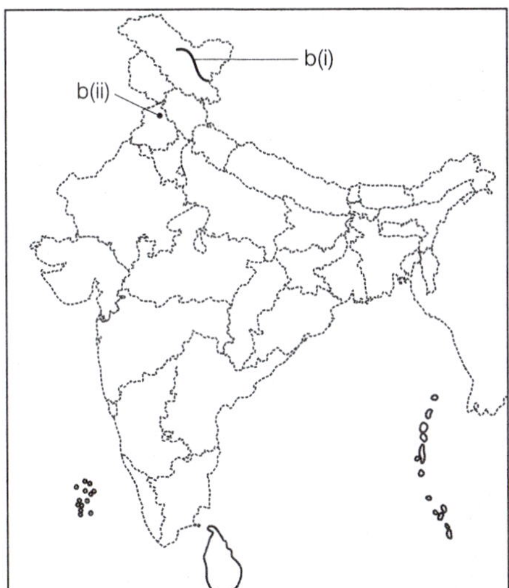

Answers

Multiple Choice Questions

1. (b)	**2.** (c)	**3.** (c)	**4.** (b)	**5.** (a)
6. (c)	**7.** (c)	**8.** (b)	**9.** (c)	**10.** (c)
11. (b)	**12.** (c)	**13.** (d)	**14.** (c)	**15.** (a)

Fill in the Blanks

1. Uraiyur
2. one
3. Government

True or False

1. True
2. False
3. True

Map Based Question

1.

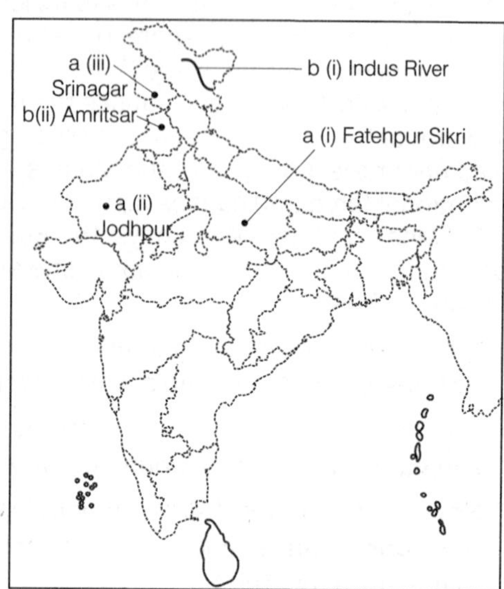